# ROLE OF ICT IN HIGHER EDUCATION

*Trends, Problems, and Prospects*

# ROLE OF ICT IN HIGHER EDUCATION

## *Trends, Problems, and Prospects*

*Edited by*

**Gopal Singh Latwal, PhD**

**Sudhir Kumar Sharma, PhD**

**Prerna Mahajan, PhD**

**Piet Kommers, PhD**

First edition published 2021

**Apple Academic Press Inc.**
1265 Goldenrod Circle, NE,
Palm Bay, FL 32905 USA

4164 Lakeshore Road, Burlington,
ON, L7L 1A4 Canada

**CRC Press**
6000 Broken Sound Parkway NW,
Suite 300, Boca Raton, FL 33487-2742 USA

2 Park Square, Milton Park,
Abingdon, Oxon, OX14 4RN UK

First issued in paperback 2021



*Apple Academic Press exclusively co-publishes with CRC Press, an imprint of Taylor & Francis Group, LLC*



**Library and Archives Canada Cataloguing in Publication**

Title: Role of ICT in higher education : trends, problems, and prospects / edited by Gopal Singh Latwal, PhD, Sudhir Kumar Sharma, PhD, Prerna Mahajan, PhD, Piet Kommers, PhD.

Names: Latwal, Gopal Singh, editor. | Sharma, Sudhir Kumar, editor. | Mahajan, Prerna, editor. | Kommers, Piet A. M., editor. | International Conference on the Role of ICT in Higher Education: Trends, Problems and Prospects (2020 : Delhi, India)

Description: Chapters are selected papers from the International Conference on the Role of ICT in Higher Education: Trends, Problems and Prospects, held at the Institute of Information Technology & Management, Delhi, India, on 14th-15th February 2020. | Includes bibliographical references and index.

Identifiers: Canadiana (print) 20200308203 | Canadiana (ebook) 20200308327 | ISBN 9781771889629 (hardcover) | ISBN 9781003130864 (ebook)

Subjects: LCSH: Education, Higher—Computer-assisted instruction—Case studies—Congresses. | LCSH: Educational technology—Case studies—Congresses. | LCSH: Information technology—Case studies—Congresses. | LCGFT: Case studies.

Classification: LCC LB2395.7 .R65 2021 | DDC 378.1/7344678—dc23

**Library of Congress Cataloging-in-Publication Data**

CIP data on file with US Library of Congress

ISBN: 978-1-77188-962-9 (hbk)
ISBN: 978-1-77463-924-5 (pbk)
ISBN: 978-1-00313-086-4 (ebk)

# About the Editors

**Gopal Singh Latwal, PhD**
*Associate Professor, Management Department, IITM, Janakpuri, New Delhi*

Gopal Singh Latwal, PhD, is an Associate Professor in the Department of Management at the Institute of Information Technology and Management, New Delhi, India. He holds an MBA in Marketing and has obtained his PhD in Management from Jai Narain Vyas University, Jodhpur, India. He has more than 14 years of academic and industry experience. He has authored two textbooks and edited two books. He has published research papers in journals of national repute and has presented a number of papers at various national and international seminars and conferences. He has delivered live expert lectures at Indira Gandhi National Open University (IGNOU), New Delhi, and regularly delivers lectures for faculty development programs. He has successfully conducted many workshops on data analysis and research methodology.

**Sudhir Kumar Sharma, PhD**
*Professor and Head of Computer Science Department, IITM Janakpuri, New Delhi*

Sudhir Kumar Sharma, PhD, is currently working as Professor and Head of the Department of Computer Science at the Institute of Information Technology and Management, affiliated with Guru Gobind Singh Indraprastha University (GGSIPU), New Delhi, India. He has rich experience of more than 20 years in the field of computer science and engineering. He obtained his PhD degree in Information Technology from the University School of Information and Communication Technology, GGSIPU, New Delhi, India. He obtained his MTech degree in Computer Science and Engineering from the Guru Jambheshwar University, Hisar, India, and his MSc degree in Physics from the University of Roorkee (now IIT Roorkee), Roorkee, India. He is interested in the machine learning, data mining and security. He has published several research papers in international journals and at international conferences. He is a life member of the Computer Society of India and the Institution of Electronics and Telecommunication Engineers. He is an associate editor for the *International Journal of End-User Computing and Development* (IJEUCD), IGI Global, USA. He is editor of proceedings of ICETIT-2019. He is a convener of ICRIHE-2020.

**Prerna Mahajan, PhD**

*Professor and Director, IITM Janakpuri, New Delhi*

Prerna Mahajan, PhD, is Director and Professor in the Department of Computer Science at the Institute of Information Technology and Management, Janakpuri, New Delhi, India. She has worked on several research projects funded by the Indian government and private bodies. She has been a member of several conference committees. She has a wide range of experience both in academics and administration, ranging from monitoring, faculty coordination, mentoring, software development, accreditation processes, and interfacing with external agencies. She has also published and presented research papers at conferences and in international and national journals. She is a certified trainer for data science and machine learning courses. She has conducted several faculty development programs and in-service training programs and workshops for researchers, faculty, and students. Dr. Mahajan earned her PhD in Computer Science at Banasthali University, India. She graduated with a BSc (Hons) in Mathematics from Delhi University, earned her MCA from Gurukul Kangri University, and obtained a PhD in Computer Science from Banasthali University, India.

**Piet Kommers, PhD**

Piet Kommers, PhD, is an early pioneer in media for cognitive and social support. His doctoral research explored methods for hypertext and concept mapping in learning. He has been developing educational technology for teacher training since 1982. He is an Associate Professor at the University in Twente, The Netherlands, and adjunct/visiting professor in various countries. He taught many advanced level courses and has supervised more than 30 PhD students. He instigated and coordinated the NATO Advanced Research Workshop on Cognitive Technologies in 1990 and a large series of Joint European Research Projects on authoring multimedia, web-based learning, teacher education, virtual 3D worlds, constructivist learning, social media, web-based communities, and international student exchange. UNESCO awarded his work in ICT for Education in Eastern Europe with the title of Honorary Professor. The Capital Normal University in Beijing awarded him the title of Honorary Doctor. He is member of the advisory boards in the ministries of education and academia of sciences in Singapore, Finland, and Russia. Dr. Kommers is the initiator of the *International Journal for Web-based Communities* on societal applications and the overall chair of the IADIS conferences on societal applications of ICT. He has given more than

40 invited and keynote lectures at conferences in the fields of education, media, and communication. His books and journal articles address the social and intellectual transformations at each transition from "traditional" into the "new" media.

# Contents

# Contributors

**Ammani Abubakar**
Department of Office Technology and Management, College of Administration and Management Studies, Hassan Usman Katsina Polytechnic, Katsina State, Nigeria.
E-mails: abubakar752000@yahoo.co.uk; comradeammani8@gmail.com

**Himanshu Agarwal**
Faculty of Commerce and Business Administration, D N (PG) College, Meerut, India

**M. Afshar Alam**
Depatment of CSE, School of Engineering Sciences and Technology, Jamia Hamdard, New Delhi 110062, India

**Deepika Arora**
Department of Management, Institute of Information Technology and Management, New Delhi, India.
E-mail: deep2581@yahoo.com

**Lakshya Bhalla**
Department of MCA, Bhai Parmanand Institute of Business Studies

**Jyoti Bhambhani**
Management Department, Institute of Information Technology and Management, New Delhi, India.
Email: drjyotiiitm@gmail.com

**Vikas Bharara**
Department of Management, Institute of Information Technology and Management, New Delhi, 110058, India. E-mail: vikas.bharara@iitmipu.ac.in

**Manjunatha Byrappa**
School of Foreign Languages, University of Mysore, Humanities Block, Manasagangothri Campus, Mysuru, Karnataka, India. E-mails: bmn2304@gmail.com; sofluom@gmail.com

**Sunakshi Chadha**
Department of Management, Assistant Professor, IITM Janakpuri, Dehi, 1100058, India.
E-mail: sunakshichadha@gmail.com

**Pooja Chaturvedi**
Department of Computer Science, School of Management Sciences, Varanasi, Uttar Pradesh.
E-mail: chaturvedi.pooja03@gmail.com

**Renu Choudhary**
IITM, New Delhi, India

**A. K. Daniel**
Department of Computer Science and Engineering, M. M. M. University of Technology, Gorakhpur, Uttar Pradesh

**Vaishali Dubey**
Department of Education, University of Delhi, Delhi, 110007, India

**Tamanna Goel**
Department of Management Studies, Institute of Information Technology & Management, Janakpuri, New Delhi, India. E-mail: goel.tamanna1502@gmail.com

**Akanksha Gupta**
School of Education, Devi Ahilya University, Indore 452012, Madhya Pradesh, India.
E-mail: akankshagupta1981@gmail.com

**Leena Gupta**
Department of Information Technology, Institute of Information Technology & Management, Janakpuri, New Delhi, India

**Aleena Ilyaz**
PaperPedia Private Limited, Noida, Uttar Pradesh, 201301, India. E-mail: aleenailyas2801@gmail.com

**Naman Jain**
Director (Development), Silverline Prestige School, Ghaziabad, India. E-mail: jain.naman31@gmail.com

**Diwya Joshi**
School of Education, DAVV, Indore, 452001, Madhya Pradesh. E-mail: diwyajoshi01@gmail.com

**Vinod Kumar Kanvaria**
Department of Education, University of Delhi, Delhi, 110007, India. E-mail: vinodpr111@gmail.com

**Bhatt Komalben**
Department of English, Hemchandracharya North Gujarat University, Patan, Gujarat 384265, India.
E-mail: komalbhatt890@gmail.com

**Gaurav Kumar**
MJPR University, Bareilly, Uttar Pradesh, India

**Rakesh Kumar**
Department of Law, University School of Law and Legal Studies, GGSIPU, Sector 16C, Dwarka, New Delhi, India. E-mail: rakesh.law@gmail.com

**S. Logesh Kumar**
Ramakrishna Mission Vivekananda Educational and Research Institute, Faculty of Disability Management and Special Education, Vidyalaya Campus, SRKV Post, Coimbatore, 641020, India

**Daisy Kurien**
Institute of Management Studies, Indus University, Ahmedabad, Gujarat, India.
E-mail: daisynevin@gmail.com

**Gopal Singh Latwal**
Department of Management Studies, Institute of Information Technology & Management, Janakpuri, New Delhi, India. E-mail: gopalsinghusl@gmail.com

**Himanshu Matta**
Amity University, Uttar Pradesh, India. E-mail: mattahimanshu@gmail.com

**Kaushal Mehta**
Department of CSE, Graphic Era University, Dehradun, Uttarakhand. E-mail: Kpu_713@yahoo.com

**Ekata Mehul**
Blazing Arrows, Vadodara, India. E-mail: ekata.mehul@blazingarrows.org

**Rama Mishra**
School of Education, Devi Ahilya University, Indore 452012, Madhya Pradesh, India

**Tejal Nathadwarawala**
M.S. University of Baroda, Vadodara, India. E-mail: chandaranatejal@gmail.com

**Ashish Kumar Nayyar**
Institute of Information Technology & Management, New Delhi 110058, India

**Sunita Negi**
School of Basic & Applied Sciences, G.D Goenka University, Gurugram, Haryana 122103, India.
E-mail: negisunita.81@gmail

**Sujata Oak**
Ramrao Adik Institute of Technology, Nerul, Navi Mumbai 400706, Maharashtra, India

**Pallavi Pal**
Department of Law, University School of Law and Legal Studies, GGSIPU, Dwarka, New Delhi, India

**Rashid**
Faculty of Commerce and Business Administration, D N (PG) College, Meerut, India.
E-mail: rashid.638@gmail.com

**Sunitha Ravi**
Department of Management, Institute of Information Technology & Management,
D-29, Institutional Area, Janakpuri, New Delhi 110058, India. E-mail: sunitharavi21@gmail.com

**Anam Saiyeda**
Depatment of CSE, School of Engineering Sciences and Technology, Jamia Hamdard,
New Delhi 110062, India. E-mail: anamsaiyeda@jamiahamdard.ac.in

**Hiren Kumar Deva Sarma**
Department of Information Technology, Sikkim Manipal Institute of Technology, Sikkim, 737136,
India. E-mail: hirenkdsarma@gmail.com

**Anitha Senathi**
Ramrao Adik Institute of Technology, Nerul, Navi Mumbai 400706, Maharashtra, India.
E-mail: anita.senathi@rait.ac.in

**Anmol Sharma**
Department of MCA, Bhai Parmanand Institute of Business Studies

**Sudhir Kumar Sharma**
Institute of Information Technology & Management, New Delhi 110058, India.
E-mail: sudhir_sharma99@yahoo.com

**Keith Sherringham**
A.C.N. 629 733 633 Pty. Ltd., Sydney, NSW, 2000, Australia. E-mail: keith.sherringham@gmail.com

**Ambalika Sinha**
Motilal Nehru National Institute of Technology, Prayagraj, Uttar Pradesh

**Malavika Srivastava**
IITM, Janakpuri, New Delhi. Email: malavika.iitm@gmail.com

**Kshipra Tatkare**
Ramrao Adik Institute of Technology, Nerul, Navi Mumbai 400706, Maharashtra, India

**Shanti Tejwani**
Shri Vaishnav College of Teachers Training, Indore, 452009, Madhya Pradesh

**Fr. Baiju Thomas**
Ramakrishna Mission Vivekananda Educational and Research Institute, Faculty of Disability Management and Special Education, Vidyalaya Campus, SRKV Post, Coimbatore, 641020, India.
E-mail: rtobaiju@gmail.com

**Bhuvan Unhelkar**
College of Business, University of South Florida Sarasota-Manatee Campus, Sarasota, FL, 3424, USA

**Savita Waswani**
Department of Management, Institute of Information Technology & Management, D-29, Institutional Area, Janakpuri, New Delhi 110058, India

# Abbreviations

| | |
|---|---|
| AWS | Amazon Web Services |
| AI | artificial intelligence |
| CMS | content management system |
| COs | course outcomes |
| DBaaS | Database as a Service |
| DC | digital communication |
| ETD | electronic thesis and dissertation |
| ERP | enterprise resource planning |
| HNGU | Hemchandracharya North Gujarat University |
| HE | higher education |
| HEI | higher education institutions |
| HR | human resource |
| PHP | hypertext preprocessor |
| ICTINF | ICT infrastructure |
| ICTF | ICT usage by faculty |
| ICT | information communication and technology |
| IT | information technology |
| IaaS | Infrastructure as a Service |
| IMEI | International Mobile Equipment Identity |
| IoT | Internet of things |
| LA | learning analytics |
| LMSs | learning management systems |
| MOOC | Massive Online Open Courses |
| NDL | National Digital Library |
| OTM | office technology and management |
| OMR | optical mark reader |
| PaaS | Platform as a Service |
| PPT | PowerPoint |
| PMJDY | Pradhan Mantri Jan-Dhan Yojana |
| POs | program outcomes |
| PTR | pupil–teacher ratio |
| ROC | region of curve |
| SAR | Self-Assessment Report |
| SIM | self-instructional e-module |

| | |
|---|---|
| SaaS | Software as a Service |
| SE | student engagement |
| SSICT | student satisfaction on ICT usage |
| SWAYAM | Study Webs of Active Learning for Young Minds |
| TAC | Type Allocation Code |
| USSD | Unstructured Supplementary Service Data |

# Preface

The *Role of ICT in Higher Education: Trends, Problems, and Prospects* provides an informative collection of chapters on ICT and data analytics in the education sector leading to a digital revolution in higher education. Its substrands are skill development through ICT, artificial intelligence in education, policies for integrating ICT in higher education, and so on.

As we see from the long list of chapter titles in this volume, there is a fascination for the wide mix of the learning/teaching spectrum: worldwide massive open online courses (MOOCs), learning analytics (using artificial intelligence for diagnosing learning characteristics), equity (providing fair learning opportunities to students from all socioeconomic strata), 21st century new citizen skills, etc. In each of them, ICT plays a crucial role. The recent interest is to use social media and web-based communities to motivate students to invest in each other "collaborative learning." How can this approach be reconciled with the ongoing university regimes where uniform test criteria are ruling? This is the question to be solved during in this volume through the in-depth discussions on the research works presented here.

Subsumed into several sections, the authors address a wide variety of issues, including applications in:

- ICT in education
- data analytics in education sector
- digital revolution: higher education
- skill development through ICT
- technological advancement for effective teaching learning outcomes

This volume will be beneficial for students, researchers, academicians, and professionals in the area of ICT who are keen to explore its wide application in the area of education.

The chapters are selected papers from the International Conference on the Role of ICT in Higher Education: Trends, Problems and Prospects, held at the Institute of Information Technology & Management, Delhi. India, on 14th–15th February 2020. Efforts taken by peer reviewers contributed to improve the quality of papers and provided constructive critical comments; improvement and, corrections to the authors, who are gratefully appreciated. We are very grateful to the authors who submitted papers in large numbers.

We finally selected 32 quality papers from the 107 submittel papers that relate to different themes of the conference from six overseas countries, which make the chapters of this book.

**—Gopal Singh Latwal**
**Sudhir Kumar Sharma**
**Prerna Mahajan**
**Piet Kommers**

# Foreword

In order to predict the next decade's evolution in education, it might be good to learn from history. Looking back from the old Indian, Chinese, and Greek scholarly traditions, we may say that learning was always seen as primarily the dialogue between wise experts and novices. Be aware that dialogue implies much more than the transfer of knowledge; it is a mutual process where the teacher needs the interaction with students, as otherwise the teacher misses the incentives to reformulate and tune to the individual learner constantly.

The printing of books was a game changer: It relies upon the belief that expertise can be consolidated, transported, and consumed by the learner. Plato explicitly refrained from handing over his text to readers. Even if the topic looked rather straightforward, he would prefer a dialogue to be sure so that both persons in the conversation understood each other. Up to today, the written word is seen as the ultimate modality to feed learning. The most recent turnpike in revaluing the conversational format for learning has been made by Lev Vygotsky, as he saw learning essentially as a social process in which the transition from conceptual imagination to formulation in language was the basis for learning.

As we see the long list of chapter titles in this volume, there is a wide mix on the learning/teaching spectrum: World-wide massive open online courses (MOOCs), learning analytics (using artificial intelligence for diagnosing learning characteristics), equity (providing fair learning opportunities to students from all socioeconomic strata), 21st century new citizen skills, etc. In each of them, information and communication technology (ICT) plays a crucial role. Even we may ask ourselves if ICT is regarded as 1. the goal in itself, 2. a method for making learning more flexible and more efficient, or 3. ICT as a cosmetic layer in order to suggest a "modern" way of learning. After you think about these three alternatives, you will find that in any real situation, it is a mix of the three of them. Maybe most essential is that the role of ICT so far has been a catalytic one: It transforms traditional goals, content, and values in new ones. What new values in learning do we face at the moment?

It is a pity to see that almost all educational innovations have tried to superimpose a new dominant view by disqualifying and supplanting prior conceptions of learning. A prominent example is the introduction of the instructional metaphor based upon the need to select and train more and more military candidates. Its method was to discern, sequence, and test small steps in knowledge and skill, in order to be sure that the learning process could be regulated and controlled according to an analytic template. With the arrival of computer-based instruction this cybernetic approach reached its apotheosis. As an antidote to this instructional paradigm, the constructivist approach evolved. Its attempt was to see in learning mainly in its idiosyncratic nature; incidental prior knowledge and experiences make every student different.

The recent interest is to use social media and web-based communities to motivate students to invest in each other's "collaborative learning." How can this approach be reconciled with the ongoing university regimes where uniform test criteria are ruling? This is the question to be solved in this volume.

Wishing you a good mood for discussions in the coming days.

**—Piet Kommers**
UNESCO Professor of Learning Technologies
University of Twente
The Netherlands

# CHAPTER 1

# Identifying the e-Learning Facilities for Teaching and Learning Office Technology and Management Courses in Nigerian Tertiary Institutions

AMMANI ABUBAKAR

*Department of Office Technology and Management,*
*College of Administration and Management Studies,*
*Hassan Usman Katsina Polytechnic, Katsina State, Nigeria.*
*E-mails: abubakar752000@yahoo.co.uk; comradeammani8@gmail.com*

## ABSTRACT

e-Learning is the type of learning where electronic technologies are utilized to access educational curricula outside the conventional classroom. e-Learning is the main information communication and technology (ICT) tool used for teaching and collaborating learning. e-Learning usually refers to the structured and managed learning experience and maybe provided partially or wholly via a web browser or through the Internet and intranet or multimedia platform. Tertiary institutions are mandated to create, adapt, and disseminate knowledge to individuals with better professional competencies. This could be achieved using e-learning facilities in the classroom instructions. Specifically, the office technology and management (OTM) courses are expected to comply with 21st- century technologywise since the secretaries are the custodians of the technologies. This paper focused on identifying the e-learning facilities for teaching and learning OTM courses in Nigerian tertiary institutions. The total population was 229 OTM and ICT lecturers used as a respondent all drawn from the seven tertiary institutions in northwest Nigeria. The whole population was used as a sample of the study because the population is manageable in size. The research was guided by three research questions. A structured questionnaire was the instrument used to collect data. It was categorized as SA = (strongly agree), A= (agree), D = (disagree), and SD = (strongly disagree). All of the categories have points of 4 and 1, respectively, in order of their importance. The analysis of data was done using mean and standard deviation to answer the research questions with a benchmark of 2.50. Conclusions and recommendations were also drawn based on the findings. Among others, the paper recommended that the e-learning approach should be used in teaching the OTM courses in tertiary institutions; the management of the institutions should encourage teachers and students to access the facilities that were not accessible as they collaborate and enhance teaching and learning, and special grant for intervention should be provided by the government to collaborate e-learning instructional delivery in tertiary institutions.

## 1.1 INTRODUCTION

e-Learning refers to learning where technologies are utilized to administer educational curriculum outside the conventional class. e-Learning is the main information communication and technology (ICT) tool for instructional delivery. e-Learning means to structure and manage learning experience provided partially or wholly via a web browser or through the Internet, palmtop, e-book, world wide web, etc. The changes occur in most business environments. Tertiary institutions are mandated to create, adapt, and disseminate knowledge to individuals with better professional competencies. This could be achieved using e-learning facilities in the classroom instructions. Specifically, the office training and management (OTM) courses are expected to comply with 21st century technologywise since the secretaries are the custodians of the technologies. This paper focused on identifying the e-learning facilities suitable for the instructional delivery of OTM courses in Nigerian tertiary institutions.

Anderson and Glem (2003) posit that ICT refers to a connection of many different types of computer networks linked together globally. They added that those technologies are used to communicate information are called ICTs. These technologies include computers and its devices, including software and hardware applications used to access the Internet networking infrastructures, video conferencing, and many more.

ICT has essentially entailed in collecting, processing, storing, retrieving, as well as transmitting and communicating data in different forms, such as audiovisual or audio and visual formats (UNESCO, 2002). The concern on how the OTM curriculum is delivered in the Polytechnics, Colleges of Education, and Universities in contemporary times is very important to our educational system. This can be achieved by accessing the e-learning facilities in the instructional delivery situation to improve the academic effectiveness and efficiency of OTM students in modern organizations. The challenges faced by educators in these institutions are neither centered on covering the course contents nor adopting the appropriate pedagogical aids by collaborating e-learning in the teaching and learning process.

The integration of information technology (IT) in teaching is to ensure the quality of the OTM courses. There are two reasons for incorporating ICT facilities in teaching and learning of OTM. First, students would be familiar with the facilities since all jobs in the society rely upon ICT. Second, the pedagogy of OTM courses using e-learning resources would improve the quality of OTM graduates by making them more attractive and effective in the labor market. ICT is significant and plays a very vital role in society. It makes them to have the skills, adapt them, and apply them in processing the information (Aribasala in Apagu and Wakili, 2015).

Furthermore, information is raw facts, while communication, on the other hand, means sending a message from the sender to the receiver. By doing so, communication becomes information (Mukerjee, 2008). As such, only when data is processed, organized, and interpreted, it can be used in decision making. Additionally, technology could be any knowledge that can be used to devote and create tools and process actions while extracting the materials (Ramey, 2013). Technology means embracing the tools, people as well as the organizations put together to get things done quickly, easily, and efficiently.

Ammani (2019) has a view that the greatest challenges in today's world business faced by secretaries are the deficiency in computer skills and understanding of international business trends. So, the rapid advancement in ICT is offering new potentials for producing and distributing knowledge electronically. These technologies are fundamentally altered by how we live and work as well as how we learn and have transformed into a global community. Therefore, there is a need for OTM courses to meet the 21st century computer wise. The OTM as a course, offered by Nigerian Polytechnics, Monotechnics, Universities, and Colleges of Education, was established to provide business knowledge with multiskill knowledge to workers to manage information effectively (Okoro and Amago, 2008). OTM focused on the use of modern technologies for processing and distribution of data and communicate the information in an organization for administration and planning purposes in the office. However, the course is offered in the polytechnics for the acquisition of skills needed to manipulate office machines and equipment. The Federal Government in collaboration with UNESCO reviewed the secretarial education curriculum in polytechnics in 2004, intending to keep pace with modern realities with emphasis on technology revolution by changing the nomenclature from Secretarial education to OTM, which will be very efficient, effective, productive, and functional for self-reliance and self-actualization.

The UNESCO-Nigeria Project (2014) described OTM as a program that is purposely designed to enable students to acquire skills for employment as office managers in public or private organizations. Students in the program will be offered professional, foundation, and general education courses to enable them to acquire vocational and interpersonal skills in the OTM for effective professional competencies at their workstations. It is posited that the OTM program is said to be the composition of office technical skills and adequate relevant knowledge to solve the problems of organizational. The essence of the OTM course was to produce the professional administrative who respond to demands of the 21st century computerwise. This means that the OTM program equips its graduates with adequate knowledge and skills in computer, self-reliance, self-confidence, motivational skills, communicative skills, planning skills, and managerial and human relations.

In a nutshell, the objectives of this study are to identify the required e-learning facilities for instructional delivery of the OTM courses in tertiary institutions and to ascertain the accessibility of the facilities.

## 1.2 RESEARCH DESIGN

The research design for this study was a descriptive survey. The design was considered to seek opinions and views of respondents, and it describes and explains what is in existence or nonexistence (Aliyu, 2006). Therefore, in this design, the researcher uses respondents' views, opinions, and facts from literature to collect analyze and provide answers to the research questions; this, therefore, means that information about the subject of investigation is gathered and is described in their natural setting without manipulating any variables. Nworgu posited that a descriptive survey is the most appropriate, especially for seeking individual's opinions and perceptions in their natural settings (Nworgu, 2007). The present study fits into the above description since it seeks the respondents' opinion on e-learning resources for teaching the OTM courses in Nigerian tertiary institutions of learning.

## 1.3 POPULATION

The population of this study was derived in seven institutions in northwest, Nigeria as follows:

| | |
|---|---|
| Federal College of Education, Katsina | 23 |
| Federal College of Education (Technical), Bichi | 28 |
| Federal College of Education, Kano | 36 |
| State College of Education, Kano | 42 |
| Hassan Usman Katsina Polytechnic | 34 |
| Nuhu Bamalli Polytechnic, Zaria | 30 |
| Kano State Polytechnic | 36 |
| | **229** |

## 1.4 METHODOLOGY

The descriptive statistic was used to analyze the data by using mean and standard deviation to answer the research questions. For any research question to be accepted, its grand mean must not be less than 2.50, else rejected otherwise. The research was guided by three research questions. The instrument designed to collect data was the structured questionnaire that was developed by the researcher and has only one section that was designed to elicit information related to the availability, accessibility, and challenges of e-learning resources in teaching the OTM courses in Nigerian tertiary institutions.

A four-point rating scale was used as follows: SA = (strongly agree), A = (agree), D = (disagree), and SD = (strongly disagree). The research study was carried out in seven tertiary institutions, all in northwest, Nigeria. The target population consists of 229 lecturers who teach OTM and ICT courses in the seven institutions in northwest, Nigeria. The instrument was subjected to face validation by the three experts, two from the Department of Office Technology Management and one from the Mathematics and Statistics Department of Hassan Usman Katsina Polytechnic. The essence was to ascertain the validity of the instrument before administering to the target respondents, as well as the suitability of the instrument in terms of the relevance of content, avoiding ambiguity in the item statement and ensuring the appropriateness of the rating scales adopted, and the statistics applied in analyzing the research questions. Some errors were detected and pointed out by validates, and all were noted and corrected.

## 1.5 CONCEPTUAL FRAMEWORK

### *1.5.1 DEFINING e-LEARNING*

e-Learning is known as a course management system, learning management system or virtual learning environment. This is designed to offer learners the opportunities to collaborate and interact with an icon-based user interface. This offers tools for test building, assignments, reporting, messaging, forum, chats, surveys, calendars, and many more (NITDA, 2018). eLearningNC.gov (2019) describes e-learning as learning that adequately utilizes different technologies to acquire educational curriculum without going to a conventional classroom for instructions. Therefore, e-learning can be viewed as pedagogy instructions offered on the Internet, rather conventional classrooms.

e-Learning refers to a learning system that learners can obtain through the Internet by using a technology device(s) (Market Business News, 2019). The word "online," in this context, means instructions with an Internet connection. Also, e-learning refers to the knowledge and skills acquired by individuals in a settlement or community. Therefore, e-learning is training that can be acquired via the Internet or other means using technologies to collaborate the learning process at any given time and anywhere all over the globe. The Economic Times (2019) opines e-learning as a system of learning using electronic facilities to deliver the curriculum contents learners without having physical contact between the instructor and the students.

E-learning can also be described as the transfer of skills and knowledge to deliver education to a large number of recipients. When it was introduced in early times, it was not accepted wholeheartedly as it was assumed that the system lacked the human element required in learning. Technologies like smartphones, tablets, etc. are nowadays relevant and applicable to the e-learning classrooms. With this development, books, journals, and bulletins will be a history and the archives will also be gradually replaced. Nkemjurumuafo (2016) opines the concept of the e-learning system like the the one among the best that has brought a tremendous improvement in today's Nigerian educational system, more especially in the field of OTM education. So, the use of technologies and other resources are the major improvements to education.

It is an online course for students in which the Internet helps to learn courses related to a variety of techniques, such as presentations, group discussions, video recordings, quizzes, games, surveys, and others (Sain, 2019). e-Learning guides learners to take complete education and training through the Internet. It is an ongoing process of technology in mobiles, computer systems, laptops, and overall technological gadgets for an e-learning environment. It infers that any learning process that will take place by using technology that is connected to Internet outside the conventional learning environment is called e-learning.

Gros and García-Peñalvo (2016) opine that e-learning as a system of learning that could be delivered through the use of the Internet in the learning process, where both the instructors and learners virtually interact without having physical contact in the conventional learning environment, While Aasha at. el. (2016) saw e-learning as a pedagogical way for student-centered learning. Therefore, e-learning includes all computer-assisted programs via Internet connectivity to collaborate and simplified the teaching and learning process.

## 1.6 LEARNING FACILITIES FOR INSTRUCTIONAL DELIVERY OF OTM COURSES

Some of the e-learning resources for teaching and learning OTM courses are listed as follows:

### *1.6.1 VISUAL PRESENTER*

Visual presenter is also called document camera, visualizer, or digital overhead. According to Smart Classroom Equipments (2014), a visual presenter could be used by tutors and learners for displaying images and animations stored on the camera for interactive display on the magnetic whiteboard. A visual presenter also is a mechanism used to present content with a visual display in training rooms, boardroom, classrooms, video conferences, science laboratories, and presentations of all kinds including medical research.

### *1.6.2 IPAD*

iPad refers to a tablet computer that is designed and developed by Apple Inc., who runs the Operating System (Wikipedia, 2019). Wikipedia asserted that the first iPad was released in 2010, while the most recent models are those released in 2018; the fifth-generation iPad Mini was released in 2019. The system has user interface, multitouch screen, and also a keyboard use for data input. According to Wikipedia (2019), iPad computers can be connected using Wi-Fi. Furthermore, iPads can be used to play music, take photos, shoot videos, and perform various Internet functions. Wainwright (2013) asserts that the use of iPads by instructors was to present assignments, questions, and comments.

### 1.6.3 COMPUTERS WITH INTERNET CONNECTIVITY

The computer has overtaken almost all aspects of human life. It is a technology that affects the education sector, economy, health, manufacturing industries including OTM education. In education, computers are used to teach students, thereby solving the problems associated with the overcrowded classrooms. A computer can even enhance the distance learning program.

### 1.6.4 EDUSAT AND e-LEARNING

EduSat is an exclusive satellite used for serving the educational sector. EduSat is configured for audio–visual medium, employing digital interactive classrooms with multimedia systems. The satellite has multiple regional beams covering different parts of India—five Ku-band transponders with spot beams covering northern, north-eastern, eastern, southern, and western regions of the country, a Ku-band transponder with its footprints covering the Indian mainland region, and six C-band transponders with their footprints covering the entire country. The EduSat network provides satellite-based education facilities to students and tutors of the engineering colleges across the country.

### 1.6.5 SMARTPHONES

TechTerms (2010) sees a smartphone as an advanced gadget used for making phone calls and sending text messages. Techopedia (2019) also explains that a smartphone has a powerful CPU, adequate RAM storage, greater connectivity options, and a larger screen that is entirely different from a regular cell phone. In the view of Hope (2019), a smartphone device is designed with a touch screen to allow users to interact with them. Furthermore, Techopedia

(2019) says that typical smartphone are those with touch screen displays, an Internet connection, a browser, and the ability to accept Internet applications. However, Gros and García-Peñalvo (2016) in García-Peñalvo and Seoane-Pardo (2015) have an opinion on the history of e-learning when web emerged. After the evolution of the e-learning model, it was inextricably linked to the evolution of the web.

Moreover, the other e-learning resources include visual instructor-led training, social networking apps, e-mail, online forums, You Tube, teleconferencing, visual learning environment, learning activity management systems, podcasts, world wide web, blogs, e-books, e-libraries, and many more that are not even conversant to the Nigerian educational system.

## 1.7 RESEARCH QUESTIONS

The following research questions are formulated to guide the study:

1. What are the e-learning facilities available for teaching and learning OTM education courses in Nigerian Colleges of Education and Polytechnics?
2. What are the e-learning resources accessible for teaching and learning OTM education courses in Nigerian Colleges of Education and Polytechnics?
3. What are the challenges of using e-learning facilities available for teaching and learning OTM education courses in Nigerian Colleges of Education and Polytechnics?

### *1.7.1 RESEARCH QUESTION 1*

What are the e-learning facilities available for teaching and learning OTM education courses in Nigerian Colleges of Education and Polytechnics? Table 1.1 presents the mean and standard deviation on the availability of e-learning facilities.

Table 1.1 reveals that items 1–18 with lower mean scores 2.92–3.69 indicate that all the e-learning resources are available for teaching the OTM Courses. This is because the mean scores of the items are up to 2.50, which is the benchmark. No item in the table shows that the facilities are not available. Therefore, they are considered as identified e-learning facilities for teaching the OTM courses.

**TABLE 1.1** Mean Rating and Standard Deviation of the Respondents on the Availability of e-Learning Resources for Teaching OTM courses in Nigerian Colleges of Education and Polytechnics

| Sr. No. | Items | N | Mean, X | SD | Decision |
|---|---|---|---|---|---|
| 1. | e-Mail | 229 | 2.94 | 1.06 | Available |
| 2. | Online forums | 229 | 2.95 | 1.03 | Available |
| 3. | World wide web | 229 | 2.92 | 1.01 | Available |
| 4. | Visual learning environment | 229 | 3.00 | 0.95 | Available |
| 5. | Visual presenter | 229 | 3.19 | 0.86 | Available |
| 6. | Computers with Internet connectivity | 229 | 3.23 | 0.83 | Available |
| 7. | iPad | 229 | 3.21 | 1.34 | Available |
| 8. | Learning activity management system | 229 | 3.03 | 1.01 | Available |
| 9. | Smartphone | 229 | 3.10 | 1.04 | Available |
| 10. | EduSat (e-learning) | 229 | 3.13 | 0.92 | Available |
| 11. | Blogs | 229 | 3.46 | 0.66 | Available |
| 12. | e-Books | 229 | 3.52 | 0.68 | Available |
| 13. | e-Libraries | 229 | 3.45 | 0.74 | Available |
| 14. | Social networking apps | 229 | 3.57 | 0.63 | Available |
| 15. | Podcast application | 229 | 3.30 | 0.66 | Available |
| 16. | Teleconferencing | 229 | 3.69 | 0.70 | Available |
| 17. | Internet services | 229 | 3.68 | 0.58 | Available |
| 18. | YouTube (video streaming services) | 229 | 3.32 | 0.97 | Available |

**Source:** Administered Questionnaire, 2019

### *1.7.2 RESEARCH QUESTION 2*

What are the e-learning resources accessible for teaching and learning OTM education courses in Nigerian Colleges of Education and Polytechnics? Table 1.2 presents the mean and standard deviation on the accessibility of e-learning facilities.

Table 1.2 shows that items 19, 20, 21, 24, 27, 29, 30, 31, 32, 34, 35, and 36 with mean scores 3.05–3.42 are all e-learning resources that are accessible for teaching and learning OTM Courses in Nigerian Tertiary Institutions. This is because the mean scores of the items are up to 2.50, which is a benchmark. However, on the other hand, items 22, 23, 25, 26, 28, and 33 with mean ratings of 1.86–2.02 fall below the benchmark of 2.50, which indicates that these are not accessible to both the teachers and learners.

**TABLE 1.2** Mean Rating and Standard Deviation of the Respondents on the Accessibility of e-Learning Facilities for Teaching and Learning OTM Courses in Nigerian Colleges of Education and Polytechnics

| Sr. No. | Items | N | Mean, X | SD | Decision |
|---|---|---|---|---|---|
| 19. | e-Mail | 229 | 3.32 | 0.97 | Accessible |
| 20. | Online forums | 229 | 3.42 | 0.73 | Accessible |
| 21. | World wide web | 229 | 3.07 | 0.93 | Accessible |
| 22. | Visual learning environment | 229 | 1.85 | 0.91 | Not accessible |
| 23. | Visual presenters | 229 | 2.02 | 0.99 | Accessible |
| 24. | Computer with Internet connectivity | 229 | 3.10 | 0.93 | Accessible |
| 25 | iPad | 229 | 2.02 | 0.99 | Accessible |
| 26. | Learning activity management system | 229 | 1.91 | 0.95 | Not accessible |
| 27. | Smartphone | 229 | 3.05 | 0.99 | Accessible |
| 28. | EduSat (e-learning) | 229 | 1.98 | 0.98 | Not accessible |
| 29. | Blogs | 229 | 3.08 | 0.93 | Accessible |
| 30 | e-Books | 229 | 3.05 | 0.97 | Accessible |
| 31 | e-Libraries | 229 | 3.06 | 0.98 | Accessible |
| 32 | Social networking apps | 229 | 3.07 | 0.96 | Accessible |
| 33 | Podcast application | 229 | 1.86 | 0.94 | Not accessible |
| 34. | Teleconferencing | 229 | 3.05 | 1.04 | Accessible |
| 35. | Internet services | 229 | 3.39 | 0.79 | Accessible |
| 36. | YouTube (video streaming services) | 229 | 3.16 | 0.84 | Accessible |

**Source:** Administered Questionnaire, 2019

### *1.7.3 RESEARCH QUESTION 3*

What are the challenges of using e-learning facilities available for teaching and learning OTM education courses in Nigerian Colleges of Education and Polytechnics? Table 1.3 presents the mean rating and standard deviation on the challenges of using e-learning resources.

Table 1.3 reveals that all items from 37 to 47 with a lower mean rating of 2.45–3.68 are above the benchmark of 2.50. Therefore, the items are accepted as challenges of using e-learning facilities in teaching OTM courses. No item was rejected.

**TABLE 1.3** Mean Rating and Standard Deviation of the Respondents on the Challenges of Using e-Learning Resources for Teaching OTM Courses in Nigerian Colleges of Education and Polytechnics

| Sr. No. | Items | N | Mean, X | SD | Decision |
|---|---|---|---|---|---|
| 37. | Lack of social interaction | 229 | 3.08 | 0.93 | Accepted |
| 38. | Lack of instant Internet connection | 229 | 3.05 | 0.99 | Accepted |
| 39. | Difficult to understand the content for courses that need physical contact | 229 | 3.13 | 0.92 | Accepted |
| 40. | Lack of required ICT skills to integrate e-learning models in both parties | 229 | 3.03 | 1.01 | Accepted |
| 41. | High cost of the facilities | 229 | 2.94 | 1.06 | Accepted |
| 42. | Lack of constant electricity | 229 | 2.92 | 1.01 | Accepted |
| 43. | Curriculum content-related factors | 229 | 2.95 | 1.03 | Accepted |
| 44. | Environment-related factors | 229 | 2.45 | 0.74 | Accepted |
| 45. | Lack of specific government policies | 229 | 3.07 | 0.93 | Accepted |
| 46. | Cost of maintenance of the facilities | 229 | 3.12 | 0.96 | Accepted |
| 47. | Difficult to operate by rural settlers | 229 | 3.68 | 0.58 | Accepted |

**Source:** Administered Questionnaire, 2019.

## 1.8 DISCUSSION OF FINDINGS

The result of the analysis in Research Question 1 shows that to deliver e-learning the items 1–18 need to be available for communication between a tutor and students. This would allow e-learning to take place. This is inconsonant with Nmeremikwu-Fiac and Onwukwe in Ngwoke and Nomonde (2011), who opine that computers with Internet and other electronic gadgets globally provide too many opportunities in education. The e-learning facilities have collaborated in no measure for delivery of learning and imparting knowledge and dissemination of information within the shortest possible of time. Odili (2016) has also mentioned some of the e-learning devices like online forums, computers, teleconferencing, Internet, virtual learning environment, and learning activity management system as e-learning tools for distance learning. This supported the items mentioned in Table 1.1 as the right facilities needed for teaching the OTM courses.

However, the result of Research Question 2 revealed that all e-learning items like 19, 20, 21, 24, 27, 29, 30, 31, 32, 34, 35, and 36 are properly accessible. This collaborates the effort of Ammani (2019) that most of the ICT facilities are accessible for learning in Katsina State, Nigeria. He further said that the facilities are highly accessible to enhance the teaching process. This confirmed that the e-learning resources listed in Table 1.2 were accessible for teaching and learning OTM courses, while items 22, 23, 25, 26, 28, and 33 were not accessible. This could be due to the cost or scarcity of the facilities in the market. The result collaborates the effort of Onojetah (2014) who revealed that many of these new technologies are not accessible for teaching and learning.

The result obtained for Research Question 3 presented in Table 1.3 shows that all the 11 items presented are considered to be constraints to the effective use of e-learning facilities in tertiary institutions. The finding was supported by Mmeremikwu-Fiac and Onwukwe (2016) who conducted similar research on the extent of utilization of e-learning opportunities for effective teaching of business education courses. Their findings revealed that out of 17 constraints to the effective use of e-learning facilities, only one item (lack of motivation) was rejected.

## 1.9 FUTURE PROSPECTS

Based on the research findings, the future prospects/recommendations are adumbrated below:

1. Since a majority of the e-learning resources are available, e-learning could take up for teaching the OTM courses in tertiary institutions of learning.
2. The management of the institutions should encourage teachers and students to access those facilities that were not available as they collaborate and enhance teaching and learning.
3. It is recommended that e-learning approaches should be used in teaching OTM courses in tertiary institutions.
4. Government at all levels should as matter of urgency imbibe e-learning in all tertiary institutions in Nigeria.
5. For other nontechnology courses, the sensitization lectures should be delivered from time to time to catch the attention of both students and lecturers to engage in the e-learning process.
6. The government should formulate policies on e-learning pedagogy for tertiary institutions.
7. Special grants for intervention should be provided by the government to collaborate e-learning instructional delivery in tertiary institutions.

## 1.10 CONCLUSION

Conclusively, e-learning facilities for teaching the OTM courses in Nigerian tertiary institutions are those electronic facilities that are connected with the Internet and can be used for virtual classroom instruction. Due to the urgent need for globalization, the resources should be available and accessible for instructional delivery in tertiary institutions of learning. This would help boost the education sector and make it possible for those that could not be able to enroll in the conventional learning environment. As such, this would increase the number of literates who could be professional in various fields. If the facilities are not available and cannot be accessed by both the tutor and the learner, it might be difficult to adopt e-learning in our tertiary education, and this would be a setback for the country's educational development. Similarly, the success on executing e-learning depends purely on the availability and accessibility for both the learners and tutors to realize the goals and objectives of the program. Having got them available and accessible, the OTM programs could be run on a virtual process. This will meet up the 21st-century computer wise. Finally, the knowledge gained from this paper should be used for all tertiary institutions for them to adopt e-learning in the instructional delivery of their courses offered in the institutions.

## KEYWORDS

- **e-learning**
- **facilities**
- **OTM**
- **tertiary institutions**

## REFERENCES

Aasha, V., Rohini G., and Kimaya S. A new trend e-learning in education system. *International Research Journal of Engineering and Technology*, **2016**, 3(4), 299–302. e-ISSN: 2395-0056. Available: https://s3.amazonws.com /academia.edu.documents

Ademuluyi, A. and Bello G.A. *Survey of Polytechnic Secretarial Education as an Instrument of Self-Reliance*, **2017**. Available: www.academia.edu/953

Agholor, S.I., Office technology and management educators' self-appraisal on information and communication tecnology competencies. *International Journal of Advanced Research*, **2019**, 5(3), 34–43.

Aliyu, A. *Information and Communication Technology and Enhancement of Education in the 21st Century*. Umunze: Research and Conference Unit, FCE(T), **2004**.

Ammani, A. *Availability and Utilization of Information Communication Technology in Instructional Delivery of Business Education Courses in Federal Colleges of Education in Northwest, Nigeria* (Unpublished M.Sc. Dissertation). Abakaliki: Ebonyi State University, **2019**, pp. 38–57.

Anderson, L.W. and Glem D.R. (2003). *Model Selection and Multi-Model Inference: A Practical Information—Theoretical Approach*. New York: Springer Science, **2003**.

eLearning. Décimo Aniversario. Education in the Knowledge Society, **2019**, 16(1), 119–144. doi: 10.14201/eks2015161119144. Available: https://repositorio.grial.eu/bitstream/grail/812/1/eLearningChapter_preprint.pdf

e-LearningNC.gov. *What is e-Learning?* Available: http://www.elearningnc.gov/about_elearning/what_is_elearning, **2019**.

García-Peñalvo, F.J. and Seoane-Pardo, A.M. Una revisión actualizada del concepto de eLearning. Décimo Aniversario. *Education in the Knowledge Society*, **2019**, 16(1), 119–144. doi: 10.14201/eks2015161119144. Available: https://repositorio.grial.eu/bitstream/grail/812/1/eLearningChapter_preprint.pdf

Gros, B. and García-Peñalvo, F.J. *Future Trends in the Design Strategies and Technological Affordance of e-Learning*, **2016**, p. 1. Available: https://repositorio.grial.eu/bitstream/grail/812/1/eLearningChapter_preprint.pdf

Hope, C. *Smartphone*, **2019**. Available: https://www.computerhope.com/jargon/s/smartphone.htm

Market Business News. *What is e-Learning? Definition and Examples*, **2019**. Available: https://marketbusinessnews.com/financial-glossary/e-learning/

Mukerjee,H.S. *WhatistheDifferenceBetweenInformationandCommunication?* **2008**.Available: https://www.quora.com/What-is-the-difference-between-information-and-communication.

Ngwoke, D.U. and Nomonde, D. *Optimizing e-Learning Opportunities for Effective Education Service Delivery: A Case Study of e-Textbook in Schools*, **2011**. Nsukka: Publication of Institute of Education, University of Nigeria, pp. 192–212.

NITDA. *e-Learning Facilities*, **2018**, p. 1. Available: https://nitda.gov.ng/nit/e-learning-facilities/

Nkemjurumuafo, O.G. Impact of e-learning on office technology and management education. *Nigerian Journal of Business Education*, **2016**, 3(2), 33–41.

Nmeremikwu-Fiac, C. and Onwukwe, V.E. Assessment of the extent of utilization of e-learning opportunities for effective teaching and learning business education. *Nigerian Journal of Business Education*, **2016**, 3(2), 212–221.

Nworgu, B.G. The indispensability of ICT in educational research in information and communication technology in the service of education, in D.N. Ezeh, Nkadi Onyegegbu (Eds.): Enugu: Timex Publication, 2007, 112–129.

Odili, S.O. e-Learning: Tools for Distance Learning in Business Education. *Business Education Journal,* 3(2), **2016**, 42–51.

Okoro, P.U. and Amago, E.K. Office education competencies required for effective entrepreneurship development in Delta. *Business Education Journal*, **2008**, 1(3), 205–208.

Onojetah, S.O. Business education curriculum and integration of new technologies. *Nigerian Journal of Business Education*, **2014**, 2(1), 139–141.

Ramey, K. *What Is Technology—Meaning of Technology and Its Use*, **2013**. Available: https://www.useoftechnology.com/what-is-technology/

The Economic Times. *Definition of 'e-Learning'*, **2019**. Available: https://economictimes.indiatimes.com/definition/e-Learning

Techopedia. *Smartphone*, **2019**. Available: https://www.techopedia.com/definition/2977/smartphone

TechTerms. *Smartphone Definition*, **2010**. Available: https://techterms.com/definition/smartphone

UNESCO. *ICT in Education*, **2002**. Available: http://www.askjeve.com

Wainwright, A. *Five Smart Ways to Use iPad Technology in the Classroom*, **2013**. Available: https://www.securedgenetworks.com/blog/5-Smart-Ways-to-Use-iPad-Technology-in-the-Classroom

Wikipedia. *Interactive Whiteboard*, **2019**. Available: https://en.wikipedia.org/wiki/ interactive_whiteboard

## APPENDIX I

*Questionnaire Instrument*

### *Question 1*

What are the e-Learning Facilities Available for Teaching OTM Courses in Nigerian Colleges of Education and Polytechnics?

| Sr. No. | Items | SA | A | D | SD |
|---|---|---|---|---|---|
| 1. | E-mail | | | | |
| 2. | Online Forums | | | | |
| 3. | World Wide Web | | | | |
| 4. | Visual Learning Environment | | | | |
| 5. | Visual Presenter | | | | |
| 6. | Computer with the Internet connectivity | | | | |
| 7. | iPad | | | | |
| 8. | Learning Activity Management System | | | | |
| 9. | Smartphone | | | | |
| 10. | Edusat (e-Learning) | | | | |
| 11. | Blogs | | | | |
| 12. | E-books | | | | |
| 13. | E-library | | | | |
| 14. | Social Networking Apps | | | | |
| 15. | Podcast Application | | | | |
| 16. | Teleconferencing | | | | |
| 17. | Internet services | | | | |
| 18. | YouTube (video streaming services) | | | | |

### *Question 2*

What are the e-Learning Resources Accessible for Teaching OTM Courses in Nigerian Colleges of Education and Polytechnics?

| Sr. No. | ITEMS | SA | A | D | SD |
|---|---|---|---|---|---|
| 19. | E-mail | | | | |
| 20. | Online Forums | | | | |
| 21. | World Wide Web | | | | |
| 22 | Visual Learning Environment | | | | |
| 23. | Visual Presenter | | | | |
| 24. | Computer with Internet connectivity | | | | |
| 25 | iPad | | | | |
| 26. | Learning Activity Management System | | | | |
| 27. | Smartphone | | | | |
| 28. | Edusat (e-Learning) | | | | |
| 29. | Blogs | | | | |
| 30 | E-books | | | | |
| 31 | E-library | | | | |
| 32 | Social Networking Apps | | | | |
| 33. | Podcast Application | | | | |
| 34. | Teleconferencing | | | | |
| 35. | Internet services | | | | |
| 36. | YouTube (video streaming services) | | | | |

## *Research Question 3*

What are the Challenges of Using e-Learning Facilities Available for Teaching and Learning OTM Education Courses in Nigerian Colleges of Education and Polytechnics?

| Sr. No. | ITEMS | SA | A | D | SD |
|---|---|---|---|---|---|
| 37. | Lack of social interaction | | | | |
| 38. | Lack of instant Internet connection | | | | |
| 39. | Difficult to understand content for courses that need physical contact | | | | |
| 40. | Lack of required ICT skills to integrate e-Learning model for both parties | | | | |
| 41. | High cost of the facilities | | | | |
| 42. | Lack of constant electricity | | | | |
| 43. | Curriculum contents related factors | | | | |
| 44. | Environmental related factors | | | | |
| 45. | Lack of specific government policy | | | | |
| 46. | Cost of maintenance of the facilities | | | | |
| 47. | Difficult to operate for rural settlers | | | | |

# CHAPTER 2

# Students' Perspective Toward Online vs Offline Modes of Examination

TAMANNA GOEL

*Department of Management Studies, Institute of Information Technology & Management, Janakpuri, New Delhi, India.*
*E-mail: goel.tamanna1502@gmail.com*

## ABSTRACT

Twenty-first century has seen an intensified trend toward online education. Ranging from primary classes to professional courses, technology has deeply embedded itself through various modes. While many research studies observe that the online education system is superior to that of its traditional counterpart, a few also conclude that there is not much difference between the two in terms of efficiency. The current study tries to focus on the role of technology in the mode of examination. Most of the competitive exams have shifted from traditional optical mark reader sheet filling to computer-based technology. This study has analyzed the students' perspective toward both the modes of examination. A comparison has been made between the two through a questionnaire.

## 2.1 INTRODUCTION

The advancement of technology can be seen everywhere today. From online shopping to online bookings to online learning, the Internet has been an effective complement to its traditional counterpart. While this technology has been a boom in many of the ways, a majority of us are still not very comfortable with the use of technology everywhere.

The main purpose of conducting examinations is to test the students' knowledge. Then, finally, these exams are evaluated to put a score on that knowledge. Competitive exams, on the other hand, can be very tricky. The purpose of these exams is not only to judge the capability of the candidates but also to find the best suitable candidates among all the capable ones (Maiya and Shivaprasad, 2014). Today, many of the competitive exams have been transferred to online modes through the Internet.

In the online mode of examination, an institution conducts the exams with the help of the Internet (Omoregbe et al., 2015). A candidate is given a login ID through which he/she begins to attempt the paper. A clock timer is set, and the answers are autosaved when the timer stops. The candidate has to scroll through the questions, can mark the questions for review, and can access any question at a click of a button. Answers can be easily marked and can also be changed without a single error (Parmar and Kumbhrana, 2016). It requires the installation of a lot of systems with Internet connections if the exam has to be conducted on a very large scale. However, this method is considered very economical in terms of the resources required. It has eliminated the use of any study material required. A lot of time and effort is also saved as the evaluation of these exams is also very quick (Hewson, 2012). Since the answers are marked online only, there a very minimal chance of any error on part of the candidate as well on part of the evaluator while evaluating these answers. Result analysis can be done very quickly with the utmost accuracy, eliminating any human error (Anakwe, 2008).

While quoting all the pros of this online mode of examination, the cons however cannot be missed out. Everyone, from administrating staff, evaluators to students have to familiarize themselves with this new mode of examination. Low confidence of the candidate can sometimes hinder the performance. Power failures and slow Internet connections can cause blunders for the students appearing in the paper (Maiya and Shivaprasad, 2014). In such cases, the student might have to reappear or remark all the answers attempted so far. Readability of an online paper is also a serious concern causing stress to the candidate as he/she goes through the paper. Noting the wrong figures from the screen to the paper, in case of practical problems, is a common error.

The traditional pen and paper method (Elliott, 2008), on the other hand, has been in history for long. Many still feel safe and confident with this method as a mode of examination. Easy readability and accessibility to question make this method also a desirable one. However, the shift from this traditional method to online was long due as the traditional method was a very expensive one. From seating arrangements to large faculty and staff to abundant study material required, this method does not score very high in terms of being economical. Also, the tiring and time-consuming process of filling the optical mark reader (OMR) sheet cannot be missed out. Every bubble has to be marked correctly and completely. Half-filled bubbles and overdrawn bubbles are not considered as a correct answer. If a candidate fills a wrong bubble, then there is no chance of redemption. What is worse than not knowing the answer is knowing the answer and still not getting any marks for it? On the contrary, the online method took care of such issues very efficiently.

Having understood the pros and cons of both online and offline modes of examination, it is now very important to understand students' perception of them. How do students perceive the transformation from the traditional offline method to the online mode of examination? Whether the accuracy of the online mode over the offline method is beneficial for them in terms of fairness or the level of confidence or ease of readability that they have in the traditional method is still a preferred choice (Juchnowski and Atkins, 1999; Rarvitz, 1998). With the upgradation of technology, undoubtedly, the online method is a preferred choice. However, with the analysis of students' preference, it can be ascertained that what can be done to make online methods more student-friendly.

## 2.2 LITERATURE REVIEW

Singh et al. (2012) focused on the efficiency of online courses vs their traditional in-class counterparts. The efficiency was defined in terms of the quantitative score, students' viewpoint, and students' level of satisfaction. This study concluded that students taking online course formats are much more efficient than their offline counterparts. The preference of online course work increases, mostly due to the convenience and the flexibility it offers to the students. Lieber and Syverson (2010) focused on the competition that the buyers and sellers face and make a comparison between online marketing and offline marketing. They concluded that the online channels have brought substantial changes in the market economic fundamentals. The markets where online channels have developed are growing at a faster rate. This channel is more evidently seen in the retail and service sectors. Frankl and Schrat-Bitter (2012) presented a secure exam environment in response to the circumstances that occur while conducting an exam. They conducted online testing of approximately 200 students. This research concluded that e-learning has a comparative advantage. Constructive feedback and immediate results help students in detecting deficiencies and fostering learning to improve performance. The results of this study were collected through a brief survey tool to obtain feedback from the participating students.

Omoregbe et al. (2015) provided a report on the implementation of a web-based examination system. In this report, Convenant University was used as a case study. This paper explains the proper method through which online examinations are conducted. Through the use of the Internet or intranet, the institution can conduct an online examination anywhere, anytime. Anakwe (2008) revealed that in different accounting courses, there was no difference in the students' test scores in the online test and the in-class test. However, since the performance of the students remains unaffected, the benefit of the online test can be ripped. These include instant grading and feedback to the students. Maiya and Shivprasad (2014) concluded that since the number of students and examinations have increased, the universities must go for online examinations, which are both qualitative and cost-effective. However, they also mentioned that it is a twin-edge sword; therefore, the university should carefully design the online examination strategy.

## 2.3 RESEARCH GAP

There have been quite a few research studies that compare the online mode of examination, but none has focused on the students' perspective toward both the modes of examination. A comparison between the two has also not been done based on students' perspective. This study has primarily focused on competitive examinations as most of them have been shifted to the online mode. Since the offline competitive exams have now been a thing in the past, it is very important to know that, according to the students, this shift has brought a positive change or not.

## 2.4 RESEARCH METHODOLOGY

Data regarding the students' perspective has been collected through a questionnaire. The questionnaire listed certain factors that will be helpful to understand the students' viewpoints. These factors are the ease of readability and accessibility to the question, economical in terms of resources (Maiya and Shivaprasad, 2014), and the accuracy of the paper (Anakwe, 2008). Students were asked to mark these factors on a scale of 1–5, 1 being the lowest and 5 being the highest. The study has been done on the students in the Delhi-NCR region within the age group of 16–25 years, as this is the age group that is exploring its career opportunities and appearing for most of the competitive exams and also this particular age group has encountered the transition from the offline mode to the online mode of the examination system. The data has been collected from a total of 185 students, out of which 181 were found to be useful. Hence, the sample size is 181 students.

Further, the information collected from the students has been statistically analyzed in SPSS using a paired sample *t*-test. Statistical analysis has been done for each factor that has been put in the questionnaire, and a collective analysis has also been done to test the overall perspective of the students regarding both the modes of examination.

## 2.5 OBJECTIVES OF THE STUDY

- Objective 1: To compare the students' perspective toward online vs offline mode of examination.
- Objective 2: To analyze certain factors that impact students' perspective toward the mode of examination.

## 2.6 HYPOTHESIS TESTING

H0: Students perceive that there is no difference between online and offline modes of examination.

H1: Students perceive that the online mode of examination is better than the offline mode of examination.

## 2.7 FINDINGS

### *2.7.1 DATA ANALYSIS*

Out of the total 181 respondents, 84 were females and 97 were males (Figure 2.1).

| | | Frequency | Percentage | Valid Percentage | Cumulative Percentage |
|---|---|---|---|---|---|
| Valid | Female | 84 | 46.4 | 46.4 | 46.4 |
| | Male | 97 | 53.6 | 53.6 | 100.0 |
| | Total | 181 | 100.0 | 100.0 | |

**FIGURE 2.1** Gender of the respondents.

The respondents were fairly distributed between the two categories of the age group. As can be seen, 50.3% of the sample size was in the age group of 16–20 and 49.7% of the population was in the age group of 21–25 (Figure 2.2).

| | | Frequency | Percentage | Valid Percentage | Cumulative Percentage |
|---|---|---|---|---|---|
| Valid | 16–20 | 91 | 50.3 | 50.3 | 50.3 |
| | 21–25 | 90 | 49.7 | 49.7 | 100.0 |
| | Total | 181 | 100.0 | 100.0 | |

**FIGURE 2.2** Age of the respondents.

The data collected also shows that almost 50% of the population has appeared for more than three competitive exams; hence, this population can easily score the factors given in the questionnaire based on their experience (Figure 2.3).

**How many competitive exams have you appeared so far?**

| | | Frequency | Percentage | Valid Percentage | Cumulative Percentage |
|---|---|---|---|---|---|
| Valid | 1 | 37 | 20.4 | 20.4 | 20.4 |
| | 2 | 28 | 15.5 | 15.5 | 35.9 |
| | 3 | 23 | 12.7 | 12.7 | 48.6 |
| | More than 3 | 93 | 51.4 | 51.4 | 100.0 |
| | Total | 181 | 100.0 | 100.0 | |

**FIGURE 2.3** Number of competitive exams appeared by the respondents.

### 2.7.2 RESULTS

The respondents were asked to give scores for the online mode of examination and the offline mode of examination based on four factors (Figure 2.4). The four variables have been coded as follows:

*V1: Ease of readability* – How comfortable do the candidates find it to read the paper with concentration through online as well as offline mode?

*V2: Ease of accessibility to the questions* – How easy do the candidates find to access any question at any time during the paper?

*V3: Economical in terms of resource used* – Since many resources are required to conduct any mode of examination like study material, faculty personnel, staff personnel, seating arrangement, computer systems, etc., how much economical do the candidates think is a particular mode of examination?

*V4: Accuracy of the paper* – Accuracy can be judged on two bases: First, on behalf of the candidate in terms of marking the answers and second on behalf of the evaluator in terms of evaluating those answers.

*V5: V1 + V2 + V3 + V4* – This is a hypothetical variable introduced to add the scores given by the respondents to each factor.

**Paired Sample Statistics**

| | | Mean | N | Std. Deviation | Std. Error Mean |
|---|---|---|---|---|---|
| Pair 1 | Easy to read the paper [online] | 3.33 | 181 | 1.234 | 0.092 |
| | Easy to read the paper [offline] | 3.85 | 181 | 1.190 | 0.088 |
| Pair 2 | Ease of accessibility to the questions [online] | 3.28 | 181 | 1.194 | 0.089 |
| | Ease of accessibility to the questions [offline] | 3.83 | 181 | 1.084 | 0.081 |
| Pair 3 | Economical in terms of resources used [online] | 3.73 | 181 | 1.219 | 0.091 |
| | Economical in terms of resources used [offline] | 3.09 | 181 | 1.246 | 0.093 |
| Pair 4 | Accuracy of the paper [online] | 3.72 | 181 | 1.171 | 0.087 |
| | Accuracy of the paper [offline] | 3.53 | 181 | 1.052 | 0.078 |
| Pair 5 | Sum of all the variables [online] | 14.07 | 181 | 3.997 | 0.297 |
| | Sum of all variables [offline] | 14.30 | 181 | 3.726 | 0.277 |

**FIGURE 2.4** Descriptive statistics of the sample.

### 2.7.3 INTERPRETATION

After running a paired sample *t*-test on the data collected in SPSS, the following results are achieved (Figure 2.5).

1. *Ease of readability of the paper (V1):* The mean value for the ease of readability for the online paper is 3.33, which is significantly less at the $p < 0.01$ level (note $p = 00$) than the mean value for V1 in the case of offline exams (3.85), and this shows that students perceive that reading on paper is much easier as compared to reading on the computer screens.
2. *Ease of accessibility to the question (V2):* The mean value for the ease of accessibility of questions in an online paper is 3.28, which is again significantly less than that for the offline paper (3.83) at $p < 0.01$

**Paired Samples Test**

| | | Paired Differences | | | | | t | df | Sig. (2-tailed) |
|---|---|---|---|---|---|---|---|---|---|
| | | Mean | Std. Deviation | Std. Error Mean | 95% Confidence Interval of the Difference | | | | |
| | | | | | Lower | Upper | | | |
| 1 | Easy to read the paper [online]–[offline] | −0.519 | 1.708 | 0.127 | −0.770 | −0.269 | −4.090 | 180 | 0.000 |
| 2 | Ease of accessibility to the questions [online]–[offline] | −0.547 | 1.641 | 0.122 | −0.788 | −0.306 | −4.484 | 180 | 0.000 |
| 3 | Economical in terms of resources used [online]–[offline] | 0.641 | 1.861 | 0.138 | 0.368 | 0.914 | 4.632 | 180 | 0.000 |
| 4 | Accuracy of the paper [online]–[offline] | 0.188 | 1.523 | 0.113 | −0.036 | 0.411 | 1.659 | 180 | 0.099 |
| 5 | Sum of all the variables [online]–[offline] | −0.238 | 5.129 | 0.381 | −0.990 | 0.515 | −0.623 | 180 | 0.534 |

**FIGURE 2.5** *t*-test results for each of the variable.

level. Therefore, according to students, it is much easier to access the questions on paper than on the computer screens.

3. *Economical in terms of the resources used (V3):* Here, the mean for the online paper is 3.73, which is significantly higher than that for the offline mode of exam (3.09) at $p < 0.01$ (note $p = 00$). So, according to students, the online mode of examination is much economical in terms of the resources used as compared to its offline counterpart.
4. *Accuracy of the paper (V4):* The mean value for the accuracy of the online mode of exam is 3.72, which is higher as compared to the mean value of accuracy of offline mode of exam (3.53). However, the $p$ value in this case is 0.099, which higher than ours (0.05). Hence, this difference is not much significant. So, this shows that according to students, a significant amount of accuracy can be achieved in both the modes of examinations and none of them is superior or inferior to each other.
5. *Aggregated value (V5):* The mean value for all the aggregated values for online exams is 14.07, which is slightly less than that for offline exams (14.3). The $p$ value in this case is 0.053, which is higher than 0.05. Hence, the null hypothesis (H0) is not rejected in this case. Thus, students do not perceive much difference between the two modes of examination on an overall basis. The positives of one mode of examination outgrow its negatives over the other one.

## 2.8 CONCLUSION

As this study that has been done on a sample size of 181, it has shown that students do not perceive much difference between both online and offline modes of examination; it can be concluded that the shift from the traditional and strenuous process of OMR filling to the online mode of examination is a positive step. As the online mode of examinations has proved to be very economical and efficient in terms of its accuracy, its implementation has been beneficial in terms of technological advancement. Confidence, which was a matter of concern with the candidates, can be gained over a period of time.

Ease of readability and accessibility to the questions can be improved in the online mode of examinations. However, many of the online examinations have now added a "question ballet," which is placed at the side of the computer screen. This ballet makes it easier for the candidate to access any question that he/she wants to by just clicking on the number of question that he/she wants to jump to. The readability of the paper is a serious concern, as it actually becomes difficult for the candidate to continuously look at the screen for hours and keep the concentration for the paper as well. Better quality of screens and properly adjusted lights could do the work. However, nonetheless, the benefits of the online mode have outgrown its disadvantages.

Faster results, time saving, improved structure, convenience, unbiased, environment friendly, up to date, less chances of cheating, quick feedback (Frankl and Bitter, 2012), and less painful are some of the benefits that have been reported by the students in the past regarding the online mode of examination. Over the time period, when candidates will get a hold of this technology, the offline mode of examinations will become a thing in the past. Moreover, we will also be able to see more favorable statistical results for online exams.

Since modernization, so far, has only been introduced with these objective types of exams, it will be interesting to see how they are applied with other types of examinations. Will the students be able to type their answers in the computer screen? While technology has excelled itself in terms of accuracy when it comes to objective-type exams? Can it prove to be as beneficial, when it comes to subjectivity? With the use of artificial intelligence, thesaurus, and other smart software, can the subjectivity of the answer be evaluated with utmost accuracy? Expensive investments will be required for system installation, and the cost associated with the maintenance of the infrastructure is a matter of concern. However, the resources, time, and efforta that will be saved will definitely be beneficial in the future. Also, the offline mode of examinations generally suffers from a "Halo effect" (Kahneman, 2011), whereby the examiner may infer one attribute of the candidate (e.g., good handwriting) with other general attributes. It can be undoubtedly inferred that the online testing methods offer more objectivity (Frankl and Bitter, 2012). Hence, this study concludes that since the students perception is indifferent toward either mode of examination, modernization and technological advancement are necessary and positive for the growth of any nation.

## 2.9 RESEARCH LIMITATIONS AND FUTURE RESEARCH

The study of this research has been limited to the Delhi-NCR region only due to the limited time and resources. Future studies can be focused on other areas also. Apart from the variables that have been analyzed in this research paper, other variables can also be studied. Analysis can also be done with respect to different areas of specializations. Results could differ according to different faculties also. The pattern of exams is different in engineering compared of management. One might be suitable for the online mode of examination, while other might not be. Hence, different studies can be done on different areas.

## KEYWORDS

- **education system**
- **higher education**
- **online education**
- **offline education**
- **role of technology**
- **students' perpective**

## REFERENCES


Anakwe Bridget; Comparison of student performance in paper-based versus computer-based testing. Journal of Education for Business, Vol. 84, Issue 1; Pages 13–17, 2008.

Frankl Gabriele and Sofie Schratt-Bitter; Online exams: Practical implications and future directions. In: Proceedings of the European Conference on e-Learning, ECEL 2012; October 26, 2012.

Maiya Umesh and Shivaprasad K.; Students' perception towards online examinations of university. International Journal of Business and Administration Research Review, Vol. 1, Issue 2; Pages 3–5; 2014.

Omoregbe Nicolas A.; Ambrose A. Azeta; Adewole Adewumi and Ajayi O. Oluwafunmilola; Implementing an online examination system. In: Proceedings of the 8th International Conference of Education, Research and Innovation, ICERI 2015, Spain; November 16–18, 2015.

Parmar Vimal P. and C.K. Kumbhrana; Analysis of different examination patterns having question answer formulation, evaluation techniques and comparison of MCQ type with one work answer for automated online examination. International Journal of Scientific and Research Publications, Vol. 6, Issue 3; Pages 459–463, March 2016

Singh Shweta; David H. Rylander and Tina C. Mims; Efficiency of online vs offline learning: a comparison of inputs and outcomes. International Journal of Business, Humanities and Technologies; Vol. 2, Issue 1; Pages 93–98, January 2012.

CHAPTER 3

# Perception of Students Toward the Use of PowerPoint Presentations as a Teaching Tool

SUNITHA RAVI* and SAVITA WASWANI

*Department of Management, Institute of Information Technology & Management, D-29, Institutional Area, Janakpuri, New Delhi 110058, India*

**Corresponding author. E-mail: sunitharavi21@gmail.com*

## ABSTRACT

Nowadays, the usage of PowerPoint as a teaching tool in class rooms has become more popular due to innovative teaching pedagogy. PowerPoint improves the clarity of presentations, helps to illustrate the message, and engages the students. PowerPoint can be used to project visuals, which would otherwise be difficult to bring to the classroom. The main objective of the study is to understand the awareness of students about the use of PowerPoint as a teaching tool in classrooms and to study the participation factor of students while PowerPoint is used. In general, most of the teachers prefer the teaching method of using PowerPoint because it delivers the material easily and the facilities in the PowerPoint make students more focused. The use of images, animations, videos, and sounds will attract the attention of students and is a part of innovation in teaching. Majority of students feel that PowerPoint is an effective tool for teaching. The atmosphere of the classroom becomes interesting when the teacher teaches using PowerPoint. The students preferred PowerPoint over the traditional lecture style in the teaching–learning process because they think it helps them to grasp the content easily.

## 3.1 INTRODUCTION

A learning process consists of various factors like teacher, students, and supporting facilities. On the basis of the mentioned factors, various teaching–learning approaches have evolved. One of them was a teacher-centered approach that includes the chalk and talk technique. This technique is considered as more of a dominated way of teaching that could not meet the need of learners. Gradually, with the progress of information and communication technology (ICT), the alternate technique was evolved known as the student-centered technique. Various technological devices and software are used to develop learners' abilities; PowerPoint (PPT) is one among those techniques.

PowerPoint is application software that is commonly used as a presentation and teaching tool in academics and the corporate world. Nowadays, it is a powerful tool for classroom teaching and learning. It is used to improve the teaching sessions by incorporating graphs and other multimedia options. The importance of PPT is quite common in this era of science and technology, driven by ICT (Gambari et al., 2015).

PowerPoint application software, developed by Microsoft in 1987, is nowadays used as a good medium of instruction (Gambari et al., 2015). The use of PPT in classrooms is very common, while its effectiveness is still being assessed. Although some studies have found that a PPT presentation is useful for students as it contains graphic content, while other researchers revealed that there is no significant difference between the scores of students taught through both the different ways (Smith, 2015).

## 3.2 LITERATURE REVIEW

Seth et al. (2010) assessed the perception of medical students and dental students toward the use of teaching aids. Primary data has been collected through questionnaires and interviews. The findings revealed that the medical students preferred the use of PPT presentations, whereas the dental students preferred the chalk and talk method. This study was failed to find the evidence-based superiority of any lecture delivery method, but it revealed that in the hands of a trained teacher any teaching aid would be appropriate and effective. This highlights the need for formal training in teaching technologies to develop good presentation skills and thus motivate the students.

Masoud et al. (2012) highlighted various ways to use PPT in the classroom teaching, such as for review, practice and drill, and conducting tests. Further, the researchers underlined several risk factors concomitant with the technology, such as equipment failure, file corruption, incompatible media, etc.

Lari (2014) carried out a study to investigate the effectiveness on use of technology on teaching English and the learners' preference toward modern teaching and traditional teaching. The data is collected from secondary school students. There were two groups of students. One group was teaching through modern technologies, like an liquid crystal display projector, PPT, etc., and the other group was teaching through tradition teaching, like face-to-face interaction, lectures, etc. The study concluded that there was a significant difference between the means of two groups. The study showed that the group that was teaching through modern technology showed better performance.

Gambari et al. (2015) studied the effectiveness of PPT for teaching technical drawing concepts in Nigerian schools. The study has been conducted by forming an experimental group and a control group comprising 100 students including high, medium, and low achievers. PPT presentation was used for the experimental group, whereas the control group was taught by the chalkboard method. The result shows that the experimental group (taught with PPT) performed better than the control group.

Zouar (2015) conducted a study to examine the impact of PPT in enhancing students' participation in the English as a Foreign Language classroom. The study focused on the perception of students toward the English class. A total of 40 students doing Baccalaureate level course were enrolled for the study. The study concluded that the participation level of students enhanced when PPT was used.

Gadicherla and Babu (2018) examined the perception of MBBS students on blackboard teaching and PPT presentation in learning biochemistry. The study concluded that 70% of the students preferred the blackboard teaching method over PPT presentation. In total, 62% of the students preferred PPT for making notes as compared to blackboard teaching. The study found that blackboard still remains the preferred teaching technique to learn.

## 3.3 RESEARCH METHODOLOGY

The study is descriptive in nature, and the source of data is primary data collected through a structured questionnaire. A five-point Likert scale was used. For the selection of the sample, the convenient sampling method was adopted, and an attempt has been made to include all the age groups and genders of every class of students from management and commerce. The sample size was restricted to 95 respondents. Sampling type is judgmental sampling, as only students have been targeted.

Following are the objectives of this paper:

- To study the perception of students toward the use of PPT as a teaching tool in classrooms.
- To study the participation factor of students while PPT is used.

## 3.4 ANALYSIS AND INTERPRETATION

Figure 3.1 indicates that 97.9% of students are aware of PPT and 2.1% of the students do not know about PPT.

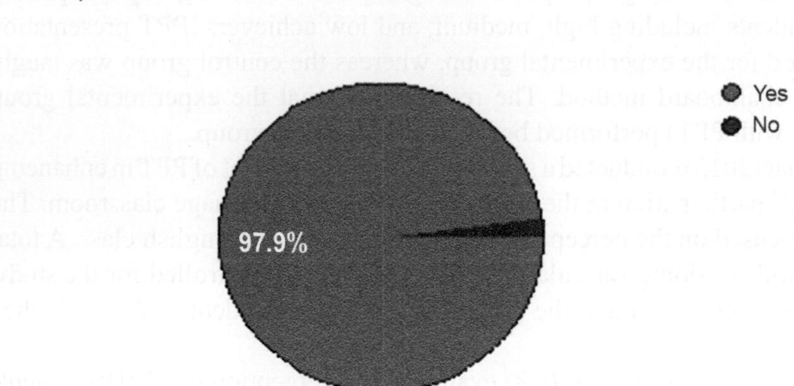


**FIGURE 3.1** Percentage showing awareness of students towards PPT.

Figure 3.2 indicates that majority of students (92.7%) says that PPT is used in their classrooms and 7.3% says that teachers follow the traditional way of teaching in classrooms.

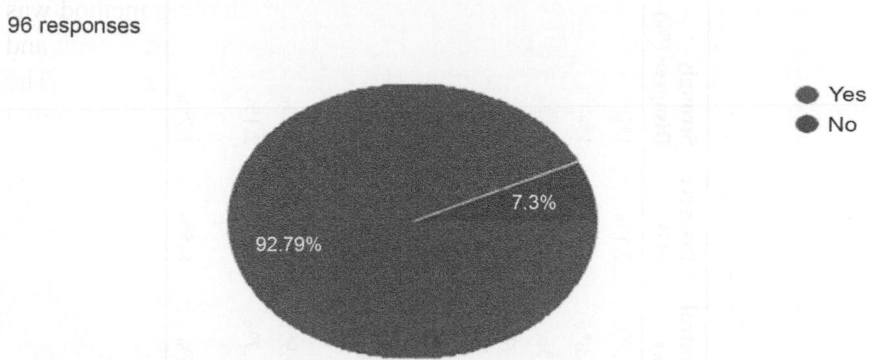


**FIGURE. 3.2** Usage of PowerPoint in classroom teaching.

Table 3.1 shows that 39.6% respondents were strongly agree and 39.6% were agree that PPT presentation is an effective tool of learning. In total, 76% respondents found it as an easy tool to understand the topics and approximately 43% of students consider it better than the chalk and talk technique.

Further, approximately 74% of the respondents perceived that the material presented through PPT is well organized and also feel that it is the best tool that draws more attention when the teacher teaches. In total, 54% students feel that the participation rate increases with the use of PPT.

In total, 52% of the students agree that use of PPT make the class atmosphere more interesting and 45.7% of the respondents agree that visual images presented in PPT lectures helps to recall the content during their final exams. Majority of the students (39.4%) disagree that the use of PPT during lectures is boring.

In total, 46.8% of the students agree that PPT should be used more as a tool for learning in classroom teaching and 43.6% of the respondents agree that they have got an exposure to PPT presentations in school too.

## 3.5 CONCLUSION

In general, most of the teachers prefer the teaching method by using PPT because it delivers the material easily and the facilities in the PPT make students more focused. The use of images, animations, videos, and sounds will attract the attention of students, and this is called innovation in teaching. In the present study, students preferred PPT over the traditional lecture style because they think it helps them to grasp the content easily. Students feel that

**TABLE 3.1** Percentage of Responses for Each Statement

| Sr. No. | Statements | Strongly Agree (%) | Agree (%) | Neutral (%) | Disagree (%) | Strongly Disagree (%) |
|---|---|---|---|---|---|---|
| 1 | PPT is an effective tool for learning | 39.6% | 39.6% | 17.7% | 2.1% | 1% |
| 2 | It is easy for me to understand the topics through PPT | 30.2% | 45.8% | 18.8% | 4.2% | 1% |
| 3 | PPT draws my attention more to the lesson/topic the teacher teaches | 29.2% | 39.6% | 24% | 5.2% | 2.1% |
| 4 | I feel that learning through PPT is better than the chalk and talk technique | 16.7% | 27.1% | 39.6% | 13.5% | 3.1% |
| 5 | I feel that PPT presents the material in a well-organized way | 23.2% | 54.7% | 15.8% | 5.3% | 1.1% |
| 6 | I feel that the participation rate of students is more when PPT is used | 16% | 38.3% | 33% | 9.6% | 3.2% |
| 7 | PPT makes the class atmosphere more interesting | 13.8% | 52.1% | 25.5% | 6.4% | 2.1% |
| 8 | Visual images presented in PPT lectures help to recall the content during exams | 35.1% | 45.7% | 17% | 1.1% | 1.1% |
| 9 | I feel that the use of PPT in lectures is boring | 6.4% | 13.8% | 30.9% | 39.4% | 9.6% |
| 10 | PowerPoint should be used more as a tool for learning in classroom teaching | 17% | 46.8% | 27.7% | 6.4% | 2.1% |
| 11 | I have got exposure to the PPT tool in schools too | 28.7% | 43.6% | 16% | 8.5% | 3.2% |

they participate more in the classroom teaching through PPT presentation. There must be projectors in every classroom of a school/college as it is the best form of innovation for teaching the students. Students and teachers both must be provided with training and workshops on the use of PPT so that it can be used effectively.

## 3.6 SCOPE OF FURTHER STUDY

For future studies, the following can be adopted:

- Greater sample size can be taken.
- Study can be conducted over a longer period of time.
- The geographical area can be enlarged.
- Expertise of academicians, IT professionals, and research scholars can be incorporated.

## KEYWORDS

- **PowerPoint**
- **teaching-learning**
- **pedagogy**

## REFERENCES

Allan M. J.; The use and abuse of PowerPoint in teaching and learning in the life sciences: A personal overview. Bioscience Education, **2003,** 2(1), 1–13. doi: 10.3108/beej.2003.02000004.

Gadicherla S., Babu R.; Comparison of blackboard and PowerPoint presentation in teaching biochemistry for MBBS students. International Journal of Biomedical and Advance Research, **2018,** 9(1), 19–22. doi: 10.7439/ijbar.v9i1.4551

Gambari A.I., et al.; Effectiveness of PowerPoint presentation on students' cognitive achievement in technical drawing. *Malaysian Online Journal of Educational Technology*, **2015,** 3(4), 1–12.

Hashemi M., et al.; PowerPoint as an innovative tool for teaching and learning in modern classes. Procedia—Social and Behavioral Sciences, **2012,** 31, 559–563. Available at: www.sciencedirect.com

Lari S.F.; The impact of using PowerPoint presentations on students' learning and motivation in secondary schools. Procedia—Social and Behavioral Sciences, **2014,** 98, 1672–1677.

Masoud H., Masoud A., Masoumeh F.; PowerPoint as an innovative tool for teaching and learning in modern classes. Procedia—Social and Behavioral Sciences, **2012,** 31, 559–563.

Seth V., et al.; PowerPoint or chalk and talk: Perceptions of medical students versus dental students in a medical college in India. Advances in Medical Education and Practice, **2010,** 1, 11–16. doi: 10.2147/AMEP.S12154

Smith E.; The Perceptions of Students about PowerPoint as a Teaching Tool in College-Level Introductory Biology Classes, **2015.** Available at: https://jewlscholar.mtsu.edu/bitstream/handle/mtsu/4512/ Smith_Honors%20Thesis.pdf?sequence=1&isAllowed=y

Zouar A.; Exploring students' perceptions of using PowerPoint in enhancing their active participation in the EFL classroom action research study. Journal of Literature, Languages and Linguistics, **2015,** 5, 36–39. ISSN: 2422-8435.

## CHAPTER 4

# A Cloud-Based Solution for Smart Education: An Extended Version

M. AFSHAR ALAM and ANAM SAIYEDA*

*Depatment of CSE, School of Engineering Sciences and Technology, Jamia Hamdard, New Delhi 110062, India*

**Corresponding author. E-mail: anamsaiyeda@jamiahamdard.ac.in*

## ABSTRACT

In the current digital era, smart is the latest buzzword, for example, smart cars, smart cities, smartphones; nowadays, technology is ubiquitous and smart. e-Learning began the era of smart education, which has now evolved to mobile-learning and smart-learning. Education is now not only limited to just one-way communication like in YouTube videos but also has become interactive and smart, leading the way to the creation of ubiquitous learning or ubiquitious-learning. This paper extends the previous model proposed to have a smart learning environment in campuses. The education environment in campuses can be made smart by integrating Internet of things, cloud computing, and education. The previous cloud-based model proposed for the smart learning environment has been extended to include more features to make it smarter by the introduction of a feedback module with form-based and log-based responses from the users. The student module has also been updated to add a discussion forum.

## 4.1 INTRODUCTION

The paradigms of education have now shifted from traditional teaching methods to smart campuses with state-of-the-art technology and devices. Smart campuses are a part of the smart cities initiative. Smart parking, smart timetable, smart energy management, smart attendance, and smart education all are subparts of this smart campus initiative.

Students of today's technology-driven world are millennials. In this era, encyclopedias and dictionaries have become obsolete to be replaced by smartphones, smartwatches, and such devices. Unidirectional, traditional, theory-based teaching is thus becoming, a thing of the past. Learning is not just merely attending the lesson. It goes beyond that. Media, especially social media, has a significant impact on learning. Therefore, learning is a long process that begins before the class and continues even after that with several factors influencing it. These smart learning techniques will lead to smart educators and smart students. The universities today need to be updated to be at par with the technologically driven environment and compete with the new e-learning and m-learning platforms, and solutions. There are a plethora of options for smart learning for students like collaborative educational platforms, Internet-based content, revising platforms, mobile apps, and offline video lessons.

To implement smart learning, a smart learning environment is needed. This environment encompasses both the virtual and the physical environment. This environment aims to become an intelligent environment. This will have all the needs of the students and educators integrated together at a place. Nowadays, not only colleges and universities but also schools are inching toward smart education. The simplest devices that introduced the students to the digital world are projectors and document cameras, which are now available in most educational institutes. To move toward smart-learning (s-learning), smart devices and technology are now being implemented. These lead to a better learning outcome of the traditional teaching–learning environment. Advanced methods and techniques like cloud computing, virtual learning environment, fog computing, Internet of things (IoT), and online virtual classrooms are being applied to education to make education and learning smart and ubiquitous. These attempt to make an interactive environment for learning. This is because unidirectional and one-way learning with students being the passive observer is no longer the best technique for education. Content, lessons, quizzes, and virtual classrooms coexist with reinforcement tools to create a new learning experience. Visual learning is a very important part of the learning paradigm. Creation of interactive video content is another crucial part of the s-learning field.

s-Learning aims to fully prepare the students for the fast-changing world. Interaction and involvement of the students in the learning environment are necessary to make the process of learning optimal. In the real world, adaptability is an important quality needed to employ these students. Thus, s-learning helps develop these skills in students. Analytics, digitalization, and assessment are also skills that educators need to learn. Teachers and learners both need to learn these skills and have adaptability needed for a digital future.

The another advantage of digital technology has been remote learning. Students in remote areas can access educational resources and learn with the help of technology. However, earlier this was a one-way communication. Now with s-learning, these students can also have interactive education. They can communicate with the teacher, post questions, have discussions, and thus have a better learning experience. s-Learning methods also enable the interaction of students with other students, all around the globe. Using virtual learning platforms, they can collaborate with other students and teachers, have online discussions, enroll in Massive Online Open Courses (MOOC), solve their doubts, and so on. Learning a virtual environment will have a greater impact on such students and make education really smart for them. s-Learning has benefits for the parents of students as well. Technology can help them by keeping them updated on their child's progress and involves them in the learning process. Machine learning and big data analytics can be applied to student and education data to create personalized courses. Individual learning styles, motivation for learning, understanding level, previous education, and all this data can enable finding of patterns, making predictions, and thus improving the process of learning. The goal will be to improve the educational outcomes of learning. This type of information and these insights are not possible in traditional learning. This leads to adaptive learning in an active learning environment. This is because s-learning aims at better teaching styles according to the student needs, progress checking of individual learning, training objectives, and continuous improvement.

Tokyo, Hong Kong, and Seoul are the top smart cities in Asia. Several countries have undertaken smart education projects like Singapore's Intelligent Nation (iN2015) Master plan (iN2015 Steering Committee, 2015), Malaysia's smart education project (Ong, Eng-Tek, 2006), and so on. In India too, several initiatives have been taken to promote smart education. One such program for smart education is the India Literacy Project. It works with Google Earth to provide a virtual reality learning experience to students in rural, isolated areas, and government schools. Educomp is an education company based in Gurgaon, India. It is India's largest K-12 content library, providing 3D multimedia educational content and modules. In India, another imitative is the collaboration between Jawahar Navodaya Vidyalayas and

Samsung (Samsung Newsroom India, 2018) that has been done to enable digital education. ERNET India set up the Smart Virtual Classroom Project. It aimed at setting up of high-end smart virtual classrooms in various states of India. Its features include central location for hosting MCU, video conferencing, scheduling s/w, electronic teaching equipments, recording/streaming solutions, and multiparty conferencing.

## 4.2 LITERATURE REVIEW

Smart learning (s-learning) is an emerging research topic that has evolved from e-learning. It now encompasses the fields of m-learning (mobile learning), u-learning (ubiquitious learning), and i-learning (intelligent learning).

IoT has taken the world by storm. Wearable technology, smartphones, e-readers, sensors, smartwatches, and IoT devices have all made technology ubiquitous. The advent of smartphones has been a game changer. The use of smartphones has increased immensely. Students of today's generation are not far behind in their use. These have become the most used devices. With the popularity of Android and iOS reaching new heights, there are a variety of learning apps available to students and educators. This has led to the development of the field of m-learning. It is a fast-growing sector. Lumosity, Evernote, Udemy, Microsoft One Note, and Khan Academy are some of the notable popular learning apps available on the mobile platform. All of these enable learning on the go. These are more popular than the learning management systems (LMSs) that are basically software to enable learning.

LMSs like Moodle (Kakasevski et al., 2008) also represent a shift from the blackboard method to the digital methods. These LMSs are useful not only for teachers and students but also for administrators. Apart from these, there are other LMSs available like Blackboard (Beatty, 2006), Shakai (Berg, 2009), and so on.

For educational purposes, Microsoft has Office 365 Education (Kasahara, 2017). This was earlier known as Office 365 (Skendzic, 2012) for education and by the name Microsoft Live@edu. It provides services and applications for students and teachers. For education institutions, it provides web-based, desktop, mobile applications along with communication tools, collaboration services, and data storage capabilities. It is a subset of Microsoft Education Solutions. It provides students access to various Microsoft applications some of which are Windows Live Spaces, Outlook Live, Windows Live SkyDrive, etc.

Google Classroom (Heggart, 2018) is another platform that enables student participation to improve learning and classroom dynamics. It has features for streamlining assignments, collaboration, document management, communication, and basic classroom management. Google Classroom provides features like a tool to add images, classroom messages, multiple choice answers to questions, organize class streams, add subjects to posts, filter streams, and find specific subjects. It also integrates with other tools provide instant feedback, track student progress, mobile application, and feedback from the teachers.

The popularity of social media can be utilized for enabling students to learn better. It provides an interactive platform for sharing of information, reviews ideas, discussions, solutions to problems, etc. Work has been done to see the effect of Twitter on medical education (Galiatsatos, 2016). The information available on social media platforms can also be analyzed through machine learning to enable better education. Recommender systems can be built using this information. A social-cum-educational portal was built with recommender systems (Jagtap, 2016).

Amazon Web Services (AWS) and Huawei have also worked in this field. Cloud-based solutions for s-learning were proposed by Huawei (2016). It made use of the Agile Controller and cloud platform for the central allocation of ICT resources. Interactive Cloud Classroom Solution, Smart classrooms, Distance Education Solution, and Education Cloud are some other services offered by Huawei. Collaborative e-learning approach was proposed by Alsumait and Fasial (2018). Flores et al. (2016) proposed a gamification technique which was challenge based in order to enable calculation of solids of revolution in engineering. Cloud Web of Things (CloudWoT) a cloud-based solution was presented by Shaaban et al. (2018) that was a reference IoT model for future smart IoT. Shawar (2017) integrated e-learning and m-learning paradigms to get benefit from both technologies. Sedayao (2008) proposed an online virtual computing lab, offering virtual computers.

MOOCs are massive open online courses that are composed of video lessons, assessments, readings, and discussion forums. MOOCs are created by universities but are distributed by course providers like Coursera, edX, FutureLearn, and Udacity. MOOCs also include auto-graded quizzes and peer-feedback assignments (graded by other students). A study by Pardos et al. (2017) enabled efficient navigation in a MOOC for students. This was done by prediction of the next page where significant time would be spent by students. To forecast this, it studied the time spent on the pages and applying a behavioral model to it.

## 4.3 PROPOSED TECHNIQUE

The proposed solution enhances the previously presented cloud-based recommender system. The previous cloud-based solution presented in Alam and Saiyeda (2020) had three layers, that is, the infrastructure layer, cloud-based services layer, and the application layer. The infrastructure layer, which was the lowest layer had devices like mobiles, tablets, and laptops. These were used to access the system. Its task was to handle these devices, their components along with ensuring the connectivity between them and the cloud. The cloud-based services layer was next, which provided storage and hosting services. The application layer is the topmost layer. It had the user portal, accessed by the users that comprised of students and teachers. The presentation and the interactive component were provided by it between the service and the user.

There were two modules in the system: the educator module and the student module. In the educator module, a course and a class were created by the educator. The classroom module allowed the uploading of study material and updating the topics taught after every class. The student module had two submodules. These were the resource viewing module and the question recommendation module or the self-evaluation module. The proposed new addition to the system adds a new feedback module to the system and a submodule in the student module. The feedback module allows the user of the mobile device to track its activities. It can enable the student to learn better by providing feedback to the user. The feedback will be in two forms. The first form will be the logs of the apps used in the device and the other will be a user-filled feedback. The user-filled feedback will rate the system in terms of usability, user-friendliness, etc. These will enable the system to perform better. The log-based feedback will serve the purpose of self-tracking. It will enable the user to get an overview of their own activities. This can enable the user to learn better by keeping track of their activities. The student module worked with the help of unique identification given to each student separately. The new addition to it is the discussion forum. This allows group discussions on topics between students and teachers. Students can collaborate with other students and teachers. They can post their queries and doubts and have discussions on these forums.

The resource viewing module remains the same and allows viewing of the study material. The self-evaluation module is a recommendation system that has questions, assignments, and quizzes. These are updated according to the topic taught in the latest class. Recommendation algorithms like collaborative filtering will be implemented in this to enable better learning. This allows active and interactive learning. The learning here is not passive and unidirectional as attempting quizzes and practice questions help students learn better and evaluate their status. Thus, an active learning environment promotes optimized and bidirectional learning (Figure 4.1).

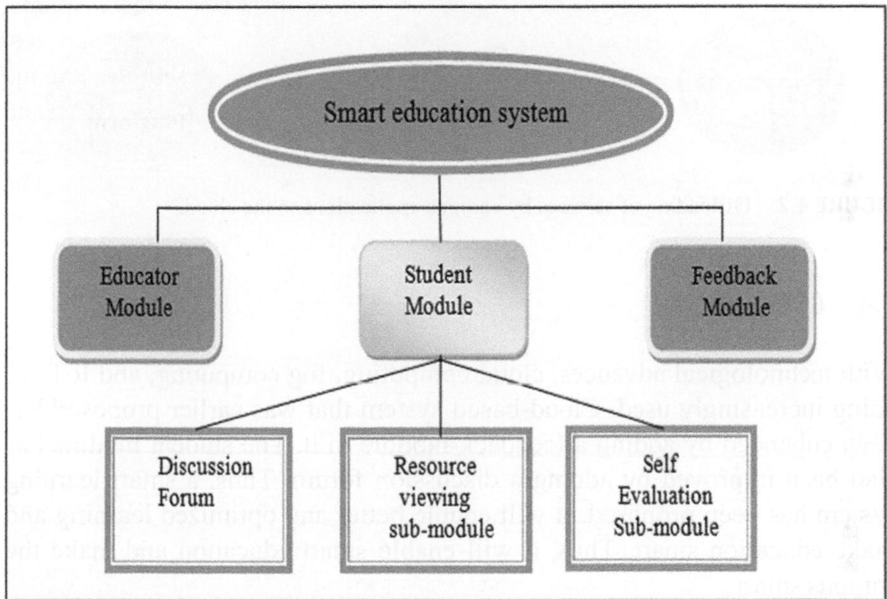


**FIGURE 4.1** Active learning environment.

Cloud computing is still used for the implementation of the system. The university's private cloud will be utilized for the smart education system. The IoT devices, mobile computing components, and storage services will be connected to the cloud. Cloud storage ensures the availability of resources and data anywhere in the campus. This ensures ubiquitous learning and promotes the smart campus paradigm (Figure 4.2).

The offloading of the services to the cloud will enable a better solution for the system. AWS, Microsoft Azure, or any such platform can be used for this. For storage Amazon S3 or such solutions can be used. The mobile devices will send the data and perform storage on the cloud. For computation tasks, Amazon Ec2 can be used or any other such cloud servers. For applications offloading to the cloud, such cloud platforms can be used.

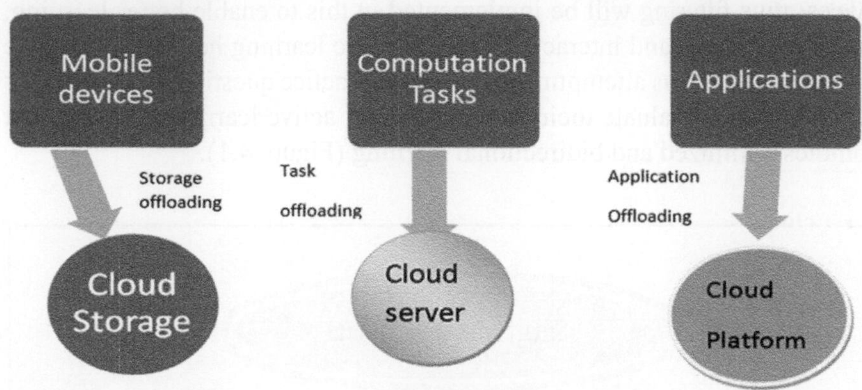


**FIGURE 4.2** Offloading of services by campus applications to the cloud.

## 4.4 CONCLUSION

With technological advances, cloud computing, fog computing, and IoT are being increasingly used. Cloud-based system that was earlier proposed has been enhanced by adding a feedback module to it. The student module has also been improved by adding a discussion forum. Thus, a smart learning system has been proposed. It will enable better and optimized learning and make education smart. Thus, it will enable smart education and make the campus smart.

## 4.5 FUTURE SCOPE

The implementation of the cloud layer will be the next phase of the work. Several platforms like ASWs, Windows Azure, etc. are available. In the future, these services will be utilized for the storage and hosting services of the campus. For data storage functionalities, i.e., the data generated by students, teachers, and cloud-based storage services like Amazon S3 and Amazon Glacier will be used. Also, the software being utilized on the campus will be hosted on the cloud to enable easy access anywhere and reduce the dependency on hardware components, systems, data servers, etc. For hosting of applications and server requirements Amazon Ec2 instances will be used. This will enable on-demand scaling-up and scale-down depending upon the need, rather than purchasing new hardware when the need arises. AWS IoT Core can be employed to easily connect the various devices available on the campus like mobiles, etc. to the cloud and also connect them to other devices, thus creating an inter-connected IoT smart campus with the least amount of investment in hardware resources.

## KEYWORDS

- **cloud**
- **smart education**
- **e-learning**

## REFERENCES

Alam, M. Afshar and Anam Saiyeda. "A cloud based solution for smart education." International Journal of Smart Education and Urban Society 11.2 (2020): 28–37.

Alsumait, Asmaa, and Maha Fasial. "CLTD: collaborative learning tool for deaf." Proceedings of the 20th International Conference on Information Integration and Web-based Applications & Services. ACM, 2018.

Al-Nadwi, Musaddiq Majid Khan, et al. "Cloud enabled e-glossary system: a smart campus perspective." International Conference on Security, Privacy and Anonymity in Computation, Communication and Storage. Springer, Cham, Switzerland, 2018.

Beatty, Brian, and Connie Ulasewicz. "Faculty perspectives on moving from Blackboard to the Moodle learning management system." TechTrends 50,4, 2006: 36–45.

Berg, Alan Mark, and Michael Korcuska. Sakai Courseware Management: The Official Guide. Packt Publishing Ltd., Birmingham, UK, 2009.

Dave, Vachik S., et al. "A combined representation learning approach for better job and skill recommendation." Proceedings of the 27th ACM International Conference on Information and Knowledge Management. ACM, 2018.

Flores, Elvira G. Rincón, María Soledad Ramírez Montoya, and Juanjo Mena. "Challenge-based gamification and its impact in teaching mathematical modeling." Proceedings of the 4th International Conference on Technological Ecosystems for Enhancing Multiculturality. ACM, 2016.

Galiatsatos, Panagis, et al. "The use of social media to supplement resident medical education–the SMART-ME initiative." Medical Education Online 21,1, 2016: 29332.

Hao, Yixue, et al. "Learning for smart edge: cognitive learning-based computation offloading." Mobile Networks and Applications, 25, 2018: 1–7.

Heggart, Keith R., and Joanne Yoo. "Getting the most from google classroom: a pedagogical framework for tertiary educators." Australian Journal of Teacher Education 43,3, 2018: 9.

Hosseinian-Far, Amin, Muthu Ramachandran, and Charlotte Lilly Slack. "Emerging trends in cloud computing, big data, fog computing, IoT and smart living." Technology for Smart Futures. Springer, Cham, Switzerland, 2018, pp. 29–40.

Huawei Technologies Solution Brief, "New ICT Building a Better Connected Education Huawei Smart Education Solutions," Huawei Industrial Base, Bantian Longgang, Shenzhen, 518129, Version No.: M3-035554-20160402-C-1, 2016.

iN2015 Steering Committee, "Innovation. Integration. Internationalisation," Report by the iN2015 Steering Committee, Singapore: An Intelligent Nation, a Global City, powered by Infocomm, Infocomm Development Authority of Singapore, June 2006.

Jagtap, Ashish, et al. "Homogenizing social networking with smart education by means of machine learning and Hadoop: a case study." Proceedings of the 2016 International Conference on Internet of Things and Applications (IOTA). IEEE, 2016.

Kakasevski, Gorgi, et al. "Evaluating usability in learning management system Moodle." Proceedings of the ITI 2008 30th International Conference on Information Technology Interfaces. IEEE, 2008.

Kasahara, Yoshiaki, et al. "Our experience with introducing Microsoft Office 365 in Kyushu University." Proceedings of the 2017 ACM SIGUCCS Annual Conference. 2017.

Kim, Svetlana, Su-Mi Song, and Yong-Ik Yoon. "Smart learning services based on smart cloud computing." Sensors 11.8 (2011): 7835–7850.

Lee, Aeri. "Authentication scheme for smart learning system in the cloud computing environment." Journal of Computer Virology and Hacking Techniques 11.3 (2015): 149–155.

Ong, Eng-Tek. "The Malaysian smart schools project: an innovation to address sustainability." Proceedings of the 10th UNESCO-APEID International Conference on Education Learning Together for Tomorrow: Education for Sustainable Development. 2006.

Pardos, Zachary A., et al. "Enabling real-time adaptivity in MOOCs with a personalized next-step recommendation framework." Proceedings of the 4th 2017 ACM Conference on Learning@ Scale. ACM, 2017.

Riahi, Ghazal. "e-Learning systems based on cloud computing: a review." Procedia Computer Science 62 (2015): 352–359.

Samsung Newsroom India, "Samsung Announces MyDream Project with UNESCO MGIEP and Navodaya Schools, 14 Samsung Smart Class in Andhra Pradesh," Samsung Newsroom India, November 26, 2018.

Sánchez, Manuel, et al. "Cloud computing in smart educational environments: application in learning analytics as service." New Advances in Information Systems and Technologies. Springer, Cham, Switzerland, 2016, pp. 993-1002.

Shaaban, Abdelkader Magdy, et al. "CloudWoT–a reference model for knowledge-based IoT solutions." Proceedings of the 20th International Conference on Information Integration and Web-based Applications & Services. ACM, 2018.

Shawar, Bayan Abu. "Neither completely M-Nor E-Learning: integrating both is the solution." Proceedings of the 2017 International Conference on Cloud and Big Data Computing. ACM, 2017.

Sedayao J. Implementing and operating an Internet scale distributed application using service oriented architecture principles and cloud computing infrastructure. Proceedings of the 10th International Conference on Information Integration and Web-Based Applications & Services, iiWAS2008; Linz, Austria. 24–26 November 2008; pp. 417–421.

Skendzic, Aleksandar, and Bozidar Kovacic. "Microsoft office 365-cloud in business environment." Proceedings of the 35th 2012 International Convention MIPRO. IEEE, 2012.

Song, Su-mi, and Yong-ik Yoon. "Intelligent smart cloud computing for smart service." Grid and Distributed Computing, Control and Automation. Springer, Berlin, Heidelberg, 2010, pp. 64–73.

# CHAPTER 5

# Impact of e-Resources in Higher Education Institutions

DEEPIKA ARORA

*Department of Management, Institute of Information Technology and Management, New Delhi, India. E-mail: deep2581@yahoo.com*

## ABSTRACT

The 21st century has been a witness to extreme levels of high competition with respect to the digitization of information and services to reach out to millions of users. People should be very well aware of the utilization of technology if used for the purpose of gaining knowledge; it also has to be channelized in the right direction. The electronic media is thus providing dynamic opportunities and possibilities for accessing information even at the global level. Electronic resources that are presently available are considered to be the pool of valuable information that is conserved by using modern information and communication technology devices. Information through e-resources can be collected to upgrade the knowledge and eliminating skill gaps that are the requirements in the present day's situation. The present study focuses on the paradigm shift from conventional resources to electronic resources. It also brings to the fore the e-resources available in various formats and their impact on higher educational institutions.

## 5.1 INTRODUCTION

In the present scenario, electronic resources are viewed as a treasure trove of information that could be delved through modern information and communication technology (ICT) tools and techniques, which can be redefined and reformed and stockpiled in cyberspace in a tangible and compressed form and can be retrieved from a large number of audiences through various points of access. Nowadays, the information/knowledge resources are transitioning from the print media into a digital format, as a result of which, there is a rapid transition from the print format to the electronic format in terms of developing a collection. The practices of acquiring resources have now been changed to cope up with the e-environment.

The Internet has revolutionized the whole concept of reading and learning, from printed books, journals, reports, conference proceedings, and monographs to e-journals, e-proceedings, e-books, and other related reports. These e-resources can be accessed over the Internet, most probably on the basis of ownership or access rights/subscriptions (Dayakar, 2018).

The present study focuses on the fundamental shift from traditional resources to electronic resources. It also underscores the e-resources available in diverse formats and their profound impact on higher educational institutions.

ICT enacts a very substantial and crucial role in teaching and learning methodology followed by several institutions. With the initiation of the recent technology in teaching, the enthusiasm of both the teachers and students can make learning more dynamic and interesting. Some of the important impact of ICT on teaching pedagogy and higher education are enumerated as follows:

### *5.1.1 MOTIVATION FOR STUDENTS*

Nowadays, students are obsessed with the Internet and smartphones, and using ICT in teaching can add motivational factors in student learning.

### *5.1.2 CONDUCTING OF ONLINE EXAMS*

Conducting online examinations not only provide benefit to students but also evaluators find it easy as results can be declared very easily along with an analysis.

### *5.1.3 24 × 7 LEARNING*

The inclusion of ICT in education overcomes time constraints in teaching–learning as well.

### *5.1.4 KNOWLEDGE SHARING AT LARGE SCALE*

One can share knowledge or gather knowledge from anywhere across the world reaching unlimited learners.

### *5.1.5 POOL OF KNOWLEDGE*

Using ICT, one can do research by utilizing a pool of knowledge available anytime, anywhere.

### *5.1.6 ADDING SKILLS*

More skills can be added through Massive Open Online Courses (MOOC) for the students as they can opt for online courses through online portals. Faculty members can also upgrade their skills by doing MOOCs.

### *5.1.7 INNOVATIVE WAYS OF TEACHING*

By taking help of ICT, faculty members can also search for innovative ways of teaching a particular subject in different institutes across the country or the world.

### *5.1.8 FEEDBACK*

Teaching is incomplete without taking feedback from students as feedback always provides scope for improvement. It is easy to find out feedback from even a bigger sample size by using appropriate methods with the help of ICT.

## 5.2 e-RESOURCES

The evolution of information technology has brought forth several alterations in the approach of transmitting the information. ICT has unraveled the innovative vistas to e-resources and media publishing in a significant manner. Electronic sources are identified as dissemination of knowledge in the automated format, such as floppy disks, magnetic tapes, and compact disc read-only memory (CD-ROMs) across the computer networks, such as e-journals and e-books.

The e-resources are essential resources that need computer access or an electronic product that would deliver a compilation of data whether it is text referring to the full text, e-journals, images anthologies, and other multimedia products (Parveen, 2015).

With the help of e-resources:

- text can be searched, except when represented in the form of illustrations;
- countless searches may be carried together on one single device;
- text-to-speech software can be used for e-resources access;
- low cost;
- resources are disseminated instantly, allowing readers to start reading at once, without the need to visit a bookstore;
- there is hardly any risk of irreparable damage on the pages.

**TABLE 5.1** Shift from Traditional Resources to Electronic Resources

| No. | Traditional Resources | Electronic Resources/Online Resources |
|---|---|---|
| 1. | Printed journals | e-Journals |
| 2. | Printed books | e-Books |
| 3. | Magazines and newspapers | e-Zines and e-newspapers |
| 4. | Off-line bibliographical databases on CDs/DVDs | On-line bibliographical databases |
| 5. | CD-ROMs (audio and video) | Web-resources—blogs, Wikipedia, e-mails, search engines |
| 6. | Dictionaries | e-dictionaries/online web dictionaries |
| 7. | Thesis and dissertations | e-thesis and dissertations |

## 5.3 TYPES OF e-RESOURCES

There are numerous kinds of e-resources:

### *5.3.1 e-JOURNALS*

An electronic journal is in fact, an e-journal that can be retrieved by employing electronic transmission. There are certain journals that are exclusively published on the web as well as in the digital format and most of the e-journals originated as print journals that are thus being evolved in the electronic version.

### *5.3.2 e-BOOKS*

An e-book is classified as a compact hardware and software system that can be used to portray a larger quantity of readable text information to the user.

### *5.3.3 e-ZINES*

e-Zines are believed to be the electronic magazine that can be used to store articles on a file server and can also be opened by using a computer network.

### *5.3.4 ELECTRONIC THESIS AND DISSERTATION (ETD)*

An ETD is well known to be an electronic file that can easily enlighten the intellectual work done by a researcher. It provides a technologically advanced instrument for communicating the concepts with the benefit of being less expensive, requiring lesser space, easy to manage, higher longevity, and therefore never become dust-ridden.

### *5.3.5 e-NEWSPAPERS*

Electronic newspapers are the compressed, refreshable, and reusable version of a traditional newspaper system that can acquire, hold complete information in newspapers that are available electronically.

### *5.3.6 CD-ROMS*

A CD-ROM is known to be the most popular series of devices that are used for storing a larger volume of data that is structured, bibliographical information, full-text information and pictures, images, and so on.

### *5.3.7 ONLINE DATABASES*

These databases are computerized and can be used for record-keeping. The significant fact about online databases is that it allows the storage of data and obtaining it easily or modifying it.

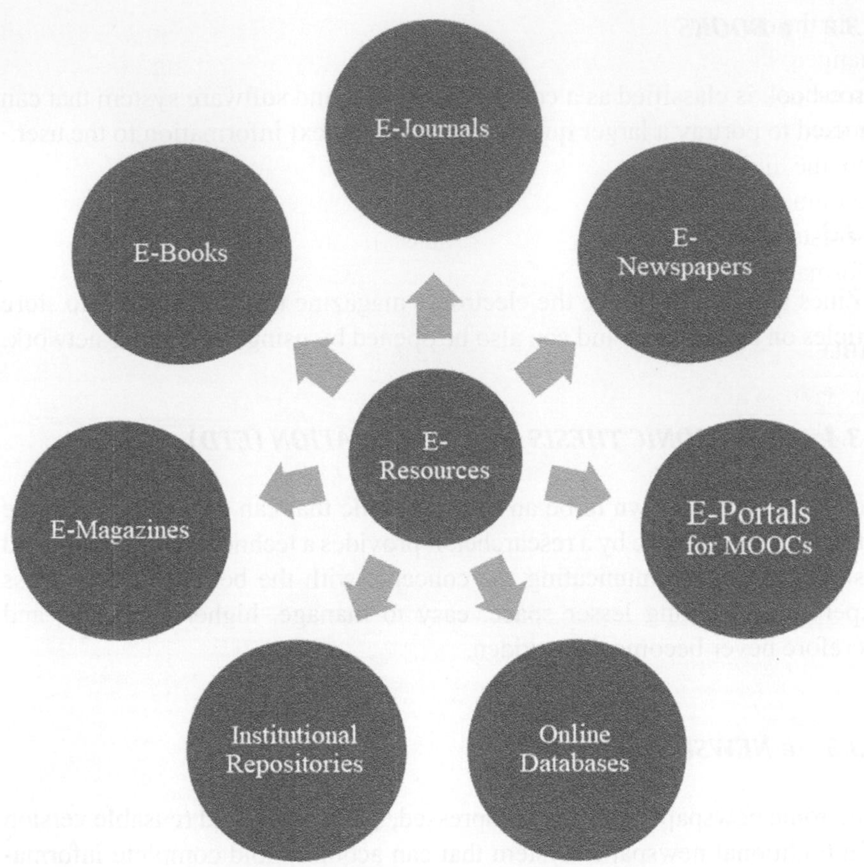


**FIGURE 5.1** Types of e-resources.

## 5.4 PROFOUND IMPACT OF e-RESOURCES IN INSTITUTIONS OF HIGHER EDUCATION

e-Resources are one of the most important components in Information Communication Process in the current stage. They excel in furnishing information of contemporary value and interest to the user community, satisfy the needs of a larger number of users. The maintenance and upkeep of e-resources are of utmost importance, without which the relative advantages cannot be achieved. Therefore to achieve the maximum benefits for the users, they should be managed more efficiently to improve the level of benefits for the users (Ron Oliver (2002).

In the era of ICT, libraries in the management institutions have drastically changed; higher education institutions have started subscribing to electronic resources to accept the ever-growing demands of the user community. The concepts of digital library, virtual library, and electronic library have come into the limelight. Presently, the resources are available in web-enabled medium and users or researchers in management institutions are more interested to access full-text publications and reference linking in a complex information space.

**TABLE 5.2** Positive and Negative Impacts of e-Resources

| No. | Positive Impact | Negative Impact |
|---|---|---|
| 1. | Easy to use | Need special equipment to access |
| 2. | Access of material any time, anywhere | Initially high infrastructure and installation cost |
| 3. | Fast and quick access to desired information | Cause of major concerns about copyright |
| 4. | Time saving | Staff training is required |
| 5. | Reduces storage space | Inconvenient and discomfort in reading |
| 6. | Helps to reduce the burden of library staff | Possibility of unawareness of relevant resources among users |
| 7. | Cheaper than print materials | Unfamiliar with the retrieval of e-resources |
| 8. | Multiaccess: a networked product can provide multiple points of access at multiple points in time and to multiple simultaneous users | Scholars and readers prefer to read print material for concentration |

## 5.5 CONCLUSION

It is a major challenge for higher education institutions to provide skilled graduates so as to cope up with the industry requirements. ICT industry engages students and increases their employability by providing a larger scope of knowledge through e-resources and MOOCs. The scenario today is demanding graduates, who are highly skilled and have a practical exposure to theoretical concepts. ICT provides a significant focus on student learning by providing a practical environment through simulations as well. e-Resources provide a pool of knowledge to enhance the teaching–learning environment. Higher educational institutions are required to provide upgraded infrastructure to their students and faculty members.

## KEYWORDS


- **e-resources**
- **information and communication technologies**
- **management institutions**
- **traditional resources**
- **higher education**


## REFERENCES


Dayakar, G. Use of e-resources in higher education: advantages and concerns. Journal of Applied and Advanced Research, 2018, 3: 17–19.

Parveen Kumari. Procurement, management and use of e-resources in current library trends: Common issues. International Journal of Digital Library Services, 2015, 5(2): 150–159.

Ron Oliver, The role of ICT in higher education for the 21st century ICT as a change agent for education. 2002, https://www.researchgate.net/publication/228920282_The_role_of_ICT_in_higher_education_for_the_21st_century_ICT_as_a_change_agent_for_education/link/09e4150cc14907835c000000/download http://ijcrt.org/papers/IJCRT1704371.pdf

# CHAPTER 6

# Application of Learning Analytics Model in Outcome-Based Education

POOJA CHATURVEDI[1*], and A. K. DANIEL[2]

[1]*Department of Computer Science, School of Management Sciences, Varanasi, Uttar Pradesh*

[2]*Department of Computer Science and Engineering, M. M. M. University of Technology, Gorakhpur, Uttar Pradesh*

[*]*Corresponding author. E-mail: chaturvedi.pooja03@gmail.com*

## ABSTRACT

The educational performance of the learners is analyzed through the process of learning analytics (LA). LA aids educational institutions in improving teaching policies and methods. The LA approaches emphasize on the application of known techniques and tools to address the issues related to the learners and institutional learning mechanisms. The traditional teaching emphasizes on the rote learning but the outcome-based education emphasizes on the development of skills that will aid in enhancing the employability skills of the learners. This chapter proposes a learning analytics model combined with classroom data analytics. The learning skills adopted by the learners are evaluated against the outcome of the course/subjects using the Naive Bayesian classification technique. The performance of the proposed classifier is evaluated against the ZeroR, SimpleCart, Random Tree, and Decision Table classification technique in terms of precision, recall, and accuracy. The results show that the output performance of the proposed model over the existing approaches is improved in terms of accuracy by a factor of 80%.

## 6.1 INTRODUCTION

There are numerous ways in which a learner observes and perceives the information from the environment. The learning process of each individual is unique and is dependent on various factors. LA-based systems emphasize on understanding and enhancing the learning process by considering and analyzing the learning environment as a whole. The main motivation of designing and developing the proposed learning analytics (LA)-based system is the lack of an all-encompassing system that adheres to the compliance with course outcome and classroom behavior (Tulbure, 2012; Brady, 2013; Mahmoud et al., 2016). The major contributions of the paper are as follows:

a. The chapter proposes a LA-based system that will aid the educators in designing and developing the course structure such that it will benefit the students of different classes.
b. The proposed system predicts the class of students on the basis of different attributes such as personal, social, and classroom information.
c. The proposed system is easy to adopt and can be applied to different.
d. The proposed system integrates the different paradigms of learners such as classroom behavior, social background, family background, and compliance with the objectives of the particular course.

The paper is organized as follows: literature review in Section 6.2, proposed model design in Section 6.3, implementation and results in Sections 6.4, and 6.5 concludes the paper.

## 6.2 LITERATURE REVIEW

LA is a relatively new term in the field of data analytics. The basic concept behind the application of the LA is to collect the data regarding the learners so as to improve the learning capabilities of the learners. There are several definitions of LA available in the literature, but to summarize it may be defined as the measurement, collection, analysis, and reporting of student's data and their environment with the aim of understanding and stimulating the process of learning and the environment in which it takes place. LA utilizes predictive models that generate information that can be worked upon by using the interdisciplinary strategy such as data processing, clustering, classification, and information technology (Junco and Clem, 2015; Xing et al., 2015; Drachsler and Kalz, 2016; Rubel and Jones, 2016).

The main application of LA is in the learning management system that emphasizes on the collection and analysis of student's data such as their environment information, behaviour information, etc. to determine student's learning styles. The basic information about the students is fed into the learning management system that may automatically recommend the learning strategy, course, and curriculum design so as to enhance the learning (Long and Siemens, 2011). The learning management systems are broadly classified into three types as Eadvising analytics, intuition specific analytics, and edge case analytics using social and biometric information. Eadvising system is designed to suggest the students about which course path to adopt based on the past success stories of their colleagues (Denley, 2012; California State University Long Beach 2014; Lewis, 2011; Parry, 2014; Campus Labs. 2014). Institutional specific analytics system spans over the entire organization and provides the administrator with the ability to provide the recommendation to the students based on their information (Glass, 2013; Long and Siemens, 2011). Edge case analytics-based systems are based on providing the recommendation according to the learner's social network data such as frequency of visiting a social networking site, time spent on a social networking site. These systems may also collect and analyze biometric related data such as temperature, heart rate, etc. (Long and Siemens, 2011; Buckingham Shum and Ferguson, 2012; Diaz and Brown, 2012; Ho, 2011; Hoover, 2012; Brazy, 2010; O'Connor, 2010; Arriba Pérez et al., 2016; Spann et al., 2017; Simon, 2012; Alcorn, 2013; Schiller, 2015).

The major challenges identified in the designing of such systems are data collection, data reporting, processing, and visualization. The paper aims to provide a model using LA that captures the learner's information and compares it with the desired level of skill of that particular subject/course and classify the learners based on their learning capabilities that are further used by the educators to provide a recommendation based on the learners' capabilities (Chatti et al., 2014).

### *6.2.1 CLASSIFICATION TECHNIQUES*

Classification is the process of organizing a given set of objects into different groups such that the intergroup similarity is minimum and intragroup similarity is maximum. The different classification techniques considered in the paper are (Witten et al., 2007):

a. *ZeroR*—Simplest classification approach. It is based on counting the frequency of each outcome and predicts the majority class.
b. *SimpleCart*—SimpleCart is basically a classification and regression technique. This approach is best suited for a numerical or categorical dataset with missing values.
c. *Random Tree*—It is a supervised learning-based classification technique that combines the approaches of a simple model tree and random forest.
d. *Decision Table*—Decision table is an accurate prediction approach based on decision trees. The output of decision table classification is set of If–Then–Else rules.
e. *Naive Bayes*—Naive Bayesian classification technique is based on determining the posterior probability of the occurrences of the events.

Viberg et al. (2018) and Jones (2019) have proposed a detailed review of the various dimensions and concepts related to the application of LA in higher education. Fenthaler et al. (2018) have proposed a graph analysis-based LA approach to improve the learning design in context to the digital learning environment through a case study.

## 6.3 PROPOSED MODEL

The paper proposes an LA model that will aid educators in providing recommendations about the learning efficiency of the learners as shown in Figure 6.1.

### 6.3.1 *SYSTEM DESIGN*

The proposed model constitutes of two entities as learners and educators. The learners are the students currently enrolled in a particular course to acquire the required skills and knowledge. The educators are the teachers that provide the knowledge of a particular course to develop the required skills in the learners. The responsibility of educators is to enhance the learning capabilities of the learners. The advancement in the technology and emergence of a voluminous amount of data implies that the existing education system may not be able to provide the necessary capabilities to enhance the learning ability of the learners. The proposed model collects the information in different dimensions and classifies it for the learners according to their learning styles. The proposed model calculates the information of the students in the two stages: first at the time of joining the institute and second after the commencement of midsession. At both stages, the information is calculated via the well designed and precise questionnaire. The collected information is provided to both educators and learners. The learners may use it for the improvement and the educators may get benefitted from designing the curriculum and course structure.

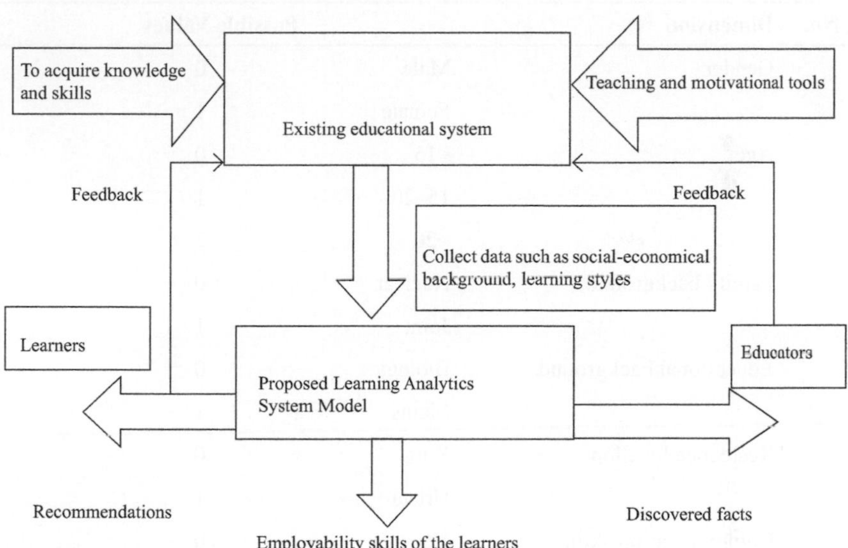


**FIGURE 6.1** Proposed Learning Analytics Model

## 6.3.2 *METHODOLOGY*

The proposed LA models comprise the following models: (1) data representation model, (2) data acquisition model, (3) data normalization model, (4) outcome model, and (5) response model. The functionalities of each model is described as follows.

### *6.3.2.1 DATA REPRESENTATION MODEL*

The data representation model consists of the following attributes as gender, age, family background, educational background, residence location, communication skills, presentation skills, programming skills, interest in course, level of query asked by the students, and the response to the classroom activities.

The communication skills, presentation skills, and programming skills are evaluated by a separate set of questionnaires. If the performance of the learner is above a threshold value, then it is assigned the value as "Yes"; otherwise, it is assigned a value "No." The collected data is represented by using the encoding mechanism as shown in Table 6.1.

**TABLE 6.1** Attribute Set with Possible Values

| Sr. No. | Dimension | Possible Values | |
|---|---|---|---|
| 1 | Gender | Male | 0 |
| | | Female | 1 |
| 2 | Age | <15 | 0 |
| | | 15–20 | 1 |
| | | >20 | 2 |
| 3 | Family background | Nuclear | 0 |
| | | Joint | 1 |
| 4 | Educational background | Biology | 0 |
| | | Maths | 1 |
| 5 | Residence location | Rural | 0 |
| | | Urban | 1 |
| 6 | Communication skills | Yes | 0 |
| | | No | 1 |
| 7 | Presentation skills | Yes | 0 |
| | | No | 1 |
| 8 | Programming skills | Yes | 0 |
| | | No | 1 |
| 9 | Interest in course | Yes | 0 |
| | | No | 1 |
| 10 | Attentiveness in class | Yes | 0 |
| | | No | 1 |
| 11 | Query | Yes | 0 |
| | | No | 1 |
| 12 | Response | Yes | 0 |
| | | No | 1 |

### *6.3.2.2 DATA ACQUISITION MODEL*

In the data acquisition phase, data is collected based on the responses of the learners. The paper is based on the case study of computer science engineering graduates, comprising 109 learners. The data obtained on the basis of the questionnaire is shown in Table 6.2.

**TABLE 6.2** Obtained Values

| Sr. No. | Dimension | Possible Values | No. of Respondents |
|---|---|---|---|
| 1 | Gender | Male | 57 |
| | | Female | 52 |
| 2 | Age | <15 | 24 |
| | | 15–20 | 81 |
| | | >20 | 4 |
| 3 | Family background | Nuclear | 73 |
| | | Joint | 36 |
| 4 | Educational background | Biology | 44 |
| | | Maths | 65 |
| 5 | Residence location | Rural | 30 |
| | | Urban | 79 |
| 6 | Communication skills | Yes | 69 |
| | | No | 40 |
| 7 | Presentation skills | Yes | 40 |
| | | No | 69 |
| 8 | Programming skills | Yes | 56 |
| | | No | 44 |
| 9 | Interest in course | Yes | 69 |
| | | No | 40 |
| 10 | Attentiveness in class | Yes | 50 |
| | | No | 59 |
| 11 | Query | Yes | 62 |
| | | No | 47 |
| 12 | Response | Yes | 25 |
| | | No | 84 |

### *6.3.2.3 DATA NORMALIZATION MODEL*

The gathered data is normalized by using the entropy values of each possible value for each dimension. The attribute space is selected on the basis of threshold value based on the information gain. The information gain of an attribute is defined in terms of entropy as

$$E(A) = \sum_{i=1}^{n} -p_i \log_2 p^i$$

Information gain is defined as the increase in the entropy value after splitting the dataset on the basis of the selected attribute. Consider the dataset consisting of two attributes A and B, information gain of this data set is determined as

$$\text{Info Gain}(A, B) = E(A) - E(A, B)$$

The information gain of the different attributes for the considered dataset is shown in Table 6.3.

**TABLE 6.3** Information of the Attributes

| Sr. No. | Attribute | Information Gain |
|---|---|---|
| 1 | Gender | 0.304 |
| 2 | Age | 0.28 |
| 3 | Family background | 0.277 |
| 4 | Educational background | 0.52[a] |
| 5 | Residence location | 0.34 |
| 6 | Communication skills | 0.54 |
| 7 | Presentation skills | 0.78 |
| 8 | Programming skills | 0.65 |
| 9 | Interest in course | 0.62 |
| 10 | Attentiveness in class | 0.54 |
| 11 | Query | 0.46 |
| 12 | Response | 0.35 |

[a]*Bold values indicates the attributes whose information gain is higher than the threshold 0.5.*

The information gain of different attributes is shown in Figure 6.2.

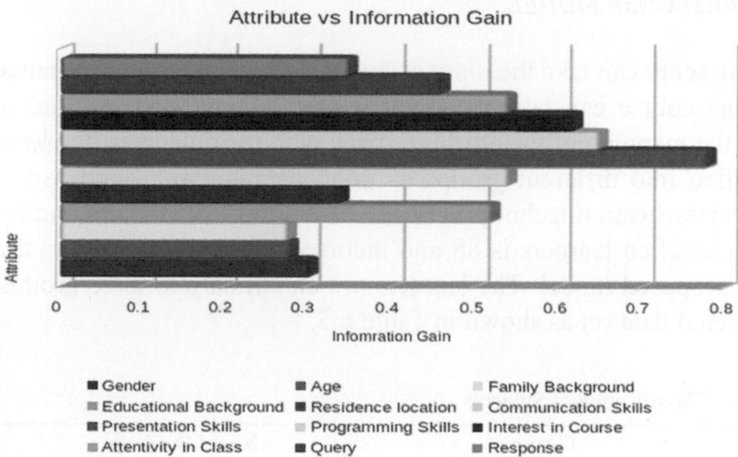


**FIGURE 6.2** Information gain values of different attributes.

Based on the information gain values, the attribute space is selected, as shown in Table 6.4. We have considered the threshold information gain as 0.5.

**TABLE 6.4** Attribute Space

| Sr. No. | Attribute |
|---|---|
| 1 | Educational background |
| 2 | Communication skills |
| 3 | Presentation skills |
| 4 | Programming skills |
| 5 | Interest in course |
| 6 | Attentiveness in class |

#### *6.3.2.4 OUTCOME MODEL*

The weighted average of the attribute space is determined for each learner. The outcome level is determined as the weighted average of the communication skills, presentation skills, and programming skills. If the weighted average of attribute space is less than 0.4, then the learner is considered as poor; if it lies between 0.4 and 0.7, then it is considered as medium; and if it is >0.7.

#### *6.3.2.5 RESPONSE MODEL*

The feature score can take the input as low, medium, and high. The outcome level of the course can take the input values as low, medium, and high. Based on the mapping of the attribute space with the outcomes, the learners are classified into different groups as poor, average, and good using the Bayesian classification technique. For the 109 total learners, the number of correctly classified learners is 88 and incorrectly classified learners are 21 using the proposed model. The learners are classified into three groups for the considered data set as shown in Table 6.5.

**TABLE 6.5** Classification of Students

| Sr. No. | Group | No. of Students |
|---|---|---|
| 1 | Poor | 62 |
| 2 | Average | 15 |
| 3 | Good | 32 |

## 6.4 IMPLEMENTATION RESULTS AND DISCUSSION

We have implemented the proposed model to determine the classification of considered 109 undergraduate learners.

### *6.4.1 PERFORMANCE METRICS*

The performance of the proposed model is evaluated in terms of the following parameters:

#### *6.4.1.1 CONFUSION MATRIX*

It is the most important measure of the efficiency of the classification algorithm. It represents the number of instances correctly classified in each class. For a binary classifier, the confusion matrix may be represented as shown in Table 6.6.

In the table, TP, FP, FN, and TN represent the classification as true positive, false positive, false negative, and true negative, respectively. True positive refers to the fact that an instance is correctly classified as positive, false positive means an instance is incorrectly classified as positive, false negative means that an instance is incorrectly classified as negative, and true negative means an instance is correctly classified as negative. The other metrics are often defined in terms of these values.

**TABLE 6.6** Confusion Matrix for a Binary Classifier

| Class | Positive Prediction | Negative Prediction |
|---|---|---|
| Positive | TP | FN |
| Negative | FP | TN |

#### *6.4.1.2 TRUE POSITIVE (TP) RATE*

The rate at which instances are classified as true positive.

#### *6.4.1.3 FALSE POSITIVE (FP) RATE*

The rate at which instances are classified as false positive.

#### *6.4.1.4 PRECISION*

It is defined as the correct results for the total number of instances. It is determined as

$$\text{Precision} = \text{TP}/(\text{TP}+\text{FP})$$

#### *6.4.1.5 RECALL*

It is defined as the ratio of the correct predicted results to the total number of classified instances. It is determined as

$$\text{Recall} = \text{TP}/(\text{TP}+\text{FN})$$

#### *6.4.1.6 F-MEASURE*

The harmonic mean estimate of the precision and recall is termed as *F*-measure and is calculated as

$$F\text{-measure} = 2 \times (\text{Precision} \times \text{Recall})/(\text{Precision} + \text{Recall})$$

#### 6.4.1.7 REGION OF CURVE (ROC)

It is used to summarize the performance of the classification approaches.

#### 6.4.1.8 ACCURACY

Accuracy is defined as the number of instances correctly classified and the total number of instances. It is calculated as

$$\text{Accuracy} = (\text{TP}+\text{TN})/N$$

where $N$ is the total number of instances.

### 6.4.2 PERFORMANCE EVALUATION OF THE PROPOSED MODEL

The values of different parameters for the proposed model are shown in Table 6.7.

**TABLE 6.7** Performance Evaluation of the Proposed Protocol

| Parameters/Class | TP Rate | FP Rate | Precision | Recall | *F*-measure | ROC |
|---|---|---|---|---|---|---|
| Low | 0.79 | 0.149 | 0.875 | 0.79 | 0.831 | 0.784 |
| Medium | 0.733 | 0.032 | 0.786 | 0.733 | 0.759 | 0.884 |
| High | 0.875 | 0.143 | 0.718 | 0.875 | 0.789 | 0.83 |
| Weighted average | 0.807 | 0.131 | 0.817 | 0.807 | 0.808 | 0.812 |

The confusion matrix for the proposed model is shown in Table 6.8.

**TABLE 6.8** Confusion Matrix for the Proposed Model

| a | b | c | Classified As |
|---|---|---|---|
| 49 | 2 | 11 | a = Poor |
| 4 | 11 | 0 | b = Average |
| 3 | 1 | 28 | c = Good |

The learning and understanding levels of all the learners in a particular course/institute are not the same. So, the LA system can aid the educators in providing the required remedial strategies for the poor learners. The proposed system classifies the learners on the basis of their responses into three groups as poor, average, and good. Out of 109 students, 62 students are classified as poor, that is, having low learning capability, 15 students are classified as average, and 32 students are classified as good, as shown in Figure 6.3.

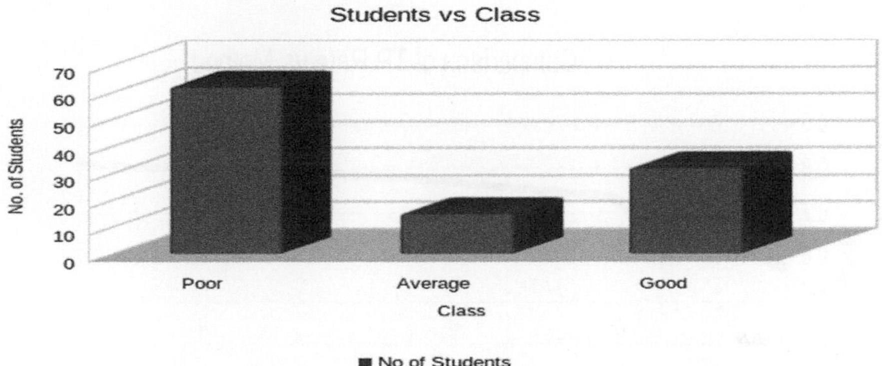


**FIGURE 6.3** Classification of students.

### 6.4.3 *COMPARISON WITH EXISTING APPROACHES*

In this section, we have compared the performance of the proposed model with the existing classification approaches such as ZeroR, SimpleCart, Random Tree, and Decision Table, as shown in Figures 6.4–6.10. It can be observed from the figures that the proposed Bayesian-based classification model outperforms the existing approaches as ZeroR, SimpleCart, Random Tree, and Decision Table in terms of TP rate, FP rate, precision, recall, *F*-measure, ROC, and accuracy. The proposed model has the highest accuracy of 80% as compared to the other approaches.

## 6.5 CONCLUSION AND FUTURE SCOPE

The paper proposed a LA system that emphasizes on the classification of learners in different groups by considering a number of attributes. By collecting and analyzing the data about the learners, the educators can effectively design the course structure, lecture plans, and teaching strategy such as to increase the efficiency of learning in the learners. The proposed system provides exhaustive information about the learners and also ensures compliance with the objectives of the course. The simulation results show that the proposed model classifies the learners into poor, average, and good classes with an accuracy of up to 80%. The results also show that the proposed model outperforms the existing classification approaches in terms of TP rate, FP rate, precision, recall, and *F*-measure. To integrate the prediction system such as Moodle with our system is our future work.

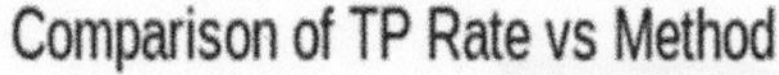


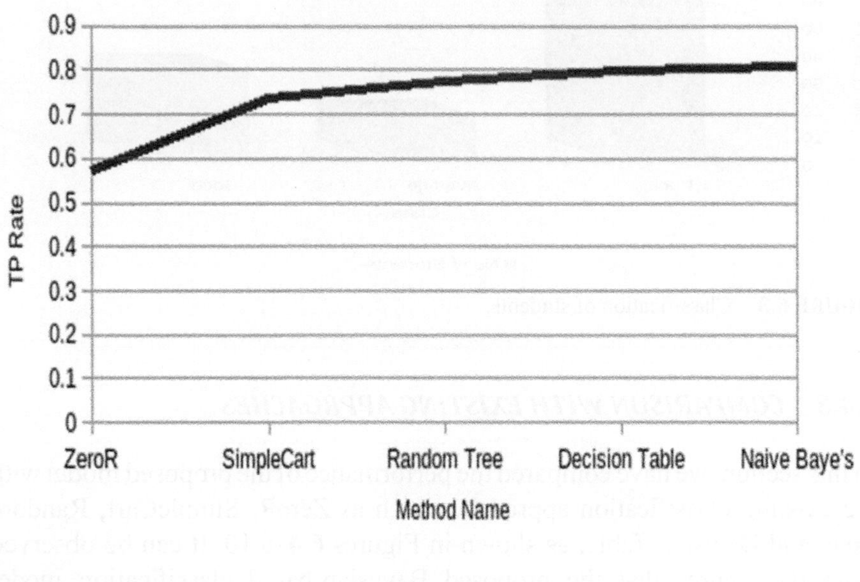


**FIGURE 6.4** TP rate.

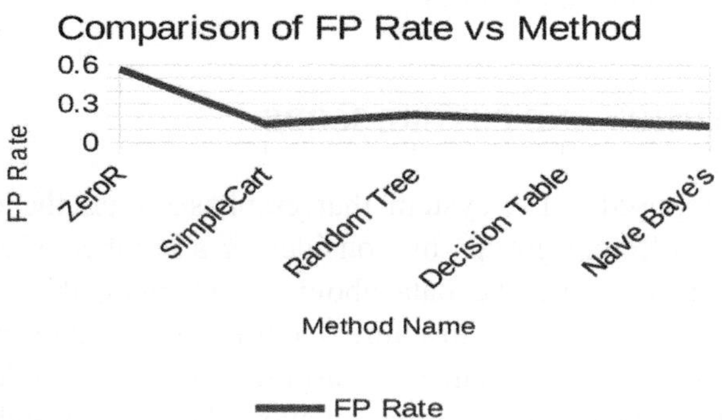


**FIGURE 6.5** FP rate.

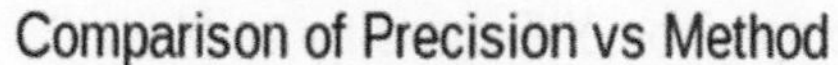


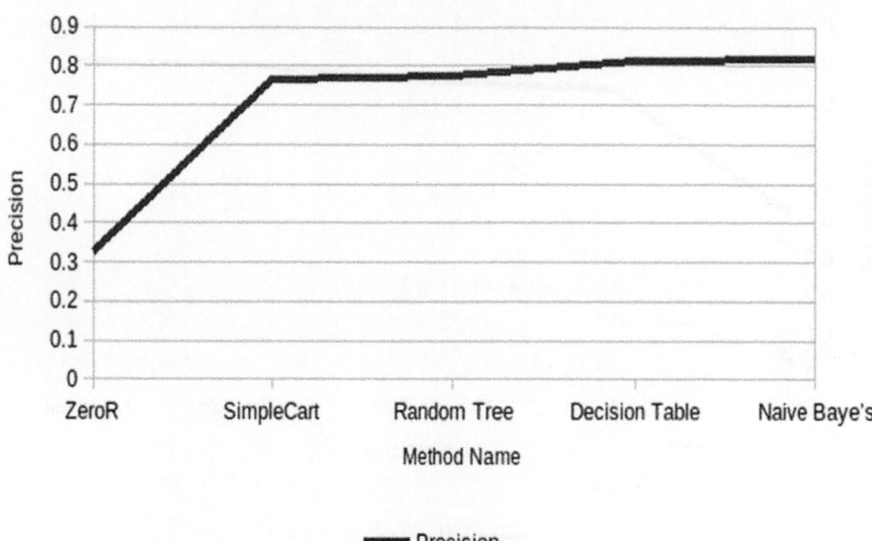


**FIGURE 6.6** Precision.

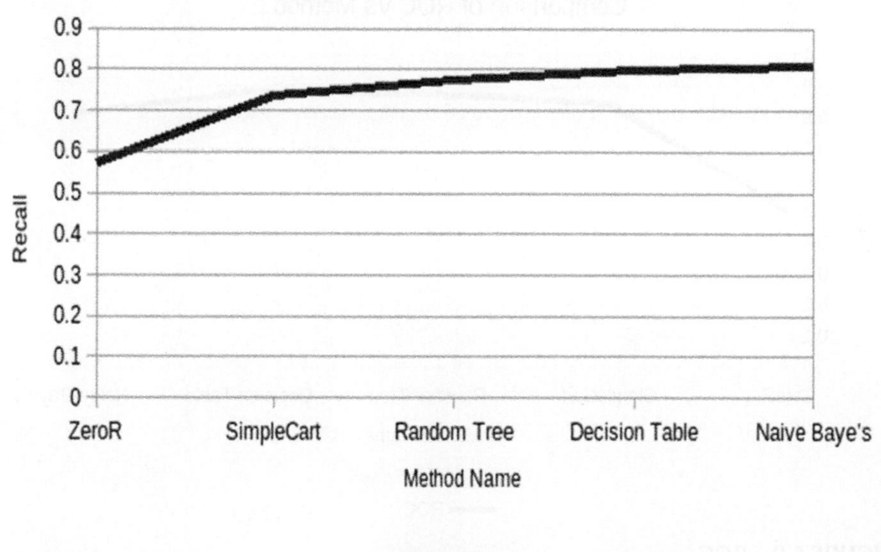


**FIGURE 6.7** Recall.

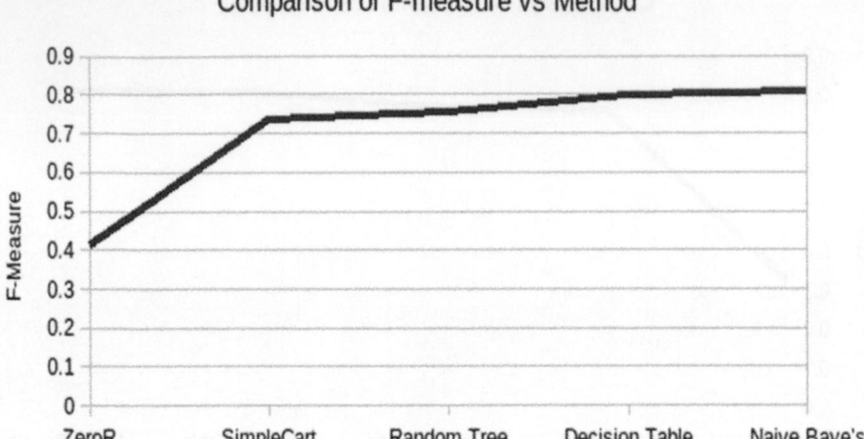


**FIGURE 6.8** F-measure.

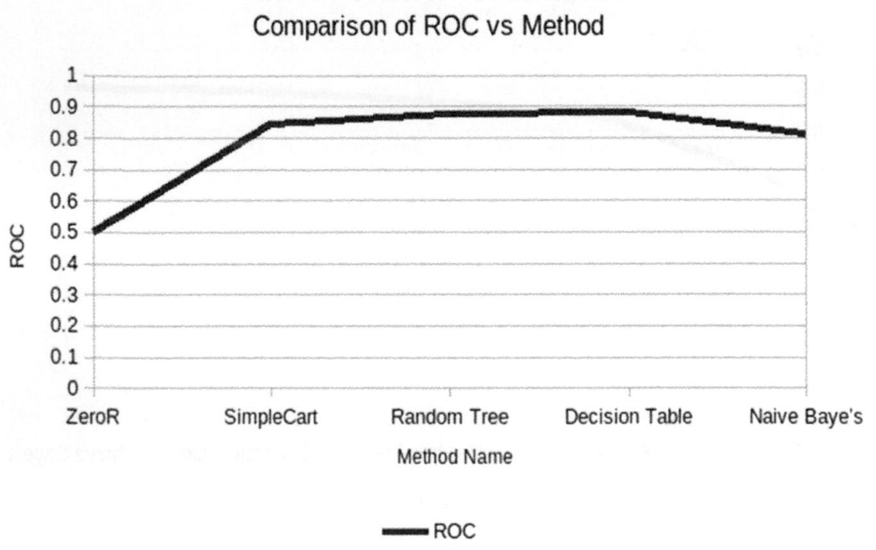


**FIGURE 6.9** ROC.

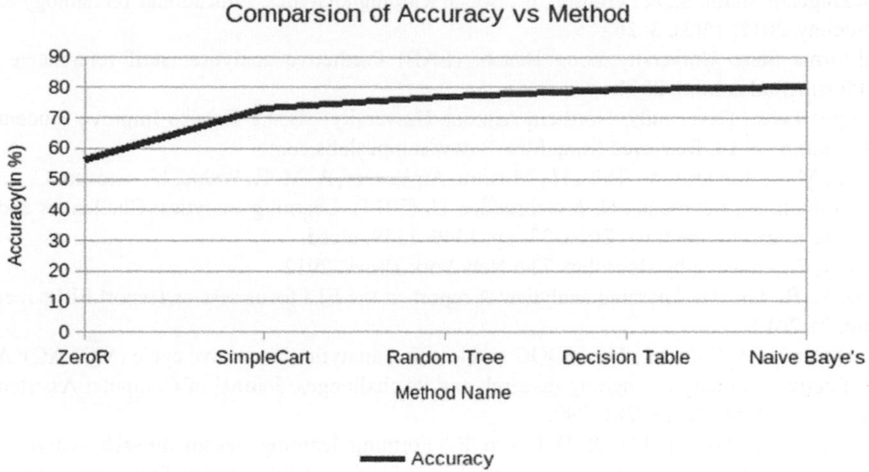


**FIGURE 6.10** Accuracy.

## KEYWORDS


- **learning analytics**
- **higher education**
- **classification techniques**
- **artificial intelligence**
- **education system**
- **data analytics**


## REFERENCES


Alcorn, S., Facial Recognition in the Classroom Tells Teachers When Students are Spacing, 2013, FastCompany. Retrieved from: http://www.fastcompany.com/3018861/facial-recognition-in-the-classroom-tells-teachers-when-students-are-spacing.

Arriba Pérez, F., Santos, J. M., & Rodriguez, M. C., Analytics of biometric data from wearable devices to support teaching and learning activities. Journal of Information Systems Engineering & Management, 2016, 1(1), pp. 41–54.

Brady, C. L., Understanding Learning Styles: Providing the Optimal Learning Experience. International Journal of Childbirth Education, 2013, 28 (2), pp. 16–19.

Brazy, D. Ariz. College to position sensors to check class attendance. The Badger Herald, 2010.

Buckingham Shum, S., & Ferguson, R., Social learning analytics. Educational Technology & Society, 2012, 15(3), 3–26.

California State University Long Beach. (EAB) Predictive analytics. staff_reference/e_advising/index.html, 2014.

Campus Labs., Case study: Northern Arizona University—Using Data to Improve Student Retention, 2014. Retrieved from: http://www.campuslabs.com.

Chatti, M. A., Lukarov, V., Thüs, H., Muslim, A., Yousef, A. M. F., Wahid, U., Greven, C.

Chakrabarti, A., Schroeder, U. & Schroeder, U. (2014). Learning analytics: Challenges and future research directions, 2016, 37, pp. 1349–1359, eleed.

Denley, T., Advising by algorithm. The New York Times, 2012.

Diaz, V., Brown, M., Learning analytics: A report on the ELI focus session (report ELI paper no. 2), 2012.

Drachsler, H., & Kalz, M., The MOOC and learning analytics innovative cycle (MOLAC): A reflective summary of ongoing research and its challenges. Journal of Computer Assisted Learning, 2016, 32, pp. 281–290.

Fenthaler D.I., Gibson I.D. & Dobozyn E., Forming learning design through analytics: Applying network graph analysis, Australasian Journal of Educational Technology, 2018, 34(2), pp. 117–132.

Glass, A., The state of higher education 2013 (Report).

Ho, C., Companies tracking college athletes' tweets, Facebook posts go after local universities, 2011,The Washington Post. Retrieved from: https://www.washingtonpost.com/business/capitalbusiness/companies-tracking-college-athletes'-tweets-Facebook-posts-go-after-local-universities/2011/10/10/glQAyHZ9oL_story.html.

Hoover, E. Facebook meets predictive analytics. The Chronicle of Higher Education, 2012, world.edu. Retrieved from: http://world.edu/facebook-meets-predictive-analytics/.

Jones, K. M. L., Learning analytics and higher education: a proposed model for establishing informed consent mechanisms to promote student privacy and autonomy, International Journal of Educational Technology in Higher Education, 2019, pp. 16–24.

Junco, R., & Clem, C., Predicting course outcomes with digital textbook usage data. The Internet and Higher Education, 2015, 27, pp. 54–63.

Lewis, B., New initiative advances ASU's effort to enhance student success. ASU News, 2011.

Long, P., & Siemens, G., Penetrating the fog: Analytics in learning and education. Educause Review, 2011, 46(5), pp. 30–40.

Mahmoud, C. B., Azaiez, I., Bettahar, F., & Gargouri, F., Discovery Mechanism for Learning Semantic Web Service, International Journal on Semantic Web and Information Systems, 2016, 12 (4), pp. 23–43.

O'Connor, M. C., Northern Arizona University to use existing RFID student cards for attendance tracking. RFID Journal, 2010, 7628, pp. 1–3.

Parry, M. Big data on campus, 2012, The New York Times. Retrieved from: http://www.nytimes.com/2012/07/22/education/edlife/colleges-awakening-to-the-opportunities-of-data-mining.html.

Rubel, A., & Jones, K., Student privacy in learning analytics: An information ethics perspective. The Information Society, 2016, 32(2), 143–159.

Schiller, B., It'll be a lot harder to cut class with this classroom facial-recognition application, 2015.

Simon, S., Biosensors to Monitor Students' Attentiveness, 2012, Reuters. Retrieved from: http://www.reuters.com/article/2012/06/13us-usa-education-gates-idUSBRE85C0182010613.

Spann, C. A., Schaeffer, J., & Siemens, G., Expanding the scope of learning analytics data: Preliminary findings on attention and self-regulation using wearable technology. In Proceedings of the Seventh International Learning Analytics & Knowledge Conference, Canada, 2017, pp. 203–207.

Tulbure C., "Learning Styles, Teaching Strategies and Academic Achievement in Higher Education: A Cross- Sectional Investigation" Procedia—Social and Behavioral Sciences, 2012, 33: pp. 398–402.

Viberg, O., Hatakka, M., Bälter, O., & Mavroudi, A., The current landscape of learning analytics in higher education, Computers in Human Behaviour, 2018, 89, pp. 98–110.

Witten, I. H., Frank, E., & Hall, M. A., Data Mining Practical Machine Learning Tools and Techniques, Third Edition, Elsevier, 2007, ISBN978-0-12-374856-0.

Xing, W., Guo, R., Petakovic, E., & Goggins, Participation-based student final performance prediction model through interpretable Genetic Programming: Integrating learning analytics, educational data mining and theory. Computers in Human Behavior, 2015, 47, pp. 168–181.

CHAPTER 7

# Higher Education Elaboration through ICT

MALAVIKA SRIVASTAVA[1*], and AMBALIKA SINHA[2]

[1]*IITM, Janakpuri, New Delhi*

[2]*Motilal Nehru National Institute of Technology, Prayagraj, Uttar Pradesh*

[*]*Corresponding author. Email: malavika.iitm@gmail.com*

## ABSTRACT

Information technology (IT) has made a significant impact on the extension of higher education. Knowledge can be transferred through IT, and people can get all content through computer usage. Persons living in every part of the country, hills, planes, seaside, and urban areas are all getting educated through open universities like IGNOU, Rajshree Open University, etc. This paper will study the impact of information communication and technology (ICT) on the elaboration of education far and wide and its impact on economic enhancement, social development, psychological impact, and knowledge enhancement in society.

This involved assessing the broadening of the mental makeup of persons with higher education, the degree to which persons have changed because of higher education, their belief systems, attitude toward life, and interactional impact on society and their employability.

The empirical study was performed on professionals who are gaining knowledge through ICT and what benefits they are achieving by availing education enhancement through ICT. Significant correlations were found between ICT and knowledge enhancement, economic enhancement, social developments, and psychological impact. This has proved that ICT is a boon to society and has made every interaction very convenient and facilitative.

## 7.1 INTRODUCTION

Information communication and technology (ICT) tools include various electronic devices, computer networks, etc. Examples of such devices are radio, television, and equipment and services associated with these technologies, such as video conferencing and electronic mail (e-mail). With the advent of new technology and innovations, communication involves the transfer of information worldwide.

Computer knowledge spread technology has escalated the utility of ICT in reducing the world into a manageable arena, which includes rural, urban, north, south, east, and west, and has lightened the minds of all to gain more and more knowledge. It has become feasible for all to enhance their skills and be more aware.

Via Internet, we do all activities from eating, drinking, sleeping, and daily activities. If we want to eat, we order through Swiggy; if we want to drink, we can order; we can watch our steps through smartwatches to maintain our health; and we can get educated through Internet connectivity with societies and its culture in a daily life communication and now create relationships on the Internet. Professional and social groups are being formed to connect with relatives, friends, and professionals via social media like Facebook,WhatsApp, email, etc. We can also connect internationally for sharing knowledge and obtaining career-related and business information.

The Internet provides various new communication techniques for interacting with society all round. Today, a wider audience can be assessed on various issues related to academic, social, personal, economic, and environmental topics through blogs, social media, videos, podcasts, e-books, newsletters, and infographics. Students of all ages can benefit from grasping knowledge about areas of their interest. Job seekers get employment opportunities through ICT. Business houses of all sizes and types are making entry into the international arena for gaining more business. All products and all services are reaching to all who want it anywhere, online degrees have become a reality, and online classes are being conducted in various institutes and organizations. Growth and development in society has become possible.

Dr. Babasaheb Ambedkar (1927) said that the various educational institutions provide education facilities to all persons with the intellectual curiosity to gain knowledge, but who cannot avail these facilities due to fund scarcity or are living in remote areas or due to disability may be deprived of these facilities. ICT provision in various institutions may upgrade and enrich the cognitions and enhance the social and human values of the student community and can propel all students of every age and gender toward greater enlightenment. Academicians' skills may also be enhanced and they may also be able to impart the latest knowledge and developments as they grasp novel skills and techniques through implementation of e-learning facilities. Students gain knowledge of whatever they want through Internet surfing that has made gaining knowledge easier. Training the trainer through Internet usage has become very common today. Whatever topic is not available in hardcopy is surfed out through the Internet and this has made trainers more confident about what they teach. Two substantial changes via ICT are available both for teaching and training; first, everything is approachable, we can reach out to all topics and gain knowledge about them. Second, the facilitation of learning from all parts of the world has made every information available to all who want to learn. Knowledge interchange between the teacher and the students has given wings to fast academic growth. In the last few decades, a greater number of persons are getting opportunities to quench their thirst for knowledge, which has also provided them with higher chances of getting respectable jobs, whether they are young, old, male, and female.

This drastic ICT intervention has revolutionized the universe, it has equalized all civilization, provided better conditions all over the world, the organizations are now all around, always learning organizations requiring novelty in an employee's performance, and demanding higher literacy among them. Therefore, both poor and rich, urban and rural, all are getting high quality and quantity of education, now all from any part of the world can do various courses through open education and e-learning mode. According to Soares and Almeida (2002), the uplifting and transformative potentials of the ICT in higher education in India have created a greater craving for higher education through part-time and distance learning schemes. It has overcome economic issues of the cost of education and demand for a few teachers but really good ones. as well as overcome time and distance barriers as viewed by Mc Gorry (2002).

## 7.2 LITERATURE REVIEW

Ozdemir and Abrevaya (2007) said that the use of e-learning is proving economic to all students, this in turn has increased the admission of students and has helped employees to learn more while in jobs without hindering their work, i.e., they are professionals and learners both. Srivastava et al. (2014) examined the role of information technology (IT) in higher education from the learners' perspective in various rural medical schools. They found that value addition occurred through the usage of technology in education and may prove a boom for the citizens if available in adequate measures by education providers. A study by Pegu (2014) on "Information and communication technology in higher education in India: challenges and opportunities" revealed that ICT-enabled education will spread higher education to all those who desire to study, no one will be hampered by distance, or expense, or disability. According to Manisha (2014) study on the role of ICT in higher education in India it was revealed that ICT is changing various educational practices. Apart from cost reduction, transparency in knowledge spread to all has been made possible. The education system has brought radical changes in the educational sphere. India has provided higher standards of educational studies to all learners through Information and Communication technology. For example, Gyan Darshan broadcasted educational programs for school kids, university students, and adults from the year 2000 onward. Similarly, institutions such as IGNOU and IIT broadcasted Gyan Vani programs. UGC took country-wise classroom initiative in bringing education programs via Gyan Darshan and Doordarshan national channel every day. e-Gyankosh was introduced by IGNOU to preserve digital learning resources in 2005. Almost 95% of IGNOU's printed material has been presented to learners as e-learning material. The National Programme for Technology Enhanced Learning was launched in 2001 by IITs and IISC jointly.Sristi, the Society for Research and Initiatives for Sustainable Technologies and Institutions, is enhancing the working of entrepreneurs linked with environmental issues for grass root level problems. Benefits of the use of ICT in education are many and they solve various issues, some slowly and some very fast.

### 7.2.1 ADVANTAGES OF ICT IN EDUCATION

1. *Motivating factor:* The Internet drives people toward their development through technology that is communicated to them. People are enthralled by Internet usage that in turn improves their self-efficacy. The country should capitalize on the knowledge enhancement through ICT for the progress of India, the Internet is available whenever we want hence we do not feel deprived if we are not learning in formal setups.
2. *Fast communication:* Virtual learning has removed worldwide barriers. People can work jointly even when living in different parts of the universe.
3. *Co-operative learning:* The Internet facilities have led to interactive learning; through video conferencing, it becomes easy to hold interactive classes for discussions. For example, Global Initiative of

Academic Networks is used in the various institutions to have live sessions with high knowledge holders with students from all parts of the country. There are programs that will allow students to get involved in class discussions through emails in a way not possible within four walls of the classroom.

4. *Locating research materials:* Researchers are benefitting to a very great via the Internet. They can review fast, can get data collection done through emailing tools, and can also learn about the usage of statistical packages easily.
5. *Acquiring varied writing skills:* Book writing and paper publication have also become faster through Internet usage. Learners can also learn writing skills through ICT.

## 7.3 OBJECTIVE OF THE STUDY

The objective of this study is to assess the actual benefits that learners are experiencing because of IT communication. People are becoming more knowledgeable and more aware of their rights.

This study attempted to observe Indian learner's perception of ICT and try to answer the question regarding its impact on professionals. Variables studied are related to the impact of ICT given in the review of the literature but in a different form. They included the following variables: economic impact, social impact, psychological impact, and knowledge development.

## 7.4 HYPOTHESES OF THE STUDY

1. ICT will have a positive impact on economic growth.
2. Technology will have a positive impact on psychological growth.
3. ICT will positively impact social impact.
4. ICT will positively lead to the enhancement of knowledge.

## 7.5 RESEARCH DESIGN

A descriptive method was used for data collection.

The subjects were 100 professionals. The survey was conducted using a questionnaire developed using five-point Likert scale format, with 1 denoting no impact, 2 denoting slight impact, 3 denoting impact to some extent, 4 high impact, and 5 meaning very high impact. The questionnaire was administered to subjects in group settings. After data collection, the subjects were thanked for their cooperation.

## 7.6 RESULT AND ANALYSIS

Statistical analysis was done on data collected from professionals. For all the four variables studied as dependent variables, Table 7.1 presents mean and SD.

**TABLE 7.1** Statistics

| | mean_know | mean_eco | mean_psy | mean_social |
|---|---|---|---|---|
| Mean | 3.4286 | 3.1276 | 3.1054 | 3.3605 |
| Std. deviation | 0.74305 | 0.69654 | 0.80604 | 0.59815 |

Means reveal that the impact of ICT on knowledge enhancement, economic growth, psychological impact, and social impact is above average. Standard deviation reveals that the greatest deviation from mean was in the psychological arena. Pearson Correlation was calculated to assess the impact of IT on the four dependent variables.

Table 7.2 presents the correlations of ICT with knowledge development, economical enhancement, social development, and psychological growth.

**TABLE 7.2** Correlations

| | | mean_know | mean_eco | mean_psy | mean_social |
|---|---|---|---|---|---|
| mean_know | Pearson correlation | 1 | 0.655** | 0.444** | 0.580** |
| | Sig. (two-tailed) | | 0.000 | 0.000 | 0.000 |
| | *N* | 98 | 98 | 98 | 98 |
| mean_eco | Pearson correlation | 0.655** | 1 | 0.512** | 0.712** |
| | Sig. (two-tailed) | 0.000 | | 0.000 | 0.000 |
| | *N* | 98 | 98 | 98 | 98 |
| mean_psy | Pearson correlation | 0.444** | 0.512** | 1 | 0.483** |
| | Sig. (two-tailed) | 0.000 | 0.000 | | 0.000 |
| | *N* | 98 | 98 | 98 | 98 |
| mean_social | Pearson correlation | 0.580** | 0.712** | 0.483** | 1 |
| | Sig. (two-tailed) | 0.000 | 0.000 | 0.000 | |
| | *N* | 98 | 98 | 98 | 98 |

******Correlation is significant at the 0.01 level (two-tailed).*

Correlations between ICT and knowledge enhancement, economic enhancement, psychological development, and social growth were significant at 0.01 level. All the dependent variables are being affected by ICT positively. This proves that technology is having a very vast impact on all-round development of professionals. This has also been proved by the study conducted by Manisha (2014).

The study revealed that ICT was bringing all-round changes among many educational practices. They highlighted motivational role, communication advantages, and knowledge enhancement role. Mobile technology and its social survey in 2018 also revealed positive changes in the economy and educational growth in various countries like South Africa, Vietnam, Mexico, etc. Spring Global Attitude Survey (2014) revealed the positive impact of the Internet on education, economy, politics but low impact on morality.

## 7.7 DISCUSSION

This study has proved that ICT is a boon for higher education. It has facilitated the overall development of learners in society. The programs should be upgraded as per new inventions and innovations to spread their knowledge for the betterment of society. It leads to a maximum realization of potentials in human resources, the confidence level of learners has increased because of the availability of information on the Internet that is usually present all the time with learners in the form of laptops, mobiles, tablets, PC, etc. The impact of ICT on peoples' social, economical, and all-round development can be observed globally. Practically, the Internet has empowered societies globally. This has proved to be the greatest benefit for accelerating the knowledge and understanding of human rights and duties. The social approach to life is more rational as it is governed by the education that is dripping down to all through Internet usage. Although people criticize youths on long term use of mobiles and laptops but cannot themselves be blind to communications through them. The biggest positive impact of the Internet on society is that societies around the globe are becoming stronger, developed, and more intelligent because most technologies are interlinked with the Internet. Life in isolation no longer exists.

## 7.8 RECOMMENDATIONS

Purpose-oriented quality programs should be developed and broadcast. If the stakeholders perceive the various educational programs as meeting their needs and expectations, ICT is a boon for enhancing knowledge, which, in turn, is an enlightening happening for the human resource and for the nation and also for the globe. All are benefiting. Furthermore, ICT policies in all business and service sectors are increasing the speed of interaction so funding for increasing ICT applications in various agencies and organizations should be provided. This will empower the various sectors to initiate, develop, promote, review, and implement ICT policies. This reveals that ICT seed should be sowed and grown into a healthy plant in the educational sector to make people competent in ICT usage and will be able to join any sector and run ICT wherever they go. As the computer software and other ICT requirement are becoming costlier the higher education system must persuade various organizations to fund in higher education through ICT as it will ultimately profit them only in the long run. Even the Ministry of Information Technology should also be incorporated in taking funds as the nation will benefit most with new developments and growth.

## 7.9 CONCLUSION

Various educational practices like getting leaning material, conducting an online exam, and paying online fees have aggravated the utility of ICT in higher education and have initiated new improved teaching and learning processes, and has facilitated e-learning of learners who were previously deprived of the same because of many hindrances like time factor, expense factor, distance, etc. ICT has proved to be the only way out for all who want to enhance their knowledge and gain benefit from it.

## KEYWORDS

- **information communication**
- **technology**
- **psychological impact**
- **social impact**
- **economic development**
- **knowledge enhancement**

## REFERENCES

Manisha, Anju 2014. The role of ICT in higher education in India. International Journal of All Research Education and Scientific Methods. 3 (11) 16–19.

Mc Gorry, S. Y. (2002), Online but on target? Internet based MBA courses: a case study. The Internet and Higher Education. 5 (2) 167–175.

Ozdemir, Z. D. and Abrevaya, J. (2007). Adoption of technology mediated distance education: a longitudinal analysis. Information and Management, 44(5), 467–479.

Pegu, Uttam Kr. (2014). Information and communication technology in higher education in India: challenges and oppurtunities. International Journal of Information and Communication Technology, 4(5) 513–518.

Srivastava, Tripti K., Lalitbhushan S., Arunita T. Jagzape, Alka T. Raweker. 2014. Role of information communication technology in higher education: learners perspective in rural medical schools. Journal of Clinical and Diagonostic Research 4(5) 163–169 3.

www.ijcrt.org © 2017 IJCRT | Volume 5, Issue 4 December 2017 ISSN: 2320-2882 IJCRT1704371 International Journal of Creative Research Thoughts (IJCRT) www.ijcrt.org 2813.

## REFERENCES

Manisha, Anju 2014. The role of ICT in higher education in India. International Journal of All Research Education and Scientific Methods. 2 (11) 16–19.

M. Geroy, S. Y. (2002). Online but on target? Internet based MBA courses: a case study. The Internet and Higher Education. 5 (2) 167–175. – 1

Ozdemir, Z. D. and Abrevaya, J. (2007). Adoption of technology mediated distance education: a longitudinal analysis. Information and Management, 44(5) 467–479.

Page, Gaurav Kr. (2014). Information and communication technology in higher education in India: challenges and opportunities. International Journal of Information and Communication Technology, 4(5) 513–518.

Srivastava, Tripti K., Lalitbhushan S., Arunav J., Jagzape, Alka T., Rawekar. 2014. Role of information communication technology in higher education: learners perspective in rural medical schools. Journal of Clinical and Diagnostic Research 4(5) 163–165. – 1

www.ijcrt.org © 2017 IJCRT | Volume 5, Issue 4 December 2017 | ISSN: 2320-2882 IJCRT1704371 International Journal of Creative Research Thoughts (IJCRT) www.ijcrt.org 2913.

## CHAPTER 8

# Students' Perceptions of ICT Usage in Higher Education: A Study

BHATT KOMALBEN

*Department of English, Hemchandracharya North Gujarat University, Patan, Gujarat 384265, India. E-mail: komalbhatt890@gmail.com*

## ABSTRACT

The present study investigates the impacts of information and communication technologies (ICTs) on higher education and also to identify impediments that resulted in slow motion penetration of ICTs at the university level in the Gujarat state. The methodology employed for this paper follows a mixed method by using the primary source of data. The structured questionnaires were administered to the students pursuing postgraduation from the Hemchandracharya North Gujarat University (HNGU) ($N = 8056$, $n = 309$) in various disciplines by considering factors such as ICT infrastructure, digital communication, and student satisfaction on ICT usage and ICT usage by faculty. IBMSPSS.25 is used for data analysis as a statistical tool. The results explore the need for strong ICT infrastructure in rural colleges of HNGU and student-centric policy on ICT usage in the university.

## 8.1 INTRODUCTION

### *8.1.1 BACKGROUND OF THE STUDY*

Information and communication technology (ICT) application in higher education and its influence on student's performance are as well as two sides of the same coin. ICT usage as a tool is proved as a time and money saver in the academic world. It also reduces the tension of big data solutions. The data collection process becomes easier in comparison to the manual data collection process in case of ICT usage. ICT usage also provides institutions and members support strategies through customer consultants, collaboration, resource sharing, and webinars. Hemchandracharya North Gujarat University (HNGU) is one of the leading public universities of Gujarat state, India. ICT usage is given priority in most of the aspects associated with administration and student-oriented activities. The university is ornamented with facilities as high-speed Internet-connected computers, e-library, Wi-Fi facility, and audio–visual classrooms. Such facilities contribute immensely to the realization of institutional goals through adequate, timely, and effective information to students, faculty, and other concerned community. HNGU is known for its contribution to the holistic development of students. The present study aims to evaluate post-graduate (PG) students' perception of ICT usage by various categorical human powers including students.

The value of ICT in academics and its related research conducted by academicians, researchers, professionals, and scholars is not up to the level of expectations in higher education of Gujarat state. This problem is also associated with another state of India and developing countries. For example, Borgman (2008) pointed that relatively little research is conducted on ICT usage in higher education and its effectiveness in easy communication. Meyer and Dutton (2009) indicated that there is little related knowledge and awareness on the use of ICT in higher education and its impact on students' academic performance. Pegu (2014) also concludes that ICT usage has changed the academic world but the desired level of information technology (IT) usage is yet to be obtained. The author also adds that ICT enabled education will ultimately lead to the democratization of education and it has the potential for transforming higher education in India. Such studies have necessitated conducting research on ICT usage in HNGU and its impacts on students' and faculty performance.

### *8.1.2 SIGNIFICANCE OF THE STUDY*

The present study focuses on PG students' perception of ICT usage in the HNGU and its student-oriented outcomes. Indian higher education is on the infancy stage on using ICT in higher education, especially in rural areas of Gujarat state. HNGU has an almost 70% district youth population that belongs to the tribe and needs to uplift their higher education at par with metro or urban Gujarat or India. The state government has adopted a sound policy on higher education policy but barriers to using advanced technology in every discipline of studies such as professional courses and nonprofessional courses. The use of social media for academic purposes and skill development is yet to reach a maturity stage. The demographic and low motivational level on career making leads to downsizing employability oriented higher education literacy ratio. In these circumstances, ICT can play a magnificent role in enhancing students' attitudes on the importance of higher education in rural Gujarat. So, the present study engages PG students' perception of ICT usage and its role in the holistic development of students.

### *8.1.3 HYPOTHESES*

H1: No positive relation exists between PG students' satisfaction on ICT usage and ICT infrastructure in context to HNGU of Gujarat state.

H2: No positive relation exists between PG students' satisfaction on ICT usage and digital communication in context to HNGU of Gujarat state.

H3: No positive relation exists between PG students' satisfaction on ICT usage by faculty in context to HNGU of Gujarat state.

### *8.1.4 OBJECTIVES OF THE STUDY*

The following research objectives are formed with the help of identifying research gaps in the present study.

1. To study PG students' perception on ICT infrastructure in context to HNGU of Gujarat state.
2. To study PG students' perception on digital communication in context to HNGU of Gujarat state.
3. To study PG students' satisfaction on ICT usage in context to HNGU of Gujarat state.
4. To study PG students' perception on ICT usage by faculty in context to HNGU of Gujarat state.

### *8.1.5 CONCEPTUAL FRAMEWORK*

The conceptual framework explains a phenomena. It is a blueprint of the study. Figure 8.1 indicates the journey from problem statement to findings and limitations of the present study. A review of the previous literature conducted on the topic is examined after defining the problem statement. Research gaps are identified from the previous relevant literature reviewed.

Research objectives are framed on identifying research gaps. Hypotheses are constituted after determining research objectives. Research methodology is also adopted with a view to maintain proper direction of present study. The collected data from primary source and analyzed and interpreted with testing of hypotheses. The findings are concluded at the end with recommendations and limitations of the study.

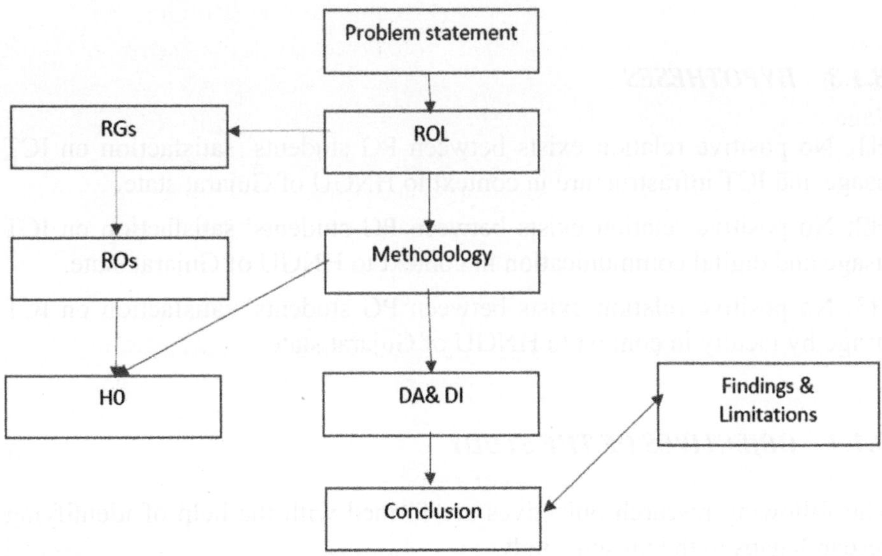


**FIGURE 8.1** Conceptual framework.

## 8.2 LITERATURE REVIEW

Mahdum et al. (2019) studied that faculty can be motivated for better performance through ICT usage in higher education. They also studied that email, PPT, smartphone use, and laptops are frequently used as a tool for using the Internet and ICT in Indonesian University. The researcher argues in this study that ICT training to faculty and faculty motivation for ICT usage is strongly associated with each other in a positive manner.

Andrey et al. (2018) concluded in their study that procedure ICT implementation in university/schooling has offer to humans significant conditions for the development of the important forces of students, their creative skills, and highbrow assets. The results of their research bolstered their conviction that the procedure of self-consciousness of students in university training indicates. On the other hand, it could serve as an inner indicator of the effectiveness of university training and the existential marker of the psychological increase of students within the manner of vocational education.

Tabassum and Shehzadi (2018) concluded that faculty attitude toward computers system is affirmative Most of the respondents are in favor of computers as they provide real advantages over conventional techniques of instructions and improve the first-rate of students gaining knowledge. Meanwhile, some of them think that computers are not suitable consistent with their curriculum and class time is not sufficient for the use of computer systems. It turned into additionally located that they had been receiving a low stage of effect from different people almost about the use ICTs and of their notion the use of ICTs would preclude the era from gaining knowledge of their traditions so other social problems that want to be addressed earlier than imposing computers in education. They also observed that the institutions need to set up training regarding ICTs for them to have a capable faculty who has to shape the destiny of the United States.

Girish and Kumar (2017) studied that ICT-enabled teaching and learning processes toward influencing and empowering teachers and students should shake hands with new initiative methods to obtain knowledge. The author also observed that ICT usage can open the doors to improving students' performance in a better way. The researcher also argues that ICT usage of higher education in Indian universities with excellent infrastructure can meet global parameters of qualitative higher education.

Gasaymeh (2017) concluded that students have positive perceptions of the want of virtual competency in their formal learning. It is also determined by the authors that virtual technologies might be easy to apply and could grow students' productiveness, beautify their corporation for gaining knowledge, and provide leisure. The college students meant to use virtual technology when they have become formally integrated into their gaining knowledge. Students' perceptions of the use of digital technology in their formal mastering were not substantially specific primarily based on their gender, age, important, and perceived virtual dependency. The college students who perceived themselves to have high ranges of digital competency had higher effective perceptions of using digital technologies of their formal gaining knowledge than the scholars who perceived themselves to have low and mild tiers of digital competency.

Tiwari and Tikam (2016) studied that students can obtain necessary information in a rapid manner by using ICT and also have the facility to access information round the clock. They also added that the duties of institutions to provide good speed Internet to students for better results and knowledge. The researcher argues that student satisfaction level on ICT usage also depends on institutional policy on providing necessary tools to students.

Shin (2015) studied through two examinations and analyzed the preservice English instructors' mindfulness with respect to three primary issues, such as computerized education, reasonable utilization of advanced material, and e-wellbeing. The members of the first investigation arranged to peruse and listening exercises by utilizing on the web material and afterward assessed as far as advanced education and reasonable use. However, in the subsequent examination, the members arranged composing exercises by online system benefits and assessed as far as e-security. The entire examination inferred that more often than not preadministration educators don't think about these issues while getting ready class exercises. Familiarity with members of basic, moral, and safe utilization of IT was additionally raised by assessment exercises. It is also argued in this study that the ethical and safe use of ICT by faculty in higher education of India is inevitable.

Shrivastava et al. (2014) studied that making plans for green management of better educational institutions and obtaining the world elegance generally far vital to have stepped forward collaboration and get right of entry to data through introducing ICT in the educational sector with e-governance as security for keeping upgraded. e-Governance wishes protection for clean statistics flow, great exercise database, and superior capability for records evaluation, and so forth. With the creation of ICT, digital governance is a rising trend to re-invent the way the government works, turning into a new version of governance. Such a comprehensive and included machine also can permit the government to research the overall performance of one of the exceptional acting institutes and evaluate it with different colleges and colleges to become aware of the gaps. e-Governance will improve the pleasantness of better education devices in India. e-Governance can create transparency among universities, colleges, and students. It will bring new standards of governance, each in phrases of desires and obligations. Many problems of better training device can be solved through the public–private partnership version and e-governance.

Mathew (2014) studied that most of the library professionals have an affirmative approach toward the application of ICT in library services. The author also studied that inadequate infrastructure in Indian public universities can be one of the barriers to prepare world-class professionals or academicians. The universities also need to enhance the soft skills of associated human power with ICT services. The researcher argues that library professionals should be trained in the area of ICT and its application in universities, which can assist students and faculties to enhance their ICT skills.

Bhardwaj and Singh (2011) studied that means of computerization are confined to simply typing or browsing the web; the complete ability of ICT has no longer been explored via many universities. ICT is a very useful device to have transparency, reliability, and performance in university examination devices. There are limitless opportunities by using integrating ICT with the examination device. An automated integrated examination system will ensure performance and effectiveness within the examination device and render the comfort of on-line queries through cutting downtime and price and breaking down geographical barriers, for that reason bringing a sea of changes in the current guide examination system. The researcher supports this observation and seeks the implementation of excellent ICT infrastructure in public universities of India.

Angel et al. (2018) concluded that the students were not extremely satisfied with the interest that the faculty shows in their participation in classroom and online as well as work quality. They also concluded that the faculties have a low level of interest in incurring necessary knowledge on ICT usage in the classroom. The researcher argues that faculty should be a role model for students to follow for enhancing knowledge activities as well as career-making activities.

Krishnaveni and Meenakumari (2010) concluded that demographic factors do not have major impacts on information administration in higher education institutions. The authors also concluded that enhancing the usage of ICT in the general administration of public universities will enhance institutional performance. The researcher argues that ICT usage in general administration in public universities will be helpful to enhance the goal achievement process.

### *8.2.1 RESEARCH GAPS*

The following research gaps are identified by reviewing the previous literature conducted by scholars, professionals, and academicians.

1. ICT infrastructure is to be considered as a core issue in higher education for better performance of faculty and holistic development of students in Indian universities, particularly in public universities having a nonmetro background.
2. Digital communication is one of the core-level components among higher education institutes in Gujarat.
3. Students can also be treated as stakeholder of the university and their satisfaction level also can be taken into consideration by having excellent ICT infrastructure in Indian public universities.

4. Faculty can also be treated as stakeholder of the university and their satisfaction on ICT training and usage also effect on student academic engagement and development

## 8.3 METHODOLOGY

Table 8.1 presents the methodology employed for the purpose of the investigation. It is a mix method type of study and the target population is PG students of HNGU ($N = 8056$, valid sample size = 309). The factors such as ICT infrastructure (ICTINF), digital communication (DC), student satisfaction on ICT usage (SSICT), and ICT usage by faculty (ICTF) are included for the structured questionnaire administered to PG students of HNGU by email and in person. The total items are 60, excluding the demographic profile, and assessed with five-point Likert scale technique (strongly disagree–strongly agree). IBM's SPSS 25 is used for the purpose of data analysis.

**TABLE 8.1** Research Methodology

| No. | Title | Topic Name |
|---|---|---|
| 1 | Study type | Mix method |
| 2 | Universe | PG students |
| 3 | Target population | PG students of HNGU (8056) |
| 4 | Sampling technique | Convenience sampling technique |
| 5 | Sample size | 309 |
| 6 | Factors | ICT Infrastructure (ICTINF), Digital Communication (DC), Student Satisfaction on ICT Usage (SSICT), ICT Usage by Faculty (ICTF) |
| 7 | Items | 60 (4 × 15) |
| 8 | Statistical tool | Excel, IBMSPSS .25 |
| 9 | Statistical tests | Descriptive statistics, scale reliability, Pearson correlations |

## 8.4 DATA ANALYSIS AND INTERPRETATION

### 8.4.1 DEMOGRAPHIC PROFILE

Table 8.2 presents the results on the demographic profile consisting of gender, age, residential status, and background of respondent in terms of culture, that is, rural or urban. Female respondents are 4.8% more in comparison to male respondents. Maximum respondents are within the age group of ≤25 years (89.6%). Residential status registers that 76.6% and 74.7% of respondents have rural background. Thus, maximum respondents have rural background in the present study. The demographic profile is not a part of objectives of the present study, and as a result, an overview in general is discussed.

**TABLE 8.2** Demographics Profile of Respondents

| No | Title | Demographic | Samples | % |
|---|---|---|---|---|
| 1 | Gender | Male | 157 | 50.8 |
| | | Female | 152 | 49.2 |
| 2 | Age | ≤25 years | 277 | 89.6 |
| 3 | | 25–30 years | 32 | 10.4 |
| 4 | Residential status | Hostel | 72 | 23.3 |
| | | Other | 237 | 76.7 |
| 5 | Background | Rural | 231 | 74.7 |
| | | Urban | 78 | 25.3 |

The imported data from Excel to IBM SPSS 25 are standardized before moving to data analysis because data are generally need to put in common format before analyzing them, which increases scale reliability and equalize the range and variability of data.

### *8.4.2 DESCRIPTIVE STATISTICS*

Descriptive statistics provides basic features of data in a study. It also provides simple summaries about sample and measures. Generally, it is more suitable to quantitative data for having directions to analyze the data. It consists of elements such as *N*, minimum, maximum, mean, SD, variance, range, skewness, and qualitative data and aims to know the basic features of data to move on for further analysis.

Table 8.3 indicates the results on descriptive statistics related to ICTINF; *N*= 309. It has items from ICTINF1 to ICTINF15. Minimum is 1, and maximum is 5. The range is 4. Mean is registered within the range of 3.11–3.66. SD is registered within the range of 1.43–1.59. Variance is registered between 1.88 and 2.55. It means that students' perception on ICT infrastructure is moderate and has direction to move on for further analysis.

**TABLE 8.3** Descriptive Statistics: ICTINF

| Descriptive Statistics | | | | | | |
|---|---|---|---|---|---|---|
| | **N** | **Range** | **Minimum** | **Maximum** | **Mean** | **Std. Deviation** |
| ICTINF1 | 309 | 4.00 | 1.00 | 5.00 | 3.6634 | 1.45383 |
| ICTINF2 | 309 | 4.00 | 1.00 | 5.00 | 3.5372 | 1.43339 |
| ICTINF3 | 309 | 4.00 | 1.00 | 5.00 | 3.1100 | 1.56282 |
| ICTINF4 | 309 | 4.00 | 1.00 | 5.00 | 3.3495 | 1.59367 |
| ICTINF5 | 309 | 4.00 | 1.00 | 5.00 | 3.5372 | 1.43339 |
| ICTINF6 | 309 | 4.00 | 1.00 | 5.00 | 3.6375 | 1.46541 |
| ICTINF7 | 309 | 4.00 | 1.00 | 5.00 | 3.5437 | 1.43773 |
| ICTINF8 | 309 | 4.00 | 1.00 | 5.00 | 3.8220 | 1.37133 |
| ICTINF9 | 309 | 4.00 | 1.00 | 5.00 | 3.1392 | 1.52577 |
| ICTINF10 | 309 | 4.00 | 1.00 | 5.00 | 3.3301 | 1.59782 |
| ICTINF11 | 309 | 4.00 | 1.00 | 5.00 | 3.6537 | 1.45489 |
| ICTINF12 | 309 | 4.00 | 1.00 | 5.00 | 3.5243 | 1.43819 |
| ICTINF13 | 309 | 4.00 | 1.00 | 5.00 | 3.0971 | 1.56368 |
| ICTINF14 | 309 | 4.00 | 1.00 | 5.00 | 3.3366 | 1.59646 |
| ICTINF15 | 309 | 4.00 | 1.00 | 5.00 | 3.5243 | 1.43819 |
| Valid N (listwise) | 309 | | | | | |

Table 8.4 presents the results of descriptive statistics related to DCN = 309. It has items form DC1 to DC15. The minimum is 1, and the maximum is 5. The range is. The mean is registered within the range of 2.96–3.86. SD is registered within the range of 1.37–1.59. The variance is registered between 1.88 and 2.69. It means that students' perception on digital communication is moderate and has direction to move on for further analysis.

Table 8.5 demonstrates the results on descriptive statistics to SSICT; $N = 309$. It has items from SSICT1 to SSICT15. The minimum is 1, and the maximum is 5. The mean is registered within the range of 1.76–3.44. SD is registered within the range of 1.00–1.64. Variance is registered between 1.10 and 2.38. It means thar students' perception on student satisfaction on ICT usage is moderate and has direction to move on for further analysis.

**TABLE 8.4** Descriptive Statistics: DC

| Descriptive Statistics | | | | | | |
|---|---|---|---|---|---|---|
| | **N** | **Range** | **Minimum** | **Maximum** | **Mean** | **Std. Deviation** |
| DC1 | 309 | 4.00 | 1.00 | 5.00 | 3.6246 | 1.47099 |
| DC2 | 309 | 4.00 | 1.00 | 5.00 | 3.5437 | 1.43773 |
| DC3 | 309 | 4.00 | 1.00 | 5.00 | 3.8220 | 1.37133 |
| DC4 | 309 | 4.00 | 1.00 | 5.00 | 3.1392 | 1.52577 |
| DC5 | 309 | 4.00 | 1.00 | 5.00 | 3.3269 | 1.59543 |
| DC6 | 309 | 4.00 | 1.00 | 5.00 | 2.9612 | 1.49624 |
| DC7 | 309 | 4.00 | 1.00 | 5.00 | 3.0615 | 1.64142 |
| DC8 | 309 | 4.00 | 1.00 | 5.00 | 3.6537 | 1.45489 |
| DC9 | 309 | 4.00 | 1.00 | 5.00 | 3.5243 | 1.43819 |
| DC10 | 309 | 4.00 | 1.00 | 5.00 | 3.0971 | 1.56368 |
| DC11 | 309 | 4.00 | 1.00 | 5.00 | 3.3366 | 1.59646 |
| DC12 | 309 | 4.00 | 1.00 | 5.00 | 3.5243 | 1.43819 |
| DC13 | 309 | 4.00 | 1.00 | 5.00 | 3.6246 | 1.47099 |
| DC14 | 309 | 4.00 | 1.00 | 5.00 | 3.5437 | 1.43773 |
| DC15 | 309 | 4.00 | 1.00 | 5.00 | 3.8220 | 1.37133 |
| Valid N (listwise) | 309 | | | | | |

**TABLE 8.5** Descriptive Statistics: SSICT

| | **N** | **Minimum** | **Maximum** | **Mean** | **Std. Deviation** |
|---|---|---|---|---|---|
| SSICT1 | 309 | 1.00 | 5.00 | 3.1392 | 1.52577 |
| SSICT2 | 309 | 1.00 | 5.00 | 3.3269 | 1.59543 |
| SSICT3 | 309 | 1.00 | 5.00 | 2.9612 | 1.49624 |
| SSICT4 | 309 | 1.00 | 5.00 | 3.0615 | 1.64142 |
| SSICT5 | 309 | 1.00 | 5.00 | 3.0777 | 1.61781 |
| SSICT6 | 309 | 1.00 | 5.00 | 2.2880 | 1.42036 |
| SSICT7 | 309 | 1.00 | 5.00 | 2.9709 | 1.62842 |
| SSICT8 | 309 | 1.00 | 5.00 | 2.7443 | 1.48674 |
| SSICT9 | 309 | 1.00 | 5.00 | 3.2427 | 1.57373 |
| SSICT10 | 309 | 1.00 | 5.00 | 2.8123 | 1.59251 |
| SSICT11 | 309 | 1.00 | 5.00 | 3.4434 | 1.52922 |
| SSICT12 | 309 | 1.00 | 5.00 | 3.0712 | 1.62412 |
| SSICT13 | 309 | 1.00 | 5.00 | 1.7670 | 1.00522 |
| SSICT14 | 309 | 1.00 | 5.00 | 1.6602 | 1.03089 |
| SSICT15 | 309 | 1.00 | 5.00 | 1.8155 | 1.17397 |
| Valid *N* (listwise) | 309 | | | | |

Table 8.6 indicates the results on descriptive statistics. It has items form ICTF1 to ICTF15; $N = 309$. The minimum is 1, and the maximum is 5. The range is registered as 4. The mean is registered within the range of 1.53–4.28. SD is registered within the range of 0.56–1.54. Variance is registered within the range of 1.14–2.38. It means that students' perception on ICT usage by faculty is moderate and has direction to move on for further analysis.

**TABLE 8.6** Descriptive Statistics: ICTF

| | N | Minimum | Maximum | Mean | Std. Deviation |
|---|---|---|---|---|---|
| ICTF1 | 309 | 1.00 | 5.00 | 1.9903 | 1.06748 |
| ICTF2 | 309 | 1.00 | 5.00 | 1.7508 | 1.02535 |
| ICTF3 | 309 | 1.00 | 5.00 | 2.7023 | 1.48653 |
| ICTF4 | 309 | 1.00 | 5.00 | 1.8447 | 1.11446 |
| ICTF5 | 309 | 1.00 | 5.00 | 1.8706 | 1.14078 |
| ICTF6 | 309 | 1.00 | 5.00 | 1.5372 | 0.84673 |
| ICTF7 | 309 | 1.00 | 5.00 | 1.9773 | 1.05196 |
| ICTF8 | 309 | 1.00 | 5.00 | 1.6764 | 0.97973 |
| ICTF9 | 309 | 1.00 | 5.00 | 2.7087 | 1.48781 |
| ICTF10 | 309 | 2.00 | 5.00 | 4.2848 | 0.56677 |
| ICTF11 | 309 | 2.00 | 5.00 | 4.2848 | 0.56677 |
| ICTF12 | 309 | 1.00 | 5.00 | 4.0194 | 0.91503 |
| ICTF13 | 309 | 1.00 | 5.00 | 4.0259 | .89695 |
| ICTF14 | 309 | 1.00 | 5.00 | 3.6019 | 1.36043 |
| ICTF15 | 309 | 1.00 | 5.00 | 2.1456 | 1.54420 |
| Valid *N* (listwise) | 309 | | | | |

### *8.4.3 SCALE RELIABILITY TEST*

Table 8.7 indicates the results on the scale reliability test. ICTINF, DC, SSICT, and ICTF are tested with 15 items to each. No one is excluded, and as a result, 15 items to each factors are considered as valid items. Cronbach's alpha ($\alpha$) is registered as 0.872(87.2%) for ICTINF. It means that the internal consistency among ICTINF1–ICTINF15 is 87.2% in terms of the scaling technique. Cronbach's alpha is registered as 0.821(82.1%) for DC. It means that the internal consistency among DC1–DC15 is 82.1% in terms of the scaling technique. Cronbach's alpha is registered as 0.644(64.4%) for SSICT. It means the internal consistency among SSICT1–SSICT15 is

64.4% in terms of the scaling technique. Cronbach's alpha is registered as 0.65.8(65.8%) for ICTF. It means that the internal consistency among SSICT1– SSICT15 is 65.8% in terms of the scaling technique. To conclude, Cronbach's alpha ($\alpha$) showed that the questionnaire is statistically reliable (George and Mallery, 2003).

**TABLE 8.7** Scale Reliability Test

| Sr. No | Factor | Items | Excluded Items | Valid Items | Measured Cronbach Alpha | Standard Internal Consistency | Decision |
|---|---|---|---|---|---|---|---|
| .1 | ICTINF | 15 | 0 | 15 | 0.872 | $0.8 \leq \alpha < 0.9$ | Good |
| 2 | DC | 15 | 0 | 15 | 0.821 | $0.8 \leq \alpha < 0.9$ | Good |
| 3 | SSICT | 15 | 0 | 15 | 0.644 | $0.6 \leq \alpha < 0.7$ | Acceptable |
| 4 | ICTF | 15 | 0 | 15 | 0.658 | $0.8 \leq \alpha < 0.9$ | Acceptable |

### *8.4.4 HYPOTHESES TESTING*

Table 8.8 presents the results on correlations. The hypotheses are tested with the Pearson correlation test to achieve the objectives satisfied in this study.

$H_0 1$: No positive relation exists between PG students' satisfaction on ICT usage and ICT infrastructure in the context of HNGU of Gujarat state (null hypothesis).

$H_1 1$: Significant positive relations exists between PG students' satisfaction on ICT usage and ICT infrastructure in context to HNGU of Gujarat state (alternative hypothesis).

$$H_0 1: \rho = 0$$

$$H_1 1: \rho \neq 0$$

Table 8.8 demonstrates that the significant Pearson correlations coefficient value of 0.952 (i.e. 95.2%) confirms that there is a significant positive correlation between SSICT and ICTINF. The significance level for the given value shows 0.00, which is less than 0.01. It is theoretically said that the significance level for the formulated hypothesis test is a value for which a $p$-value is less than 0.05 and 0.01 (i.e., $p < 0.01$ and $p < 0.05$); $N = 309$. In this case, significance correlation is observed, and as a result, $H_0 1$ is rejected and $H_1 1$ is accepted.

$H_0 2$: No positive relation exists between PG students' satisfaction on ICT usage and digital communication in context to HNGU of Gujarat state (null hypothesis).

$H_1 2$: No positive relation exists between PG students' satisfaction on ICT usage and digital communication in context to HNGU of Gujarat state (alternative hypotheses).

$$H_0 2: \rho = 0$$

$$H_1 2: \rho \neq 0$$

Table 8.8 demonstrates that the significant Pearson correlations coefficient value of 0.571 (i.e., 57.1%) confirms that there is significant positive correlation between SSICT and DC. The significance level for the given value shows 0.00, which is less than 0.01. It is theoretically said that the significance level for the formulated hypothesis test is a value for which the *p*-value is less than 0.05 and 0.01 (i.e., $p < 0.01$ and $p < 0.05$); $N = 309$. In this case, significance correlation is observed, and as a result, $H_0 2$ is rejected and $H_1 2$ is accepted.

$H_0 3$: No positive relation exists between PG students' satisfaction on ICT usage by faculty in context to HNGU of Gujarat state (null hypothesis).

$H_1 3$: Positive relation exists between PG students' satisfaction on ICT usage by faculty in context to HNGU of Gujarat state (alternative hypothesis).

$$H_0 3: \rho = 0$$

$$H_1 3: \rho \neq 0$$

Table 8.8 demonstrates that the Pearson correlations coefficient value of 0.191 (i.e., 18.1%) confirms that there is positive correlation between SSICT and ICTF. The significance level for the given value is 0.01, which is less than 0.05. It is theoretically said that significance level for the formulated hypothesis test is a value for which a *p*-value is less than 0.05 (i.e., $p < 0.05$); $N = 309$. In this case, a positive correlation is observed, and as a result, $H_0 3$ is rejected and $H_1 3$ is accepted. Generally, Pearson coefficient above 0.6 is considered as significant positive correlations, but in this case, it is registered as 0.191 (i.e., 19.1%) so that positive correlation exists in a poor manner but not observed as negative relations.

## 8.5 CONCLUSION

The PG students of HNGU responded on ICT infrastructure do not match with the private higher education sector. It should be made available to the students as easy accessible. The monitoring issues of ICT infrastructure are over looked in this case. The digital communicative system is also gets interrupted in a regular manner. The government should be initiative within the issue. The students should be given equal opportunities for their holistic development through ICT usage and government benefits during the study. The students also feel that the satisfaction level on ICT usage can be enhanced by eliminating routine hurdles, such as poor attention toward complaints, power supply problems, and slow Internet accessibility. The students also seek their growth at par with private institutions.

**TABLE 8.8** Pearson's Correlations Test

| | | **Correlations** | | | |
|---|---|---|---|---|---|
| | | **ICTINF** | **DC** | **SSICT** | **ICTF** |
| ICTINF | Pearson correlation | 1 | 0.952** | 0.571** | 0.191** |
| | Sig. (2-tailed) | | 0.000 | 0.000 | 0.001 |
| | N | 309 | 309 | 309 | 309 |
| DC | Pearson correlation | 0.952** | 1 | 0.555** | .164** |
| | Sig. (2-tailed) | 0.000 | | 0.000 | 0.004 |
| | N | 309 | 309 | 309 | 309 |
| SSICT | Pearson correlation | 0.571** | 0.555** | 1 | 0.141* |
| | Sig. (2-tailed) | 0.000 | 0.000 | | 0.013 |
| | N | 309 | 309 | 309 | 309 |
| ICTF | Pearson correlation | 0.191** | 0.164** | 0.141* | 1 |
| | Sig. (2-tailed) | 0.001 | 0.004 | 0.013 | |
| | N | 309 | 309 | 309 | 309 |

****Correlation is significant at the 0.01 level (2-tailed).*

**Correlation is significant at the 0.05 level (2-tailed).*

## 8.6 RECOMMENDATIONS AND LIMITATIONS

HNGU authorities can strengthen ICT infrastructure by keeping students in center. HNGU administration can also raise funds for better ICT infrastructure facilities to the students. HNGU management can engage efficient ICT service provider with eminent and trained human power, which can train faculty members and students, also. Faculty can be motivated by given adequate knowledge. HNGU can associate the students with ICT-based extracurricular activities with strong digital communication and infrastructure. HNGU management can enhance ICT usage by motivating students and faculty for better student academic engagement.

This is academic research and has certain limitations, such as time constraints and funding issues. Further research can be conducted by incorporating more factors and extending number of universities.

## KEYWORDS


- **ICT**
- **higher education**
- **digital communication**
- **student satisfaction**
- **faculty**


## REFERENCES


Andrey I. et al., The use of modern ICT to provide students' self-realization in Russian higher school, Espacios, 2018, Vol. 39, No. 43, pp. 15–21.

Angel F. et al., The use of modern ICT to provide students' self-realization in Russian higher school, Espacios, 2018, Vol. 39, pp. 1–15.

Bhardwaj Mohini, Singh Amar Jeet, Automated integrated university examination system, *Himachal Pradesh University Journal,* 2011, Vol. 20, No. 3, pp. 1–10.

Borgman C.L., What can studies of e-learning teach us about collaboration in e-research? Some findings from digital library studies. Computer Supported Cooperative Work, 2006, Vol. 15, No. 4, pp. 359–383.

Gasaymeh Al-Mothana M., University students' perceptions of the use of digital technologies in their formal learning: A developing country perspective, IJLD, 2017, Vol. 7, No. 3, pp. 149–164.

George D. and Mallery P., SPSS windows step by step: A simple guide and reference, 11.0 update. Allyn & Bacon, 4th ed., 2003, pp. 131–138.

Girish S.R. and Kumar S., ICT in teaching learning process for higher education: Challenges and opportunities. IOSR JCE, 2017, Vol. 19, No. 4, Ver. III (Jul.–Aug. 2017), pp. 24–28.

Krishnaveni R. and Meenakumari J., Usage of ICT for information administration in higher education institutions—A study, IJESD, 2010, Vo. 1, No. 3, pp. 282–287.

Mahdum et al., Exploring teacher perceptions and motivations to ICT use in learning activities in Indonesia, JITER, 2019, Vol. 18, pp. 294–316.

Mathew S., Impact of information communication technology (ICT) on professional development and education needs of library professionals in the universities of Kerala, 2014, Dissertation Submitted to KU.

Meyer E.T. and Dutton W.H. Top-down e-infrastructure meets bottom-up research innovation: The social shaping of e-research. Prometheus, 2009, Vol. 2, No. 3, pp. 239–250.

Pegu Uttam Kr, Information and Communication Technology in higher education in india, challenges and opportunities, IJICT, 2014, Vol. 4, No. 5, pp. 513–518.

Shin, W.S., Teachers use of technology and its influencing factors in Korean elementary schools Technology, Pedagogy and Education, 2015, Vol. 24, No. 4, pp. 461–476.

Shrivastava R.K., et al. Role of e-governance to strengthen higher education system in India, IOSR-Jimmie, 2014, Vol. 4, No. 2, pp. 57–62.

Shahida Tabassum and Kiran Shehzadi, ICT Awareness among Faculty Members of The Public Sector Women Universities of Pakistan, Proceedings of the RAIS Conference I, February 19–20, 2018, pp. 128–142.

Tiwari Riya and Tikam Swati. Awareness and use of ICT by B.Ed. students of Pt. Ravishankar University, JRU, 2016, Part A, pp. 44–48. ISSN-0970-5910.

## CHAPTER 9

# Role of ICT in Research and Development in Higher Education

SUNITA NEGI

*School of Basic & Applied Sciences, G.D Goenka University, Gurugram, Haryana 122103, India. E-mail: negisunita.81@gmail*

## ABSTRACT

Information and communication technology (ICT) has been very common in almost every aspect of life. It helps change the practices and procedures that are followed in our day to day life. ICT has helped people to improve their communication, work style, and their living standards to a much extent. The role of ICT in education especially in higher education is even more important. It has helped the student and the teacher interaction to a larger extent. The students are now being able to access a variety of data and services through ICT that helps them in pursuing their higher education. Research is an integral part of higher education as it has become mandatory in almost every curriculum. Thus, ICT also plays an important role in research and development in higher education. In this paper, we discuss the main components of ICT, its major role in higher education, and the importance of ICT in research in higher education.

## 9.1 INTRODUCTION

Information and communication technology (ICT) has changed almost every aspect of our lives. It plays a major role in various fields such as education, marketing, engineering, etc. In the last few decades, it has almost become the necessity of our lives. We are almost dependent on ICT for performing every day-to-day work in our lives. But in the earlier stages, it remained quite far from the higher education sector. Many people have tried to explore and study the lack of activity in the education sector (Soloway and Prior, 1996; Collis, 2002).

According to the study done by various stakeholders, there had been a number of challenges involved in incorporating ICT in higher education. The funding support was less to incorporate ICT in education. Also, there was a lack of awareness in the teacher's community to accept it for teaching methodology (Starr, 2001). In recent times, the support has increased to a larger extent for incorporating ICT in higher education. Also, the teachers are well oriented for its use and application.

In this paper, we would explore the role and importance of ICT in higher education. Further, the role of ICT in research development in higher education would be discussed. Various factors governing the research and development activities in higher education are discussed. In the future prospect, we also discuss further changes that could be incorporated for better availability of ICT for research in higher education.

## 9.2 IMPACT OF ICT IN HIGHER EDUCATION

The conventional sources of teaching involved one too many teaching methods where one teacher would be engaged in imparting knowledge to many students in the class. This method mainly involved the usage of textbooks. Over the past few decades, with the increase in the number of resources available more and more teachers have started using various ICT methods for their classroom teaching (Oliver and Short, 1996, Oliver, 2000). It provides an edge as the teaching now shifts from one to many to one to one. The teaching quality also improves with ICT aids. The quality of teaching also improves as the teacher and the students get access to higher bandwidths. The teachers can make use of presentations, audios, and videos to explain a topic to the students in the class. Other than this, the teachers can also make use of various other modes such as software and online portal to discuss a particular topic with the students.

### *9.2.1 BENEFITS TO THE STUDENTS*

The usage of ICT in higher education mainly impacts the way and how the student would learn a topic. In the conventional methods of teaching and learning, the students were restricted to a scheduled class or lecture in which the teacher used to give them information and knowledge. With the

ICT incorporated methods, the student are flexible to learn on their own whenever they have time and access. Other then what is being taught in the class, the student can gather other supporting information as well. In this way, the ICT-based method of teaching and learning can be considered as a student-centric methodology (Duffy and Cunningham, 1996). This would enhance the knowledge of the student to a great extent and also improve the personality development of the student as the student can now take part in a group discussion with all this knowledge. The student also gets a choice over the content which they want to access.

### 9.2.2 *BENEFITS TO THE TEACHERS*

The conventional methods of teaching do not provide a choice of time and place for teaching and learning. With the advanced methods of ICT, the teacher is now able to prepare well for his lecture. Also, he gets the flexibility to revise and rewind the topics taught in a particular class/lecture. The teacher gets access to the online course where he/she can upload the notes and the covered in the lecture. The other major advantage of using ICT is the usage of any place for the delivery of the program (Moore and Kearsley, 1996). The teacher also gets access to what is being taught in the class.

## 9.3 ROLE OF ICT IN RESEARCH IN HIGHER EDUCATION

ICT also plays a very important role in the research areas in higher education. The various components of ICT for research in higher education are as shown in Figure 9.1. The students/researchers mainly use ICT to gather knowledge for their work and to ease the knowledge gathering process and to enhance resource development. The students/researchers use the ICT tools to identify and solve their research problems in the most effective manner. It also helps them to discuss their ideas and research with the peer groups.

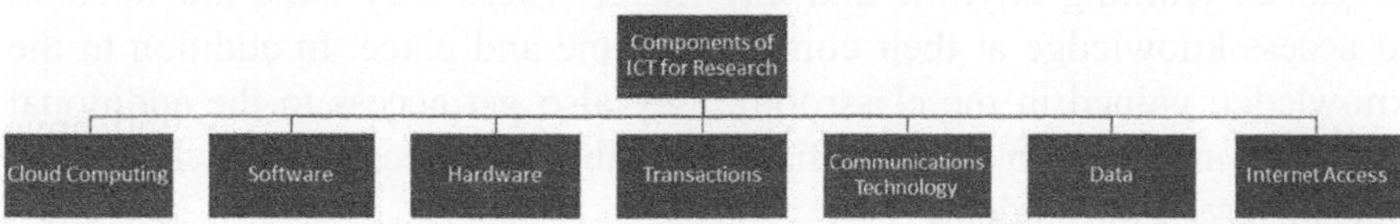


**FIGURE 9.1** Components of ICT for research.

The researchers make use of ICT for a number of applications such as to do a literature survey, analyze the information, perform analytical tasks, and analyze the data of the research. ICT tools are also used by the researchers to manage the information in a better way and perform their analysis. Generally, ICT is used by the researcher for performing the following tasks:

1. access the information source;
2. analyze information;
3. manage information;
4. literature survey;
5. perform study;
6. analyze results;
7. publish results; and
8. communicate with peer groups.

## 9.4 FUTURE PROSPECTS OF ICT USGAE IN RESEARCH IN HIGHER EDUCATION

As discussed in the previous section, ICT plays a very important role in the area of research in higher education. This usage can further be enhanced with the wider availability of resources of ICT to a much larger research community. This can be done with the involvement of industry in the education sector that can provide ICT to a much larger research and education community on a reasonable rate.

## 9.5 SUMMARY AND CONCLUSIONS

This paper has explored the role of ICT in higher education and in particular in research in higher education. Various advantages of using ICT-based methods in teaching and learning are discussed. The role of ICT is enormous in imparting knowledge to the students. It adds an extra edge over the conventional classroom methods of teaching and learning. ICT helps students to pursue learning anytime and anywhere, where they have the freedom to access knowledge at their convenient time and place. In addition to the knowledge gained in the classroom, they also get access to the additional information related to the same field. It further enhances the knowledge and personality of the student.

In addition to this, the paper also discusses the importance of the role of ICT in research and development in higher education. The various aspects of ICT usage in various research areas are discussed. The researcher makes use of ICT for the literature survey to begin with. The research work is also dependent on ICT in many of the cases. After this, the data generated in the study is also analyzed with the help of various ICT tools available. In short, it can be concluded that ICT plays a very crucial role in higher education and in particular in pursuing research in higher education.

## KEYWORDS

- **literature survey**
- **research and development**
- **data analysis**

## REFERENCES

Collis, B. (2002). Information technologies for education and training. In Adelsberger, H., Collis, B, & Pawlowski, J. (Eds.) *Handbook on Technologies for Information and Training.* Berlin, Germany: Springer Verlag.

Duffy, T., & Cunningham, D. (1996). Constructivism: Implications for the design and delivery of instruction, *Handbook of Research for Educational Telecommunications and Technology* (pp. 170–198). New York, NY, USA: Macmillan.

Moore, M. & Kearsley, G. (1996). *Distance Education: A Systems View.* Belmont, CA, USA: Wadsworth.

Oliver, R. & Short, G. (1996). The Western Australian Telecentres Network: A model for enhancing access to education and training in rural areas. International Journal of Educational Telecommunications, 2(4), 311–328.

Oliver, R. (2000). Creating meaningful contexts for learning in web-based settings. *Proceedings of Open Learning 2000.* (pp. 53–62). Brisbane, Queensland, Australia: Learning Network Queensland.

Soloway, E. & Pryor, A. (1996). The next generation in human-computer interaction. Communications of the ACM, 39(4), 16–18.

Starr, L. (2001). *Same Time This Year.* [on-line]. Available at http://www.education-world.com/a_tech/tech075.shtml [Accessed July 2002].

# CHAPTER 10

# Blended Learning Strategies for Management Students in Metro and Nonmetro Cities

RENU CHOUDHARY[1], and DAISY KURIEN[2*]

[1]*IITM, New Delhi, India*

[2]*Institute of Management Studies, Indus University, Ahmedabad, Gujarat, India*

[*]*Corresponding author. E-mail: daisynevin@gmail.com*

## ABSTRACT

With time, the teaching–learning process has witnessed a plethora of changes. Management teaching too has evolved and academicians have moved on from traditional modes of teaching to using digital aids. Due to the digitalization of society, teaching approaches such as blended learning, described as the combination of online and face to face instructions have become more prevalent in instructional strategies. This blend of using traditional in-classroom and online learning brings in a new dimension with exposure to more content and holistic learning. This redefining of traditional educational experience is challenging as most of the students in India have been less exposed to online learning.

The researchers approached 151 students from management colleges in Ahmedabad and Delhi and studied their attitude, liking, and preferences toward blended learning. Understanding these challenges will help educators to better implement blended learning strategies and ensure better learning.

## 10.1 INTRODUCTION

Online learning has evolved gradually from web-based, distance learning programs and has paved a way in redesigning courses, the use of advanced tools, and digitized content for instructional delivery. Online learning has completely transformed the pedagogy of teaching and learning. Innovative ways of learning aids to strengthen communication between students and teachers and enriches each student's learning experiences through robust personalized learning. Even in recent times, numbers of courses are not taught in different universities or colleges, and for such courses, online learning presents the only viable means of providing good-quality course options within their area.

In recent years, a shift has been observed from the traditional learning methods to modern methods of learning. Academicians have changed their pedagogy of interaction with their students so as to connect them with the real world. Textbooks are rapidly supplementing with Web-based content and resources. Online learning not only increasing effective communication and timely feedback but also alliance and learning extend beyond the corners of the classroom (Law et al., 2019). In the early stage of this revolution, very few techno-savvy academicians desire to achieve new ways to provide enriching and engaging content and to extend learning beyond the hour and location restrictions. Initially, results garnered the attention of top management institutions that attempted for making blended learning options available to students across the country. Previously, these institutions were reluctant to share innovative practices, but gradually grew into scalable new blended learning models with the goal of offering every student a quality education. This process of widening of blended learning models that combine the best of digital learning and one-to-one communication has been an encouragement for using more and better quality digital resources, and alternative platforms. These new learning models aid teachers to personalize instruction to students according to their learning requirements.

Many academicians and institutions are conspiring learning environments for students with a more customized approach. Blended learning models, evolved from early experimentation, position the learner at the middle point of the learning process, applying the technological power to design more enchanting, systematic, and goal-oriented intellect atmosphere. These models work on the methodology of identifying gaps in learning and provide instructions accordingly for ensuring success. Strong support of learner and instructor applying to transform learning create powerful next-stage learning models that prepare learners for success. The changing scenario of higher education across the world suggests that, in time to come, a blended learning approach will be the most important element of the learning process.

Over the past decade, most of the institutions of higher education started opting of a blended learning approach to excel and optimize their instructional model. Blended learning models attribute elements of influence over time, pace, path, and/or place, allowing for more student-centered learning experiences. Various researches show that learners with access to both online and face-to-face instruction excel in relation to learners who have exposure to only one method of instruction. Thus, it should not be surprising that blended learning has appeared as a powerful way to scale personalized learning. The emergence of learning that constitutes both digital and one-to-one communication is not only a hypothesis but also—an informative model move being carried out by both educators and learners around the world. This paper mainly focuses on the understanding of blended learning approach, implementation in management education, and its challenges to better implement the blended learning strategies and ensure better learning.

## 10.2 BLENDED LEARNING MEANING

Blended learning described as the blend of the traditional method of learning and online learning. The traditional method includes one-to-one interaction with teachers. In the case of face-to-face learning, the teacher is an active communicator whereas in online learning, students are center of the learning process to reach curriculum diversity. Blended learning incorporates learning opportunities, both by one-to-one interaction and by the online medium:

Traditional learning + online learning = blended learning.

## 10.3 LITERATURE REVIEW

Blended learning, a new dimension to the teaching and learning process, is defined as a blend of online and face-to-face instruction and has become a very acceptable educational strategy due to the digital transformation of society (Graham, 2006). Blended learning is a very popular tool and has been accepted as a widely appreciated potential learning strategy. Previously done research work shows that the effectiveness of blended learning is more as compared to fully online or one-on-one instructional courses and also it results in successful learning (Means et al., 2013; Vella et al., 2016). Involvement in blended learning has helped build positive social outcomes, such as social inclusion of adults and social capital. Social capital also saw a rise due to the beginner involvement in MOOCs (Joksimović et al., 2017). The study showed that people who were highly educated and were working largely participated in MOOCs. On the other hand, people with limited monetary resources faced more hurdles for MOOCs (Van de Oudeweetering and Agirdag, 2018). Comparing blended learning courses with MOOC courses, the former has been found to be a strong medium for self-development and has led to the empowerment of adults. This is because of its online nature and its ability to provide one-to-one instructional support.

Interaction is the base of all learning (Vygotsky, 1979), and it plays an important role in adding to the quality of online teaching and creating good learning experiences (Anderson, 2008). Blended learning supports direct communication between two parties or via online communication, which is carefully designed and is a well thought out strategy of the educational approach (Fryer et al., 2018). At higher levels of cognition and influence, a strong system of communication is required and the need for a group of learners is established, which is an alternative through which societal capital (Bourdieu, 1986) and societal inclusion (Rüber et al., 2018) is improved.

With the wide acceptance of technology in the educational system to enhance the pedagogy of teaching and learning, blended learning has been growing at its pace. Blended learning has primarily redesigned the entire approach of teaching and learning. Adoption of the Blended learning approach may replace classroom-attending time with computer-supported online techniques (Garrison and Vaughan, 2008). Acceptance of blended learning demands a complete redesign of courses with the aim of extending access to online learning opportunities. Studies conducted to illustrate that combining technology with conventional teaching and learning can surely improve access to information and the learning experience (Bai et al., 2016; Darling-Aduana and Heinrich, 2018).

The blended learning strategy has positive impact on learning performance and it has been verified that learner's contentment in blended courses was found to be greater than of traditional classroom teaching (Black, 2002) and also contributed toward better students' learning progression (Gunter, 2001; Sanders and Morrison-Shetlar, 2001). Students these days prefer blended courses than conventional courses because of their greater time flexibility and convenience (Hogarth, 2010). Blended learning strategy is a complex topic and includes various factors that decide the efficacy of a blended learning course.

## 10.4 RESEARCH OBJECTIVES

1. To understand the attitude, liking, and preferences of students from management colleges in Ahmedabad and Delhi, for blended learning.
2. To understand blended learning strategies that can be adopted by educators in management colleges, to ensure better learning.
3. To understand the impact of demographics on challenges perceived by management students.

## 10.5 ANALYSIS

Data was collected from 151 respondents, and from Table 10.1, it is clearly seen that 69.5% of the respondents understood the term blended learning, however, the rest 30.5% did not understand its meaning. The researchers, however, explained the meaning to the students, before administering the other questions given in the questionnaire.

**TABLE 10.1** Understanding of the Term "Blended Learning"

| | Frequency | Percent |
|---|---|---|
| Yes | 105 | 69.5 |
| No | 46 | 30.5 |
| Total | 151 | 100.0 |

Students were asked whether they were ever a part of the blended learning approach as a part of their management education. As given in Table 10.2, approximately 97% said that they have been subjected to the blended learning approach while approx. 3% denied the exposure.

**TABLE 10.2** Being a Part of the Blended Learning Approach in Management Education

| | Frequency | Percent |
|---|---|---|
| Yes | 147 | 97.4 |
| No | 4 | 2.6 |
| Total | 151 | 100.0 |

The surveyed students comprised 48% females and 52% male students (Table 10.3).

**TABLE 10.3** Gender of Students

| | Frequency | Percent |
|---|---|---|
| Female | 72 | 47.7 |
| Male | 79 | 52.3 |
| Total | 151 | 100.0 |

The researchers had chosen leading management colleges in Delhi and Ahmedabad, as their place of survey (Table 10.4). Approximately 50% of data was collected from each city.

**TABLE 10.4** Place of Survey

| | | Frequency | Percent |
|---|---|---|---|
| Valid | Delhi | 76 | 50.3 |
| | Ahmedabad | 75 | 49.7 |
| | Total | 151 | 100.0 |

From Table 10.5, it is evident that students (of both cities) agreed most that blended learning techniques are very effective. Students agreed to the fact that they had not been exposed to blended learning techniques in school. However, they also opined that blended learning techniques give them comparatively less access to information than face-to-face interaction.

## 10.6 FINDINGS

- Students (of both cities) agreed most that blended learning techniques are very effective. Their exposures in undergraduate and postgraduate colleges and the efforts of present age management colleges for teaching–learning process cannot be ignored.
- Students still believe that face-to-face interactions gives them more access to information than using blended learning techniques. This is a drawback too, as our Indian students who have since ages been exposed to classroom teaching may still feel comfortable in having a teacher in front of them to explain, solve their queries, and learn.

**TABLE 10.5** Descriptive Analysis of the Perception of Students for Blended Learning (in Order of Descending Mean)

| | Descriptive Statistics | | | | |
|---|---|---|---|---|---|
| | **N** | **Minimum** | **Maximum** | **Mean** | **Std. deviation** |
| Blended learning is ineffective as compared to conventional learning | 151 | 1 | 5 | 2.97 | 1.238 |
| I have got exposure to blended learning in school too | 151 | 1 | 5 | 3.25 | 1.255 |
| I get access to more information through blended learning than face to face interaction | 151 | 1 | 5 | 3.61 | 1.143 |
| Blended learning gives me opportunities to pursue other courses as per my convenience | 151 | 1 | 5 | 3.81 | 1.057 |
| Blended learning should be used more as a tool for learning and teaching | 151 | 1 | 5 | 3.86 | 1.039 |
| It is easy to handle e-learning tools | 151 | 1 | 5 | 3.91 | 0.938 |
| It is easy for me to understand the topics | 151 | 1 | 5 | 3.92 | 1.023 |
| Blended learning helps me to manage my time as per my convenience | 151 | 1 | 5 | 3.97 | 0.979 |
| Blended learning has made learning interesting | 151 | 1 | 5 | 3.98 | 0.983 |
| Management colleges across India should adopt blended learning | 151 | 1 | 5 | 3.98 | 1.010 |
| Blended learning encourages me to learn more through online learning platforms | 151 | 1 | 5 | 4.01 | 1.033 |
| Learning through Blended learning techniques is effective | 151 | 1 | 5 | 4.02 | 0.948 |
| Valid *N* (listwise) | 151 | | | | |

- Online platforms provide encouragement to students to learn more. Most management colleges have their own portals on which course curriculum, updates, session plans, chapter notes, power points presentations, exercises, assignments, marks, and feedback is uploaded. Students have access to such information that makes it quicker for them to learn, unlearn, and relearn.

- Students find learning through blended learning techniques to be effective. It has been much debated whether marks are the real criteria to judge the effectiveness of the teaching–learning process, hence researchers have not compared students' academic scores with effectiveness. Further research may be done in this area.

## 10.7 CONCLUSION

India is changing, and so it is imperative for management colleges and academicians to incorporate new strategies of learning, blended learning being one of them. Knowledge should be accessible to all. There are a number of government initiatives (Swayam, NPTEL, ARPIT) and sponsored platforms that provide a plethora of courses that can be pursued online. Teaching–learning can be made easier by adapting to new changes and by putting in continuous efforts to evolve new and simpler processes. Blended learning approaches make it easy for more and more learners to acquire knowledge regardless of age, gender, and geographical boundaries. It would also help more and more students having an urge to learn to build knowledge that will help them learn new skills and competencies for a better tomorrow.

## KEYWORDS

- **blended learning**
- **strategies**
- **management students**
- **educators**
- **metro**
- **nonmetro**

## REFERENCES

Anderson ML. Multiple inference and gender differences in the effects of early intervention: A re-evaluation of the Abecedarian, Perry Preschool, and early training projects. Journal of the American Statistical Association. 2008; 103(484):1481–95.

Bai K, Chang NB, Gao W. Quantification of relative contribution of Antarctic ozone depletion to increased austral extratropical precipitation during 1979–2013. Journal of Geophysical Research: Atmospheres. 2016;121(4):1459–74.

Black G. A comparison of traditional, online, and hybrid methods of course delivery. Journal of Business Administration Online. 2002;1(1):1–9.

Bourdieu P. The forms of capital: 1986. Cultural Theory: An Anthology. 2011, vol. 1: pp. 81–93, New York, NY: Wiley & Sons.

Caner M. The definition of blended learning in higher education. In: Blended learning environments for adults: Evaluations and frameworks 2012 (pp. 19–34). IGI Global.

Cocquyt C, Zhu C, Diep AN, De Greef M, Vanwing T. Examining the role of learning support in blended learning for adults' social inclusion and social capital. Computers & Education. 2019;142:103610.

Darling-Aduana J, Heinrich CJ. The role of teacher capacity and instructional practice in the integration of educational technology for emergent bilingual students. Computers & Education. 2018;126:417–32.

Fryer LK, Ginns P, Howarth M, Anderson C, Ozono S. Individual differences and course attendance: Why do students skip class?. Educational Psychology. 2018;38(4):470–86.

Garrison DR, Vaughan ND. Blended learning in higher education: Framework, principles, and guidelines. 2008, John Wiley & Sons, San Francisco.

Graham CR. Blended learning systems. The handbook of blended learning: Global perspectives, local designs. 2006, pp. 3–21, Pfeiffer Publishing, San Francisco.

Gunter H. Leaders and leadership in education. 2001, SAGE Publications Ltd.

Joksimović S, Dowell N, Poquet O, Kovanović V, Gašević D, Dawson S, Graesser AC. Exploring development of social capital in a CMOOC through language and discourse. The Internet and Higher Education. 2018;36:54–64.

Hogarth RM. Intuition: A challenge for psychological research on decision making. Psychological Inquiry. 2010;21(4):338–53.

Law KM, Geng S, Li T. Student enrollment, motivation and learning performance in a blended learning environment: The mediating effects of social, teaching, and cognitive presence. Computers & Education. 2019;136:1–2.

Means B, Toyama Y, Murphy R, Baki M. The effectiveness of online and blended learning: A meta-analysis of the empirical literature. Teachers College Record. 2013;115(3):1–47.

Rüber IE, Rees SL, Schmidt-Hertha B. Lifelong learning–lifelong returns? A new theoretical framework for the analysis of civic returns on adult learning. International Review of Education. 2018;64(5):543–62.

Sanders, D. W., & Morrison-Shetlar, A. I. Student attitudes toward web-enhanced instruction in an introductory biology course. Journal of Research on Computing in Education. 2001; 33(3):251–262.

Van de Oudeweetering K, Agirdag O. MOOCS as accelerators of social mobility? A systematic review. Journal of Educational Technology & Society. 2018;21(1):1.

Vella EJ, Turesky EF, Hebert J. Predictors of academic success in web-based courses: age, GPA, and instruction mode. Quality Assurance in Education. 2016;24(4), 586–600.

Vygotsky L. Consciousness as a problem in the psychology of behavior. Soviet Psychology. 1979;17(4):3–5.

**CHAPTER 11**

# Effectiveness of Developed Electronic Module in Terms of Achievement in Educational Administration of M.Ed. Students

AKANKSHA GUPTA* and RAMA MISHRA

*School of Education, Devi Ahilya University, Indore 452012, Madhya Pradesh, India*

**Corresponding author. E-mail: akankshagupta1981@gmail.com*

**ABSTRACT**

As we know that education is a systemize knowledge of our environment. The purpose of education is to prepare students for life. Students can learn through personal experience and by relating new information through innovative methods. In traditional methods of teaching, the focus was only on imparting the knowledge, which could not develop the understanding, practical ability, and skills in the learners. If a teacher adopts similar strategies for teachingthen students will be bored and they will stop taking interest in the learning. The present scenario is the scenario of fast changes, innovative ideas, skill-based information, and creativity. In this age of rapid change, teachers need to adopt new trends. information and communication technology (ICT) is one of them. The main aim of this paper is to explore the integration of ICT in the area of higher education. It was a pilot study whose objective was to find out the effectiveness of electronic module (e-module) in terms of achievement in the Educational Administration of M.Ed. students. The study has been carried out on purposely selected 23 students of M.Ed. who were studying at the School of Education, DAVV, Indore. The tool was developed by the researcher to measure achievement in the Educational Administration of M.Ed. students. The result of this pilot study showed that e-modules are effective in terms of achievement of M.Ed. students in Educational Administration. This module enhances student-centered learning based on ICT. Nowadays, traditional methods of teaching are not so worthy, and for that, e-modules can be a wonderful teaching aid for a skilled instructor.

## 11.1 INTRODUCTION

Education is a bipolar process in which an educator is at the one end and educant at the other. Successful teaching depends upon the approach of communicating the subject matter to the learners. As we know that education is a systemize knowledge of our environment, the purpose of education is to prepare students for life. Students can learn through personal experience and by relating new information through innovative methods. In traditional methods of teaching the focus was only on imparting the knowledge, which could not develop the understanding, practical ability, and skills in the learners. If a teacher adopts similar strategies for teaching then students will be bored and they will stop taking interest in the learning. In this age of rapid change, teachers need to adopt new trends related to information and communication technology (ICT).

## 11.2 PRESENT SCENARIO OF TEACHING AND LEARNING

Nowadays, education is based not only on psychology but also on technology. With the growth of technology, students can take responsibility for their own learning, with the help of the teacher. A teacher can guide their pupils for setting the goals and then by making a plan he can facilitate them to follow the plan for reaching the goal. This process can make their pupils self-regulating and self-evaluating. In the whole process, ICT can help the pupils as a powerful tool.

## 11.3 NEED AND SIGNIFICANCE OF ICT IN HIGHER EDUCATION

The fact emerges that in higher education children find learning to be most difficult. The most important reason for not learning is poor teaching. If teaching is not well planned, then it will be ineffective. In this technological scenario, a teacher has to be ready with his objectives, tools, and techniques. For a wonderful teaching, tool should be powerful, the technique should be innovative, and the teacher should be motivated. A teacher should understand that individuals are coming from different backgrounds, they are having different talents, ideas, and interests. These ideas and talents need execution, which is possible only through contemporary teaching. Contemporary teaching involves group work, more expression, discussion of ideas, evidences, argumentation, etc. Thus, for various skill development in pupils, recent trends are needed. In these recent trends, ICT is one of them. The electronic module enhances student-centered learning based on ICT.

## 11.4 e-MODULE

Personalized system of instruction involves a self-instructional e-module (SIM). SIM ensures "learner participation" and involvement by presenting answers to them. This ensures that the learner "evaluates" his progress. The answers provided to the questions help him do so and they act as "reinforcement in learning." SIM's has one thing in common with textbooks and that is "self-pacing" or the possibility for the learner to proceed with learning at a speed convenient to him.

### *11.4.1 DEFINITION OF MODULE*

According to W.R. Houston (1972); "e-Module is a set of experiences designed to facilitate the learner's demonstration of specified objectives."

According to R. L. Amends "Module is a set of learning activities intended to facilitate the student's achievement of an objective or set of objectives."

### *11.4.2 ADVANTAGES OF e-MODULES*

e-Modules have the following possible advantages in the administration:

a) Students can study e-modules within their own environment. This means they can be used not only within teaching institutions but also on the job.
b) Students can study e-modules with minimum disruption to their normal duties and responsibilities. While this applies to both students and teachers and it is particularly true for teachers who can use e-modules as resources for staff development.
c) e-Modules may be administered to a single user, small groups, or large groups according to need.

d) e-Modules programs can be easily revised and upgraded by replacing one module by another amending aspect of a single module.
e) e-Module programs are flexible in the sense that they can be implemented through a variety of scheduling patterns.
f) e-Modules are cost-effective and economical to use.

## 11.5 RATIONALE

A module is one of the most popular forms of self-instructional material. Many research studies have been conducted in this field that were developmental and experimental in nature.

Johnson (1986), Lee (1987), Knotts (1988), Cook (1994), Rodriquez (1995), Rowland (1999), Al-Quattam (1989), Joshi (1999) developed and designed module for different target groups.

Some researchers studied the effectiveness of modules with various variables like achievement, attitude, and the reaction of students toward the module (Pankiewiez, 1985; Odhuno, 1989; Swearingen, 1993; Cap, 1995; Sansanwal and Joshi, 1990; Dhamija, 1993; Senapati, 1998; Singh, 2001).

The module can be an effective tool for instructions. A module was already developed in various subjects at different levels, but there is no study in the field of Educational Administration. We are living in the age of democracy. The success of democracy depends on education. A democratic country must have good educational planning and decision-making. M.Ed. students of today are the educational administrators of tomorrow.

So, it is necessary for them to have knowledge of various theories regarding conflict, motivation and decision-making, and system approach. These theories help them to solve their future problems regarding their job. These theories are helpful for an administrator in resolving the conflict in an institution, to motivate their pupils in goal-directed behavior and to take a fair decision. A module is the best means to achieve this quality. They can study e-module with self-pacing and critical thinking. Researchers could not find any study related to the development of the e-module in theories of Educational Administration.

## 11.6 STATEMENT OF THE PROBLEM

*Effectiveness of Developed Electronic Module in terms of Achievement in Educational Administration of M.Ed. Students*

## 11.7 OBJECTIVE OF THE STUDY

The following objective was proposed for this research work:

- To compare the mean scores of achievement in the Educational Administration of M.Ed. students toward developed e-module at the pre- and poststage.

## 11.8 HYPOTHESIS

The following hypothesis was studied:

There is no significant difference in mean rank scores of achievement in the Educational Administration of M.Ed. students toward the developed e-module at the pre- and post-test stage.

## 11.9 LIMITATIONS OF THE STUDY

1. The sample size only comprised of 23 students of M.Ed. who have chosen Educational Administration as their optional paper at the School of Education, DAVV, Indore.
2. Purposive sampling method was used to collect the sample.
3. Criterion reference test was nonstandardized and developed by the researcher.
4. The effectiveness of treatment was assessed only with the help of achievement scores.
5. The developed e-module was created only with one unit of subject code 626: Educational Administration of School of Education, DAVV, Indore.
6. The e-module was developed in the English language only.

## 11.10 SAMPLE

The sample consisted of 23 students of M.Ed. studying at the School of Education, DAVV, Indore. The sample comprised both male and female students. The purposive sampling technique was used. The students were of the age group between 22 and 45 years. They belonged to different socio-economic backgrounds. All the students were able to understand, read, and write English properly.

## 11.11 EXPERIMENTAL DESIGN

The study was based on the pretest, post-test single group design. The pretest by the Criterion Reference Test was administered, and then, each student of the sample was provided a copy of the developed e-module via e-mail. The researcher instructed them to study the e-module at their own pace. After one-month, the CriterionReference Test was administered on the group.

### *11.11.1 LAYOUT OFTHE EXPERIMENTAL DESIGN*

$$O_1 \times O_2$$

where $O_1$ =pretest (followed by the criterion reference test)
$\times$ =treatment (e-module was provided via e-mail)
$O_2$=post-test (followed by the criterion reference test).

## 11.12 TOOL

Tools are necessary for collecting the data. The tools were selected according to the objective of the study. So, the selection of the tool is an important aspect of research activity. The achievement was the dependent variable of the study. e-Module was taken as a means of treatment. The achievement of students in the subject "Educational Administration" (subject code 626) of M.Ed., School of Education, DAVV, Indore was observed with the help of a Criterion Reference Test that consisted of 50 questions. The test has been divided into five sections A, B, C, D, and E. Section A consisted of fill in the blanks, Section B consisted of true/false questions, Section C consisted of multiple-choice questions, Section D consisted match the columns, and Section E consisted of answers in one word. The maximum marks for the test were 50. Each question carried 1 mark. The total time given for completing the test was 1 h.

## 11.13 PROCEDURE OF DATA COLLECTION

The pretest for the assessment of achievement was administered on the sample. The module has been developed by the researcher on theories of conflict, motivation, decision-making, and system approach. Then, each of the students has been provided a copy of the e-module via e-mail and asked them to study at their own pace. After one month, the achievement test was re-administered to the group.

## 11.14 STATISTICAL ANALYSIS

The following statistical technique was used for analyzing the data:

- *Nonparametric Wilcoxon test* was computed for studying the effectiveness of the e-module on the basis of pre- and postmean rank scores of students.

## 11.15 INTERPRETATION OF RESULTS

The objective was "To compare the mean scores difference of achievement in Educational Administration of M.Ed. students toward developed module at the pre- and poststage." The data from post-test and pretest obtained for all 23 students are entered in the statistical software SPSS, and Wilcoxon signed-rank test for the related sample was applied. The results are given in Table 11.1.

**TABLE 11.1** Results of the Wilcoxon Signed-Rank Test to Compare the Pretest–Post-test Educational Administration Achievement Scores of the Students in the Experiment

| Achievement Post-test–Pretest | N | Mean Rank | Sum of Ranks | Z | p |
|---|---|---|---|---|---|
| Negative ranks | 1 | 7.50 | 7.50 | −3.760 | 0.000* |
| Positive ranks | 20 | 11.18 | 223.50 | | |
| Ties | 1 | | | | |
| Total | 22 | | | | |

**The difference is significant at 0.01 level.*

*Post-test > pretest.*

The observed value of *Z* is 3.760, which is greater than its critical value 2.585 for two-tailed tests; hence, it is significant at 0.01 level of significance. So, the null hypothesis,that is,"There is no significant difference in mean rank scores of achievement in Educational Administration ofM.Ed. students toward the developed module at the pre- and post-test stage" has been *rejected* at 0.01 level of significance. Further, the sum of their negative ranks for the experimental group (M.Ed. students) achievement in Educational Administration scores was found to be 7.5, while their sum of positive rank was 223.5. The observed difference is in favor of positive ranks or in other words, the post-test scores of M.Ed. student's achievement in Educational Administration are greater. So, we can say that the e-module was found to be effective.

## 11.16 FINDINGS AND CONCLUSION

From the study, it was found that the e-module developed for teaching Educational Administration was effective in terms of students' achievement and it can be a better option of teaching in the present scenario. The role of the teacher in the e-module will be acquiring, processing, analyzing, integrating the content, and then designing it according to the need of the learner. Then, preparing a powerful tool for their pupils and communicating them to how to use the tool, which can make them self-evaluating, self-regulating. This technology offers so many benefits for the learners and instructors but technology can never be a good substitute for a teacher. So, here also the teacher has to be present as a guide or facilitator. Nowadays, traditional methods of teaching are not so worthwhile, for that e-module can be a wonderful teaching aid for the skilled instructor.

## 11.17 IMPLICATIONS

The present study has wide implications for persons working in the field of education. It provides guidelines to text-book writers, curriculum designers, teacher educators, principals, teachers, students, parents, and researchers. These are given in different captions in detail.

- *Textbook writers*
  The module developed for the present study can provide guidelines to the text-book writers. The module has been prepared in a pictorial form. Some different facilities are also incorporated to make it more and more interactive and effective.
- *Teacher educators*
  There is a need to upgrade and up to date the knowledge of teacher educators. e-Module is an effective means for them.

- *Administrators*

  This e-module is very much beneficial for administrators. It provides a guideline to them that how to motivate their employees? How to resolve conflict in their institution, how to do strong decision making? andhow to run a system in an integrated way?Either of these administrators can keep the self-learning material in the library. The Principal can organize the proper teacher training programs to upgrade and up to date knowledge of various innovations that have been done in the area of education through organizing workshops, seminars, and refresher courses, etc.
- *Teachers and students*

  For imparting knowledge teacher may use e-module. Teachers can develop modules at various topics to enhance the achievement of students.
- *Researchers*

  It is an important area of research for the researcher. e-Module is the need of learners and demands of the present society. It is observed that there is a need to develop self-learning material.

## KEYWORDS


- **information and communication technology (ICT)**
- **e-Module (electronic module)**
- **achievement**
- **innovative strategy**


## REFERENCES


Cap, I. A Study of the Usefulness & Effectiveness of a Self Instructional Print Module on Multicultural Behavior Changes in Apprentices in Manitoba, The Florida State University, Ph.D., DAI, Vol. 56, No. 4, 1995.

Cook, M.L. The Design of a Course Module for Addition Counselors using a System Approach to training (SAT) Format, Florida International University EDD, IGNOU, Curriculum & Instruction (Course ES-331), 2000, Akash Deep Printers, New Delhi, India, 1994.

Joshi, K. Development of a Module on Educational Technology, its Effectiveness & Comparison with Traditional Method in Terms of Scholastic Achievement at Bed level. Ph.D. in Education, IOE, DAVV, Indore, 1999.

Knotts, D.M. Development & Validation of an issue Oriented Conservation Module for 5th & 6th Grade Students. Doctoral Dissertation, DAI, Vol. 50, No. 6, 1989.

Lee, K. Development & Evaluation of a Cardio Vascular Health Module for Korean High School students. Doctoral Dissertation, DAI, Vol. 48, No. 10, 1988.

Mangal, S.K. and Mangal. U, Essentials of Educational Technology, PHI Publication; New Delhi, India, 2011.

Odhuno, O. Effectiveness of a Global Education Module on the Knowledge & Attitudes of Home Economics of University students. Doctoral Dissertation, DAI, Vol. 45, No. 9, 1990.

Pandey, L., Effectiveness of Computer Based Classroom Instructions on Information Communication Technology in terms of Achievement, Attention & Reacton of B.Ed. Students of Indore District. Unpublished Dissertation SOE, DAVV, Indore, 2013.

Pandya, S.R., Administration & Management of Education, Himalaya Publishing House, Mumbai, Maharastra, India, 2011.

Pankiewicz, P.R. The Effects of a Self Designed Introductory Junoir High School Organic Chemistry Module on selected students characteristics. Doctoral Dissertation, DAI, Vol. 45, No. 7, 1985.

Rao, U., Educational Technology, 2001, Himalaya Publishing House, Mumbai, Maharastra, India.

Rodriguez, D.M., Application of Geographic Information System in School Administration. A Teaching Case of School Restricting, Columbia University Teachers College, EDD, DAI-A 56/07, January 1996.

Rowland, S., The Development & implementation of an Instructional Module that Prepares Preservice Teachers to Address the needs of students with Attention Deficit Hyperactivity Disorder (ADHD), The University of Mississipi, EDD.DAI-56/06, December 1995.

Sampath, K., Educational Technology, 2000, New Age International Publishers, New Delhi, India.

Sansanwal, D.N., Buddhisagar, M., Different styles of Writing Instructional Material, The Progress of Education, Volume, LVI, No. 7, 1982.

Senapati, K., Effectiveness of a Module on Guidance & Counselling at B.Ed. level in Terms of Achievement & Reaction Towards Module, M.Ed. Dissertation, IOE, DAVV, Indore, 2001.

Sharma, R.A., Advanced Educational Technology, Loyal Book Depot, Merrut, Uttar Pradesh, India, 1993.

Sharma, Y. Bed Course ke Vishay Mapan & Mulyankan ke Chayanit Prakarano Ke Nirman & Uski Prabhavita ka Vidyarthiyon ki Upalabdhi, Adhyayan Sanbandhi Aadaton & Pratikriyaon ke Sandarbh me Adhyayan. Master's Dissertation, DAVV, Indore, 2013.

Sindhu, I.S., Educational Administration & Management ofEducation, Mumbai, Maharastra, India: Darling Kindersley, Pearson, 2012.

Singh, H., Shaikshik Sansathaon ka Prabandha B,Ed. Course Par Vikasit Pramap avam Paramparagat shikshan ka Upalabdhi, Atamvishwas Tatha Adhyayan Sambandhi Aadaton Ke Aadhar par Tulnatmak Adhdhayan (in Hindi), Unpublished M.Ed. Dissertation, IOE, DAVV, Indore, 2001.

Swearingen, K.D., A Study of the Effectiveness of the Inclusion of a Music Appreciation Learning Module as a Supplement to the Traditional High School Band Performance Curriculum University of Southern California. DAI, 154/84, October, 1993.

Tripathi, P.C., Successful Organizational Management, Abhinav Publishing Industry, Delhi, India, 1992.

## CHAPTER 12

# Changes, Innovations, and Reforms in Education from Traditional Learning to 21st Century Learning

JYOTI BHAMBHANI

*Management Department, Institute of Information Technology and Management, New Delhi, India. Email: drjyotiiitm@gmail.com*

### ABSTRACT

Changes, innovations, and reforms in education are some of the main factors that help in the development of the education sector in any country. Nowadays, educational institutions and universities are facing a number of challenges due to the evolution of new techniques for the teaching–learning process. Adopting new ways of teaching not only brings new opportunities but also improves traditional learning system. Most of the universities and institutes have transformed themselves by adopting 21st century learning processes. The term "21st century learning" has become an integral part in the education sector. It refers to digital literacy, better communication skills, leadership skills, productivity, critical thinking, problem-solving skills, etc. In fact, 21st century learning fosters students' creativity. Both teachers and students benefit from new ways of teaching and learning. These skills help students in planning their career in a much better way. This paper is based on the conceptual study and throws light on the changes, innovations and reforms that have evolved recently in the education sector. The study is based on finding out the need for adopting these changes and innovations in education sector.

### 12.1 INTRODUCTION

In the case of traditional learning methods, teachers and students gather together at a particular place, usually known as school/college, and learn during a specified time period. It includes class rooms teaching, boards, paper-based assignments, exams etc. This system is also known as conventional education, customary education, old-fashioned way of teaching, or face-to-face learning. The traditional system has been in practice from the ancient times. Here, 40–50 students in a classroom are asked to recite in groups and are expected to learn and also to appear in exams. In this system, the students are rewarded on the basis of efforts put by them. This system has several disadvantages. In some cases, teachers are not able to hear an individual student's voice. In fact, teachers cannot work on each student's performance. Each student does not get sufficient speaking time to work on his/her skills. Students of shy nature do not try to ask questions. In some cases, reading comprehension and writing ability improves a lot, but communication skills of students do not develop.

Considering that all the students do not have same level of understanding, the system of progressive educational practices is given more importance. Indian literacy rate is 74.04%, while world literary rate is 84% of all nations (2011 data) (Yadav, 2017). To make studies interesting, the 21st century learning focuses on skill building, values, big ideas, and overall development of students. The 21st century learning methods are considered better than traditional learning as there is more emphasis on participation of each student in the teaching–learning process. The students who want to learn in an interesting way can develop their creative skills. Their critical thinking and creativity are also developed. This way of teaching produces performance at the individual level. Hence, the 21st century learning methods based on using the latest technology from projectors to laptops bring active participation of most of the students in the teaching–learning process.

### *12.1.1 LITERATURE REVIEW*

Bhoyar et al. state that India is the biggest market for e-learning after the United States. India is growing in every field like banking sector, insurance sector, automobile sector, and also education sector. The education sector is one of the biggest sectors in India. However, still, one-fourth of the population of India is illiterate. One of the biggest challenges for the government is to eradicate illiteracy. For this, Prime Minister Shri Narendra Modi has started the Digital India movement in India that covers universal digital literacy. Although there is no any provision for e-education, with this movement, provisions for education would also increase (Bhoyar et al., 2016).

According to Saini et al., traditional learning gives the students a chance to create interest in studies. The students can clarify their doubts immediately. The teachers can also understand student's psychology while teaching and can deal with questions raised by students. Teachers can also motivate them by appreciating when they perform well. But nowadays Internet is part of our education system. Web-based courses are the cost effective and have more control on students. Web-based learning is useful in improving students' performance and increases the outcome of learners in comparison to traditional learning. The outcome can be shown in students' learning, satisfaction, and performance. Saini et al. did their research by taking samples from professional graduate and under graduate courses. They concluded that learning through web based tool is better than the learning through traditional learning. It helps the teachers and students to improve overall learning process as it can be used from basic classes to higher education, computer science to noncomputer science courses, and diploma to degree courses (Saini et al., 2014).

According to Ghavifer and Rosdy, the education system of late 20th century has changed rapidly. The easy access technology today is very advanced and provides comprehensive teaching and learning environment. Ghavifer and Rosdy did their research and found out that online educational videos help to improve student's ability in language learning skills such as reading, writing, listening, and speaking.

Further, students are encouraged to communicate more with their classmates and also participate actively in the class. The results of their study show that technology-based teaching and learning is more effective as compared to traditional learning. They also suggested that further studies are required to know what barricrs teachers are facing in using ICT in their daily classrooms in schools (Ghavifekr et al., 2015).

According to Fındıkoğlu and İlhan, the educational system of any country changes the people and their societies. The societies always transform, and with themselves, they transform the inner dynamics of the country they belong to. Use of technology in education can be a part of using innovative practices that brings innovation in education. It has been found in literature and research that there is a very close relationship between innovation in education and technology adoption to education. Now, those people are required who can work on critical and creative thinking skills to solve problems as a team (Fındıkoğlu and Dilek, 2016).

According to Al-Omari and Salameh, the universities are making headways in the use of computing and information technology in the past decade. Everyone, be students or faculty members, is using technology either to fulfil their scholarship or for research purpose. Therefore, studies are being carried out over the years to focus on some specific computing and information technology concerns. They concluded that students firmly believe that e-learning has a great role in supporting and enhancing their university learning experience. However, it is also necessary to combine face-to-face classes with online activities for better understanding. In their survey, the students felt that e-learning could sometimes be used as an alternative to face-to-face activities (Aieman, 2012).

### 12.1.2 RESEARCH METHODOLOGY

The proposed study is exploratory in nature. It is based on secondary data only. The documents of articles and websites have been used in this study. Some people were interviewed about traditional learning and 21st century learning.

### 12.1.3 OBJECTIVES OF THE STUDY

The following are the objectives of the study.

1. To find out in detail about traditional learning and 21st century learning by making a comparison.
2. To find out changes, innovations, and reforms in education from traditional learning to 21st century learning.

### 12.1.4 ANALYSIS OF CHANGES, INNOVATIONS, AND REFORMS IN EDUCATION

#### 12.1.4.1 COMPARISON BETWEEN TRADITIONAL AND 21ST CENTURY LEARNING

- In the olden times, the concept of 21st century learning was not considered good, but nowadays, the concept of traditional learning is not considered good.
- The main objective of traditional learning is to pass on the values to the next generations, while the objective of 21st century learning it to develop various skills of the students.

- Students were made to sit in the class room in case of traditional education, while in case of 21st century learning, the students can learn anywhere even on their mobiles.
- There is less practical work in case of traditional education, while there is more practical work in case of 21st century learning.
- The relationship between teachers and students were of *Guru* and *Shishya* in case of traditional education, while the relationship between teachers and students is of friends in case of 21st century learning.
- Online courses/training were not popular case of traditional education, while online courses/training have become extremely popular case of traditional education

By analyzing various papers, the following changes, innovations, and reforms in education have been noted

### *12.1.4.2 ONLINE NETWORK AND DAY AND NIGHT CONNECTIVITY*

The increasing use of Internet and round the clock connectivity has increased the scope of 21st century learning. Internet is used in every field, including education. In fact, Internet is the blessing for the students. It is very convenient to learn through this facility as it can be availed even in mobiles. Not only the students get solution of their problem but also they get tutorials and other kinds of assisting material, which is used to academically improve and enhance their learning.

### *12.1.4.3 SLIDE PROJECTORS AND VISUALS*

Everyone would agree that visual images always have a better appeal as compared to words. Using projectors and visuals to aid in learning is another form of great technological use. Almost all the institutes use Power Point presentations and projections to keep the learning interactive and interesting for students. Students also like to see appealing visuals that motivate them to think rather than just reading (Raja and Nagasubramani, 2018).

### *12.1.4.4 INNOVATIVE TEACHING METHODS*

These are the methods that involve an interesting way of interaction between teachers and students. Various innovative teaching methods are used in today's era like brainstorming, group teaching, case studies, etc. The following are the different type of innovations.

- Introducing absolutely new technology is called an absolute innovation.
- Introducing significantly improved technology is called a modernized innovation.
- Introducing slightly improved technology is called a modified innovation.
- An innovation may be introduced in a new territory or to a new field.

Most of the teachers in academics have been introducing new methods and technologies to motivate the students' cognitive activity (Aigerim et al., 2017).

### *12.1.4.5 POSITIVE ENVIRONMENT*

The teachers create positive environment to cope up with issues and challenges in the 21st century. The major challenges are quality education, access of education, cost of education, unemployment, poverty, corruption, privatization of education, etc. The teachers believe that students learn by doing. Education should be valuable not only in college but also in shaping up career of students. Teachers today do not believe in physical punishment. Government is trying to achieve 100% literacy rate in India. So our teachers are trying to provide value based and skill based education. In this era of globalization, the students have to face global problems. Curriculum should be designed in such a way to enable the students to cope up with global issues (Yadav, 2017).

### *12.1.4.6 FOUR C'S OF 21ST CENTURY LEARNING*

Everyone would agree with 4C that are used in 21st century learning. These are critical thinking, communication, collaboration, and creative problem solving. For much of the 1990s and in the early of 2000s, 21st century skills were almost synonymous with computer and information communication technology skills. The learners are "grounded in purposeful learning by doing" in 21st century learning. In fact, education in 21st century learning requires a deep engagement with the question of the larger purposes of education and students are being prepared for the realities of a global economy. This educational vision makes perfect sense as technical, pragmatic, and instrumental criteria (Patrick, 2007).

### *12.1.6 LIMITATIONS OF THE STUDY*

The study is based on secondary data only. A few people were approached for discussion. Further, a few changes in 21st century have been analyzed.

### *12.1.7 CONCLUSION*

Traditional learning, which includes classroom teaching, boards, paper-based assignments, etc., is the conventional education system, which is not popular nowadays. This system has several disadvantages. In some cases, teachers are not able to hear an individual student's voice. The teachers cannot assess each student's performance. Further, each student does not get sufficient speaking time to work on his/her skills. Due to these problems, most of the universities and institutes have transformed themselves by adopting the 21st century learning process, which is interesting and also creates interest of students in studies. Twenty-first century learning has several advantages like digital literacy, better communication skills, leadership skills, productivity, critical thinking, problem-solving skills, etc. In fact, 21st century learning fosters students' creativity. Huge resources are required by institutes for implementing system of modern learning. Hence, there is a big challenge to maintain a sufficient level of resources to adequately meet with increasing computing and information technology demands.

**KEYWORDS**

- **education**
- **traditional learning**
- **21st century learning**

**REFERENCES**

Aieman Al-Omaria, "e-Learning versus Traditional Learning as Perceived by Undergraduate Students in Jordanian Universities," E-Learning and Digital Media, Vol. 9(2), 2012 issue retrieved on January 04, from https://journals.sagepub.com/doi/pdf/10.2304/elea.2012.9.2.223

Aigerim Mynbayeva, Zukhra Sadvakassova, Bakhytkul Akshalova, "Pedagogy of the twenty-first century: Innovative teaching methods, An open access peer-reviewed chapter, Dec., 2017 issue retrieved on January 04, 2020 from https://www.intechopen.com/books/new-pedagogical-challenges-in-the-21st-century-contributions-of-research-in-education/pedagogy-of-the-twenty-first-century-innovative-teaching-methods

Bhoyar Pravin Kumar, Sharma Aadya, Kadam Pratik, "Online versus Traditional Learning: A Comparative Study," Journal of Advances in Social Science—Humanities, 2016 issue, retrieved on January 02, 2020 from file:///C:/Users/Jyoti%20Bhambhani.IITMDC/Downloads/109-Article%20Text-405-1-10-20161111%20(2).pdf

Fındıkoğlu Fuat, İlhan Dilek, "Realization of a desired future: Innovation in education," Universal Journal of Educational Research, Vol. 4(11), 2016 retrieved on July 09, from http://www.hrpub.org/journals/article_info.php?aid=5255.

Ghavifekr Simin, Athirah Wan and Rosdy Wan, "Teaching and learning with technology: Effectiveness of ICT integration in schools," International Journal of Research in Education and Science, Vol. 1(2), Summer 2015, retrived on January 02, 2020 from https://files.eric.ed.gov/fulltext/EJ1105224.pdf

Patrick, Howard G. "Twenty-first century learning as a radical re-thinking of education in the service of life," Education Sciences, Retrieved on January 07, from https://www.mdpi.com/2227-7102/8/4/189/htm

Raja R. and Nagasubramani P.C., "Impact of modern technology in education," Journal of Applied and Advanced Research, 2018 issue, retrieved on January 03, 2020 from file:///C:/Users/Jyoti%20Bhambhani.IITMDC/Downloads/Impact_of_modern_technology_in_education.pdf

Saini Kavita, Wahid Abdul, Purohit G. N., "Traditional learning versus web based learning: Performance analysis," International Journal of Computer Science an Information Technologies, Vol. 5 (4), 2014, retrieved on December 31, 2019 from http://ijcsit.com/docs/Volume%205/vol5issue04/ijcsit2014050479.pdf

Yadav Sagar Vidya, "Educational issues and challenges in the 21st century in India," Educational Trends, Feb. and Aug. 2017 issue, retrieved on January 06, 2020 from https://www.researchgate.net/publication/331327294_educational_issues_and_challenges_in_the_21st_century_in_india

CHAPTER 13

# Anytime Learning vs Classroom Teaching: A Comparative Perception Study

HIMANSHU MATTA

*Amity University, Uttar Pradesh, India*

*E-mail: mattahimanshu@gmail.com*

## ABSTRACT

In this study, the researcher will compare the perception of students toward anytime learning facilities like through mobile applications like Udemy, BYJU'S, etc., YouTube videos, and other e-learning facilities from the Government of India like NIPCCD e-learning, massive online open courses (MOOCs), etc. and compare them to perception toward classroom teachings. As e-learning or anytime learning is a comparatively emerging trend in India, this study will give insights into or viewpoints about the most impacted people, that is, students. The researcher will empirically study the comparative perceptions of students of management courses from various B-schools in the Delhi-NCR region using structured questionnaires, and the results will be drawn using SPSS software. The results have shown a positive overall perception of respondents toward anytime learning.

## 13.1 INTRODUCTION OF e-LEARNING AND ANYTIME LEARNING

ASTD defined e-learning as "anything delivered, enabled, or mediated by electronic technology for the purpose of learning." This includes "applications and processes, such as web-based learning, computer-based learning, virtual classrooms, etc."

Content can be delivered using internet, intranet, audio and video forms, etc. According to the E-Content Report (2004), e-learning is "any type of learning that depends on or is enhanced by electronic communication using the latest information & communication technologies."

The features of e-learning are listed below:

- *Personalization:* The contents in the learning modules of can be personalized to suit the level and pace of the learner.
- *Reusability:* e-Learning modules can be reused for different students in different steams at different time, which makes it cost effective.
- *Flexibility:* Courses can be generated in different formats and students can use various kinds of devices with different processor speeds and memory capacities, for example, personal computers, laptops, and mobile devices such as smartphones to access the learning content.
- *Convenience:* Anytime learning modules enable students to learn at their convenience speed and at their home comfort.

## 13.2 LITERATURE REVIEW

Various researchers have focused on the effectiveness of anytime learning or e-learning, like Karen Swan (2003). In their paper reviews, the literature focuses on the learning effectiveness of asynchronous online environments. Research concludes with a summary of what the various researches tells us and its implications for online learning. While Valentina Arkorful (2014) in their study reviews literature by various researchers on the concept of e-learning, mainly its usage in teaching and learning in higher educational institutions. The study unveils some views that people and institutions have shared globally on the adoption and integration of e-learning technologies in education through surveys and other observations. It also looks at the advantages and disadvantages of its implementation.

Stöhr (2017) in their paper studied the use of mobile computing devices and its effects on learning in MOOCs. The paper analyzes how learners accessed and watched video lectures of the MOOCs to identify whether there are differences between browser and mobile application users. The results indicated that only 12% of all learners accessed course content via mobile device and they are younger compared to exclusive browser users. The research concludes with a discussion of the implications for the further development and use of MOOCs and mobile devices as global educational resources.

However, some researchers have studied m-learning; for example, Mohamed Sarrab (2012) in their paper have discussed the history of mobile learning and how it can be used to enhance the e-learning system. The paper presents the m-learning approach using empirical study as the next generation of e-learning and also stated the benefits and future challenges of m-learning in our educational environments. Moreover, Romana Martin (2013) in their paper focused on identifying what motivates students to use mobile devices for learning and to engage in m-learning. For the study, seven classes from three Australian universities were included. The findings revealed that "convenience and mobility was the main motivator for the use of laptops."

## 13.3 RESEARCH METHODOLOGY

### *13.3.1 TYPE OF RESEARCH*

This study is a descriptive research as we compare the perception of students toward anytime learning facilities and compare them to perception toward classroom teachings.

### *13.3.2 OBJECTIVES OF THE STUDY*

- To compare the perception of students toward anytime learning and classroom teaching.
- To identify the hurdles in successful implementation of anytime learning in India.

### *13.3.3 RATIONALE OF THE STUDY*

Perception plays a significant role in adoption of innovation or change; thus, through this study, the researcher will study the perception of students toward anytime learning to identify the problems in successful implementation of anytime learning in India.

### *13.3.4 DATA COLLECTION TOOL*

This study is done using both secondary and primary data. The tools used to analyze the data are cross-tabs using SPSS software.

### *13.3.5 AREA OF THE STUDY*

For this study, the respondents will be selected from the NCR region.

### *13.3.6 RESEARCH APPROACH*

For this study, the questionnaire method is used for collecting data.

### *13.3.7 SAMPLING TECHNIQUE AND SAMPLE SIZE*

The convenience sampling method is used, and the sample size is 30.

## 13.4 DATA ANALYSIS AND INTERPRETATION

This section will include the responses of the respondents to the questionnaire primarily designed to understand their perceptions.

Table 13.1 lists the count of the responses given to the question: Are you aware about the anytime learning or e-learning term-ology?

**TABLE 13.1** Age-wise Awareness Level

| | | No | Yes | Total |
|---|---|---|---|---|
| Age (years) | 15–20 | 4 | 22 | 26 |
| | 20–25 | 0 | 2 | 2 |
| | 25–30 | 0 | 2 | 2 |
| Total | | 4 | 26 | 30 |

It can be interpreted from the table that 15% of young respondents/students are unaware of the anytime learning term-ology, but most of the respondents were aware of anytime learning.

Table 13.2 lists the count of the responses given to the question: Are you aware about the anytime learning or e-learning term-ology?

It can be interpreted from the table that a few male respondents (16%) were unaware of the anytime learning or e-learning termology, while 100% female respondents were aware.

**TABLE 13.2** Gender-wise Awareness Level

| | | No | Yes | Total |
|---|---|---|---|---|
| Gender of respondents | Female | 0 | 6 | 6 |
| | Male | 4 | 20 | 24 |
| Total | | 4 | 26 | 30 |

Table 13.3 lists the count of the responses given to the question: Anytime learning is convenient in terms of no need to travel than classroom teaching.

**TABLE 13.3** Perception Toward Anytime Learning in Terms of Convenience

| | | Highly Disagree | Disagree | Neutral | Agree | Highly Agree | |
|---|---|---|---|---|---|---|---|
| Age (years) | 15–20 | 2 | 1 | 7 | 5 | 11 | 26 |
| | 20–25 | 0 | 0 | 1 | 1 | 0 | 2 |
| | 25–30 | 0 | 0 | 0 | 0 | 2 | 2 |
| Total | | 2 | 1 | 8 | 6 | 13 | 30 |

It can be interpreted from the table that most of the young respondents (15–20 years old) highly agree that anytime learning is convenient in terms of no need to travel than classroom teaching.

Table 13.4 lists the count of the responses given to the question: Anytime learning is low in cost as compared to classroom teaching?

**TABLE 13.4** Perception Toward Anytime Learning in Terms of Cost

| | | Highly Disagree | Disagree | Neutral | Agree | Total |
|---|---|---|---|---|---|---|
| Age (years) | 15–20 | 3 | 2 | 7 | 14 | 26 |
| | 20–25 | 0 | 1 | 1 | 0 | 2 |
| | 25–30 | 0 | 0 | 1 | 1 | 2 |
| Total | | 3 | 3 | 9 | 15 | 30 |

It can be interpreted from the table that most of the young respondents (15–20 years old) highly agree that anytime learning is low in cost than classroom teaching.

Table 13.5 lists the count of the responses given to the question: Anytime learning is free from any distractions from fellow classmates as compared to classroom teaching?

**TABLE 13.5** Perception Toward Anytime Learning in Terms of Distractions

| | | Highly Disagree | Disagree | Neutral | Agree | Highly Agree | Total |
|---|---|---|---|---|---|---|---|
| Age (years) | 15–20 | 2 | 3 | 5 | 8 | 8 | 26 |
| | 20–25 | 0 | 0 | 0 | 1 | 1 | 2 |
| | 25–30 | 1 | 0 | 0 | 1 | 0 | 2 |
| Total | | 3 | 3 | 5 | 10 | 9 | 30 |

It can be interpreted from the table that most of the young respondents (15–20 years old) agree that anytime learning is free from any distractions from fellow classmates than classroom teaching.

Table 13.6 lists the count of the responses given to the question: Does Anytime learning lacks personal touch of teacher?

**TABLE 13.6** Perception Toward Anytime Learning in Terms of Personal Touch of Teacher

| | | Highly Disagree | Disagree | Neutral | Agree | Total |
|---|---|---|---|---|---|---|
| Age (years) | 15–20 | 3 | 5 | 7 | 11 | 26 |
| | 20–25 | 0 | 0 | 2 | 0 | 2 |
| | 25–30 | 0 | 1 | 0 | 1 | 2 |
| Total | | 3 | 6 | 9 | 12 | 30 |

It can be interpreted from the table that a few young respondents (15–20 years old) agree that anytime learning lacks personal touch of the teacher.

Table 13.7 lists the count of the responses given to the question: Anytime learning lacks easy doubt clearing advantage of classroom teaching

**TABLE 13.7** Perception Toward Anytime Learning in Terms of Doubt Clearing

| | | Highly Disagree | Disagree | Neutral | Agree | Highly Agree | Total |
|---|---|---|---|---|---|---|---|
| Age (years) | 15–20 | 2 | 1 | 4 | 11 | 8 | 26 |
| | 20–25 | 0 | 0 | 0 | 1 | 1 | 2 |
| | 25–30 | 0 | 0 | 0 | 0 | 2 | 2 |
| Total | | 2 | 1 | 4 | 12 | 11 | 30 |

It can be interpreted from the table that a few young respondents (15–20 years old) agree that anytime learning lacks easy doubt clearing advantage of classroom teaching.

Table 13.8 lists the count of the responses given to the question: Do you prefer e-learning over classroom teaching?

**TABLE 13.8** Preference of e-Learning Over Classroom Teaching vis-a-vis Age

| | | No | Yes | Total |
|---|---|---|---|---|
| Age (years) | 15–20 | 14 | 12 | 26 |
| | 20–25 | 1 | 1 | 2 |
| | 25–30 | 1 | 1 | 2 |
| Total | | 16 | 14 | 30 |

It can be interpreted from the table that more than 50% of young respondents (15–20 years old) prefer e-learning over classroom teaching.

Table 13.9 lists the count of the responses given to the question: Do you prefer e-learning over classroom teaching?

**TABLE 13.9** Preference of e-Learning Over Classroom Teaching vis-a-vis Gender

| | | No | Yes | Total |
|---|---|---|---|---|
| Gender of respondents | Female | 3 | 3 | 6 |
| | Male | 13 | 11 | 24 |
| Total | | 16 | 14 | 30 |

It can be interpreted from the table that female respondents prefer anytime learning more as compared to the male respondents.

Table 13.10 lists the count to the responses to the question: Which anytime learning method do you prefer the most?

**TABLE: 13.10** Cross Table Between Age Group and Preference to Anytime Learning Methods

| | | Free of Cost YouTube Video-Based Learning | Government Online Courses | Mobile Application-Based Learning | Online Live Classes | Total |
|---|---|---|---|---|---|---|
| Age (years) | 15–20 | 12 | 1 | 7 | 6 | 26 |
| | 20–25 | 2 | 0 | 0 | 0 | 2 |
| | 25–30 | 0 | 1 | 0 | 1 | 2 |
| Total | | 14 | 2 | 7 | 7 | 30 |

It can be interpreted from the table that young respondents (15–20 years old) prefer free of cost YouTube video-based learning, while mature respondents (25–30 years old) preferred government online courses.

Table 13.11 lists the count of the responses given to the question: Which anytime learning method do you prefer most?

**TABLE 13.11** Preference for Anytime Learning Method

| | | Free of Cost YouTube Video-Based Learning | Government Online Courses | Mobile Application-Based Learning | Online Live Classes | Total |
|---|---|---|---|---|---|---|
| Gender of respondents | Female | 3 | 1 | 1 | 1 | 6 |
| | Male | 11 | 1 | 6 | 6 | 24 |
| Total | | 14 | 2 | 7 | 7 | 30 |

It can be interpreted from the table that most of the respondents prefer free of cost YouTube video-based learning.

Table 13.12 lists the count of the responses given to the question: Do you think anytime learning is successful in India?

**TABLE 13.12** Cross Table Between Gender and Opinion Toward the Success of Anytime Learning

| | | No | Yes | Total |
|---|---|---|---|---|
| Gender of respondents | Female | 0 | 6 | 6 |
| | Male | 7 | 17 | 24 |
| Total | | 7 | 23 | 30 |

It can be interpreted from the table that a few male respondents (29%) think anytime learning is not successful in India.

Table 13.13 lists the count of the responses given to the question: What do you think is the major hurdle for the full implementation for anytime learning in India?

**TABLE 13.13** Hurdles in Implementation

| | | High Cost of Internet | Lack of Digital Literary | Slow Internet Penetration | Slow Present Internet Connections | Total |
|---|---|---|---|---|---|---|
| Gender of respondents | Female | 1 | 5 | 0 | 0 | 6 |
| | Male | 0 | 19 | 3 | 2 | 24 |
| Total | | 1 | 24 | 3 | 2 | 30 |

It can be interpreted from the table that most of the respondents (80%) think lack of digital literacy as the major hurdle for the full implementation for anytime learning in India.

Table 13.14 lists the count of the responses given to the question: Do you think anytime learning or e-learning is the future of Indian education advancement?

**TABLE 13.14** Future of the Education System

| | | No | Yes | Total |
|---|---|---|---|---|
| Age (years) | 15–20 | 9 | 17 | 26 |
| | 20–25 | 1 | 1 | 2 |
| | 25–30 | 0 | 2 | 2 |
| Total | | 10 | 20 | 30 |

It can be interpreted from the table that all respondents belonging to age group of 25–30 years see any time learning as future of education in India.

Table 13.15 lists the count of the responses given to the question: Do you think anytime learning is the future of the education in India?

**TABLE 13.15** Future of the Education System

| | | No | Yes | |
|---|---|---|---|---|
| Gender of respondents | Female | 2 | 4 | 6 |
| | Male | 8 | 16 | 24 |
| Total | | 10 | 20 | 30 |

It can be interpreted from the table that 33% of female respondents think anytime learning is not the future of the education in India, while 67% of female respondents think anytime learning is the future of the education in India. In total, 35% of male respondents think anytime learning is not the future of the education in India, while 65% of female respondents think anytime learning is the future of the education in India.

## 13.5 FINDINGS AND CONCLUSIONS

In total, 15% of young respondents/students are unaware of the anytime learning term-ology, but most of the respondents were aware of the anytime learning. A few male respondents (16%) were unaware of the anytime learning or e-learning termology, while 100% female respondents were aware. Most of the young respondents (15–20 years old) highly agree that anytime learning is convenient in terms of no need to travel than classroom teaching.

A few young respondents (15–20 years old) agree that anytime learning lacks easy doubt clearing advantage of classroom teaching. Most of the young respondents (15–20 years old) highly agree that anytime learning is convenient in terms of no need to travel than classroom teaching. However, more than 50% of young respondents (15–20 years old) prefer e-learning over classroom teaching. Female respondents prefer anytime learning more as compared to the male respondents.

Young respondents (15–20 years old) prefer free of cost YouTube video-based learning, while mature respondents (25–30 years old) preferred government online courses. Most of the respondents prefer free of cost YouTube video-based learning. A few male respondents (29%) think anytime learning is not successful in India. Most of the respondents (80%) think lack of digital literacy as the major hurdle for the full implementation for anytime learning in India. All respondents belonging to age group of 25–30 see any time learning as future of education in India. In total, 33% of female respondents think anytime learning is not the future of the education in India, while 67% of female respondents think anytime learning is the future of the education in India. Moreover, 35% of male respondents think anytime learning is not the future of the education in India, while 65% of female respondents think anytime learning is the future of the education in India.

Hurdles in successful implementation of anytime learning in India as identified through the above survey identify that lack of digital literacy as the major hurdle for the full implementation for anytime learning in India.

## 13.6 CONCLUSIONS

Mature respondents above 25 years of age are more aware of and have positive perception of anytime learning courses by the government. Most of the respondents see anytime learning as the future of education in India if barriers like low digital literacy are eliminated. Female respondents are having more positive perception and behavior toward anytime learning as compared to male respondents.

Anytime learning has lots of potential in India as it can break the physical barriers. People who are living in remote villages having limited access to formal education can now study through online courses, especially MOOCs by the Government of India.

There are some limitations of this paper like for more realistic view the sample size needs to be increased. Also, the researcher has used cross-tabs as a tool of analysis, which has its own limitations. For more detailed analysis of data, collection methods like the interview method can be used. Future research studies can compare government and private anytime learning programs to find out the best features of anytime learning modules.

## KEYWORDS

- **anytime learning**
- **e-Learning**
- **perception**
- **MOOC**
- **comparative perception**

## REFERENCES

E-Content Report, 2004. http://ijariie.com/AdminUploadPdf/E__CONTENT__AN_EFFECTIVE_TOOL_FOR_TEACHING_AND_LEARNING_IN_A_CONTEMPORARY_EDUCATION_SYSTEM_C_1289.pdf

Karen Swan, J. C. An Examination of Social Presence in Online Courses in Relation to Students' Perceived Learning and Satisfaction. Journal of Asynchronous Learning Network. March 2003, 7, 1.

Mohamed Sarrab, L. E. Mobile learning (m-learning) and educational environments. International Journal of Distributed and Parallel Systems, July 2012, 3, 31–38. https://www.researchgate.net/publication/262488863_Mobile_Learning_M-Learning_and_Educational_Environments.

Ozdamli, Fezile and Cavus, Nadire. Basic elements and characteristics of mobile learning. Procedia- Social and Behavioral Sciences, 2011, 28, 937–942. 10.1016/j.sbspro.2011.11.173.

Romana Martin, T. M. Learning anywhere, anytime: Student motivators for M-learning. Journal of Information Technology Education: Research, January 2013, 12, 51–67. http://www.jite.org/documents/Vol12/JITEv12ResearchP051-067MartinFT51.pdf

Stöhr, C. (2017). Anywhere and anytime? An analysis of the use of mobile devices in MOOCs. Proceedings of the INTED2017 Conference, Valencia, Spain. 2017, 11.

Valentina Arkorful, N. A. The role of e-learning, the advantages and disadvantages of its adoption in higher education. International Journal of Education and Research, December 2014, 2, 397–410. https://www.ijern.com/journal/2014/December-2014/34.pdf

## CHAPTER 14

# Learners' Satisfaction with MOOCs: A Cross-Sectional Study

GOPAL SINGH LATWAL[1,*] and LEENA GUPTA[2]

[1]*Department of Management Studies, Institute of Information Technology & Management, Janakpuri, New Delhi, India*

[2]*Department of Information Technology, Institute of Information Technology & Management, Janakpuri, New Delhi, India*

[*]*Corresponding author. E-mail: gopalsinghusl@gmail.com*

## ABSTRACT

In the fast-changing environment, massive open online coursers (MOOCs) are also growing substantially. MOOCs use electronic tools or the Internet to deliver educational content to learners to facilitate learning. MOOCs are now a synonym for online learning.

MOOCs are beneficial to instructors, trainer, and lecturers through which they can provide or share course material with learners and their colleagues outside the classroom. There are a number of problems pertaining to e-learning, that is, isolation, lack of human interaction, self-discipline, and self-initiative from the learners. Lack of self-motivation may reduce course engagement, thus resulting in deviation in their satisfaction level with the course content. Even with these requirements, more and more learners seek online courses and training.

This study attempts to conduct a cross-sectional study of the satisfaction of MOOC learners. The research is quantitative. Quantitative data is collected by a structured questionnaire. Convenience sampling techniques are used. The response is collected through Google Docs from 250 respondents. The collected data is analyzed for frequency, correlation, and regression analysis using SPSS software.

Respondents mainly prefer Coursera, NPTEL, and EdX for MOOCs. Business Administration course is a highly preferred course. Obtaining more knowledge is one of the key factors for pursuing a course. Lack of time and motivation leads to quitting the MOOCs. The majority of respondents are satisfied with the course contents, learning environments, evaluation, and teaching methods.

This study will help to understand the area where significant steps need to be taken for improving the satisfaction level of learners. Other aspects of satisfaction can also be explored in further research.

## 14.1 INTRODUCTION

In the fast-changing environment, the development of information and communications technology makes it possible to use digital platforms and tools to diffuse knowledge. Massive open online coursers (MOOCs) are also growing substantially. MOOCs use electronic tools or the Internet to deliver educational content to learners to help in learning.

In the early 1990s, e-learning was in the form of distance learning, which was synonymously known as computerized learning or online learning. Initially, the lectures were conducted without the physical presence of students in the schools or colleges. Subsequently, with the arrival and extensive use of Internet technology, e-learning has become very famous and widely used means of education. It is well known as online learning or web-based learning.

Online learning is learning done on computers, mobile, tablets, etc., using the Internet. It breaks the traditional learning and makes it available to masses. In recent years of improvement, easy, and economical accessibility of the Internet and information technology has caused tremendous growth in online learning.

Distance education is the way to provide knowledge to learners through their teachers or trainers even when they are separated from a distance but connected through certain electronic media in such a manner that they can enhance their knowledge according to their time and place. This provides flexibility to the students who are not in a state to reach the school and college or those who have to work for their family or because of any other reason are not able to reach the learning place they get the opportunity to learn.

e-Learning provides large educational opportunities to trainers or educators to approach a wide student audience, also reduces their investment in construction, and resolves the problem of strength of students in a particular class. MOOCs can provide consistent and effective training content; as per students' need at low cost (Tucker, 2001).

Zapalska and Brozik (2006) propose that it is possible to define an appropriate context and content if we understand students' learning styles. They have identified four main learns based on their learning styles, namely, (i) auditory learners, (2) visual learners, (3) kinesthetic learners, and (4) read/write learners. According to them, online learning can be improved by providing instruction as per the students' learning style. At the same time, instructors must ensure that they sufficiently expose students to different learning styles to help them to become a versatile learner. Holsapple and Lee-Post (2006) introduced the e-Learning Success Model, which summarizes that the overall success of e-learning systems depends on system design, system delivery, and system outcome.

e-Learning provides many benefits to instructors, trainers, and lecturers as a medium through which they can provide or share course material with learners and their colleagues outside the classroom. e-Learning also works as a preparatory and presentation tool for them who help them to create a world better understood by the students. In e-learning, the instructors and trainers can also combine information and communication technology into their lecture delivery.

With lots of solutions for different problems, that is, time–space, distance, etc., there are a few problems pertaining to e-learning, namely, isolation and lack of human interaction, as it needs lots of self-discipline and initiative by the learner, so a lack of self-motivation will result from the difficulty in engagement with the subject and, therefore, affect the satisfaction level with the course content. Even with these requirements, more and more learners seek online courses and training.

This paper is an attempt to measure the satisfaction level of MOOC learners and to understand learners' behavior toward MOOC.

## 14.2 MASSIVE OPEN ONLINE COURSES (MOOCS)

MOOCs is the platform through which an educator can provide open access through the Internet to a large number of students by elite professors across the globe.

The uniqueness of MOOCs is that it is massive, open, and online. Massive means a course that can contain plentiful students. Open means free for everyone. Online means the delivery of the courses through the Internet.

MOOCs are more than just an online course compared to other online courses that provide only online lectures; MOOCs are the complete learning package that provides proper instruction with lectures. The courses provide lectures and assignments, the instructors provide various assignments or homework after class, and the students can receive feedback after the assignment is assessed. In addition, online discussion forums (students can interact with the teachers and other students) make it more attractive. After completing the course and passing the exams, the learners obtain certification. MOOC builds on the active rendezvous of several hundred to several thousand "students" who customize their participation as per their learning goals, knowledge, skills, and interests.

### *14.2.1 CMOOC AND XMOOC*

Bates (2012, 2014), in their paper, "Comparing xMOOCs and cMOOCs: philosophy and practice," stated that MOOCs are a relatively new phenomenon and is still evolving in its design. There are two quite different philosophical positions of MOOCs, namely, xMOOCs and cMOOCs.

cMOOC is based on four key design principles, such as autonomy, diversity, interactivity, and openness. cMOOC allows sharing of knowledge between different learners that may or may not be separated by long distance. cMOOC is based on a networked approach, that is, each autonomous learner shares its experience, learning, and content with other learners sitting apart, connected with the Internet.

In the "xMOOCs teaching model," high-quality contents (audio and video delivery, computer-based assessment for student feedback) are primarily focused on the transmission of information to all the participants. There is a lack of direct interaction between an individual participant and the mentor.

## 14.3 CHALLENGES AND ISSUES OF MOOCS

MOOC is growing rapidly and has many advantages, yet it faces challenges. The problems MOOC faces are as follows:

1. *Low completion rates*:
   MOOC's enroll size is very big in comparison to completion rates. Some of the reasons for low completion rates are due to learners' low self-motivation, less interaction among participants, etc. According to NPTEL, only about 10% of total enrolled learners are completing their course (https://nptel.ac.in).

2. *Lack of interaction*:
   MOOCs are online so sometimes it becomes difficult for a learner to complete or continue their course without interacting with an instructor or other participants. Downes criticized that MOOCs are laying less stress on "interactive and dynamic" but more on "static and passive" learning (Parr, 2013).
3. *No accreditation*:
   For such courses, there is nothing to measure their quality only a few organizations are providing certificates for completion of course. These certificates are not for the quality measures but to show that learners have knowledge of that particular course.
4. *Authenticity issues*:
   The parties (professors, facilitators, institutes, evaluators, and professional bodies) involved have raised their concern over the authenticity of the course contents. There is a lack of standards, terms and conditions that make authenticity issue a major challenge.

## 14.4 CHALLENGES FOR INDIA

India is the second largest populated country and first in the age group of 25–35 years. It is the largest contributor to the workforce worldwide. Following are the major challenges encountered by the Indian education system:

1. Mismatch of curricula and industry needs.
2. *Lack of skilled workforce:* India is a developing country and requires a large number of colleges to equip the workforce with necessary skills (survey from MHRD, GoI). MOOCs play an important role to provide skills, but its availability to masses is a major challenge.
3. *Diversity:* India is rich in diversity, particularly in terms of languages. This diversity makes it difficult to meet the expectations of diverse learners.
4. *Lack of infrastructure:* Availability of adequate infrastructure (Internet, computes, etc.) in the rural area is challenging.
5. *Lack of evaluation:* Crediting the marks for the course required verification and validation. Different evaluation and assessment methods make it more challenging.
6. *Rate of completion:* In MOOCs, the completion rate is less, as learners are engaged only in discussions and do not complete their courses.

## 14.5 MOOC PLATFORMS IN INDIA

Education is the basic right of everyone living in India. A county like India has a huge diversity in language, so providing education to all in different learning categories is a tedious job. Many high-ranked institutions are providing the courses through MOOCs. To improve the accessibility of education, THE first dedicated "Educational Satellite" EDUST was launched on September 20, 2004. The Indian government has taken several steps to provide open resources in the form of e-books, repositories, libraries, etc.

### *14.5.1 NPTEL*

NPTEL began providing online courses in March 2014. Successful learners get certificates from the IITs/IISc. Currently, faculty from the IITs and some other reputed institutes such as CMI, IMSc, etc. are providing online courses.

#### *14.5.1.1 HIGHLIGHTS OF NPTEL*

National Programme on Technology Enhanced Learning (NPTEL) is one of the largest online repositories providing coursed in engineering, basic sciences, humanities, and social sciences:

a. It has more than 471 million views (http://nptel.ac.in).
b. NPTEL on the Youtube channel is the most subscribed educational channel with more than 1.5 million channel subscribers and more than 404 million views.
c. It has more than 56,000 hours of video content.
d. It has more than 52,000 hours of transcribed contentand more than 51,000 hours of subtitled videos.

### *14.5.2 MOOKIT*

IIT Kanpur has started MOOC in 2012 with a course on software architecture. IIT Kanpur has not only delivered MOOCs but also developed tools and technologies for delivering MOOCs such as MooKit, a MOOC management system. It is a lightweight MOOC management system built to adapt to local needs, managing the hosting of software. MooKit has been used in more than 60 courses in India and abroad (https://www.mookit.in/architecture).

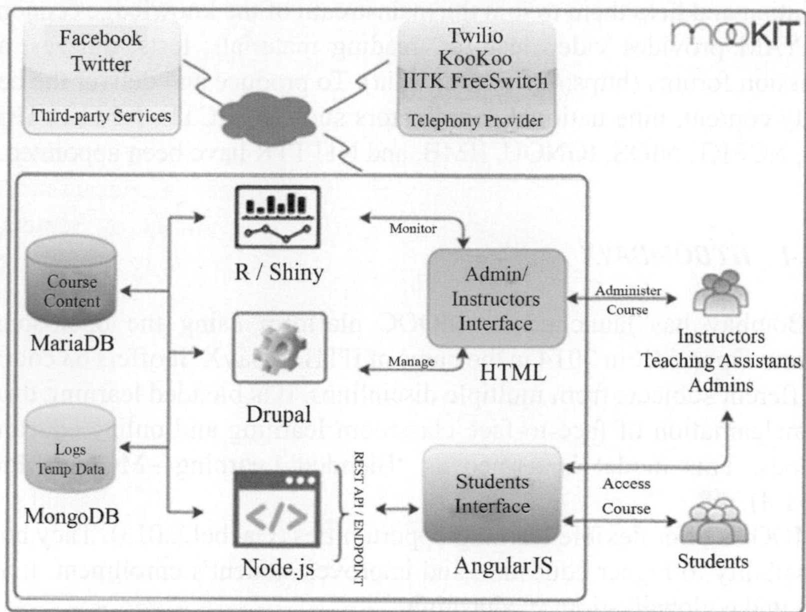


**FIGURE 14.1** MooKit architecture.

*Source*: Reprinted from https://www.mookit.in/architecture. https://creativecommons.org/licenses/by-sa/3.0/us/

Key features of MooKit are as follows:

1. delivery of contents as per available bandwidth,
2. exhaustive discussions and interactions,
3. permission to access Twitter or Facebook forums,
4. easy blend of new language,
5. assessments through the evaluation of assignments,
6. online issuance of course certification, and
7. course customization.

### *14.5.3 SWAYAM*

SWAYAM is an online program started by the Government of India. It is designed to attain the three fundamental principles of education policy, namely, access, equity, and quality. The main objective of this SWAYM is to provide the best teaching–learning resources to everyone. SWAYAM seeks to bridge the digital divide for students who are deprived of the digital revolution and help them to join the mainstream of the knowledge economy. SWAYAM provides video lectures, reading materials, tests, quizzes, and discussion forums (https://swayam.gov.in). To produce and deliver the best-quality content, nine national coordinators such as AICTE, NPTEL, UGC, CEC, NCERT, NIOS, IGNOU, IIMB, and NITTTR have been appointed.

### *14.5.4 IITBOMBAYX*

IIT Bombay has launched its MOOC platform using the open-source platform Open edX in 2014 in the name of IITBombayX. It offers 63 courses on different subjects from multiple disciplines. It is blended learning that is an amalgamation of face-to-face classroom learning and online education methods. This model is termed as "Blended Learning—MOOC Model (BLMM)".

MOOCs offer flexible learning opportunities (Gaebel, 2013). They boost accessibility to higher education and improves student's enrollment. It also helps in the globalization of education.

## 14.6 RESEARCH METHODOLOGY

This study is a cross-sectional study measuring the satisfaction of MOOC learners. This research is quantitative. Quantitative data is collected by a structured questionnaire. The questionnaire comprises of two sections. The first section of the questionnaire designed to collect demographic and basic information of the respondents. The second section of the questionnaire collected data pertaining to the satisfaction of various aspects of MOOCs.

Convenience sampling techniques are used. The questionnaire was e-mailed to the participants through Google Docs. The data was collected from 250 respondents. The collected data is analyzed using SPSS software. Frequency analysis, correlation, and regression analysis were carried out.

## 14.7 DATA ANALYSIS AND FINDINGS

Table 14.1 depicts the demographic profile of respondents. Only 44% ($n$ = 110) are male and remaining 56% ($n$ = 140) are females. In total, 53.2 % ($n$ = 133) belongs to the 17–20 year age group. In total, 49.8% ($n$ = 67) respondents are from 21 to 24 years of age. In total, 51.2% ($n$ = 128) of respondents hold a UG degree or pursuing UG program and 42.8% ($n$ = 107) of respondents are pursuing/completed postgraduation (PG), while 6% ($n$ = 15) respondents have other education qualification. In total, 74% ($n$ = 185) of participants are students, 17.2% ($n$ = 43) of respondents are doing services.

**TABLE 14.1** Demographic Profile of Respondents

| Particulars | No. of Respondents | % |
|---|---|---|
| **Gender** | | |
| Male | 110 | 44.0 |
| Female | 140 | 56.0 |
| Total | 250 | 100.0 |
| **Age group (years)** | | |
| 17–20 | 133 | 53.2 |
| 21–24 | 67 | 49.8 |
| Total | 200 | 100.0 |
| **Educational background** | | |
| UG | 128 | 51.2 |
| PG | 107 | 42.8 |
| Others | 15 | 6.0 |
| Total | 250 | 100.0 |
| **Profession** | | |
| Student | 185 | 74.0 |
| Services | 43 | 17.2 |
| Self-employed | 22 | 8.8 |
| Total | 250 | 100.0 |

Respondents usually prefer Coursera, NTPEL, and EdX for MOOC. The three most preferred platforms are the Coursera (32%, $n$ = 80) and NTPEL (37%, $n$ = 20), and 18% ($n$ = 45) of respondents use EdX (Table 14.2).

**TABLE 14.2** Commonly Used MOOC Platforms

| MOOC Platforms | No. of Respondents | % |
|---|---|---|
| Coursera | 80 | 32.0 |
| NTPEL | 20 | 20.0 |
| EdX | 45 | 18.0 |
| Swayam | 30 | 12.0 |
| Udacity | 37 | 14.8 |
| Others | 8 | 3.2 |
| Total | 250 | 100.0 |

The first three preferred course for MOOCs are business administration (40%, $n = 100$), statistics (38%, $n = 95$), and computer science (37%, $n = 93$), followed by economics (35.2%, $n = 88$), and data science (34.8%, $n = 87$) (Table 14.3).

**TABLE 14.3** Courses Attended by Respondents

| Courses Attended | No. of Respondents | % |
|---|---|---|
| Business administration | 100 | 40.0 |
| Statistics | 95 | 38.0 |
| Computer science | 93 | 37.0 |
| Economics | 88 | 35.2 |
| Data science | 87 | 12.0 |
| Social science | 75 | 30.0 |
| Education | 55 | 22.0 |
| Others | 30 | 12.0 |

**Note:** The sum of the respondents is more than the sample size, as these are multiple option questions.

Majority of the respondents (54%, $n = 135$) enroll in a single course; 32% ($n = 80$) of respondents enroll in 2–4 courses. Only 2% ($n = 5$) respondents enrolled in more than eight courses are able to complete the courses (Table 14.4).

**TABLE. 14.4** Number of Courses Attended by Respondents

| Number of Courses | No. of Respondents | % |
|---|---|---|
| 1 | 135 | 54.0 |
| 2–4 | 80 | 32.0 |
| 5–8 | 30 | 12.0 |
| More than 8 | 5 | 2.0 |
| Total | 250 | 100.0 |

A large number of respondents (87%, $n = 218$) could finish 1–3 courses. Only 4.8% ($n = 12$) participants complete more than seven courses (Table 14.5).

Obtaining more knowledge (66%, $n = 165$), improving existing skills (64%, $n = 160$), and increasing specialized knowledge (61%, $n = 153$ are the three major purposes of doing MOOCs. In total, 8% ($n = 20$) of participants are doing MOOCs for improving communication and the other 4% ($n = 10$) are doing for effective utilization of time (Table 14.6).

**TABLE 14.5** Numbers of Courses Finished by Respondents

| Number of Courses | No. of Respondents | % |
|---|---|---|
| 1–3 | 218 | 87.2 |
| 4–7 | 20 | 8.0 |
| More than 7 | 12 | 4.8 |
| Total | 250 | 100.0 |

**TABLE 14.6** Purpose of Doing MOOCs

| Purpose of Doing a Course | No. of Respondents | % |
|---|---|---|
| To obtain more knowledge | 165 | 66.0 |
| To improve skills | 160 | 64.0 |
| To increase specialized knowledge | 153 | 61.2 |
| To improve communication | 20 | 8.0 |
| For effective utilization of time | 10 | 4.0 |
| Others | 2 | 0.8 |

**Note:** The sum of the respondents is more than the sample size, as these are multiple option questions.

Many respondents enroll in MOOCs but unable to finish due to various reasons. The main reason is that the respondents lack the time (75.2%, $n = 188$). A total of 62.8% ($n = 157$) and 42.8% ($n = 107$) of respondents fail to complete the MOOC course due to lack of motivation and difficult course content respectively. In total, 24.8% ($n = 62$) of respondents quit the courses as they fail to submit the assignments (Table 14.7).

**TABLE 14.7** Reasons for Quitting MOOCs

| Reasons | No. of Respondents | % |
|---|---|---|
| Lack of time | 188 | 75.2 |
| Lack of motivation | 157 | 62.8 |
| Difficult content | 107 | 42.8 |
| Nonsubmission of assignments | 62 | 24.8 |
| Others | 12 | 4.8 |

**Note:** The sum of the respondents is more than the sample size, as these are multiple option questions.

Table 14.8 depicts the satisfaction of respondents with the course content of MOOCs. In total, 51.2% ($n$ = 128) of respondents are strongly satisfied with the structure of the contents and only 13.6%, ($n$ = 34) respondents are neutral; 65.2% ($n$ = 163) of respondents strongly agree that they are satisfied with up-to-date contents and only 4.8% ($n$ = 12) of respondents are neutral; 76.8% ($n$ = 192) of respondents strongly agree that they are satisfied with the availability of course contents; 70% ($n$ = 175) of respondents strongly agree that MOOCs content are able to meet their requirement and 70% ($n$ = 175) of respondents are strongly satisfied with the quality of course content and only 12% ($n$ = 30) of respondents are neutral.

**TABLE 14.8** Satisfaction Level with Course Content

| Particulars | Strongly Agree | Agree | Neutral |
|---|---|---|---|
| Satisfied with the structure of contents | (128) 51.2% | (88) 35.2% | (34) 13.6% |
| Satisfied with updates (up-to-date contents) | (163) 65.2% | (75) 30.0% | (12) 4.8% |
| Satisfied with the availability of course recourses | (192) 76.8% | (38) 15.2% | (20) 8.0% |
| Satisfies with the meeting the requirements | (175) 70.0% | (65) 26.0% | (10) 4.0% |
| Overall satisfaction with the quality of the course contents | (175) 70% | (45) 18% | (30) 12% |

Table 14.9 depicts the satisfaction of the teaching methods. In total, 68% ($n$ = 170) of respondents strongly satisfied with the teaching approach to promote learning and only 8.8% ($n$ = 22) respondents are neutral; 66% ($n$ = 165) of respondents strongly satisfied with the factors that teaching methods improving learners skills and only 12% ($n$ = 30) of respondents are neutral; 54% ($n$ = 135) of respondents strongly satisfied with the encouragement they received in communication; 56% ($n$ = 140) of respondents strongly agree that they are satisfied with the encouragement of team works through learners' cooperation by teaching methods; and 68% ($n$ = 170) of respondents are strongly satisfied with the teaching methods of MOOCs and 8.8% ($n$ = 22) are neutral.

Table 14.10 depicts the satisfaction of respondents with the learning environment of MOOCs. In total, 63% ($n$ = 153) of respondents strongly satisfied with MOOCs platform and its operations and only 11.6% ($n$ = 29) of respondents are neutral; 58% ($n$ = 145) of respondents strongly satisfied with the technical supports and only 10% ($n$ = 25) of respondents are neutral;

64% ($n$ = 160) of respondents strongly satisfied with the ease of uploading assignments; and 67% ($n$ = 168) of respondents are strongly satisfied with the overall learning environment of MOOCs and 8.8% ($n$ = 22) are neutral.

**TABLE 14.9** Satisfaction Level with Teaching Methods

| Particulars | Strongly Agree | Agree | Neutral |
|---|---|---|---|
| Satisfied with a different teaching approach to promote learning | (170) 68.0% | (58) 23.2% | (22) 8.8% |
| Satisfied with the improvement of learners skills | (165) 66.0% | (55) 22.0% | (30)12% |
| Satisfied with the encouragement in communication | (135) 54.0% | (80) 32% | (35)14% |
| Satisfied with the encouragement of team works through learners' cooperation | (140) 56% | (80) 32% | (30)12% |
| Overall satisfaction with teaching methods | (170) 68% | (58) 23.2% | (22)8.8% |

**TABLE 14.10** Satisfaction Level with the Learning Environment

| Particulars | Strongly Agree | Agree | Neutral |
|---|---|---|---|
| Satisfied with the MOOC platform and its operations | (153) 61.2% | (68) 27.2% | (29) 11.6% |
| Satisfied with technical supports | (145) 58.0% | (80) 32.0% | (25) 10.0% |
| Satisfied with the quality of audio–video | (160) 64.0% | (70) 28.0% | (20) 8.0% |
| Satisfied with the uploading of assignments | (165) 66.0% | (63) 25.2% | (22) 8.8% |
| Overall satisfaction with the learning environment | (168) 67.2% | (60) 24.0% | (22) 8.8% |

Table 14.11 depicts the satisfaction of respondents with the evaluation and assessment of MOOCs. In total 59.2% of respondents are satisfied with the effectiveness of assessment tools; 49.2% ($n$ = 123) respondents are strongly satisfied with the assessment through peers; 59.2% ($n$ = 148) respondents are strongly satisfied with the feedback in improving learning; 53.2% ($n$ = 133) of respondents are strongly satisfied with the final exams; and 58% ($n$ = 145) of respondents are overall satisfied with the assessment of MOOCs.

Table 14.12 depicts the overall satisfaction of respondents with the MOOCs. In total, 72% ($n$ = 180) of respondents are strongly satisfied with the MOOCs, 23.3% ($n$ = 58) are satisfied, and only 4.8 % ($n$ = 12) respondents are neutral with the satisfaction from MOOCs.

**TABLE 14.11** Satisfaction Level with Evaluation and Assessment

| Particulars | Strongly Agree | Agree | Neutral |
|---|---|---|---|
| Satisfied with the effectiveness of assessment tool | (148) 59.2% | (73) 29.2% | (29) 11.6% |
| Satisfied with the peer assessment | (123) 49.2% | (80) 32.0% | (47) 18.8% |
| Satisfied with the feedback in improving learning | (148) 59.2% | (78) 31.2% | (24) 9.6% |
| Satisfied with the final exams | (133) 53.2% | (80) 32.0% | (37) 14.8% |
| Overall satisfaction with the assessment of MOOCs | (145) 58.0% | (80) 32.0% | (25) 10.0% |

**TABLE 14.12** Overall Satisfaction with MOOC

| Particulars | Strongly Agree | Agree | Neutral |
|---|---|---|---|
| Overall satisfaction with MOOC | (180) 72% | (58) 23.2% | (12) 4.8% |

Table 14.13 depicts the correlations between variables of course content, teaching methods, evaluation, and learning environments. Different aspects of MOOCs show significant relationships with overall satisfaction with MOOCs. The overall satisfaction with the learning environment has the maximum correlation ($r = 0.645$, $p < 0.01$). The overall satisfaction also highly correlated with teaching methods ($r = 0.605$, $p < 0.01$) and whether the course has rich content ($r = 0.568$, $p < 0.01$) and the overall satisfaction with MOOCs with course content ($r = 0.568$, $p < 0.1$).

Table 14.14 shows that the independent variables significantly predict the overall satisfaction with MOOCs. Approximately, 63% of the variance of overall satisfaction can be explained by four predicators.

The overall satisfaction with course content ($t = 2.655$, $p < 0.01$), teaching methods ($t = 4.314$, $p < 0.001$), evaluations system ($t = 2.449$, $p < 0.005$), and the learning environment ($t = 6.378$, $p < 0.001$) is significantly predicts the overall satisfaction with MOOCs.

## 14.8 SUMMARY AND CONCLUSION

MOOCs are emerging as an important domain of knowledge building and being used in various subjects/specialization. MOOCs are generally adopted by service people and students who want to acquire more skills and knowledge. People usually do MOOCs for obtaining more knowledge and utilizing time. A large number of respondents do 3–4 courses simultaneously. Respondents mainly prefer Coursera, NPTEL, and EdX for MOOCs. Business

Administration course is a popular course among learners. Learners pursue a course to improve skills and obtain more knowledge. Lack of time and motivation leads to quitting the MOOCs. The majority of learners are highly satisfied with MOOC's course contents, learning environments, evaluation, and teaching methods.

**TABLE 14.13** Correlation between Overall Satisfaction and Satisfaction with Other Aspects

| | Overall Satisfaction with Course Content | Overall Satisfaction with Methods | Overall Satisfaction with Evaluation | Overall Satisfaction with the Learning Environment | Overall Satisfaction with MOOC |
|---|---|---|---|---|---|
| Overall satisfaction with course content | 1 | | | | |
| Overall satisfaction with methods | 0.651** | 1 | | | |
| Overall satisfaction with evaluation | 0.535** | 0.593** | 1 | | |
| Overall satisfaction with learning environment | 0.591** | 0.576** | 0.641** | 1 | |
| Overall satisfaction with MOOC | 0.568** | 0.605** | 0.563** | 0.645** | 1 |

***Correlation is significant at the 0.01 level (two-tailed).*

**TABLE 14.14** Multiple Regression—Overall Satisfaction with MOOCs ($n = 250$)

| Model | Unstandardized Coefficient | | Standardized Coefficient | t | Sig. |
|---|---|---|---|---|---|
| | B | Std. Error | Beta | | |
| (Constant) | 1.543 | 0.189 | | 7.772 | 0.000 |
| Overall satisfaction with content | 0.108 | 0.040 | 0.133 | 2.655 | 0.008 |
| Overall satisfaction with methods | 0.176 | 0.040 | 0.214 | 4.314 | 0.000 |
| Overall satisfaction with evaluation | 0.107 | 0.043 | 0.124 | 2.449 | 0.14 |
| Overall satisfaction with environment | 0.289 | 0.043 | 0.314 | 6.378 | 0.000 |

*Dependent variable*: overall satisfaction with MOOCs.

MOOCs have the prospective to increase knowledge and skills and they are indeed supplementing education. Despite the various advantage of

MOOCs, MOOCs are open and cost-effective, as they are based on self-paced learning and lacks direct supervision.

Respondents pursue a course to obtain more knowledge. Lack of time and motivation leads to quitting the MOOCs. Assessment of learning, peer assessment, and creating a learning environment are the major issues in MOOCs.

This study will help instructors and teachers to understand the area where significant steps need to be taken for improving the satisfaction level of learners. This study is confined to Delhi only, and four areas of satisfaction are explored. This study can be further researched for other aspects of satisfaction.

## KEYWORDS

- **course content**
- **evaluation**
- **learning environment**
- **MOOC**
- **satisfaction**

## REFERENCES

Bates, T. What's Right and What's Wrong about Coursera-style MOOCs. **2012** Retrieved from http://www.tonybates.ca/2012/08/05/whats-right-and-whats-wrong-about-coursera-style-moocs/

Bates, T. Comparing xMOOCs and cMOOCs: philosophy and practice. **2014** Retrieved from http://www.tonybates.ca/2014/10/13/comparing-xmoocs-and-cmoocs-philosophy-and-practice/

Downes, S. Connectivism and Connective Knowledge: Essays on Meaning and Learning Networks. **2012** Retrieved from http://www.downes.ca/me/mybooks.htm

Gaebel, M. MOOCs—Massive open online courses. European University Association. **2013** Retrieved from http://www.eua.be/Libraries/publication/EUA_Occasional_papers_MOOCs

Holsapple, C.W and Post. A.L. Defining, assessing, and promoting e-learning success: An information systems perspective, Decision Sciences, **2006,** 4(1),67–85 Retrieved from https://onlinelibrary.wiley.com/doi/abs/10.1111/j.1540-4609.2006.00102.x

Parr, C. MOOC creators criticise courses' lack of creativity. *Time Higher Education*. **2013** Retrieved from https://www.timeshighereducation.com/news/mooc-creators-criticise-courses-lack-of-creativity/2008180.article

Tucker, S. Distance education: better, worse, or as good as traditional education? *Online Journal of Distance Learning Administration,* **2001,** *4*(4). Retrieved from !http://www.westga.edu/~distance/ojdla/winter44/tucker44.html

Zapalska, A. and Brozik, D. (2006). Learning styles and online education. *Campus-Wide Information Systems,* **2006** *23*(5), 325–335.

Wikipedia. Massive open online course. **2016** Retrieved from https://en.wikipedia.org/wiki/Massive_open_online_course

http://www.educause.edu/blogs/cheverij/moocs-and-intellectual-property-ownership-and-use-rights

https://www.mookit.in/features

https://docserv.uni-duesseldorf.de/servlets/DerivateServlet/Derivate-41685/Yuquin%20Yin_PDFA.pdf

http://www.g2collective.com/2013/05/01/top-5-issues-with-moocs/

http://www.educause.edu/blogs/cheverij/moocs-and-intellectual-property-ownership-and-use-rights

https://nptel.ac.in/about_nptel.html

https://www.mookit.in/architecture

https://pdfs.semanticscholar.org/67a5/8c66b1c2f5e3675c69662198838b12470a1b.pdf.

https://swayam.gov.in/about

Wikipedia. Learning community. **2016** Retrieved from https://en.wikipedia.org/wiki/Learning_community

# CHAPTER 15

# Survey of Awareness of Massive Open Online Courses in Delhi, India

SUDHIR KUMAR SHARMA* and ASHISH KUMAR NAYYAR

*Institute of Information Technology & Management,*
*New Delhi 110058, India*

*Corresponding author. E-mail: sudhir_sharma99@yahoo.com*

## ABSTRACT

Teaching–learning trend has changed over the course of time owing to the advancements in information and communication technology (ICT). Massive Open Online Course (MOOC) is one of the most recent innovations in higher education. *Massive* refers to a large number of simultaneous learners and *open* means anyone can sign up and join the course online free of charge. It offers a lifelong learning opportunity to anyone. This opportunity is made possible by innovation, experimentation, and the use of the latest ICT. This chapter explores the opportunities and challenges for introducing MOOCs in higher education. This chapter also examines the awareness and usability of MOOCs among the students and professionals in Delhi, India. We employed an online method for the collection of data and data was analyzed using the latest software and tools. The findings suggest that ICT must be used more effectively in higher education. MOOCs will promote lifelong learning and motivate students' self-development.

## 15.1 INTRODUCTION

India is the second most populated country in the world. The most significant feature of our Indian population is its adolescent population. One-fifth of India's population comprises adolescents. Better infrastructures and human expertise equipped with the latest technology are needed to provide quality education among the masses.

The teaching–learning process has been changed due to the advancement of science, technology, and information and communication technology (ICT) since the 1960s. The major technologies which have been used over the past decades are tabulated in Table 15.1. The objective of using these technologies is to provide an overall improvement in all the dimensions of teaching–learning. e-Learning can be defined as an online and on-campus learning, whereas off-campus e-learning comes under online distance learning.

**TABLE 15.1** Role of ICT in Higher Education

| Sr. No. | Technology | Year of Establishment |
|---|---|---|
| 1 | Massive Open Online Courses | 2008 |
| 2 | Virtual campus | 2000 |
| 3 | Learning management systems | 1999 |
| 4 | Virtual university | 1999 |
| 5 | Open learning | 1995 |
| 6 | e-Learning | 1993 |
| 7 | Computer-mediated learning | 1990 |
| 8 | Educational telemetric | 1988 |
| 9 | Computer-based learning | 1980 |
| 10 | Computer-assisted instructions | 1960 |

Massive Open Online Courses (MOOCs) were initiated in 2008 in Canada by Stephen Downes and George Siemens but gained popularity in the United States when Stanford University professor Sebastian Thrun held a free online course on Artificial Intelligence in 2011 (Nana-sinkam, 2014).

In the last three years, over 25 million people from around the world have enrolled in MOOCs offered by different platforms.

The purpose of this study can be summarized as follows:

- To summarize the facts of MOOCs.
- To explore the initiative of the Government of India to introduce MOOCs to provide quality education to the mass learners.
- To determine the latest trends in the field of massive open learning.
- To conduct a survey of awareness among many stakeholders in Delhi, India.

The remainder of the paper is organized in the following seven sections. Section 15.2 discusses MOOCs. Section 15.3 discusses Study Webs of Active

Learning for Young Minds (SWAYAM). The latest trends are discussed in Section 15.4. The survey of awareness is discussed in Section 15.5.

Results and discussion are given in Section 15.6. The paper is concluded in the last section.

## 15.2 MASSIVE OPEN ONLINE COURSES

### *15.2.1 INTRODUCTION*

MOOCs have recently received great attention from the student community, teachers, and professionals. It can be considered as a breakthrough in the education system that is breaking the barriers in providing quality education to anyone, anytime, and anywhere.

MOOCs are based on the characteristics of massiveness, openness and, connectivity philosophy.

Some details are as follows:

- *Massive:* More than 10,000 students can enroll for a single course at a time.
- *Open:* Learner can study any course, anywhere at any time.
- *Online:* As opposed to face to face or blended learning.
- *Course:* The diversity of the courses expands to academic subjects, professional courses, and research-oriented topics.

An overall characteristic of MOOCs can be explained by Figure 15.1.

### *15.2.2 DEVELOPMENT HISTORY*

The major developments in MOOCs (Yuan et al., 2013) are depicted in Figure 15.2.

The major MOOC platforms that emerged in the last decade are as follows:

- Coursera[1] was started by two Stanford professors, namely, Daphne Koller and Andrew Ng. A conducive environment was created by the company, and the company built a learning platform and subsequently engaged more than 30 university partners in developing the course content (as per a report of Voss, 2013).

[1] www.coursera.org

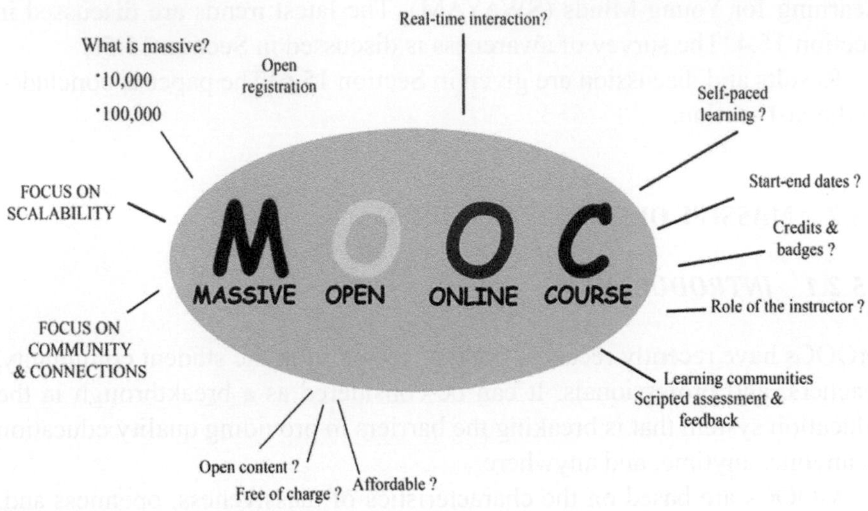


**FIGURE 15.1** MOOC poster adapted from Wikipedia.[1]

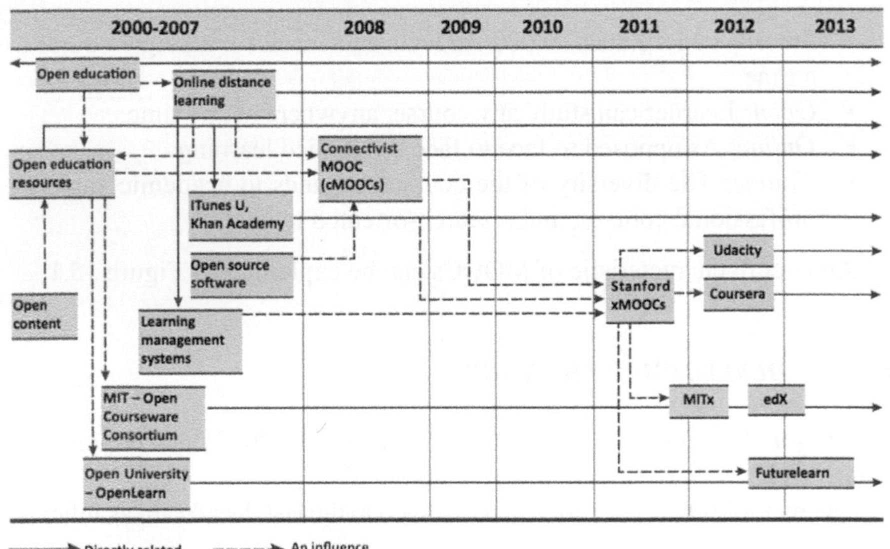


**FIGURE 15.2** MOOCs development history.

*Source*: Adapted from Yuan et al., 2013.

- edX[2] was started as a partnership between Harvard and MIT. edX then expanded to include the University of California at Berkeley,

[2] www.edx.org

the University of Texas System, Wellesley College, and Georgetown University in December 2012. It offered 15 courses in Spring 2013.

- Udacity[3] was begun by Stanford Professor Sebastian Thrun with Mike Sokolsky and David Stavens and then joined by Prof. David Evans from the University of Virginia. Udacity offered around 20 courses in Spring 2013.
- Udemy[4] was established by Eren Bali and Oktay Caglar. This platform was built to invite individuals (rather than institutions) to offer online courses.

MOOCs can also be classified in a number of ways. The two major types of MOOCs that are encouraged by the institutions are cMOOCs and xMOOCs. cMOOCs are based on principles that indicate that material should be aggregated, remixable, and repurposable. cMOOCs are based on collaborative learning with no predefined course structure. xMOOCs follow a properly-defined course structure. The structure is defined as per the syllabus of recorded lectures and self-test problems. In xMOOCs, instructor is supposed to provide his knowledge to the students, and students can ask for assistance and advise each other on difficult points.

A study from Stanford University's Learning Analytics group identified four types of students (Wikipedia, 2020):

- *Auditors:* who watched video throughout the subject but took a few exams or quizzes.
- *Completers:* who viewed most lectures content and took part in most assessments.
- *Disengaged learners:* who quickly dropped the subject.
- *Sampling learners:* who might only occasionally watch lecture content?

The percentage of learners from these four categories is tabulated in Table 15.2.

**TABLE 15.2** Four Types of Learners as per Stanford University

| Course | Auditing | Completing | Disengaging | Sampling |
|---|---|---|---|---|
| High School | 6% | 27% | 29% | 39% |
| Undergraduate | 6% | 8% | 12% | 74% |
| Graduate | 9% | 5% | 6% | 80% |

(https://en.wikipedia.org/wiki/Massive_open_online_course)

[3] www.udemy.com
[4] https://in.udacity.com/

## 15.3 INITIATIVE OF THE GOVERNMENT OF INDIA: STUDY WEBS OF ACTIVE LEARNING FOR YOUNG MINDS (SWAYAM)

The Government of India started working on MOOC early in August 2014. This initiative was known as SWAYAM[5] (Study Webs of Active Learning for Young Aspiring Minds). This project was launched in August 2016. UGC5 published some documents about the initiative on its website that include a list of MOOCs, and its framework, and guidelines. In the first phase, 244 free MOOCs were announced on the SWAYAM[6] platform. These courses are categorized into six different categories. The details are given in Figure 15.3.

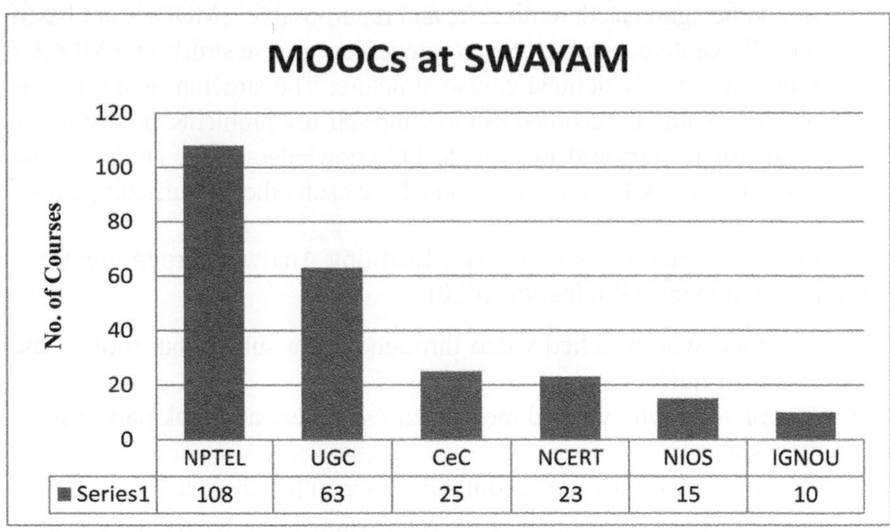


**FIGURE 15.3** MOOCs at SWAYAM (2016).

More than 600 free online courses have been started in January and February 2020. These courses are categorized into 13 different disciplines (MOOC Class Central Report, 2020). The details are given in Figure 15.4.

Approximate 2000 courses are expected to be available for catering up to three crore students across the country. The objective was to provide high-quality education on various disciplines from the school level to undergraduates and postgraduate students.

---

[5] https://swayam.gov.in/

[6] http://www.ugc.ac.in/ugc_notices.aspx?id=1453

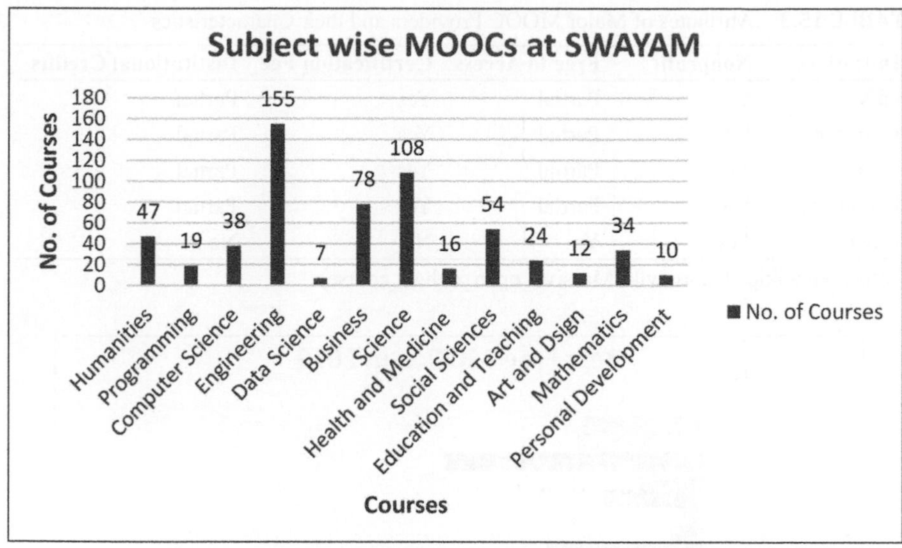


**FIGURE 15.4** Subject-wise MOOCs at SWAYAM in January and February 2020.

*Source*: MOOC Class Central Report, 2020.

## 15.4 LATEST TRENDS

The number of learners on these platforms is increasing day by day. The number of learners who signed up for at least one course crossed 35 million at the end of the year 2016. edX platform crossed 10 million learners in February 2017. These learners have watched approximately 230 million videos and solved 119 million problem sets. On this achievement, Dr. Anant Agarwal, CEO of edX was awarded Padma Shri by the Government of India. Many other open online course providers like Khan Academy, Moodle, Peer-to-Peer University, ALISON, etc. are similar to MOOCs. They are not considered under MOOCs as per the latest trend. The xMOOCs are gaining more popularity among learners nowadays. A comparative study of the most popular MOOCs in terms of their attributes and characteristics are presented in Table 15.3 (Wikipedia, 2020).

As per the Class Central MOOC report, 2500 MOOCs were initiated first time ever in 2019 by 450 universities worldwide. Of them, 147 were introduced for the first time (MOOC Course Report, February 2019). Top 15 and most reviewed MOOCs are listed in Figure 15.5.

**TABLE 15.3** Attributes of Major MOOC Providers and their Characteristics

| Initiatives | Nonprofit | Free to Access | Certification Fee | Institutional Credits |
|---|---|---|---|---|
| **edX** | Yes | Partial | Yes | Partial |
| **Coursera** | No | Partial | Yes | Partial |
| **Udacity** | No | Partial | Yes | Partial |
| **Udemy** | No | Partial | Yes | Partial |
| **P2PU** | Yes | Yes | No | No |

(https://en.wikipedia.org/wiki/Massive_open_online_course)

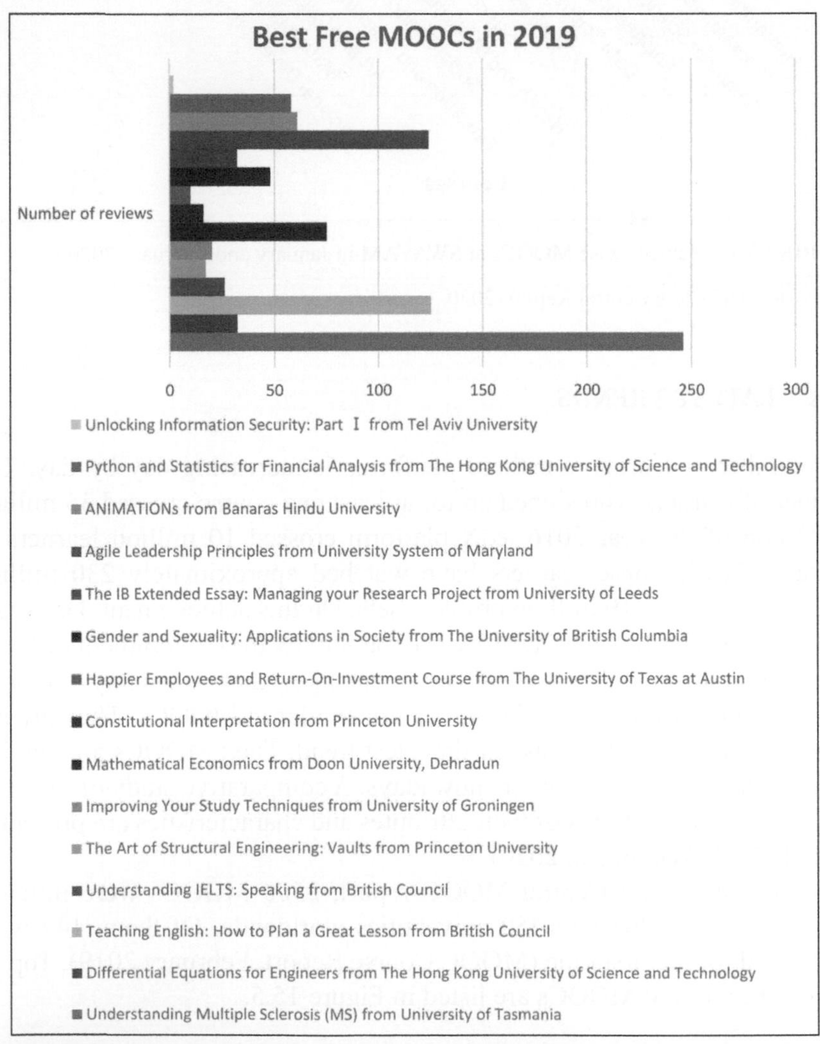


**FIGURE 15.5** Best free MOOCs in 2019. (MOOC Course Report, 2019).

There are many survey studies that are available in the literature. Many survey studies have been done by the MOOC providers. These studies emphasize more around the enrolled learners on these platforms. A survey report on students' profile provided by Coursera in 2013 is presented in Figure 15.6.

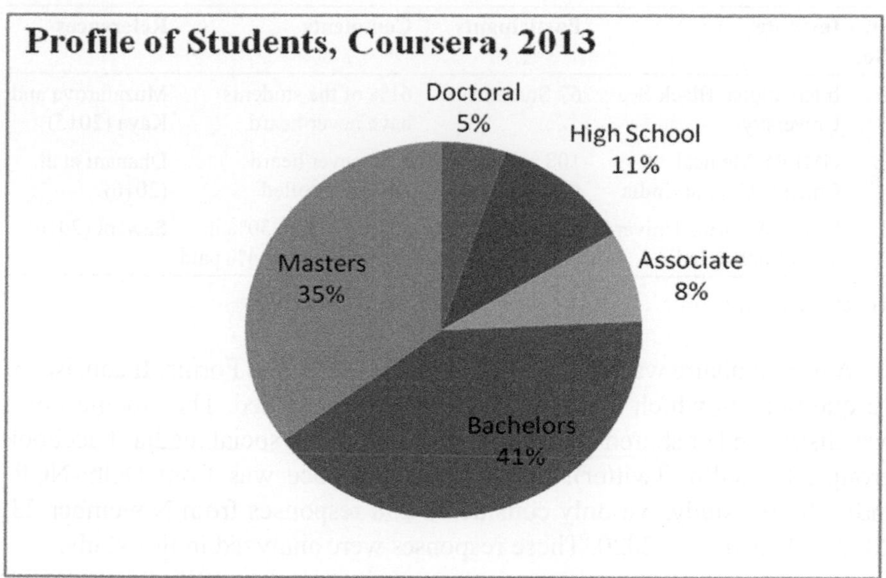


**FIGURE 15.6** Profile of students.

The survey report is summarized online in the form of a table (Ho et al., 2015). This survey report was based on demographics and outcomes by curricular content area and calculated as the average of course-level statistics.

We have selected some latest surveys conducted for assessment of awareness of MOOCs. A comparative study is presented in Table 15.4.

## 15.5 SURVEY OF AWARENESS OF MOOCS

The objective of this survey was to cover different aspects of awareness of MOOCs in a diversified user community. These include students from class 9 up to graduates and masters, research scholars, and teacher community in higher education.

The objective of the survey can be summarized as follows:

- to examine the awareness of MOOCs among different users,
- to know their opinion about the benefits of MOOCs, and
- to find out the challenges in adapting lifelong learning.

**TABLE 15.4** Literature Review on Awareness on MOOCs

| Sr. No. | Institute | Participants | Comments | References |
|---|---|---|---|---|
| 1. | International Black Sea University | 67 Students | 61% of the students have never heard | Muzafarova and Kaya (2015) |
| 2. | GMERS Medical College, Gujarat, India | 108 medical teachers | 81% never heard 14/108 enrolled | Dhanani et al. (2016) |
| 3. | SNDT Women's University, Mumbai, India | 102 library science teachers | 22% enrolled, 30% in the free course, 4% paid | Sawant (2016) |

(Ho et al., 2015)

A questionnaire was created with the help of Google Forms. It consists of 12 questions in which three questions were open-ended. The Google Form was distributed or shared with the help of emails and social media (Facebook groups, LinkedIn, Twitter). The targeted audience was from Delhi-NCR, India. In this study, we only considered 238 responses from November 23, 2019 to January 10, 2020. These responses were analyzed in this study.

## 15.6 RESULTS AND DISCUSSIONS

The results of the survey are presented in the form of a pie chart. These pie charts are given in Figure 15.7.

About 67% of participants were students of graduates and masters level students. More than 31% of the students are from an engineering background. The usage of open educational resources is evenly distributed. Around 25% of the students who participated in the survey are not familiar with the MOOC concept. Students are interested in the free courses much than attaining a verified certification course. Coursera among udacity, edx, and other institutions is preferred the most. More than 57% of the participants think that MOOCs will have a positive impact on the education system. This survey shows a clear picture of the number of students willing to enroll in the upcoming MOOCs next year. The main reasons for enrolling in a MOOC were to learn new technologies but a fair amount of students could not complete the course due to the time constraints.

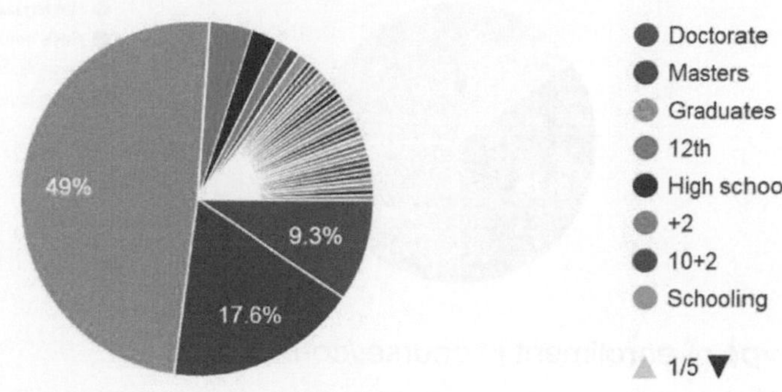


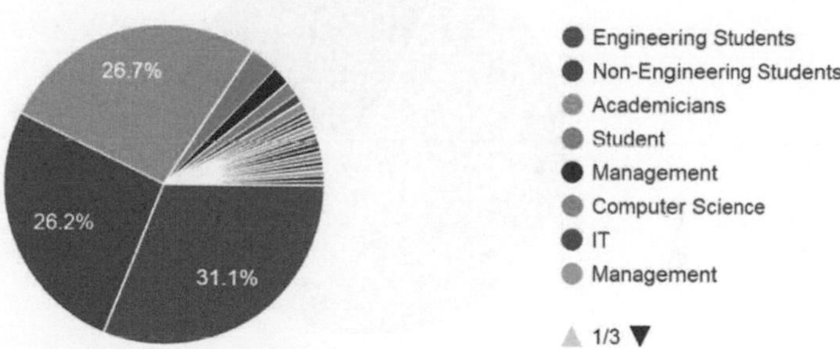


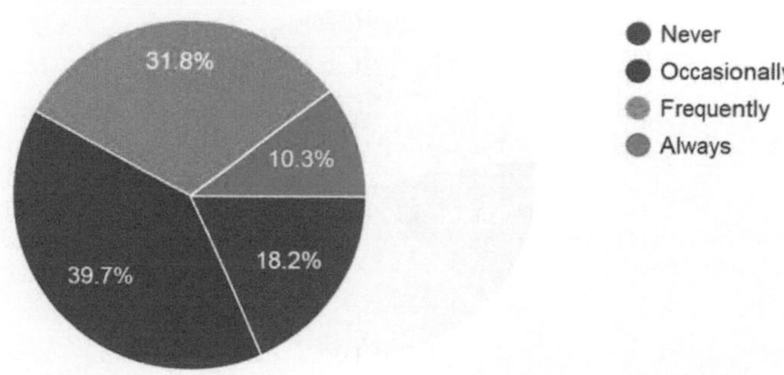


**FIGURE 15.7** *(Continued)*

How would you rate your familiarity with MOOCs?
213 responses

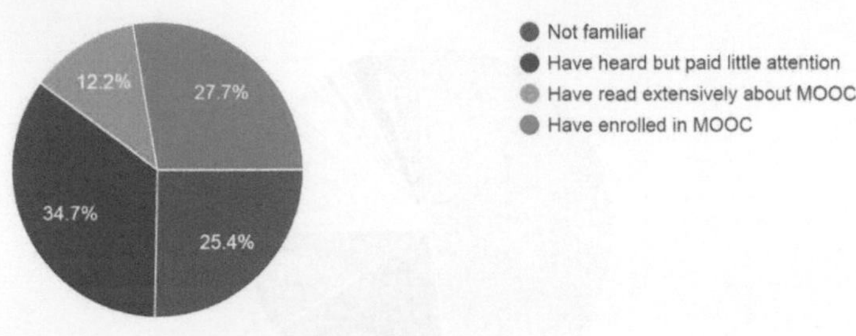


Type of enrollment in course /courses?
211 responses

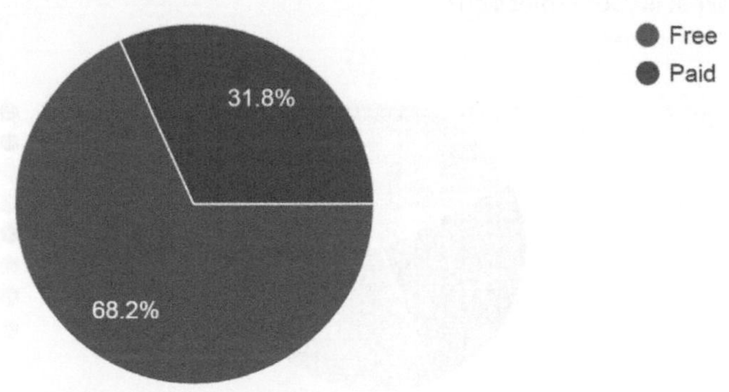


Which is a best MOOC platform according to you?
190 responses

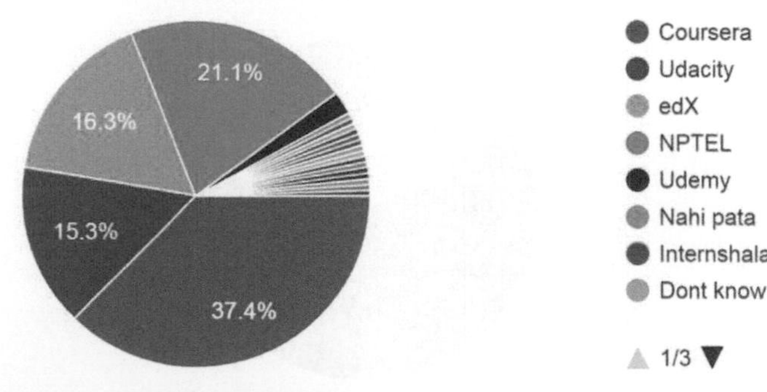


**FIGURE 15.7** *(Continued)*

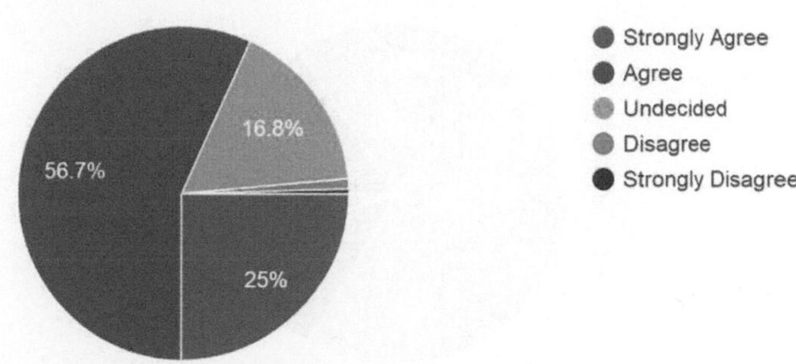
MOOCs are an innovation that will have a positive impact on education.
208 responses
56.7%
16.8%
25%
Strongly Agree
Agree
Undecided
Disagree
Strongly Disagree

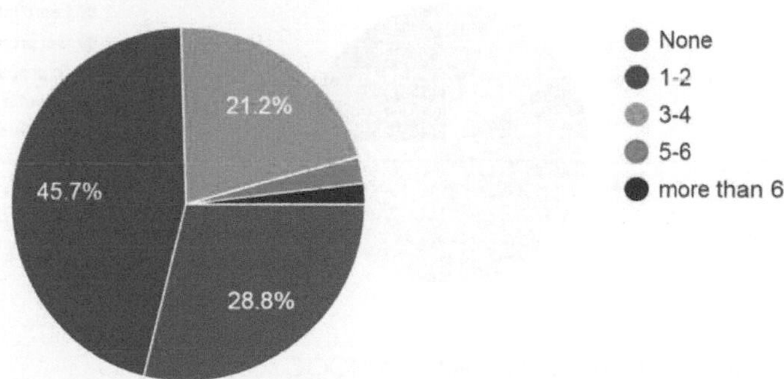
How many MOOCs have you enrolled in as a learner?
208 responses
45.7%
21.2%
28.8%
None
1-2
3-4
5-6
more than 6

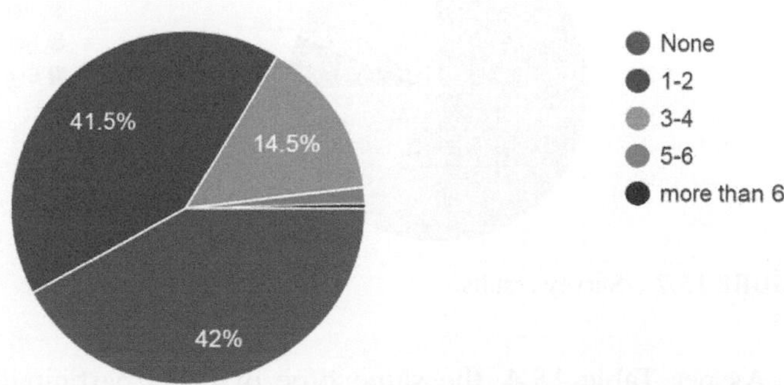
How many MOOCs have you successfully completed with score card?
207 responses
41.5%
14.5%
42%
None
1-2
3-4
5-6
more than 6

**FIGURE 15.7** *(Continued)*

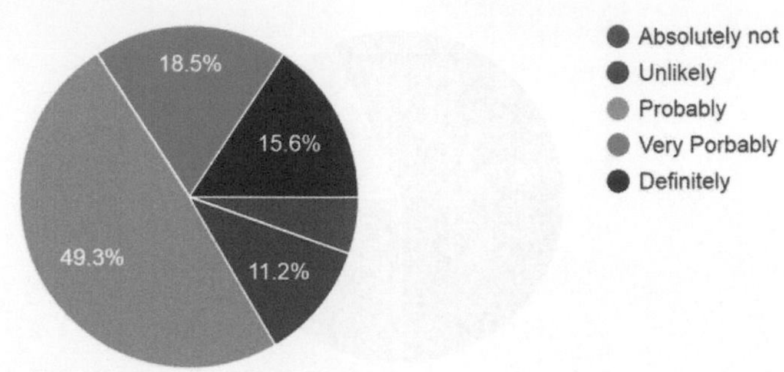


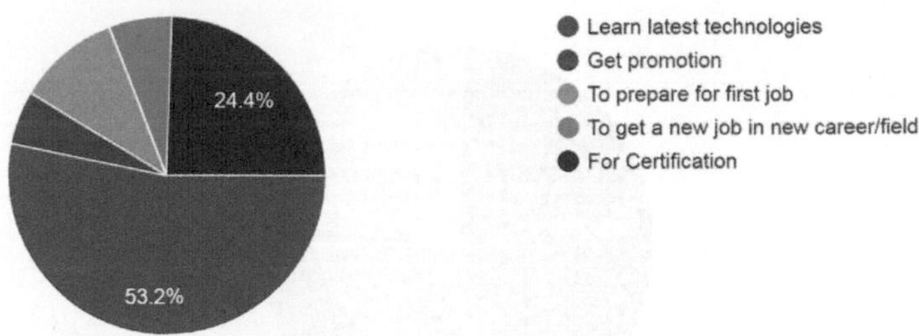


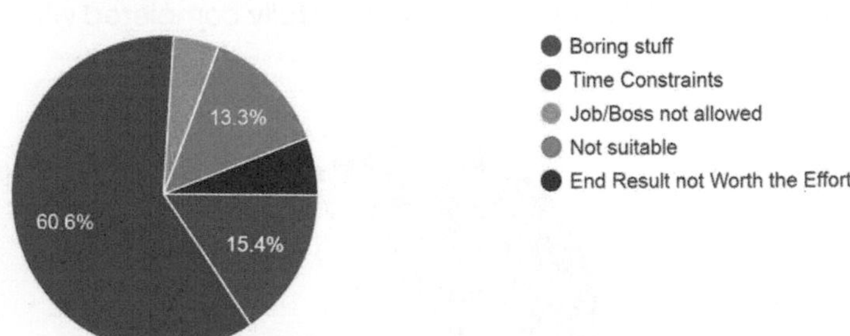


**FIGURE 15.7** Survey results.

As per Table 15.4, the same type of users participated in the surveys conducted earlier. The diversified users participated in this survey. A total of

217 users participated in this survey that exceeds the count of participants in the previous surveys. There is a lack of awareness among the students on how to utilize the full potential of the MOOCs. Initiatives by the government organizations and institutions should be taken to spread awareness among the different users.

## 15.7 CONCLUSIONS

The objective of this survey was to get a fair idea about the familiarity of MOOCs among a diversified community. A total of 217 users participated in this survey from November 23, 2019 to January 10, 2020. This survey concludes that users are not familiar with the expected margin and the users who are already familiar are continuously benefiting from these MOOCs. Students pursuing undergraduate and masters are extensively using MOOCs to learn new technologies and for pursuing new careers. One indirect benefit to the students who participated was that the students who were not familiar with this concept also became aware and will create a spark to look forward and get enrolled in the MOOCs. Seminars regarding the utilization of MOOCs in schools, colleges, and universities should be encouraged by the government.

## KEYWORDS

- **information and communication technology (ICT)**
- **massive online open courses (MOOCs)**
- **Study Webs of Active Learning for Young Aspiring Minds (SWAYAM)**

## REFERENCES

Chavda, J. V., Patel, N., & Tandel, K. (2016). Awareness and utilization of massive open online course (MOOC) and video series as continuous learning tools for faculties. International Journal of Medical Science and Public Health, 5(8), 1540–1543.

Ho, A. D., Chuang, I., Reich, J., Coleman, C. A., Whitehill, J., Northcutt, C. G., Williams J., Hansen J., Lopez G. & Petersen, R. (2015). Harvardx and mitx: Two years of open online courses fall 2012-summer 2014. MITx Working Papers 15.

Khalil, M., Ebner, M., Kopp, M., Lorenz, A., Kalz, M., editors (2016). Proceedings of the European Stakeholder Summit on experiences and best practices in and around MOOCs (EMOOCS 2016). BoD—Books on Demand; Feb. 2.

Massive Open Online Course (2019). Wikipedia information. Retrieved from https://en.wikipedia.org/wiki/Massive_open_online_course.

MOOC Course Report (2019). Class Central Report. Retrieved from https://www.classcentral.com/report/top-moocs-2019-edition.

MOOC Class Central Report, 2020. Retrieved from https://www.classcentral.com/report/swayam-moocs-course-list/.

Muzafarova, T., & Kaya, E. (2015). Survey of Awareness of Massive Open Online Courses (MOOC)—A Case of International Black Sea University Students, Georgia. Journal of Education, 3(2), 15–19.

Nana-Sinkam, A. (2014). Education technology in the international context: A critical analysis of massive open online: Course innovation in sub-Saharan Africa. Master's thesis. Stanford University, Department of Communication: Stanford, CA, USA.

Sawant, S. (2016). MOOCs as a means of continuing professional development for LIS educators in India.

Shah, D. (2019). The 100 Most Popular Free Online Courses of 2019 https://www.classcentral.com/report/100-most-popular-online-courses-2019.

Voss, B.D. (2013). Massive Open Online Courses (MOOCs): A Primer for University and College Board Members. An AGB White Paper. Association of Governing Boards of Universities and Colleges. Mar 2013.

Yuan, L., Powell, S., & Cetis, J. (2013). MOOCs and open education: Implications for higher education. 10.13140/2.1.5072.8320.

## CHAPTER 16

# Online Students' Feedback Management System for Higher Education

SUDHIR KUMAR SHARMA[1*], GAURAV KUMAR[2]

[1]*Institute of Information Technology & Management, New Delhi 110058, India*

[2]*MJPR University, Bareilly, Uttar Pradesh, India*

[*]*Corresponding author. E-mail: sharmasudhir08@gmail.com*

### ABSTRACT

In general, to access the quality teaching in higher education, students' feedbacks are collected and then processed manually for generating the reports of each teacher. This traditional system is not only time consuming but also not so useful in instant decision making. Software development cell of IITM Janakpuri, New Delhi automates the traditional student's feedback system. This paper explores those companies providing enterprise resource planning (ERP) solutions for schools/colleges/Universities. Some of them are Campuspedia[1], Academiaerp[2], Softwaresuggest[3], Cloudems[4], etc. The services provided by these companies are not only paid but also not providing online students feedback management system. This paper presents an application of information and communication technology (ICT) in higher education that is an online student's feedback management system. The proposed system is based on client–server computing. The front-end is designed using HTML pages. Programming *javascript* is used for client-side validation purposes. All business logics are implemented

[1] http://www.campuspedia.org/
[2] https://www.academiaerp.com/
[3] https://www.softwaresuggest.com/
[4] https://www.icloudems.com/

through hypertext preprocessor (PHP) language in the middle layer. The third tier of this system employs MySQL database. Apache as a web server is required to start working on this application as a development environment and PhpMyAdmin as a database. This system is developed using the Iterative Enhancement software life cycle model. System architecture design employs a Divide and Conquer paradigm. The built software has been implemented successfully.

## 16.1 INTRODUCTION

Education in India has emerged as a giant industry as more and more institutions are opening and providing various types of courses to students. The quality of education is certainly dependent upon the teacher and student's communication. Sometimes a highly qualified teacher is not able to deliver the subject knowledge as per the expectations of students. Therefore, to improve the two-way communication there is a need for a feedback system that must surface out the gaps which are required to be addressed for an overall improvement of education system points associated with teachers and teaching pedagogy. With the given approach, teachers can focus upon learner-centric approach for the overall delivery of knowledge to the aspiring students. In our institution in a regular approach for gathering feedback, it is seen that a feedback form is given to every student at a regular interval of time to gather information about faculty's teaching quality at IITM Janakpuri, New Delhi. Students filled a feedback form by assigning marks for each parameter ranging from 1 to 5. A feedback report is provided to each faculty member at the end of the semester. This report helps teachers to improve his/her performance for forthcoming semesters. The feedback system helps in determining a few aspects of the good teaching and qualities of a particular faculty member.

Now the problem with these forms is that they do not get filled if a student is absent on that particular day when feedback is taken during working hours. Also, it is a hectic job to find those average scores for a particular faculty member. Analysis of feedback forms obtained from students is a very time-consuming process. It takes from weeks to months for getting the final feedback reports of each faculty member. It has been decided that the feedback system must be online so that feedback reports must be generated instantly. The proposed system is a module of enterprise resource planning for colleges, schools, and universities. This module can be used in any institutes and college after some changes.

The paper furnished over here tried to give the approaches used in the past to gather the feedback of the students and various aspects and parameters taken care.

The reaming paper is organized into seven sections: Section 16.2 discusses the literature review. Section 16.3 discusses the software requirement specification document. The experimental setup is discussed in Section 16.4. The design phase is discussed in Section 16.5. Coding and testing being discussed in Section 16.6. Results and discussion are given in Section 16.7. The chapters has been concluded in Section 16.8.

## 16.2 LITERATURE REVIEW

The system design started from the study of feedback system which was already available and an insight into such system has been brought out by Franklin et al. (1994)

Hatziapostolou and Paraskakis (2010) have given an overview of the feedback system, which points out that the use of the feedback system is quite prevalent and can be effectively used if the students are given, as per their personal addressing, the criteria and within a stipulated time. There are certain issues associated with the approach that students are not motivated and the expected outcome is not furnished out due to the same reason. Online Feedback System is an e-tool that results in an alternative to decisive feedback. Their aim was to enhance the feedback quality by the way of communication change with the students. As a simple approach for students about sharing their views in feedback that certainly puts a better approach for the feedback submission. The results of such development suggested the overall improvement in the motivation of students and the efficiency of the system data processing related to the feedback system. The usage of online feedback certainly provided an encouraging response.

(Houten and Hill, 1975) have given their view on developmental input is instrumental within the learning involvement of a student. It can be compelling in advancing learning on the off chance that it is convenient, individual, sensible, motivational, and in coordinate connection with appraisal criteria. In their paper, they display the Online Feedback Framework, an e-learning apparatus that viably underpins the arrangement of developmental input. Our points are to improve criticism gathering and to fortify the quality of criticism through the way input is communicated to the students. They propose that a successful input communication component ought to be coordinated into a student's online learning space and it is expected that this arrangement will propel students to lock in with criticism.

This work had put an emphasis on the applicability of the feedback system in case of medical studies. Students are given some parameters which were taken from the majority and individual parameters were evaluated. The majority of teachers have also responded that a good feedback system also gives a glimpse of their efforts which must be corrected to the right direction as per response (Husain and Khan, 2016).

These works discussed the continual improvement in the system, based on regularity perception associated with the feedback system, which tell about the psychotherapist improvement in the overall system (Wiggins, 1993).

Based on the above literature review, Software development cell of IITM Janakpuri, New Delhi proposes the state of the art student feedback management system.

## 16.3 SOFTWARE REQUIREMENT AND SPECIFICATION DOCUMENT

Feedback-form is to provide anytime service for the students as well as for the faculty. It simplifies the task and reduces the work regarding the feedback process. It manages the details of all the students and their entered feedbacks into a database. It minimizes the time of calculating the average scores for each faculty. Feedback system is comprised of following components:

### *16.3.1 ADMIN*

The admin module is required for signing up the students according to the university registration number (unique), so that students will be eligible to fill up the feedback form.

### *16.3.2 LOG-IN MODULE FOR STUDENTS AND FACULTY*

A Log-in module for a particular student is required for filling up the feedback form. The same is required for faculty so that they can view their feedback reports in their particular subject.

### *16.3.3 FEEDBACK MODULE*

The feedback module is the core part of the whole academic system as it is the form that is required to provide marks/grading to the faculties by the students through the feedback form. Students can access the form once after signing in through their log-in module using their university registration number (unique) as a username and password (provided during signing up).

At present, Feedback form has 12 parameters/attributes.

## 16.4 EXPERIMENTAL SETUP

### *16.4.1 TOOLS USED*

*XAMPP SERVER*: It contains Apache and MySQL.

### *16.4.2 LANGUAGE USED*

HTML, to create the front end and PHP for back end or running data query Software Life Cycle.

### *16.4.3 MODEL USED*

Iterative Enhancement life cycle Model.

## 16.5 DESIGN PHASE

We have designed the Data Flow diagram and ER diagrams in this phase (Figure 16.1). We also designed database in MySQL. All tables are normalized in the database.

## 16.6 CODING AND UNIT TESTING AND SCREENSHOTS

### *16.6.1 LOGIN FORM*

Details are to be entered by students.

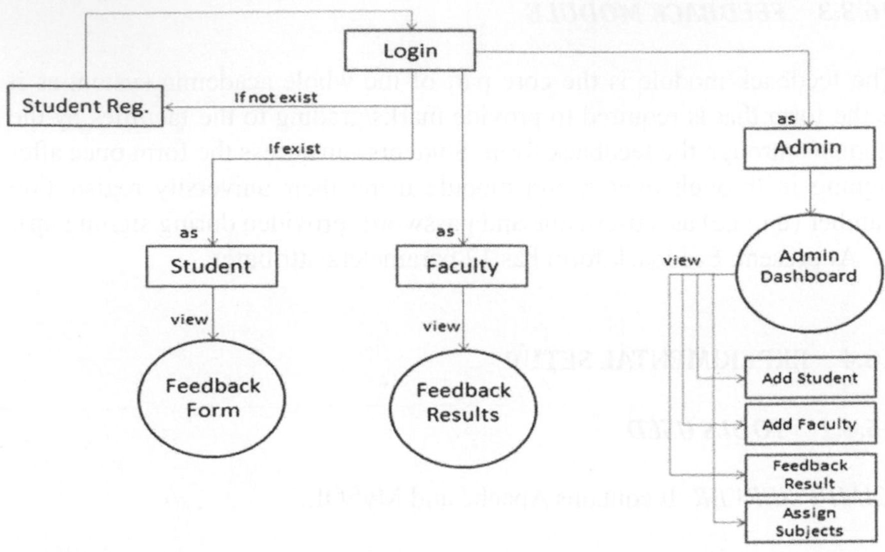


**FIGURE 16.1** Data flow diagram for the project.

Figure 16.2 shows the login form which is to be filled by students to see the feedback form shown in Figure 16.3, which is required to be filled by the student. It contains 12 questions which students have to answer by giving marks between 1 and 5.

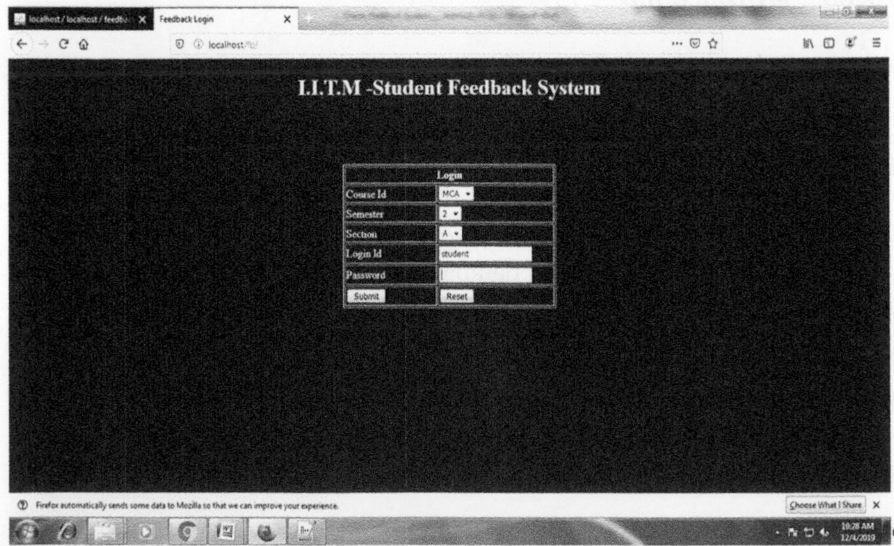


**FIGURE 16.2** Login form.

### 16.6.2 FEEDBACK FORM

localhost / localhost / feedba… | Untitled Document

localhost/fb/feedbackmain.php

skip

I.I.T.M Student Feedback System

Faculty Name: Dr. Sandhaya Maitra Subject Name: Computer Graphics

Points Reflection 1(Poor) 2(Fair) 3(Good) 4(Very Good) 5 (Excellent)

| | |
|---|---|
| Q1. | The Syllabus and learning objective were properly defind with clarity about the depth in each. 1 2 3 4 5 |
| Q2 | Coverage of sylabus is through, Comprehensive and done in time. 1 2 3 4 5 |
| Q3 | The Faculty act as a role model and regular without missing any class. 1 2 3 4 5 |
| Q4 | The faculty clearly set fourth his/her expectationsof the students. 1 2 3 4 5 |
| Q5 | The faculty is able to handle the doubts and clarifications quite effectively and satisfactorily 1 2 3 4 5 |
| Q6 | Faculty voice and expression are loud and clear. 1 2 3 4 5 |
| Q7 | The faculty is able to control the class and create confidence among the students. 1 2 3 4 5 |
| Q8 | Outside the class the faculty provides help in solving my problems. 1 2 3 4 5 |
| Q9 | The class is interactive with faculty providing enough opprtunity for the two way communication. 1 2 3 4 5 |
| Q10 | The faculty uses teaching aids (Like White board , OHP, Power point etc.) effectively. 1 2 3 4 5 |
| Q11 | Faculty is very systematic, objective and unbiased in my evaluation. 1 2 3 4 5 |
| Q12 | Overall evalulation for the faculty for the course is? |

Firefox automatically sends some data to Mozilla so that we can improve your experience.

**FIGURE 16.3** Feedback form.

### 16.6.3 ADMIN LOGIN PANEL

Figure 16.4 shows admin login which is filled by admin to access all the admin privileges. Admin Dashboard shown in Figure 16.5 contains the following four subpanels. Take a backup, change the password of students, upload data, generate reports, and logout.

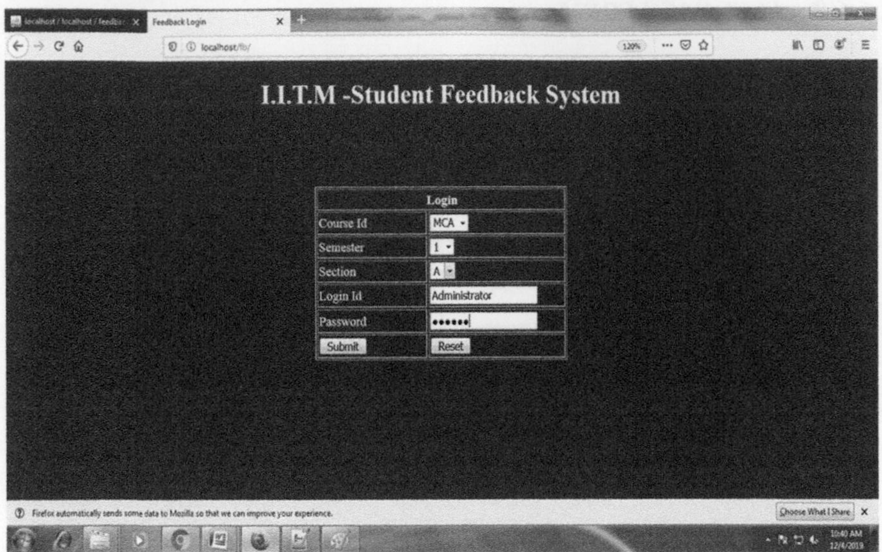


**FIGURE 16.4** Admin Login window is the same with the only difference that the User Name is Administrator.

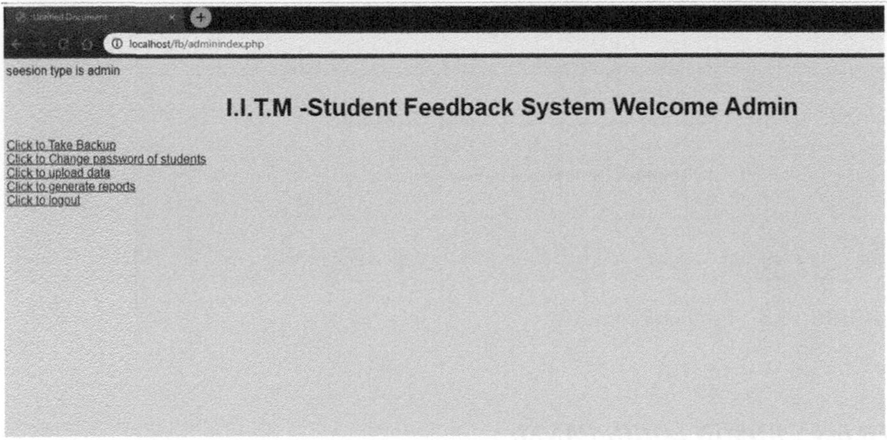


**FIGURE 16.5** Admin Panel showing various options.

**FIGURE 16.6** Admin Login window to take backup.

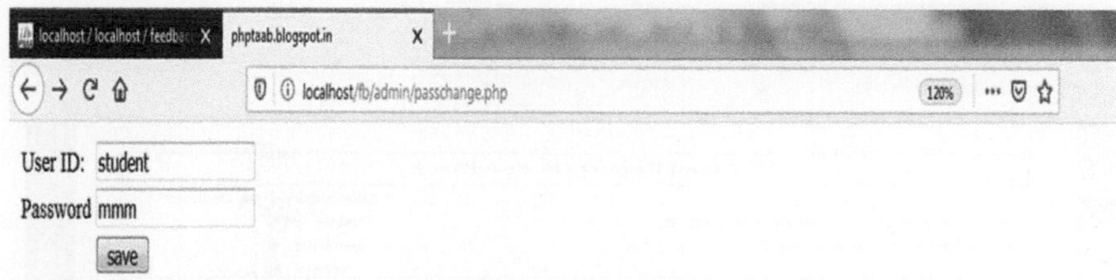


**FIGURE 16.7** Admin Login window change student password.

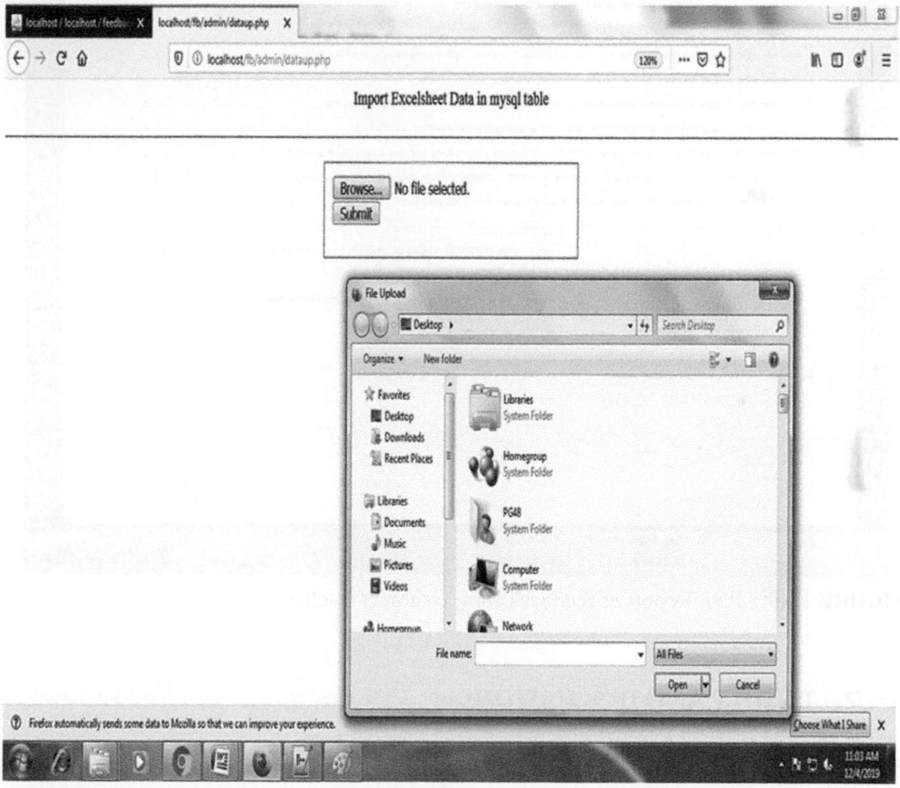

**FIGURE 16.8** Upload data Window for admin.

During coding, our team tested each and every step to ensure that flow of the software is correct and fixes all the bugs. Only college students are applicable for signup and login into this system. If registration ID and Password do not match or not found into the record then it ensures that the student is not able to login to the system. Students also can't fill the form if already filled for that particular period. The feedback form is only filled by the students.

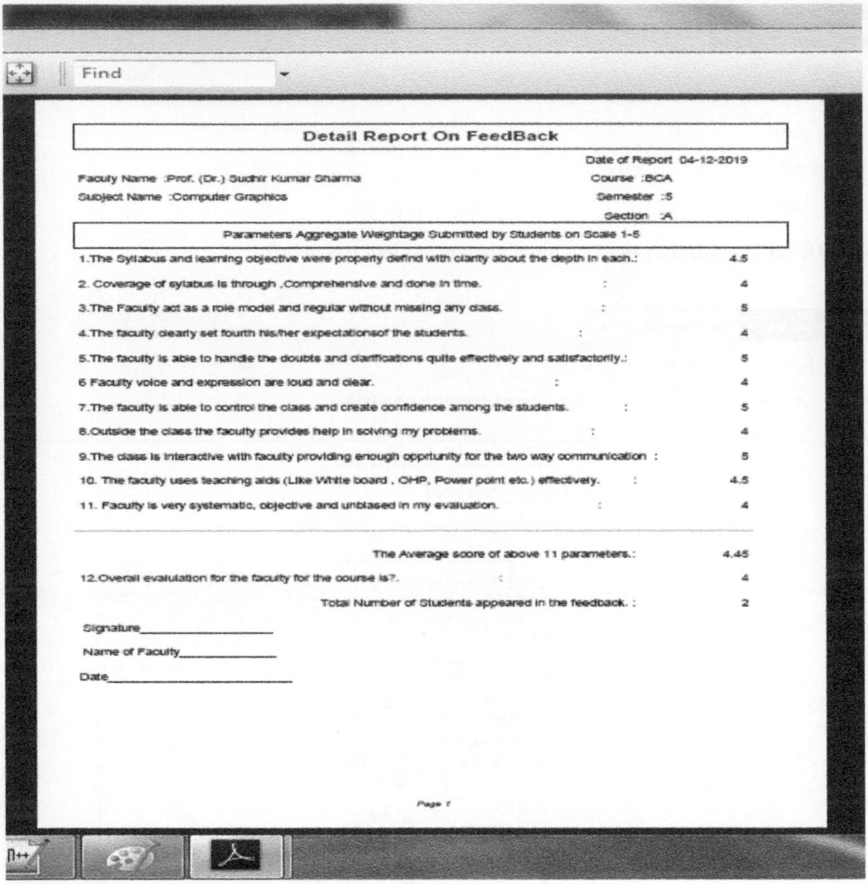

Find

**Detail Report On FeedBack**

Date of Report 04-12-2019

Facuty Name :Prof. (Dr.) Sudhir Kumar Sharma — Course :BCA

Subject Name :Computer Graphics — Semester :5

Section :A

| Parameters Aggregate Weightage Submitted by Students on Scale 1-5 | |
|---|---|
| 1.The Syllabus and learning objective were properly defind with clarity about the depth in each.: | 4.5 |
| 2. Coverage of sylabus is through ,Comprehensive and done in time. : | 4 |
| 3.The Faculty act as a role model and regular without missing any class. : | 5 |
| 4.The faculty clearly set fourth his/her expectationsof the students. : | 4 |
| 5.The faculty is able to handle the doubts and clarifications quite effectively and satisfactorily.: | 5 |
| 6 Faculty voice and expression are loud and clear. : | 4 |
| 7.The faculty is able to control the class and create confidence among the students. : | 5 |
| 8.Outside the class the faculty provides help in solving my problems. : | 4 |
| 9.The class is interactive with faculty providing enough opprtunity for the two way communication : | 5 |
| 10. The faculty uses teaching aids (Like White board , OHP, Power point etc.) effectively. : | 4.5 |
| 11. Faculty is very systematic, objective and unbiased in my evaluation. : | 4 |
| The Average score of above 11 parameters.: | 4.45 |
| 12.Overall evalulation for the faculty for the course is?. : | 4 |
| Total Number of Students appeared in the feedback. : | 2 |

Signature________________

Name of Faculty______________

Date____________________

Page 1

**FIGURE 16.9** PDF Report of feedback for the subject teacher.

## 16.7 RESULT AND DISCUSSIONS

Some characteristics of this ICT application for higher education are as follows: Student's feedbacks directly entered in the database, final feedback reports will be generated within minutes, teachers can see their reports from their terminals, this application helps in improving their teaching/lecture delivering process, feedbacks can be taken easily many times within semester, head of the department, dean of the department, and director/principal and management can view the feedback report of any faculty member. They can access comparative feedback class-wise online from their terminals.

A sample copy of a feedback report is reported in the appendix. Class-wise and department-wise consolidated reports are also generated. This online feedback software is successfully implemented at IITM Janakpuri, New Delhi. This software can be used in any school and college after some changes.

## 16.8 CONCLUSION

This paper presented a module of the ERP system for college. This module is known as "Online Students' Feedback Management System for Higher Education." The proposed system is based on three-tier architecture. The first tier is designed using HTML pages. Programming JavaScript is used for client-side validation purposes. The second tier is implemented through PHP language at the middle layer. The third tier of examination system employs MySQL database. The proposed software is successfully executed at the end of last semester at IITM Janakpuri, New Delhi.

## KEYWORDS

- **information and communication technology**
- **online students' feedback management system**
- **client–server computing**
- **HTML**
- **PHP**

## REFERENCES

Franklin, G. F., Powell, J. D., Emami-Naeini, A., Powell, J. D. *Feedback Control of Dynamic Systems*. Addison-Wesley: Reading, MA; 1994.

Hatziapostolou, T., Paraskakis, I. Enhancing the Impact of Formative Feedback on Student Learning Through an Online Feedback System. *Electronic Journal of e-Learning*, 2010, 8(2), 111–22.

Houten, R. V., Hill, S., Parsons, M. An Analysis of a Performance Feedback System: The Effects of Timing and Feedback, Public Posting, and Praise Upon Academic Performance and Peer Interaction 1. *Journal of Applied Behavior Analysis*, 1975, 8(4), 449–57.

Husain, M., Khan, S. Students' Feedback: An Effective Tool in Teachers' Evaluation System. *International Journal of Applied and Basic Medical Research*, 2016, 6(3), 178.

Wiggins, G. P. Assessing Student Performance: Exploring the Purpose and Limits of Testing. Jossey-Bass; 1993.

## CHAPTER 17

# The Role of ICT in Higher Education: Emerging Issues and Challenges

PALLAVI PAL[1] and RAKESH KUMAR[2*]

[1]*Department of Law, University School of Law and Legal Studies, GGSIPU, Dwarka, New Delhi, India*

[2]*Department of Law, University School of Law and Legal Studies, GGSIPU, Sector 16C, Dwarka, New Delhi, India*

[*]*Corresponding author. E-mail: rakesh.law@gmail.com*

## ABSTRACT

Education has always been identified as a priority sector for all the elected Government to emancipate masses at large from abject ignorance and illiteracy and recognized as important instruments for economic development, technological progress, reduction in poverty, and eradication of social inequalities in a country. The prime concern of this paper is to examine the significance the Information Technology as a facilitator in enabling Higher Education in light of the current status of admission/enrolment of students particularly in higher educational institutions and the factors that disable them to enroll themselves for the higher studies. To tackle the issues of low enrollment the Government of India has adopted a number of significant measures to make educational rights a practical reality by incorporating the information and technology as a facilitator in its endeavor to ensure education for all in new and emerging India. The emerging information and communication technology (ICT) trends, introduced in educational platforms like MOOCs, SWAYAM, etc., to ensure education easily accessible and affordable for a large section of society in a practical sense.

## 17.1 INTRODUCTION

Education is one of the most significant ingredients for translating and realizing human resources potential and for enabling any nation to become knowledge superpower on the knowledge landscape. It is intrinsically related to the right to preserve distinct features and the single most important instrument for nation's economic development, cultural reproduction, socialization, identity formation, and transmission.

"According to Census data of 2011, the total population of India in 2011 was 121.09 crore. The person professing Hindu religious belief and persuasion comprises of 79.8%; Muslim 14.2%; Christian 2.3%; Sikh 1.7%; Jain 0.4%; Buddhist 0.7%; other religions and persuasions 0.7% and people not stated their religion comprises of religion not stated 0.2%" (Census, 2001;2011). If the existing population profile is being examined from the perspective of literacy and numeracy, the literacy rate of various religious groups reflects diversity in the same fashion as their religious beliefs and practices. The literacy rate of the Hindu population is 64.5%, Muslim 60%, Christian 80.3%, Sikh 70.4%, Buddhist 73%, Jains 95%, and other minority groups are having a literacy rate of 50% (Census, 2001;2011).

In complete contrast to literacy rate, that is, those who can write and read, the "total enrolments in higher educational institutions are merely 37.4 million consisting of 19.2 million male scholar and 18.2 million girl scholars reflecting very sorry states of affairs. The girl scholars comprises of 48.6% of the total enrolment in higher education. In India, Gross Enrolment Ratio in Higher education quantified as a mere 26.3%, between the age group of 18 and 23 years. Gross Enrolment Ratio for boy scholars is 26.3% and for girl scholars it is narrowly better at 26.4%. From a social justice perspective, the marginalized section of Indian society consisting of Scheduled Castes and Scheduled Tribes, it is 23% and 17.2%, respectively, in contrast to the national GER of 26.3%. At All India level pupil–teacher ratio (PTR), works out to be 26 and 24 if only regular enrolment in educational institutions is considered. For the University and its affiliated colleges, the PTR is 29 for regular mode" (AISHE, 2018–2019).

The educational attainment of various groups demonstrates that the majority of our population is illiterate and ignorant. Education is considered to be the single most powerful instrument for the progress and emancipation of such huge populations. The Supreme Court of India in this regard rightly observed this by saying, "The State, with its grossly inadequate budgetary allocation, slow-moving and insensitive, and unresponsive administrative setup, miserably failed to fully harness the genius of the Indian people. Invariably, the unbiased education that is transmitted by the state-controlled machinery, lacking updated teaching material that makes the students having merely bookish knowledge without any vocational training as a result adequate number of jobs are not available" (TMA Pai Foundation v State of Karnataka, 2002). NEP, 2019 also pointed out "The world is witnessing rapid changes in the knowledge fields. With the invention of cloud computing, machine learning, and artificial intelligence, many semi- and unskilled jobs throughout glove are expected to be taken over by machines while the need for skilled manpower, especially involving mathematics, computer science, data mining, and deep learning, will be increasing in demand." (TMA Pai Foundation v State of Karnataka, 2002).

In this backdrop where there is an absence of quality learning and education and absence of a sufficient number of Schools and Colleges with an adequate number of teachers, an attempt is being made to analyze the role of ICT in facilitating access of secondary and higher education to masses at large. This paper is divided into five parts:

1. The status of an educational institution at a higher education level.
2. Steps taken by the Government of India and the recommendation of various committees.
3. ICT initiative techniques initiated by the Government of India to enhance the standard and quality of education.
4. Agenda for change.
5. Concluding observation.

1. *Status of Education and Educational Institution*: AISHE Report, 2019, noted that throughout India the "total number of recognized universities, colleges, and standalone institutions by UGC, AICTE, and other regulatory bodies comprises of 99,339 and 10,725, respectively, out of which 298 Universities are affiliating, that is, having colleges; 385 universities are under private management. From a spatial distribution perspective, rural areas are having 394 Universities and for catering the educational needs of women exclusively merely 16 University have been established." (Article 15(3) of Indian Constitution enjoins the State to make special provisions for the empowerment of women and children). "Further, privately managed colleges comprise of 77.08% out of which 64.3% are unaided and 13.5% aided by the state. The southern states, such as Telangana, Andhra Pradesh, Tamil Nadu, and Uttar Pradesh, having

a bulk of private-unaided colleges over 85%, whereas Assam has 16.0% private-unaided colleges" (TMA Pai Foundation v State of Karnataka, 2002) (AISHE, 2018–2019).

The issues of low enrolment ratio may be attributed to a shortage of well-trained teaching faculties, poor infrastructure, administrative difficulties in getting affiliation and recognition, unsustainable expenses in terms of unaffordable tuition fees, and expensive and outdated reading material, irrelevant curricula, absence of library, etc.

The increasing dropout ratio may be attributed to nonaffordability of higher studies fees structure which is increasing every year irrespective of the quality of education provided in those institutions.

2. *Steps taken by the government and recommendations of various committees:* Since the post-independence period, the Government is regularly reviewing the policies on Higher Education in India to make it compatible with the changing needs of the people and their aspirations. The first such attempt was made by The Radhakrishnan Commission Report (University Education Commission, 1948–1949), which was appointed with the aim of identifying and reporting the shortcomings in India's University education system and suggest measures that may be advisable for the present, as well as future requirements, of the nation. It was reinforced by the University Education Commission Report (Commission, University Education Commission, 1964–1966), that is, "Kothari Commission." The objective behind this was to augment education with modernization, enhance productivity, and ensure social and national assimilations by developing spiritual and moral percepts among students pursuing higher education to ensure holistic development. The Kothari Commission Report forms the prime basis for New Education Policy (Education, 1986) and Program of Action (Programme of Action Report, 1992). Further, the "National Knowledge Commission (National Knowledge Commission report, 2006–2009)" was set up in June 2005, "to build excellence particularly in the tertiary education system to meet the market requirements of the present century to enhance India's competitive advantage in the field application and dissemination of knowledge." (Pitroda, 2006–2009)

In pursuance to recommendations of various committees, several legislative measures have been initiated by the Government for the development of education at primary, secondary, and tertiary education levels. The 86th Amendment Act, 2002, inserted Article

21A to Constitution of India which mandate for free and compulsory education to children till completion of 14 years. Under Articles 21, the right to education has been recognized as a Fundamental Right for every citizen as a part of the right to live with human dignity. The dignified rights of worth cannot be imagined in the absence of meaningful educational attainment. The Constitution 86th Amendment Act, 2002 also amended Article 45 to provide early childhood care for all children until they complete the age of 6 years. To operationalize this amendment the Free and Compulsory Education Act, 2009, that is, "Right to Education Act, 2009" was passed by the Parliament for taking care of elementary education. For addressing the concern of Higher education, several Acts have been enacted by the Parliament. These are as follows:

1. The Central Educational Institution (Reservation in Admission) Act, 2006
2. The University Grants Commission Act, 1956
3. The National Commission for Minority Education Institution Act, 2004
4. The Central Universities Act, 2009
5. The All India Council for Technical Education Act, 1987
6. Indira Gandhi National Open Universities Act, 1985
7. National Council for Teachers Education Act, 1993
8. The Higher Education Commission of India Act, 2018.

3. *ICT techniques devised by the Government of India to enhance the standard and quality of education:* The teaching methods at Indian Universities are still conventional and traditional which are far below the international standards. None of Indian University today featured in any of top 200 institutions across the world. To address this problem of low enrolment ratio, the government has taken several initiatives by combining accessibility with affordability by incorporating the use of ICT in higher education.

The NEP, 2019 rightly recognized India's prominent position as a worldwide technology leader in information and communication. "Digital India Campaign intended to transform the entire country into a digitally empowered knowledge society. While education will play a censorious role in this transformation, technology itself will play a crucial role in the enhancement of the educational system." (Parab, 2014)

Thus, ICT tools have a significant edge when it comes to issues of imparting and disseminating education at various levels. It may be ascertained from the followings:

First, ICT provides online education which is comparatively less costly than the formal education system and that too without compromising upon the quality of information available, at the low cost of the infrastructure and vast learner base. The learning and teaching material available online will facilitate the students to realize their educational goal easily in time and space;

Second, on an online platform, the lectures and speeches are directly delivered by the best academicians ensuring high-quality teaching. It provides conceptual clarity as the online media can be replayed if students so desired.

Third, the online educational resources can be extensively used to address the most neglected rural areas where higher education reach is as low 4.5% for the male population and 2.2% for females as against 17% for urban males and 13% for the female population.

Fourth, ICT is a medium through which the youth can learn vocational training which will address unemployment issues not only in their state but even outside.

Fifth, it enhances the skills of learners as ICT provides them with various online courses and training, it helps those unfortunate classes of people who could not afford to buy expensive books and reading material thus helping the State to achieve its social welfare objective;

Sixthly, the household expense on Higher Education is bound to rise significantly providing the educational opportunity for unreached masses in higher education; the ICT can play pivotal roles.

Lastly, even the smartphones available these days will enable the students to learn without incurring expenses on buying PCs, laptops.

The Government of India renewed thrust may be ascertained from The Eleventh Five Year Plan (2007–2012) which was widely proclaimed as "Education Plan" and also known as "Second Wave" because it has set an ambitious target of 15% enrolment rate which was up from 10% enrolment target set during Tenth Plan. "For augmenting academic infrastructure in the area of higher education, total financial allocation of Rs. 47,000 crores was made resulting into in building of a significant number of Educational institutions of eminence such as IITs, IIITs, NITs, IIMs, etc. (Nair, 2015) " University Grants Commission has played a vital role in devising new policies and schemes and implementing them by transforming into an action plan.

During the Eleventh Five Year Plan, "the National Mission on Education through Information Communication Technology (NME-ICT)" was launched. Under this initiative, universities and colleges have been provided with broadband connectivity (Plan, 2012–2017)" There established virtual labs for science and engineering students. "Aakash a low-cost computing cum access device was invented for significant engagements. Through these kinds of innovative technologies, the vision of Twelfth Plan, that is, the three Es'– Expansion, Equity, and Excellence, sought to be achieved. (Plan, 2012–2017)"

The third "E," that is, Excellence in terms of quality sought to be achieved through the "Technical Education Quality Improvement Program (TEQUIP, 2003–2009)." with an investment of 1378 crores which covered about 127 Engineering Institutions. The second phase of (TEQUIP 2010–2014) extended to another 190 odd institutions. The outcome of the first phase has marked an improvement in the placement of graduates, postgraduates, and doctoral programs. It also enhanced the research quality. It may be noted here that the aim of education is not just to acquire or impart knowledge rather to ensure full development of personality beyond schooling. The holistic education imparted through various modes of teaching and learning prepares the students for life and work, thus, economically empowering the nations. Many institutions of Higher Education all over the world have implemented 'Liberal Education' through various disciplines, like Humanities, Arts, Mathematics, Sciences, etc. The Higher education commences from the undergraduate level of students and goes on to doctoral levels. At every level of education, the technology can effectively motivate the students, makes learning more interesting and lively, and renew teacher enthusiasm as they learn new skills and techniques. Technology helps the students to understand any abstract concepts clearly and easily. Information technology has become an integral component of holistic learning and teaching pedagogy. It is the need of today. ICT is helpful for those children who cannot afford higher education coaching classes or tuition fees. It provides us with new techniques, skills, and teaching for research and it has proved powerful support for innovation.

The following tools and techniques have been devised by the Government to enhance the quality of education:

1. *SWAYAM (*PIB, 2018)**:** SWAYAM "(Study Webs of Active Learning for Young Aspiring Minds) is a homemade initiative as a part of IT Massive Open Online Courses (MOOCs) (PIB, 2018) initiated by the Government of India in the year 2017 with the objective to provide best possible education system in terms of quality, equity, and accessibility so as to bring the disadvantaged sections of society into the mainstream. The MOOCs involves interactive learning to a massive number of students at the same time (Convention, 2017)" There are "four components in the MOOC scheme: (a) Video-lecture components covering the entire course; (b) E-reading resources; (c) self-assessment method to assess the students through assignments and quizzes; (d) there are discussion forums for posing queries (HRD, 2010).
2. *NPTEL:* The NME-ICT "(The National Mission on Education through Information and Communication Technology) is a nodal funding agency for NPTEL, that is, National Program on Technology-Enabled Learning." (HRD, 2010) NPTEL is combined efforts of IITs and IISCs introduced in the year 1999 with an aim to provide quality education to those students who are interested in learning from IITs. The main aim was to create web and video online courses in all branches of engineering and physical sciences at undergraduates and postgraduates levels and also in management stream at postgraduate level (PIB, 2018).
3. *SWAYAM PRABHA:* "SWAYAM PRABHA" is one of the smartest digital initiative introduced in the year 2015 comprising of 32 DTH channels with educational content with the object to promote learning telecasted 24 × 7 basis. Students can choose the time slots as per their convenience. "The DTH channels cover the various disciplines such as (a) arts, science, humanities, law, agriculture science, medical field in higher educational domain. (b) School education from grade 9th to 12th modules, preparedness for competitive examinations. (c) IIT-PAL to prepare the children of class 11th and 12th for the entrance examination of JEE Advanced." (HRD, 2010) (PIB, 2018) and help in conceptual understanding so that good quality students can enter IITs.
4. *National Digital Library* (*NDL*) (MOOC, an initiative under NME-ICT, 2018)**:** The project of the "Development of National Digital Library was assigned to IIT Kharagpur under NME-ICT by M.H.R.D." (MOOC, an initiative under NME-ICT, 2018). Its

objective is to provide online access to educational content from primary to tertiary level with intellectual inputs including technical education. The NDL is having e-resources comprising more than 7 million books, journals, and periodicals. It covers all major domains of education."

5. *National Academic Depository:* "National Academic Depository is another startup by MHRD to provide Digital Academic certificates which are accessible in a secure manner. (MOOC, an initiative under NME-ICT, 2018)" In this, the Academic Award issued by the Academic Institutions are preserved and are issued by the NAD and can be accessed by its website when and where needed. Its objective is to reduce the efforts of collecting, maintaining, and even avoiding the risk of misplacing the certificates (MOOC,an initiative under NME-ICT, 2018).
6. *E-Shodh Sindhu:* It is an initiative of M.H.R.D, Government of India, being executed by *INFLIBNET* center. Its objective is to make available the best available education resources throughout the world to all higher educational institutions through E-Shodh Sindhu. It provides numerous "international electronic journals and books. The *INFLIBNET* is one such scheme implemented at Gandhinagar (Gujarat)" (MOOC, an initiative under NME-ICT, 2018).
7. *Virtual Labs:* "The Virtual Lab provides remote experimentation to all enthusiastic and curious students who were earlier unable to perform experiments due to physical distances and lack of resources with the help of a computer with broadband connectivity" (MOOC, an initiative under NME-ICT, 2018) (MOOC,an initiative under NME-ICT, 2018). "Over 205 virtual labs in 9 engineering and science disciplines, comprising about 1515 experiments are operational and currently being accessed by more than 6 lakh students" (MOOC, an initiative under NME-ICT, 2018)
8. *Campus Connectivity:* The Government has also planned to make all the universities and campus Wi-Fi enabled in line with IITs, IIMs, and NITs.
9. *Talk to a Teacher:* It is initiated by the Institute of Information and Technology Bombay, under the broad umbrella of "NME-ICT" it provides free access to the online teachings by faculty members at IIT Bombay. It can be viewed on personal computers/

laptops having a headphone and Internet connection"(MOOC,an initiative under NME-ICT, 2018). No special registration is required for this as it is not a certificate course. It covers all major disciplines of education. It also has an "Ask-a-Question" platform through which students from across the country can ask any question relating to the course and at prescribed time slots.

10. *E-Acharya:* It is also known as an integrated E-content portal of "NME-ICT where e-content is preserved at repository platform of INFLIBNET center, Gandhinagar.
11. *E-Kalpa:* It is yet "another initiative of M.H.R.D creating learning environment through digital media in India."
12. *FOSSEE:* "*Free and Open Source Software for Education* has been promoting the use of open-source software in the field of education. It includes documentation; spoken tutorials; conferences; awareness programs, etc., makes them available for free to download." The list is never-ending as India is a developing country the technology also grows with the nation.

4. *Agenda for Change:* The increasing role of ICT was acknowledged by NEP, 2019, which provided that " the paradigm of learning involving classrooms, as well as methods of imparting teaching, is bound to witness tremendous change by application of innovations involving information technologies with the help of artificial intelligence, block chains, data mining, smart boards, other forms of educational software (Draft, 2019)."

For giving further thrust upon the advancement of research mechanism it provided for setting up "the National Educational Alliance for Technology (N.E.A.T), for the free exchange of ideas on the use of technology to enhance the process of learning, assessment, planning, administration, etc. (Draft, 2019).

Further, "the N.E.A.T is a platform where the brainstorming of experts will take place, where their expertise on the subject will be shared at the grass root level. It will facilitate in democratizing technology use among the scholar (Draft, 2019)

Besides this, a multiple variety of educational software will be developed for teaching community and intended beneficiary in all major Indian languages including students in remote areas and differently-able students. Smart classroom equipment and digital learning classrooms will be made available to teachers at all schools so that teachers can suitably integrate open educational videos into teaching–learning practices (Draft, 2019)."

Therefore, in view of the Draft NEP, 2019, the following measures may be initiated to make ICT in higher education a living reality.

1. Awareness of Information Technology has to be provided otherwise the low IT literacy will defeat the very purpose of the scheme of incorporating ICT in the education sector. The majority of the people still reside in rural areas and they do not know even the basics of computer system then how can it be expected from them to learn and take advantage of various modules of ICT.
2. Another challenge could be the poor access to the Internet for the rural population as they are already struggling to survive without electricity; the Internet is still a far-off dream for them.
3. The language barrier is yet another challenge as the information is available usually in common English medium but everyone is not expected to be well versed with the language as only "read and write" will not serve the purpose rather the objective is to understand the available information and apply that in practical life as well.
4. Proper information technology infrastructure has to be developed to ease the use of technology. Even today, in 21st century, computer system is a luxury item for a few poor classes of people.
5. To reduce the social inequalities and the gaps between rich and poor, technology will play a vital role by providing that quality of education which was once unaffordable for some.
6. In most of the villages in rural areas people could not afford basic sustenance then how can we expect them to own PCs/laptops or even smartphones.
7. "There is a need for training all stakeholders in ICT" otherwise it will give rise to a divide in the class between students who are tech-savvy and those who are not tech-savvy. Those students who have computers in their homes would understand better in class and answer quickly as compared to those who do not have.
8. It may also lead to a shift of focus from the primary goal of teaching–learning to the development of ICT skills which is the secondary goal.

## 17.2 CONCLUDING OBSERVATION

The standard of education has tremendously risen due to the adoption of Information Technology in the education sector. The quality of research and experimentation has taken a new direction; ICT provides enormous information on anything, anywhere, and anytime. No place is left untouched in terms of resources to acquire knowledge. Moreover, it provides access to education irrespective of temporal and spatial restrictions. Nonetheless, it has become an indispensable support system in the field of education especially for higher education as it could address some of the challenges in our country like insufficient resources for research which was once there but now, we can access uncountable sites. Similarly, a wide variety of course material for every discipline is available free of cost. Hence, students, who could not afford earlier, now can make use of those resources to the fullest to realize their potential and reach the zenith. ICT helps in dynamic ways whether it is teaching, learning, working online, business, governance, banking, etc. ICT enabled education has the power of transforming higher education in India as well as it will lead to the democratization of education. New emerging initiatives, such as SWAYAM, SWAYAM Prabha, e-yantra, e-Kalpa, National Digital Library, etc., have helped people from different parts of the world to access education through online resources available. No need to physically go to the library or join expensive coaching or costly books.

## KEYWORDS

- **higher education**
- **information communication technology**
- **TEQUIP**
- **NEAT**
- **University Education Commission**
- **human resource development**
- **teaching and learning**
- **Kothari Commission**
- **massive open online courses**

## REFERENCES

Agarwal, Pawan. *Indian Higher Education: Envisioning the Future*; New Delhi: Sage Publication; 2009, p. 488.

AISHE (All India Survey on Higher Education). *Annual Report (2018–2019*), "Ministry of Human Resource and Development, *department of Higher Education*", Government of India.

Census Data (2001), Office of the Registrar General and Census Commissioner, India, Ministry of Home Affairs, Government of India.

Draft of National Education Policy, 2019. Ministry of Human Resource Development, Government of India *E-Learning Project Report 2018*, Press Information Bureau, Ministry of Human Resource Development, Government of India.

Jain, C.; Prasad, N. (2018), *Quality of Secondary Education in India*; Springer Nature Singapore Pte Ltd., 2018.

Ministry of Human Resource Development, Government of India visited on www.mhrd.gov.in.

MOOCs Massive Open Online Courses An initiative under National Mission on Education through Information Communication Technology (NME-ICT) Programme, (2018). Department of Higher Education, Ministry of Human Resource Development. Government of India.

Nair, Geeta (2015), Gendered Impact of Globalization of Higher Education. H.R. College of Commerce and Economics, India, p 10.

*National Convention on Digital Initiatives on Higher Education Report,* 2017. Department of higher education. Government of India.

*National Education Policy (2019),* Ministry of Human Resource Development, Government of India, p 50 (Para 23.2–23.6)

National Knowledge Commission report, 2006–2009. Sam Pitroda. Ministry of Human Resource Development, Government of India.

National Project Implementation Unit Impact Evaluation of Technical Education Quality Improvement Programme, Phase I. 2003–2009. Government of India.

*New Policy on Education Report 1986.* Ministry of Human Resource Development, Government of India. New Delhi

Parab, Gyan. Technology use and integration-global technology accessed on https://www.gyanparab.xyz/

Pegu, U. Kr (2014), Information Communication & Technology in Higher Education: Challenges and Opportunities, *International Journal of Information & Computation Technology,* 4(5), pp 513–518.

*Programme of Action Report 1992.* Ministry of Human Resource Development, Department of Education. Government of India

*TMA Pai Foundation* v. *State of Karnataka* (2002) SCC 495 (25 November 2002).

Twelfth Five-year Plan, Education Sector (2012–2017) Report, vol. III, Ministry of Human Resource Development, Government of India.

*University Education Commission Report, 1964–1966,* Ministry of Human Resource Development, Government of India.

*University Education Commission, 1948–1949. Radhakrishnan Commission* Report. Ministry of Human Resource Development, Government of India.

CHAPTER 18

# Comprehensive Tool to Improve Program Outcome Attainment by Integrating Indirect Internal Assessment

ANITHA SENATHI*, KSHIPRA TATKARE, and SUJATA OAK

*Ramrao Adik Institute of Technology, Nerul, Navi Mumbai 400706, Maharashtra, India*

*Corresponding author. E-mail: anita.senathi@rait.ac.in*

## ABSTRACT

The National Board of Accreditation self-assessment report for Tier-II engineering institutions in the country has ten different criteria covering different aspects of providing engineering education. These criteria rigorously assess the quality of engineering education offered by different programs of a nonautonomous engineering institution affiliated to a university. The Criterion 3 assesses the program outcomes (POs) attainment with the attainment of course outcomes (COs). Different approaches have been adopted by engineering institutions for the calculation of COs and POs attainment. This paper presents details about a simplified and comprehensive tool to collect assessment details from indirect assessment methods, like workshops, seminars, expert talk, internships, etc., and integrate with the Criterion 3 tool for evaluating PO attainment. These indirect activities may contribute to the courses prescribed under University like projects, mini projects of different subjects. Such contribution and its weights are identified, its COs are evaluated and added to the university course's CO attainment. The goal is to integrate the outcomes from different indirect assessment methods conducted in educational institutions and improve the accuracy of program attainment of the course.

## 18.1 INTRODUCTION

Direct assessment includes assignments, internal assessment tests, lab performances, etc. (National Board of Accreditation Self-Assessment Report (SAR), 2015). As per NBA tier-II guidelines, indirect assessment methods include alumni feedback, exit surveys, and employer feedback (Evaluation Guidelines by NBA, XXXX). Our approach suggests collecting outcome information from other curriculum activities like workshop, expert talk, etc., and integrate with the curriculum courses to which they contribute to. For instance, training on LateX, a document preparation tool, will help students in improving the CO of curriculum courses like Project and Mini projects, where project reports have to be prepared.

## 18.2 EXISTING SYSTEM

The process of program-specific, program, and course attainment, begins with identifying suitable COs for all the courses from 1st-year engineering to the 4th year of engineering of a bachelor degree program. COs are drafted by the senior faculty members by referring to Bloom's levels (Bloom, 1956) and Anderson and Krathwohl (2001). Then a relation mapping is established between course outcomes (COs) and program outcomes (POs) in the range of 1–3, 1 represents low, 2 represents medium, and 3 represents high. A table of mapping is arranged in this regard for all courses mentioned in the bachelor program. The mappings of COs with POs are reviewed frequently by a senior faculty member committee and finalized. Using CO–PO mapping and CO attainment, PO is calculated subject wise.

The assessment process used to evaluate CO is mainly with the help of indirect and direct methods of assessment. For determining indirect attainment of POs and PSOs, self-assessment report suggests co-curricular activities, employer surveys, student exit surveys, extracurricular activities (Accreditation Manual for UG Engineering Programmes (Tier-II), 2019). The literature survey was done to understand various indirect assessment methods and evaluations of PO thereon. The student exit survey alone was considered by an author (Soragaon and Mahesh, 2016). As mentioned in literature, author suggests indirect methods like course-end surveys, program-exit surveys, employer survey as indirect survey methods (Soragaon et al., 2018). The author suggests the indirect assessment methods such as the end semester exam result analysis, faculty feedback report, and exit survey report (Bhagyalakshmi et al., 2014). Another literature suggests the co-curricular happenings, students exit surveys, extracurricular happenings, employer feedback, survey of alumni, and various competitive exams such as GATE, etc., are taken into consideration for assessing PO indirectly with a 20% of weightage (Kavitha et al., 2018). The simple and effective method to determine the course and PO has been illustrated using Excel software (Shivakumar et al., 2014). Courses are grouped and mapped against a particular PO. The PO is derived from the average of CO of all the subjects mapped under that PO using Rubric (Therese, 2015).

Table 18.1 lists direct assessment methods through which the course outcome is calculated.

**TABLE 18.1** List of Direct Internal Evaluation Components.

| | Direct Internal Assessment Methods |
|---|---|
| 1. | Term test assessment |
| 2. | Laboratory work |
| 3. | Assignments/tutorials |
| 4. | University examination |
| 5. | CO–PO feedback |
| 6. | Projects |

Figure 18.1 explains the existing system to calculate the CO attainment from direct assessment methods.

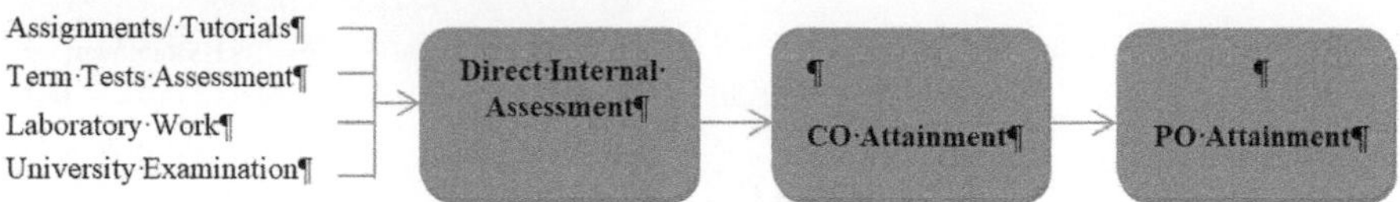


**FIGURE 18.1** Existing system.

### *18.2.1 PROPOSED SYSTEM*

There was a need to include the attainments arising from the various activities conducted in the institute related to the curriculum. This paper presents a framework to integrate the CO attainment from various indirect internal evaluation components. The indirect internal evaluation components include workshops, seminars, expert talks, hackathon/codathan, internships, project competition, and training related to training and placement. These are the events conducted in the educational institutions to enhance the knowledge of various advanced topics to the curriculum. These events can be based on some upcoming trends in the research area. We refer to such events as a course in our approach. Table 18.2 lists various indirect internal evaluation components.

**TABLE 18.2** List of Indirect Internal Evaluation Components

| | Indirect Internal Assessment Methods |
|---|---|
| 1. | Workshop |
| 2. | Seminars |
| 3. | Expert Talk |
| 4. | Hackathon |
| 5. | Internship |
| 6. | Project Competition |
| 7. | Training and Placement Training |

Figure 18.2 represents the proposed system where indirect internal assessment component is integrated with the existing system.

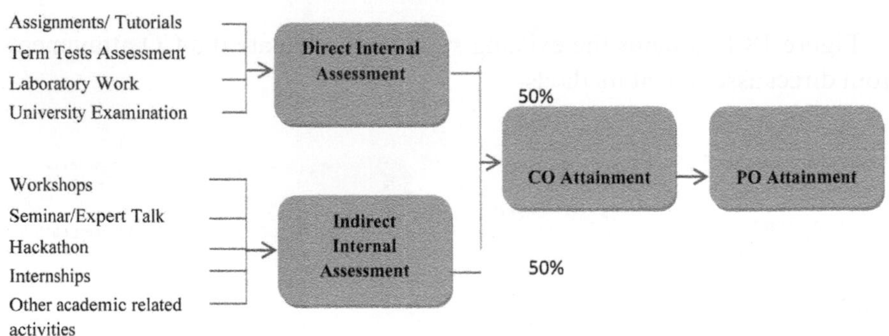


**FIGURE 18.2** Proposed system.

The workflow to collect event-related data and calculate the event attainment is depicted in Figure 18.3.

The following figures are the sample Latex workshop data collected and calculation of workshop outcome attainment. In similar fashion to curriculum courses, event objectives and event outcomes are defined by the event organizers. All the assessments are measured against these event outcomes. Figure 18.4 shows the Latex workshop objectives.

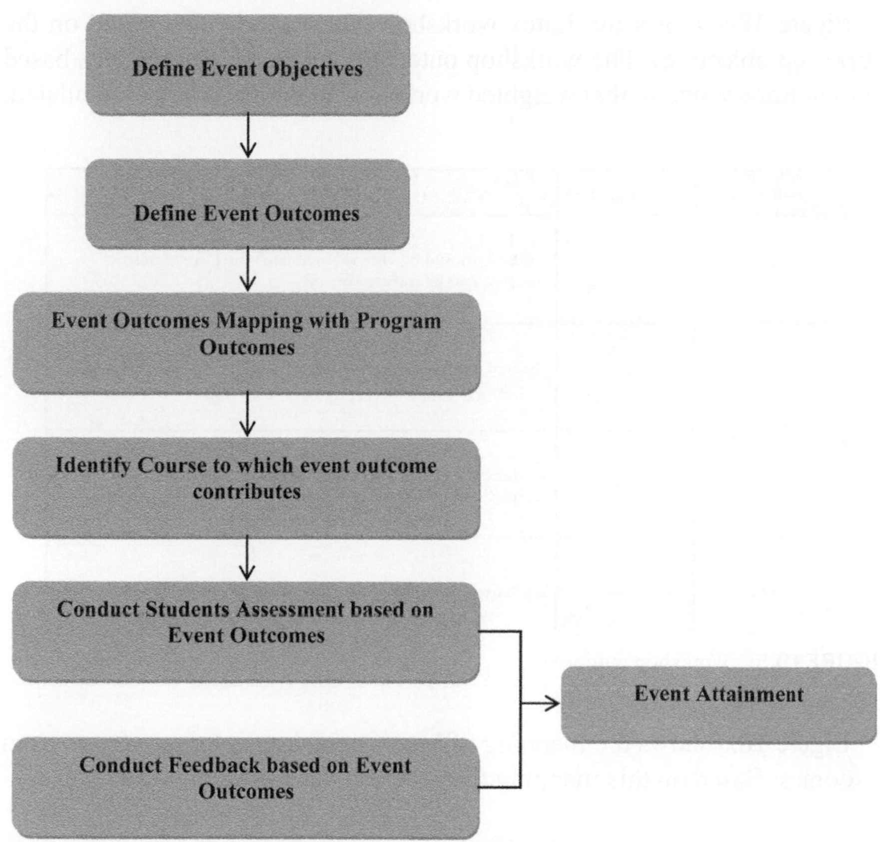


**FIGURE 18.3** Workflow to evaluate event attainment through indirect internal assessment.

| Workshop Objectives | Description |
|---|---|
| CO1 | Student should be able to document the Formulation of problem and Literature survey |
| CO2 | Student should be able to document the Specifications and Requirements |
| CO3 | Student should be able to document the Overview / design of components / Elements / System |
| CO4 | Students should be able to document the project report |

**FIGURE 18.4** Workshop objective.

Figure 18.5 shows the Latex workshop outcomes defined based on the workshop objectives. The workshop outcomes are also given weights based on their importance so that weighted workshop attainment can be calculated.

| Workshop Outcom | CO Weightage | Description |
|---|---|---|
| CO1 | 30 | Student should be able to document the Formulation of problem and Literature survey |
| CO2 | 20 | Student should be able to document the Specifications and Requirements |
| CO3 | 20 | Student should be able to document the Overview / design of components / Elements / System |
| CO4 | 30 | Students should be able to document the project report |

**FIGURE 18.5** Workshop outcome.

Figure 18.6 shows the mapping of Latex workshop outcomes to program outcomes. Based on this mapping the program outcome can be evaluated.

| Weightage | | Course Outcome | PO1 | PO2 | PO3 | PO4 | PO5 | PO6 | PO7 | PO8 | PO9 | PO10 | PO11 | PO12 | PO13 |
|---|---|---|---|---|---|---|---|---|---|---|---|---|---|---|---|
| Theory | 30 | CO1 | | | | | 3 | | | | 1 | 3 | 3 | | |
| | | CO2 | | | | | 3 | | | | 1 | 3 | 3 | | |
| | | CO3 | | | | | 3 | | | | 1 | 3 | 3 | | |
| | | CO4 | | | | | 3 | | | | 1 | 3 | 3 | | |
| | | | | | | | | | | | | | | | |
| Handson | 70 | CO1 | | | | | 3 | | | | 1 | 3 | 3 | | |
| | | CO2 | | | | | 3 | | | | 1 | 3 | 3 | | |
| | | CO3 | | | | | 3 | | | | 1 | 3 | 3 | | |
| | | CO4 | | | | | 3 | | | | 1 | 3 | 3 | | |

**FIGURE 18.6** Workshop outcome mapping to program outcome.

Figure 18.7 shows the list of regular curriculum courses and its outcomes to which the workshop outcomes attainment contributes to. Latex is used for documenting the report for the project course and mini projects of different subjects like the IoE lab. Hence, it is mapped to both these courses.

| Workshop Outcome | Subject Code | Subject Name | CO | Course Outcomes | CO Attainment |
|---|---|---|---|---|---|
| CO1 | BEITP805 | Project-I | CO1 | Formulation of problem and Literature survey | 71.21 |
| | BEITP805 | Project-II | CO1 | Formulation of problem and Literature survey | 71.21 |
| | ITL802 | Internet of Everything Lab | CO5 | To report and present of the study conducted in preffered | 71.21 |
| | | | | | |
| | | | | | |
| CO2 | BEITP805 | Project-I | CO2 | Specifications and Requirements | 57.58 |
| | BEITP805 | Project-II | CO2 | Specifications and Requirements | 57.58 |
| | ITL802 | Internet of Everything Lab | CO5 | To report and present of the study conducted in preffered | 57.58 |

**FIGURE 18.7** Workshop outcome mapped to courses.

For each of the event outcomes, the curriculum subjects getting impacted are identified as shown in Figure 18.8. The CO Attainment on the right is the total event outcomes which are measured by various means like feedback, quizzes, etc.

| Quiz No. | Course Outcome (CO) | Students Assessment |
|---|---|---|
| 1 | CO1 | Sample1 : Which command is used for horizontal spacing? a) \hspace b) \vspace c)\choice d) \CorrectChoice |
| 2 | CO1 | Sample2 : On which platform Latex can be installed? a) Windows b) MacOSX c) Linux d) All mentioned |

**FIGURE 18.8** Students assessment conducted at the end of workshop.

Figure 18.9 shows the quiz and survey/feedback is conducted at the end of workshop. The feedback questions are based on the workshop outcomes. The feedback response of the students is collected and the workshop attainment is calculated.

| Feedback Q No. | Course Outcome (CO) | Feedback Questions (Rate the following out of 10) |
|---|---|---|
| 1 | CO1 | How well will you be able to document the problem definition and literature survey? |
| 2 | CO1 | How well you understood to include figures/ tables etc? |

**FIGURE 18.9** Feedback conducted at the end of workshop.

Based on the type of event, the weights are given to students' assessment and feedback. Then consolidated event attainment is evaluated. For instance, for workshop events, 50% for assessment and 50% for feedback weights can be considered. For events like expert talk, 100% weightage can be considered for feedback as conducting assessment for the same is not in practice. Figure 18.10 shows integrating average workshop attainment with a direct internal assessment. Wherever the indirect internal assessment attaintment is available, 50% weightage is given while evaluating final internal assessment attainment. In the absence of the same, 100% course attainment would come from direct internal assessment methods.

| | | | | | Indirect Internal CO Attainment | | | |
|---|---|---|---|---|---|---|---|---|
| Subject Code | Subject Name | Sem | Div | Th / | CO | CO Attainment | | |
| BEITP805 | Project-I | | | | CO1 | 62.12 | | |
| BEITP805 | Project-II | | | | CO1 | 62.12 | | |
| BEITP805 | Project-I | | | | CO2 | 69.70 | | |
| BEITP805 | Project-II | | | | CO2 | 69.70 | | |
| BEITP805 | Project-I | | | | CO3 | 60.61 | | |
| BEITP805 | Project-II | | | | CO3 | 60.61 | | |
| ITL802 | Internet of Everything Lab | | | | CO5 | 62.12 | | |
| ITL802 | Internet of Everything Lab | | | | CO5 | 69.70 | | |
| | | | | | | | | |

Average

| Subject Code | Subject Name | Sem | Direct Internal Assessment | | Indirect Internal Assessment | | Overall Performance | |
|---|---|---|---|---|---|---|---|---|
| | | | CO Attainment | Attainment Level | CO Attainment | Attainment Level | CO Attainment | Attainment Level |
| BEITP805 | Project | 8 | 99.90 | 3 | 64.14 | 2 | 82.02 | 3 |

**FIGURE 18.10** CO attainment including Indirect Internal assessment.

## 18.3 CONCLUSION

Outcome-based education gives the clarity of what to be achieved, by the end of the curriculum. Students will know what is anticipated from them and facilitators will identify what they need to explain through the course. It also gives teachers the flexibility of conducting lectures around student's needs and assessment methods. The outcome assessment helps the institution and teachers to understand where they stand as well as indicate the areas for enlightening the process of teaching–learning. Integrating attainment from indirect internal assessment methods would improve the accuracy of PO attainment.


## KEYWORDS

- **accreditation**
- **NBA**
- **program outcome**
- **attainment**
- **indirect assessment**


## REFERENCES


Accreditation Manual for UG Engineering Programmes (Tier-II), 2019. Available from: https://www.nbaind.org/files/general-manual-of-accreditation.pdf.

Anderson, L. W., Krathwohl, D. R. *Taxonomy for Learning, Teaching, and Assessing*, Abridged Edition, Boston, MA: Allyn and Bacon, 2001.

Bhagyalakshmi, H. R., Seshachalam, D., Lalitha, S. Program Outcome Attainment Through Course Outcomes: A Comprehensive Approach. *Proc. International Conference on Transformations in Engineering Education*. India, 2014, 279–286.

Bloom, B. S. Taxonomy of Educational Objectives. Handbook I: The Cognitive Domain. New York: David McKay Co Inc.; 1956.

Evaluation Guidelines by NBA. Available from: http://www.nbaind.org/files/evaluation-guidelines-tier-ii-v0.pdf.

Kavitha, A., Immanuvel Arokia James, K., Harish, K. A., Rajamani, V. A Empirical Study On CO-PO Assessment & Attainment For NBA Tier-II Engineering Accreditation Towards Empowering The Students Through Outcome Based Education. *International Journal of Pure and Applied Mathematics*, 2018, *118*(20), 2615–2624.

National Board of Accreditation Self-Assessment Report (SAR) For Engineering Programs of Tier-II Institutions—First Time Accreditation. Available from: http://www.nbaind.org/En/1079-self-assessment-report-tier-ii.aspx [June 2015].

Shivakumar, R., Maitra, S., Mallikarjuna Babu, K. Method for Estimation of Attainment of Program Outcome Through Course Outcome for Outcome Based Education. *2014 IEEE International Conference on MOOC, Innovation and Technology in Education (MITE)*, 2014.

Soragaon, B., Mahesh, K. S. Measuring Attainment of Course Outcomes and Program Outcomes—A Simplified Approach as per Self-Assessment Report. *IOSR Journal of Research & Method in Education (IOSR-JRME)*, 2016, *6*(4), Ver. IV.

Soragaon, B., Sivakumar, V., Mahesh, K. S. On Some Aspects of Indirect Attainment of Course Outcomes and Program Outcomes in a Tier-II Engineering Institution. Presented at the World Summit on Accreditation (WOSA-2018); held at New Delhi; 7–9, September 2018.

Therese, Y. M. Measurement of Program Outcomes Attainment for Engineering Graduates by using Excel. *International Journal of Engineering and Management Research*, 2015, *5*(2), 348–352.

## CHAPTER 19

# An Appraisal of Constructive Learning Process Environment Using Intranet Based e-Content Management System for Engineering Education in Karnataka State

MANJUNATHA BYRAPPA

*School of Foreign Languages, University of Mysore, Humanities Block, Manasagangothri Campus, Mysuru, Karnataka, India.*
*E-mails: bmn2304@gmail.com; sofluom@gmail.com*

**ABSTRACT**

e-Learning is sometimes described as pedagogy empowered by digital technology. Education by means of online services has emerged over the last several years worldwide as a crucial educational ingredient to supplement contact teaching in the classroom. Similar to classical education, multimedia content and particularly video delivered on-demand directly to the student's end is one of the most powerful facets of what we call e-Learning 2.0. It is closest in impact to classroom-based live contact teaching. An intranet-based e-content-based content management system is needed in e-Learning environments, especially in scientific and engineering education. The aim of this study is to enlighten the conceptual framework adopted in intranet-based e-Content Management System (CMS), architecture of intranet-based e-content delivery, key benefits of intranet-based e-CMS to stake holders with an analysis and interpretation of first time experiences by under graduate students and their level of satisfaction with the use of intranet-based e-CMS. The study made by the researcher evaluates that the under-graduate students find very interesting in learning through this mode of technology and also the study recommends to extend this e-Platform to other educational domains.

## 19.1 INTRODUCTION

e-Learning is sometimes described as pedagogy empowered by digital technology. Education by means of online services has emerged over the last several years worldwide as a crucial educational ingredient to supplement contact teaching in the classroom.

Various studies and research worldwide have praised "e-Learning as not only Electronic learning, but also as an Effective, Exciting, Energetic, Enthusiastic, Emotional, Extended, Excellent, and Educational learning experience—Luskin (Wikipedia) (Deveci, 2015)." e-Learning can provide a highly flexible, convenient, anytime anywhere learning environment to a much broader community of learners than can be accommodated within classrooms of institutes of higher learning. It is also well established that e-Learning is most effective when blended appropriately with traditional contact teaching in the classroom. The primary enablers of e-Learning are: Network, Web and Multimedia. With the recent advances in web-based multimedia technology, we are well equipped to provide effective e-Learning environments to our students.

e-Learning is particularly critical for an emerging nation like India (Bakia, 2010). For India to live up to its claim as an emerging world leader nation, we must meet the urgent national needs to rapidly produce a very large number of science and technology graduates well trained in advanced scientific and technical disciplines. This national imperative is placing a huge demand on our higher education system across the country and stretching our university and college faculty beyond normal capacity. This is where e-Learning can play a crucial role by making high-quality education available to all students of science and technology beyond the borders of the finest national institutions.

Recognizing e-Learning as part of an agenda of national importance, Govt. of India and the various state governments have begun providing massive impetus to promote the adoption of e-Learning in the country (Swayam Central, 2019). Large budgetary outlays have been allocated by the Ministry of HRD for promotion of e-Learning systems and solutions and for content creation.

Visvesvaraya Technological University in Karnataka State has taken pioneering steps in e-Learning early on with the Education through Satellite-based EDUSAT program, network-based education program and other web-based initiatives (VTU Elearning, 2019). In order to maintain leading position among technological universities in India, the university has taken new steps to spread the new initiatives further to all of its affiliated colleges across Karnataka state. Resulting to this, there is also a need to deploy much more advanced state-of-the-art technologies such as "On-Demand Video Streaming and Community Learning" using the latest Web 2.0 technologies?

Multimedia content, particularly video, delivered on-demand directly to the student's computer screen is one of the most powerful facets of what we call e-Learning 2.0 (Kharbirymbai, 2013). It is closest in impact to classroom-based live contact teaching.

Use of Web 2.0 techniques promoting a community environment for learning is another equally powerful facet of e-Learning 2.0 (Gernsbacher, 2015). It allows leveraged group learning supported by a variety of online interaction and management tools.

However, there are some challenges of delivering multimedia content over the network since the data is usually voluminous and poses serious challenges of high latency in delivery and scarcity of client-side resources such as storage (Eastmond, 1998). To address these challenges, advanced multimedia streaming technologies, formats and protocols have been evolved that allow client side media players to play a stream as the data is being received; thus alleviating problems of client-side resources and latency.

Critical success factors for a good user experience of an e-Learning environment using a streaming multimedia solution include the following (Neo and Neo, 2004):

- Ability to deliver high-resolution video and high-quality audio
- Fast start without large latency and high throughput without stall and jitter
- Easy content management, browsing, and searching
- Free nonproprietary open-source software's and tools.

Key standards and technologies that have evolved include the following (Online Courses, 2019):

- MPEG-4/H.264 video compression and coding/decoding
- Transmission and content delivery over standard HTTP web protocol
- Web 2.0 content management techniques.

Over the last few years, electronic-based education has come into its own as the mainstay in the field of education. The incorporation of video-on-demand-based technology; the teaching and learning has earned prosperous rewards in socially, culturally, and economically (Page, 2005). e-Learning and e-Teaching have also been a boon in a more specific sense to educational institutions as it allows extremely useful contact across national and international borders.

This is principally correct in the present context, for information communication and technology (ICT)-based education that is transforming knowledge deliverance process and "Virtual Education." The newly arrived e-Learning has caused world over reflective variations in the means public learn and train, letting them to do it everywhere, at any time (Ajithkumar, 2018). Through the web browser a student can access e-Content from any point, in the campus, through an e-Content accessing system with a network connectivity medium. The network-based e-content education systems are being used for delivering of video contents and SCORM-based learning materials on demand e-Content of a particular course. The education through intranet-based network technology permits asynchronous delivery of various kinds of teaching/learning data presentations including teaching/learning resource of, server-hosted digital data, PowerPoint presentations, still pictures, simulations, animations, graphical information, question types like e-assessment, quiz poll, feedback, learning activities, data field types (for the database activity), graphical themes, authentication methods, enrollment methods, content filters, etc.

The study on the "An Appraisal of Constructive Learning Process Environment Using intranet Based e-Content Management System (CMS) For Engineering Education In Karnataka State" was made the research scholar to study the solution architecture of intranet-based e-CMS, conceptual framework adopted in teaching/learning process of intranet-based e-CMS, key benefits of intranet-based e-CMS to the stakeholders and conclude with a study on students experiences on intranet-based teaching/learning process through e-CMS and recommendations given to extend this mode of learning technology to upcoming learners and suggestions obtained toward enhancing the e-CMS application features, developing e-Contents with additional supplementary and demonstrative resources and developing e-contents for core courses.

## 19.2 ARCHITECTURE OF INTRANET-BASED e-CONTENT MANAGEMENT SYSTEM

The e-CMS solution is deployed on local high capacity servers to be installed in each college campus. Student's PCs access the streaming media content over the high-speed standard campus LAN using a web browser with plug-in of media player. All necessary software for using the e-CMS solution is freely available in open source. No special proprietary software is needed (Michael, 2012). The only tools needed on the client computer are the widely used open-source and freely available web browser and the media player plugin. There is no restriction on the client computer operating system or hardware. Any multimedia desktop PC or laptop or any handheld devices (if the campus has Wi-Fi connectivity) is sufficient for accessing content from the e-CMS server. The transmitted data includes video-based lecture sessions, e-notes, courseware materials, presentation materials, exercises, simulations, etc.

### 19.2.1 SOLUTION ARCHITECTURE OF INTRANET-BASED e-CONTENT MANAGEMENT SYSTEM

Figure 19.1 illustrates the conceptual architecture of the intranet-enabled solution.

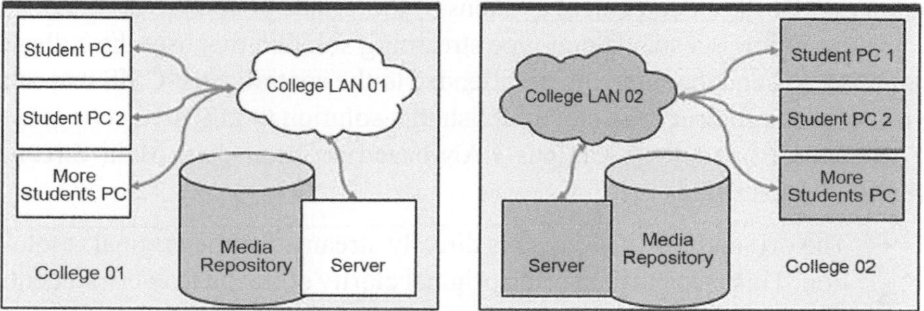


**FIGURE 19.1** Intranet-based e-content management system solution architecture.

Figure 19.1 shows a campus with its e-CMS server serving an arbitrary number of client (student) machines connected on the college campus LAN. Provision can also be made for client machines to have intranet connectivity through the campus network connection. The e-CMS solution architecture also works with any existing network firewalls, web proxies, caches, or filters.

The secure e-CMS platform provides the infrastructure for provisioning the content to users and enabling content, and community management functionalities. The media and content administrator of each campus manages the student communities and the media content of that campus independently using the highly intuitive and easy-to-use content and community management functionalities of the e-CMS platform. The e-CMS platform is built upon the world's most widely used open-source CMS and adds a highly sophisticated but extremely easy to use platform for hosting online secure social networks.

The current solution is also feasible for inclusion of National Program on Technology Enhanced Learning (NPTEL) master media server to enable automated media distribution (Nptel, 2019). In the extended solution, a new video media content uploaded by NPTEL content administrator to the NPTEL master media server is automatically pushed to the local media servers of all subscribing campuses that opt for automatic updates. This requires Internet connectivity on the campus media server. The media transfers are done using a private bit torrent network of the campus NPTEL media servers. This dramatically reduces the network load on the NPTEL master media server and makes the solution feasible. If desired, the system can even be configured to create the lecture wrapper pages corresponding to newly uploaded media automatically. This further reduces the need for campus level content administration. The extended solution pre includes the need for distribution of NPTEL content by means of physically shipped DVDs or hard disk drives to each subscribing campus. It scales automatically to hundreds of thousands hours of NPTEL video content and tens of thousands of campuses.

The solution is a standalone-type streaming solution that uses the college campus LAN and the same can be extended to the centralized e-CMS that can work over the Internet and can establish this solution to affiliated colleges.

Benefits of a college campus LAN-based solution over Main Stream Media (Phipps, 2015)

- The original MPEG4 video is directly streamed at the original resolution. This ensures delivering original clarity of media to every student. Every such MPEG4 stream can consume Between 2 and 4 Mbps of network bandwidth. Since the media are streamed from a local server over the LAN (typically 100 Mbps–1 Gbps), network bandwidth is not an issue.
- No Internet video sites are needed; therefore, no changes are needed in the Internet access control management policy of any college.
- Practically an unlimited number of students can access the platform without running into Internet access bandwidth issues since the media are streamed from a local server.
- The media carries the original source branding.
- Every subscribing college has complete control over its media server. Each college can categorize lectures in whichever way suits its specific needs independent of all other colleges.
- The solution comes with a whole range of features for community learning, comments, ratings, interactions, etc.

In addition to the specific comparative advantages described above, this solution also provides the following to the facilitated college and the students (Sheela, 2015):

- Powerful categorization and tagging facility: Using this, each college can structure the content in a completely flexible manner appropriate for its own specific needs. This also allows searching for specific lectures using a variety of criteria such as subject, lecturer, discipline, level, keywords, and source.
- A college can optionally enable community interaction among the students by allowing viewers of a lecture to write comments on the lecture and engage in group discussion.
- Local admin has the ability to remove or block any users if needed.
- Access statistics can be collected and analyzed to refine the content.
- The system can be easily expanded to enable student communities to create a variety of content themselves. The staff and faculty of the college can also create a wide variety of content to enrich the e-Learning system further. Essentially the platform can evolve into a comprehensive e-Learning portal custom made for a college and its needs.
- No complex local administrative tasks are necessary to deploy and maintain the platform. Creation of new lecture pages is fully menu driven and there is no chance of creating broken video links and such errors in the site.
- The solution is highly scalable. Addition of disk storage in direct proportion of the volume of media released by NPTEL or other sources (approximately 1 GB per hour of video) enables the solution to scale practically indefinitely. This will serve the projected needs of a college for several years to come.

### 19.2.2 SALIENT FEATURES OF INTRANET-BASED e-CMS

The basic video media content provisioning solution has the following features (Yadav et al., 2017):

- Based upon well-proven open-source components integrated using the secure e-CMS application service platform for secure social networks.
- Covers the scenario of secure provisioning of the video media content to the students in a campus along with student–teacher learning communities and community interactions built around the video media content.
- Works with the MPEG4 media directly without using flash technology and without depending upon any external services such as YouTube. The solution is highly scalable. The number and quality of concurrent streams served are not constrained in any way other than by the HTTP

throughput of the local media server and the LAN bandwidth available for media streaming.

- Supports a simple standalone version for campuses that do not provide Internet connectivity to users. An easy and seamless migration path is available to migrate from the standalone solution to the intranet-enabled solution with the full range of services from the secure e-CMS application service platform. The high-bandwidth media content is always hosted and served to users by a local media server over the LAN to ensure high quality streams and content security.
- e-CMS functionalities wrapped around the video media content significantly enhance the group learning experience of students. The platform allows rating of content and student–teacher community interaction through comments, discussion forums, and other user-generated content channels. It allows students and mentors to enhance the educational experience with a full range of community generated content on a secure structured social networking platform.
- A powerful tagging, browsing, and search facility is built-in to enable users to find relevant content of interest to them. Content can be tagged, browsed, and searched by source, by courses, by keywords, by course experts, and by target audience type. Free-form multiple tagging allows total flexibility in content categorization as per the needs of a campus.
- Low bandwidth intranet connection from the client machine is sufficient for the e-CMS functionalities of the secure e-CMS application service platform. The media is always streamed from the local media server over the high-speed local network.
- Client computers can be of any type and only require a standard Java Script-enabled web browser and any standard media player browser plug-in capable of playing MPEG4 media.
- Other types of media than MPEG4 (e.g., Flash) can be accommodated easily within the same solution.

### *19.2.3 INFRASTRUCTURE*

Commonly available infrastructural prerequisites are adequate for the campus to deploy the e-CMS solution in a suitable configuration. The following infrastructures are needed for successfully deploying and using the e-CMS solution.

- *Space:* The most appropriate way of deploying the server and storage systems is in a standard rack. 5U of total rack space is required by the two systems put together. If a rack is not available, temporarily clean and clear table top space of 8 $ft^2$ can be used to deploy the hardware.

- *Power:* Five (5) standard 3-pin universal 240 V/6 A power sockets are required to power up the e-CMSs.
- *UPS:* A minimum of 1 kVA uninterrupted power supply is required with a backup time of at least 3 h. A 2 kVA UPS is strongly recommended. It is strongly advised that the systems are not powered on without using a UPS. It is essential to ensure that the systems are not allowed to crash owing to a loss of power. Adequate administrative arrangements must be made to power down the systems using the shutdown procedure before the UPS runs out of power in case of a prolonged power failure.
- *Cooling:* Suitably air-conditioned server room or data center environment with approximately 0.5 ton cooling capacity available for the e-CMS server and storage is required. In relatively cool climates, it may be possible to run the system without AC for limited periods, but it is strongly advised that these systems are housed in AC environments.
- *Network:* Two (2) standard RJ-45 Ethernet ports are required for connectivity.
- *LAN bandwidth:* A minimum of 100 Mbps LAN is required to deploy e-CMS. A 1000 Mbps (gigabit) or faster LAN is highly recommended. It is not advisable to deploy e-CMS on a LAN slower than 100 Mbps.
- *Physical security*: It should be ensured that physical access to the e-CMS server is strictly restricted to authorized and trained local administrators. Unauthorized users should not be given access to these systems.
- *Dedicated use:* The e-CMS systems hardware should be used only for the e-CMS solution and related usage.

### 19.2.4 CONNECTIVITY

e-CMS is a complex system. Several connectivity requirements must be fulfilled for the e-CMS to work properly at college campus. For a complete and proper deployment of the new e-CMS and for the proper operation of the e-CMS meta services, it is necessary for the e-CMS server at each college campus to have network connectivity. Also, the e-CMS server deployed at each college is eligible for the e-CMS remote support service by courses to providing remote access to the e-CMS server. To ensure that the students receive maximum benefit from the e-CMS deployment, the intranet-based e-CMS facilitated colleges' needs to ensure that the following network connectivity requirements are fulfilled. These prerequisites must be completely satisfied before the actual e-CMS can be properly installed to client colleges and the remote support services provided by the client college.

- *Network ports:* Each e-CMS server requires two network ports—the first one is used for the LAN connection and the second one is used for the external intranet connection. The first port is used by the system to serve content to your users. The second port is required when remote support services are to be performed.
- *Internal static IP:* The facilitated colleges need to assign an internal static IP address for the e-CMS server. Ideally this should be a class A private IP address of the form 10.*.*.*. The recommended default IP address of the e-CMS server is 10.0.0.10. If the LAN does not use the 10.*.*.* class A addresses, the colleges can also use a class C address of the form 192.168.*.*. However, the client colleges are strongly advised to use the 10.*.*.* class A subnets for the e-CMS server. However, e-CMS servers that are assigned class C IP addresses such as 192.168.*.* may be denied access to metadata from the e-CMS Meta server.
- *LAN routing:* The client college's needs to make sure that, LAN routing is set up such that the LAN network port to be connected to the e-CMS server is able to receive network traffic addressed to the above LAN IP address. Once the e-CMS server is installed, this network port should always be connected to the server on the assigned network interface and should always be active. If this port is not active or is disconnected from the server, the e-CMS Website will not be accessible to the students.
- *Public static IP:* There is a need to get a valid dedicated public static IP address assigned to the e-CMS server. Usually the public static IP address needs to get it from valid ISP. The ISP may charge a nominal annual fee for this. The client colleges needs to double check with your ISP and confirm that the IP address provided is legal and valid. It is not allowed to connect a computer with an illegal IP address to the intranet.
- *WAN routing:* The facilitated colleges needs to make sure that the WAN routing of respective college campus is set up such that the WAN traffic from the intranet addressed to the above external IP address will be routed to the network port to be connected to the e-CMS server on the second assigned network interface. Once the e-CMS server is fully installed, this port should preferably be always

connected and active for remote monitoring. Alternatively, this port can be connected to the server on a need basis in coordination with support end—Visvesvaraya Technological University (VTU) when remote service is to be done.

- *Local host names:* The e-CMS server hosts multiple application servers and has several distinct names identifying it in your campus LAN for these services. First of all, it will be known as cms.<college domain> where < college domain > is the official domain name of e-CMS facilitated colleges. Under this name, it hosts the main e-CMS application. The e-CMS Meta Server will not serve metadata to e-CMS servers with invalid domain names.
- *Local DNS entries:* If the facilitated colleges have an internal local DNS in college campus LAN, ideally the above host names should be added in the local DNS and bound to the LAN IP address assigned in step 2 above. If the colleges do not have a local DNS, these host names and the IP address must be added to the host's file of each client computer from which users will access the e-CMS server. The VTU strongly recommend that facilitated college's needs to set up a local DNS service.
- *HTTP out connections:* The e-CMS server receives content metadata from the e-CMS Meta Server on the intranet on demand. The metadata is obtained by calling web services available on the e-CMS Meta Server over HTTP. For this mechanism to work, the e-CMS server must be able to send HTTP requests to the intranet. The client colleges need to ensure that the college campus LAN configuration allows outgoing HTTP connections to the intranet from the e-CMS server. One way to verify this setup is to connect a client PC to the LAN network port connected to the e-CMS server and verify that the client colleges can browse Websites on the intranet such as http://cms.in. Remember to connect the network port back to the e-CMS server after the check!
- *Public host names:* The e-CMS server also has three additional public names. These names are *remote-cms.<your_domain>*, *remote-moodle.<your_domain>*, and *remote-phpmyadmin.<your_domain>*.
- *Public DNS entries:* Please have these three public names added to the *public DNS* for the college domain and point all three names to the public static IP address of the server that you obtained for the e-CMS server from your ISP. You may need to contact your ISP for setting this up. These URLs are only for remote service connections. The NPTEL and VTU video content on to the college e-CMS server

cannot be accessed from the Internet through these URLs. To check that the names have been properly set up in the public DNS, ping the host name from a computer connected to the intranet.

- *High-speed LAN:* To facilitate efficient access to the content, please ensure that the e-CMS server is connected to the high-speed core segment of the college campus LAN. A minimum LAN bandwidth of 100 Mbps is required for proper operation of e-CMS. A 1000 Mbps LAN (gigabit LAN) is highly recommended.
- *LAN only use:* It is note that the NPTEL and VTU videos are bandwidth intensive. Each NPTEL and video stream served by the e-CMS server consumes between 512 Kbps and 1 Mbps network bandwidth. These streams therefore are not particularly suitable for serving to users over the intranet. The e-CMS configuration deployed in the campus is not configured for such use and we advise against allowing such access.

### 19.2.5 OPERATIONS

This section describes the overall operational framework of the e-CMS solution. Most features of the e-CMS solution are self-explanatory and all workflows are guided by the user interface. This section only provides the high level perspective.

- *Admin account:* The default e-CMS administrator account user id is "admin." The default password is handed over to respective colleges after system installation. The colleges should change the default admin password to a secure password of their choice to prevent misuse of the system. The default admin account should never be deleted from the system. Additional users can also be granted the administrator role by the default admin user.
- *Settings:* The e-CMS administrator can modify certain core settings of the e-CMS to suit the needs of particular deployment. Log in as "admin" and go to the tab: My e-CMS → Settings.
- *Local site name:* The name of the local site should be set at the time of initial deployment of the system only. If the local site name is changed post-installation, the e-CMS metadata service subscriptions will become unavailable until re-approved by the e-CMS Meta Server.
- *System e-mail:* The system e-mail address should be changed to the e-mail address of the local admin. All e-mails generated by the system

will be sent with this address in the "From:" field. To minimize the chances of mails generated by the e-CMS server being marked as SPAM by some mail services, the preferred e-mail address for this should be cms@<your_college_domain>. For received mails (e.g., new user registration notifications), this address may be set up as an alias which redistributes the received mails to the appropriate e-mail addresses. If the campus does not have a mail service, try using any other appropriate valid e-mail address as the system e-mail address.

### *19.2.6 USER ADMINISTRATION*

- *New user registration:* The e-CMS Website in respective colleges allows users to register themselves, but approval by the site administrator is required before a user account is activated. Users must provide a valid e-mail address in order to register. Account activation notifications are sent by the system by e-mail.
- *User profiles:* New e-CMS users must provide certain profile information to enable site administrators to verify the eligibility of the user to use the e-CMS site. Such information includes identification information such as local student ID, university student ID, and details of the academic program the user is registered for. Site administrators should carefully validate the user profile information provided by a user before approving the user account. Approving unverified users allows spurious users to join the community and create potentially SPAM postings such as forum posts and comments.
- *User management:* e-CMS Administrators must carefully maintain the user database and remove or deactivate expired entries, such as accounts of students who graduate.
- *Role management:* e-CMS Administrators may assign the administrative role to additional users in order to share the work and to provide for backup administrators during vacations. Such users should be selected carefully since users with administrative privileges can alter the content, remove or create videos, content, posts, comments, etc.

### *19.2.7 CONTENT ADMINISTRATION*

- *Contents:* Over 15,000 lectures are predeployed on the e-CMS server and being used by the students.

- *Future e-Content.* As new video contents become available, the respective e-Contents will be made available in e-Content updates and any necessary instructions for deploying them on the respective e-CMS server.
- *Local content.* It is possible to upload and publish additional video content over and above the content currently deployed, for example, those produced at your campus or downloaded from other sources on the intranet. Presently, only MPEG-4 videos are currently supported. You can use the "My e-CMS → Data" tab to upload new videos. Video files are stored in a hierarchy of subdirectories: <ROOT>/< channel>/<discipline>/<subject>. If you upload any local content, it is instructed to place them under the 'Local' channel to avoid the polluting of content name space available from standard channels such as NPTEL and VTU.

## 19.3 CONCEPTUAL FRAMEWORK ADOPTED IN INTRANET-BASED e-CMS

The term e-Learning covers a broad set of applications and processes including computer-based and web-based teaching and learning, virtual classrooms and digital collaboration. e-Learning is defined as the delivery of lecture, e-Contents through electronic media, be it intranet, network broadcast, audio/video tape, interactive devices, and CD/DVD.

e-Learning is self-possessed for widespread acceptance among students and faculty. e-Learning has emerged as a powerful supplement tool to conventional teaching/ learning systems. It uses the powerful multimedia and interactivity features which is compatible for currently available computing platforms to deliver teaching. The growth of World Wide Web, intranet, high-capacity networks through network, fiber optics and workstations is making learning contents available round the clock around the globe.

In the proposed e-CMS-video-on-demand-based education, the campus network infrastructure will be used for streaming of video-based lecture sessions (Manjunatha, 2019). The course matter experts use presentation materials according to standard templates, which is compatible for better viewing in network steaming mode. Such video lecture session would be captured, digitized, compressed and linked to become part of the overall e-Learning e-Contents. The e-Learning framework consists of the components as shown in Figure 19.2.

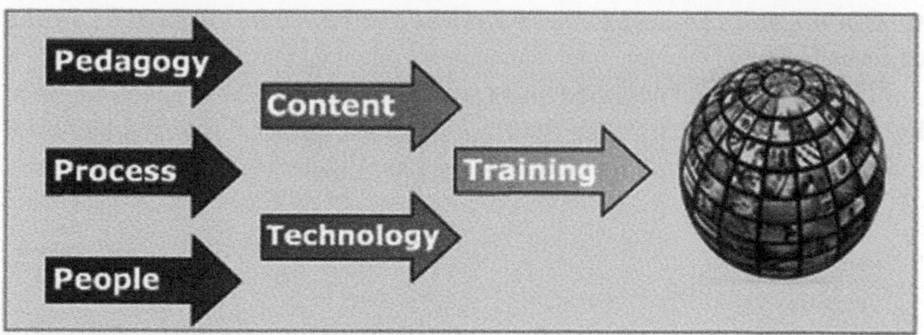


**FIGURE 19.2** Conceptual framework.

### 19.3.1 PEDAGOGY

All e-Content that is being developed will be made repository for asynchronous learning. The collection of courses envisaged for streaming through campus LAN to the target group of students and teachers of the colleges is as follows:

a. *Full semester program:* The best resource persons drawn from both academia and industry will be recorded the full semester course of the curriculum. Two/three course experts will cover one full course, which requires about 40 video sessions of one hour each.
b. *Supplementary program:* A series of 15–20 sessions on select topics of a difficult will be transmitted.
c. *Single lesson program:* It is a special lecture e-content, called "Industrial Experts Talks," which addresses one specific topic or concept providing an overview of the topic. Eminent speakers (like academicians, CEOs and CTOs) will deliver the lectures.
c. *Exam revision service:* This type of e-contents is planned to cover difficult course/subjects or difficult portions for revision, together with tests and tips.

### 19.3.2 PROCESS

The e-Learning e-Content generation process involves development of e-Content for the video-based lectures that being streamed through campus LAN and generation of high-quality Shareable Content Object Reference Model (SCORM) compliant e-Content that will be deployed on the web so that anyone can access the e-Knowledge resources at anytime in the campus LAN.

The teaching end designed four formats to convert raw Content, as given by the course experts, to the final e-Learning Content. Provision has been made to retrieve recorded video sessions (see Figure 19.3)

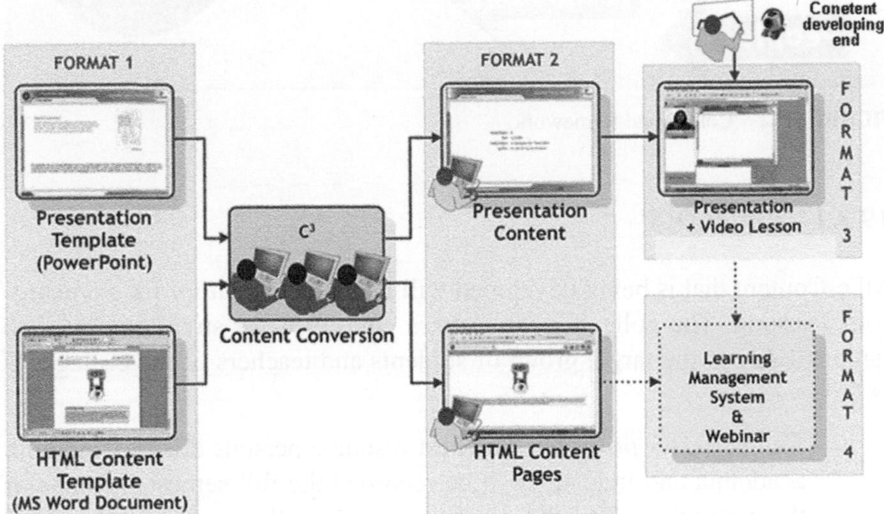


**FIGURE 19.3** Process of e-content conversion and delivery.

### *19.3.3 PEOPLE*

Successful execution of e-Learning process involves the following players of three teams (see Figure 19.4)

- e-Content Team
- Receiving End Team
  - Principal
  - Coordinator
  - Technician
  - Teacher
  - Student
- Teaching End Team
  - Course Expert
  - Technical manpower

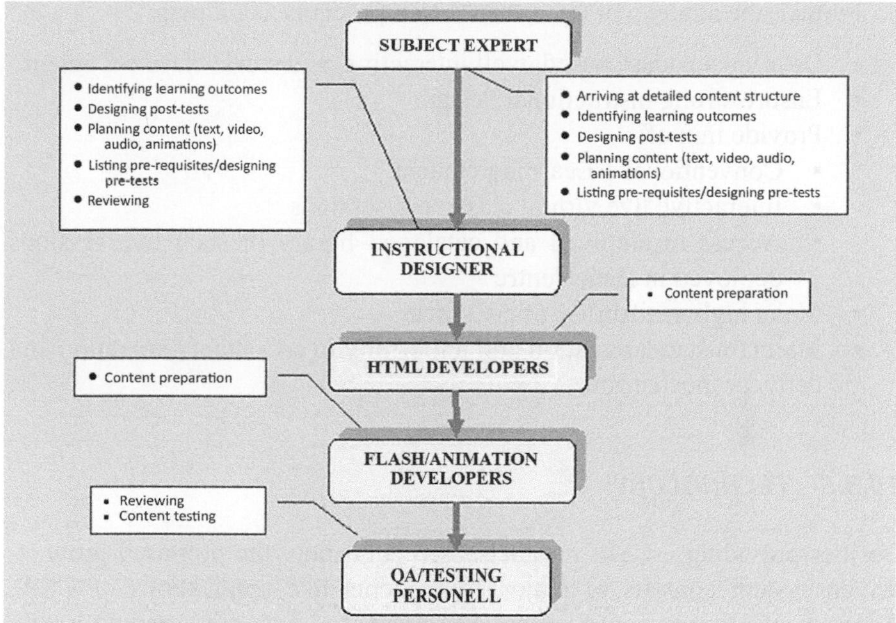


**FIGURE 19.4** People involved in e-Learning process.

### 19.3.4 CONTENT

The most significant part of any e-Learning implementation is the Content, which incorporates the pedagogies of online teaching/learning. Well planned, designed, and target-oriented e-Learning Contents are required to maximize the benefits of any learner through a network infrastructure meant for e-Learning. The key benefits of e-Learning contents are:

- Teaching/Learning objects are the basic core components of e-Learning contents, which serves as a influential tool in the hands of the faculties to make teaching/learning process more effective
- e-Content available on a network infrastructure would be an effective supplement for the students
- Helps to maintain appropriate standards and uniformity in teaching/ learning process
- Enables the learning activity of a learner of their choice anytime and anywhere in the network
- Enable study of more usable presentation in the context of learning content creation through models, practical examples and checklists

Further, the strategy of e-Content development is as follows:

- Develop standard based, well interactive, and world class e-Content
- Ensure strong instructional design
- Provide mix of:
  - Conventional e-Learning content
  - Interactive live virtual classroom sessions
  - Access to archived and cataloged library of such live sessions deployed in Data Centre
- Make high availability of e-Content
- Maintain standardization and uniformity in e-Content generation and delivery mechanism

### 19.3.5 TECHNOLOGY

Besides providing e-CMS intranet-based education, the proposed intranet-driven system consists of major components like applications of CMS, Assessment Management System, e-Content, and network computing with campus LAN infrastructure. All the student nodes ends are being connected to a single network. The delivery mechanism has been discussed in Section 19.2 of intranet-based e-CMS education.

### 19.3.6 TRAINING

Orientation, sensitize, and training are essential for the different stakeholders of e-Content-based education system. The various stakeholders are shown in Figure 19.5.

### 19.3.7 KEY BENEFITS OF INTRANET-BASED EDUCATION AND e-LEARNING

#### 19.3.7.1 TEACHING END

- Proving teaching/learning resources
- Improving quality of teaching–learning processes
- Providing a platform to collaborate with other universities
- Providing online examination
- Facilitating e-Management and e-Library

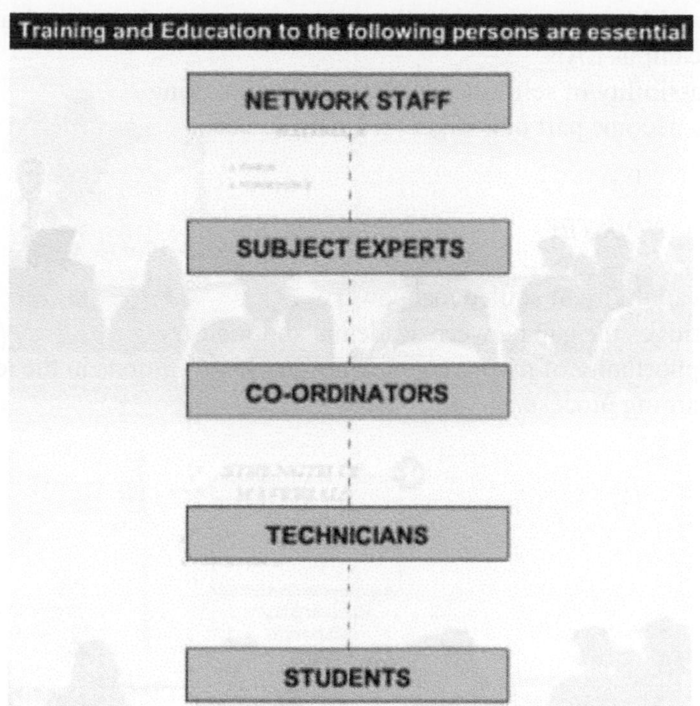


**FIGURE 19.5** Training for stakeholders of the system.

#### *19.3.7.2 FACULTY MEMBERS*

- Empower the faculties to mentor the teaching–learning process in the college end
- An innovative platform to share developed teaching, learning, and assessment resources like quizzes, question banks, and assessments to large student community or peer-group learners
- Enables peer-group interaction by teachers with the external agencies leading to technology-enhanced learning opportunities.

#### *19.3.7.3 STUDENTS/LEARNERS*

- Bridges the gap toward providing quality teaching/learning resources
- Improves the quality of learning process through standard e-Contents and resources

- Provides, self-paced, self-directed, anywhere, and anytime learning in a campus LAN
- Possibility of self-assessment and benchmarking
- To become part of a larger "learning society."

*19.3.7.4 INDUSTRY*

- Availability of skilled manpower
- Bridges the gap between academia and industry
- Opportunity of partnering with academic institutions in the teaching/learning process

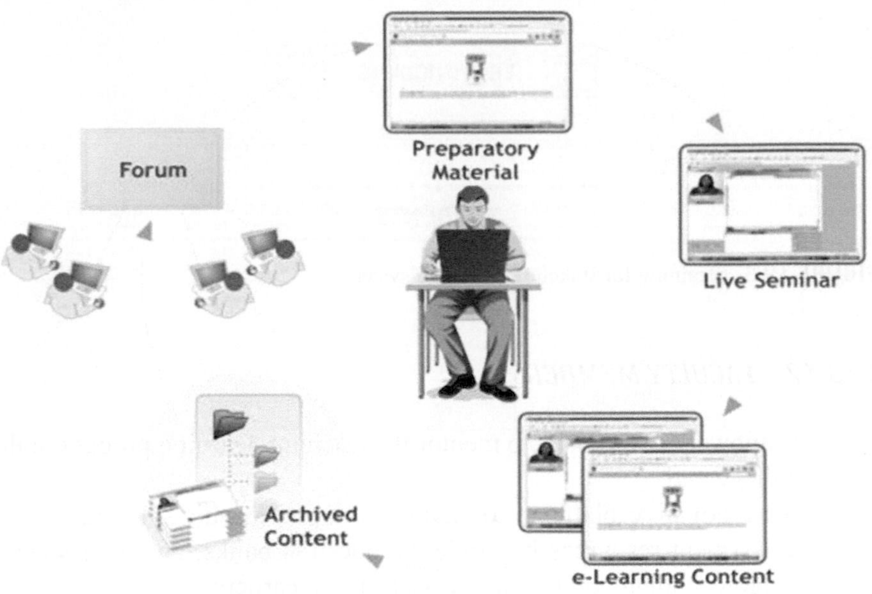


**FIGURE 19.6** Student-centric approach.

## 19.4 INTRANET-BASED e-CMS

In Karnataka, the Visvesvaraya Technological University has deployed intranet-based e-CMS to its affiliated engineering colleges (Manjunatha, 2019). The e-CMS comprises CMS Application, MOODLE LMS, NPTEL Phase-I and II videos and videos recorded through e-Learning programs.

The feedback about the deployed intranet-based e-CMS has been obtained by mentors and students from facilitated colleges to assess their attitudes and responses toward deployed intranet-based e-CMS learning process (N = 53). The research tools used for collecting feedback and seeking opinions are meeting with mentors and students from irrespective of engineering disciplines through conducting informal unstructured interviews, observations and questionnaire.

The scope of questionnaire is limited to the study of e-Content-based learning process toward overall look of the user interface of the e-CMS application, efficiency of search plug-in, layout of the video courses home page, content of the lectures, quality of audio and video and the impact of learning through intranet-based e-CMS toward gaining new concepts, gaining self-confidence in solving course-related problems and lab assignments and implementing the course-based concepts in real-time applications. The feedback has been taken by the students of all major engineering disciplines. Figure 19.7 briefs the ratio of feedback taken by the students in engineering discipline wise. The feedback was measured in a 5-point scale (1 = Poor, 2 = Average, 3 = Good, 4 = Very Good, 5=Excellent). Table 19.1 illustrates the results of the responses received by the students toward intranet-based e-CMS.

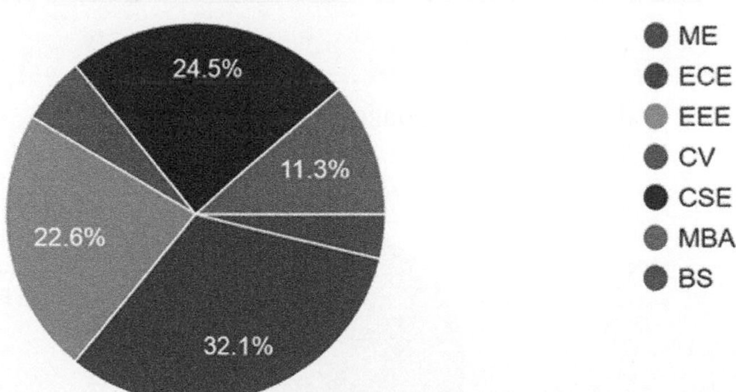


**FIGURE 19.7** Percentage of feedback taken by students according to engineering discipline.

The responses also been taken by the students regarding influences of e-Content-based learning in their regular teaching learning process toward whether the e-Content-based learning were interesting or boring; whether learning through e-Content were the students were more active or less active than their regular classes; seeking opinion were e-Content-based learning were useful or not useful and lastly, getting opinion from students e-CMS packages were useful or not useful. Figures 19.8–19.11, respectively, illustrate the responses received by the students regarding influences of e-Content-based learning in their regular teaching learning process.

**TABLE 19.1** Percentage and Total Count of the Survey Results

| Particulars | Poor | Average | Good | Very Good | Excellent |
|---|---|---|---|---|---|
| Overall look | 00% | 1.9% | 9.4% | 60.4% | 28.3% |
| | 00 | 01 | 05 | 32 | 15 |
| Efficiency of search | 00% | 7.5% | 18.9% | 37.7% | 35.8% |
| | 00 | 04 | 10 | 20 | 19 |
| Layout home page | 00% | 3.8% | 3.8% | 34% | 43.4% |
| | 00 | 02 | 10 | 18 | 23 |
| Content of lecture | 00% | 3.8% | 15.1% | 50.9% | 30.2% |
| | 00 | 02 | 08 | 27 | 16 |
| Quality of audio | 00% | 7.5% | 20.8% | 26.4% | 45.3% |
| | 00 | 04 | 11 | 14 | 24 |
| Quality of video | 00% | 9.4% | 13.2% | 39.6% | 37.7% |
| | 00 | 05 | 07 | 21 | 20 |

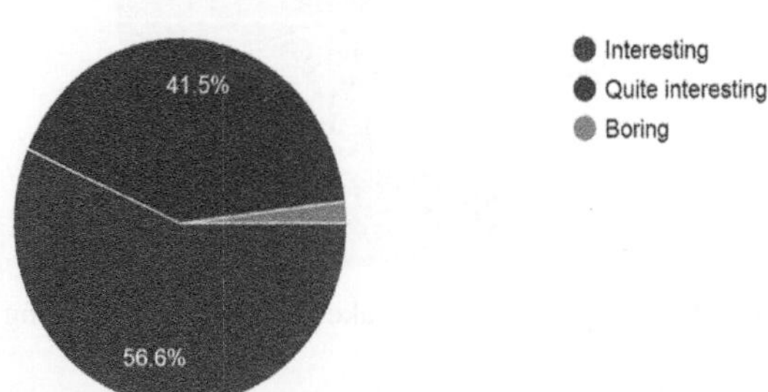


**FIGURE 19.8** Percentage of feedback taken by students regarding e-Content-based learning.

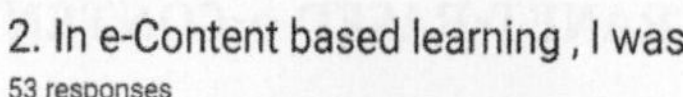


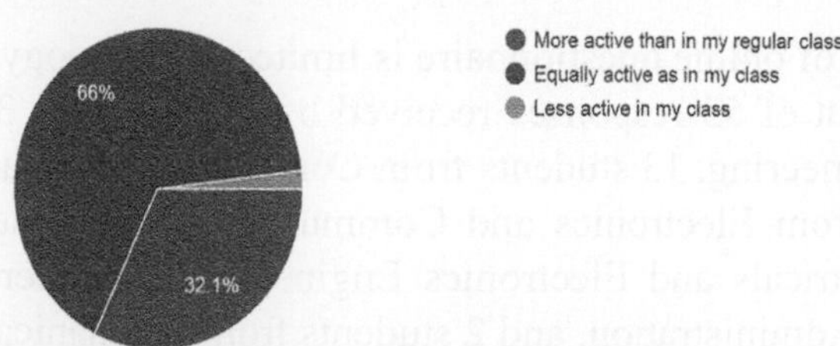


**FIGURE 19.9** Percentage of feedback taken by students regarding whether students are active or not active in e-Content-based learning.

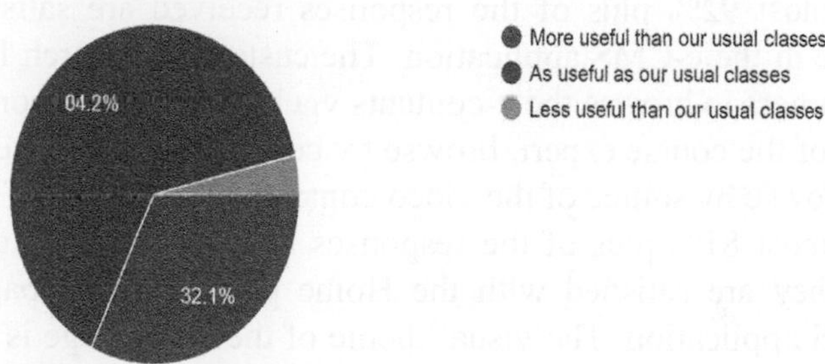


**FIGURE 19.10** Percentage of feedback taken by students regarding e-Content-based learning were useful or not useful.

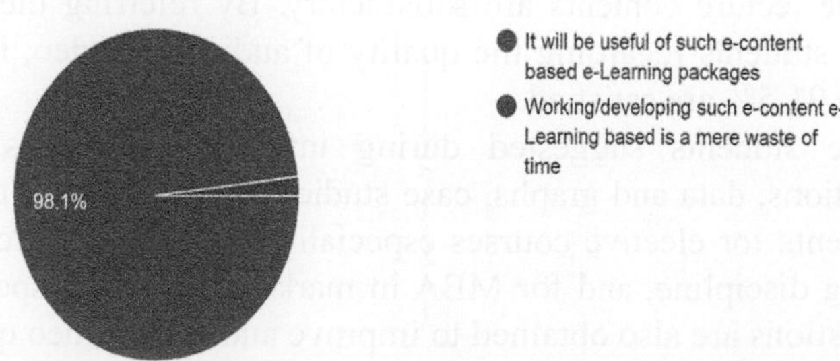


**FIGURE 19.11** Percentage of feedback taken by students regarding usefulness of e-CMS.

## 19.5 INTERPRETATIONS OF INTRANET-BASED e-CONTENT MANAGEMENT SYSTEM

The scope of online questionnaire is limited to pedagogy, process, and technology. Out of 53 responses received by the students, 3 students are from Civil Engineering, 13 students from Computer Science and Engineering, 17 students from Electronics and Communications Engineering, 12 students from Electricals and Electronics Engineering, 6 students from Master of Business Administration, and 2 students from Mechanical Engineering.

The results highlight that almost 98% plus of the participants are satisfied with the overall look of the e-CMS application. The e-CMS is developed in such a manner that the visual theme of the solution has been designed in accordance with the basic principles of simple and uncluttered layout and mild pleasing colors in order to present an academic ambiance and minimize viewer distraction.

Almost 92% plus of the responses received are satisfied with search feature in the e-CMS application. The customized search feature facilitates the learners to browse the e-contents via browse by keyword, browse by the name of the course expert, browse by course name, browse by course code, and browse by source of the video contents (NPTEL or VTU).

Almost 81% plus of the responses received by the students highlights that, they are satisfied with the Home page or index page layout of the e-CMS application. The visual theme of the home page is design in such a way that is simple and organized layout according to academic standards. The foreground colors are mild pleasing according to highlight the academic atmosphere with minimum student interruption. One click accesses to the most important features of the e-CMS.

Presently the e-CMS comprises of NPTEL Phase-I and VTU academic video and web contents. Almost 96% plus of the students have expressed that the lecture contents are satisfactory. By referring the response given by the students regarding the quality of audio and video, it is observe that almost 91.5% are satisfied.

The students suggested during informal interviews to incorporate animations, data and graphs, case studies in the lecture content, to develop e-contents for elective courses especially for Computer Science and Engineering discipline, and for MBA in marketing and HR specialization area. Suggestions are also obtained to improve audio and video quality.

By referring the feedback and survey report, it is learn that it is better to take the inputs from the students that they feel the course is difficult and inputs from the Principal's regarding the scarcity of faculties for the respective courses in their respective engineering disciplines and also considering the most detained courses in previous university examination results. By considering this methodology, the objective of intranet-based education through e-CMS can be achieved; the maximum utilization can be made. In addition to developing e-Content repository of academic courses, the special topics on current trends, emerging technologies, placement and training, soft skills, career guidance program, industry experts talks can be made available in the e-Content repository for the benefit of student community. The e-Contents on the topics on research methodologies, thesis writing, and PhD course work can also be made for research scholars.

Nearly 56.6%, that is, almost 30 participants out of 53 have stated that e-Content-based learning were interesting, about 41.5%, that is, 22 participants out of 53 stated that e-Content-based learning were quite interesting and 1 participant from MBA stated that e-Content-based learning is boring. When I approach the candidate personally to seek his reflections regarding his feedback, he replied that, watching of lecture videos without the interaction with the faculty leads to one way of learning.

Nearly 32.1%, that is, almost 17 participants out of 53 have stated that e-Content-based learning was more interesting than in their regular classes. About 66%, that is, 35 participants out of 53 stated that e-Content-based learning was equally active as in their regular classes and 1 participant stated that e-Content-based learning is less active than in their regular classes. When I approach the candidate personally to seek his reflections regarding his feedback, he replied that, watching of lecture videos without the interaction with the faculty leads to one way of learning.

Nearly 32.1%, that is, almost 17 participants out of 53 participants responded that that e-Content-based learning was more useful than their regular classes. About 64.2%, that is, 34 participants out of 53 stated that e-Content-based learning was as useful as their regular classes and 2 participants stated that e-Content-based learning is less useful than their regular classes. Whereas when I approach the candidates personally to seek his reflections regarding his feedback, the students replied that watching lecture videos without the interaction with the faculty does not fulfil the classroom environment.

Nearly 98.1%, that is, almost 52 participants out of 53 participants responded that that e-Content-based learning was useful and 1 participant stated that developing e-Content-based learning environment is mere waste of time. When I approach the candidates personally, the student replied that, developing any e-Learning packages cannot fill the faculty place. I am able to convey that the importance of e-Learning packages and their impact in student motivation through success video stories provided by NPTEL, by stating the case study that, if any student miss the important class by one or other reason. The same class can be recorded and lecture content made available in the e-CMS, the missed class can be fulfilled with the help of e-Learning package and explaining the importance given by the Government of India for ICT-based education but ultimately the candidate is able to convince about the importance of e-Learning packages.

## 19.6 CONCLUSION

In conclusion, the learning process in e-Content-based technology leads to a major paradigm shift in education with a great impact on education domain. The e-Content-based education technology can be used as the strategic instructional medium for teaching and learning process in our education system. The trends indicate that e-Content-based teaching and learning process in Karnataka will gain ground in higher education institutions and the e-Content medium will emerge as an effective platform for teaching and learning process.

## KEYWORDS

- **e-Learning 2.0**
- **e-Content**
- **intranet**
- **multimedia**
- **video on demand**
- **Web 2.0**

## REFERENCES

Ajithkumar C. ICT in Education. New Delhi: A.P.H. Publishing Corporation; 2018.

Bakia M. Internet-based education. International Encyclopedia of Education. 2010; 102–8.

Deveci H. Value education through distance learning: opinions of students who already completed value education. Turkish Online Journal of Distance Education. 2015;16(1).

Eastmond DV. Adult learners and internet-based distance education. New Directions for Adult and Continuing Education. 1998;1998(78):33–41.

Gernsbacher MA. Why Internet-based education? Frontiers in Psychology. 2015;5.

Kharbirymbai BB. ICT in Education. Guwahati: EBH Publishers (India); 2013.

Manjunatha B. An appraisal of internet-based education in Karnataka state. 2019 IEEE Tenth International Conference on Technology for Education (T4E). :238–239.

Manjunatha B. An appraisal of satellite based teaching/learning structure in Karnataka state. Quality Teacher Education vis-a-vis School Education. 2019;19;III:23–32.

Michael K. Virtual classroom: reflections of online learning. Campus-Wide Information Systems. 2012;29(3):156–65.

Naseerali MK. ICT in Education. Delhi, India: Meena Book Publications; 2017.

Neo TK, Neo M. Classroom innovation: engaging students in interactive multimedia learning. Campus-Wide Information Systems. 2004;21(3):118–24.

Nptel, online courses and certification, Learn for free [Internet]. [cited 2019Nov30]. Available from: http://www.nptel.ac.in/

Online Courses [Internet]. Online courses. [cited 2019Nov30]. Available from: https://onlinecourses-archive.nptel.ac.in/

Page T. A learner evaluation of the use of Intranet-based instructional resources and MLE in support of the teaching and learning of CAE. International Journal of Learning Technology. 2005;1(3):339.

Phipps RA. Measuring quality in internet-based higher education. International Higher Education. 2015;(20).

Sheela VP. Digital library in open universities—a review. Indian Journal of Library and Information Science. 2015;9(1):75–8.

Swayam Central [Internet]. Swayam Central. [cited 2019Nov30]. Available from: https://swayam.gov.in/

VTU Elearning | E-learning [Internet]. [cited 2019Nov30]. Available from: http://elearning.vtu.ac.in/

Yadav R, Tiruwa A, Suri PK. Internet-based learning (IBL) in higher education: a literature review. Journal of International Education in Business. 2017;10(2):102–29.

# CHAPTER 20

# Comparative Study of Four Options of ICT Systems in Management and Administration of Educational Institutions

NAMAN JAIN[1*] and BHUVAN UNHELKAR[2]

[1]*Silverline Prestige School, Ghaziabad, India*

[2]*University of South Florida, Sarasota-Manatee, FL 34242, USA*

[*]*Corresponding author. E-mail: jain.naman31@gmail.com*

## ABSTRACT

Information and communication technologies (ICT) not only enable deployment of education in a scalable manner but are also poised to provide effective measure and control of educational institutions. There are many challenges of education deployment in India including vast numbers of students, the social issue of lack of adaptability, and quality of educational IT service providers. The challenge that stands out the most is the measure and control of governance and administration of institutions. This is particularly so because of the myriad social, educational, government and financial complexities in which these institutions operate. ICT provides an opportunity to put automation and optimization in educational processes that enable the institutions to have a certain level of agility in their business. ICT has the potential to provide effective measures in terms of teaching–learning pedagogies. In this chapter, we explore the opportunities for educational institutions in India through the use of ICT such as cloud-based deployments, Teacher–Student Collaboration, Data Analytics-based measurements, predictions and corrective actions related to schedules, administration, teaching–learning outcomes and implementation of policies and procedures. There are four groups of

ICT-based systems identified that can be considered in school administration. We present these groups as a scholarly paper with detailed thoughts and strategies based on the hands-on experience of the lead author.

## 20.1 INTRODUCTION TO THE CHALLENGES OF SCHOOL EDUCATION—AN INDIAN CONTEXT

Nelson Mandela, former South African President and Noble Laureate, once observed that education is the most powerful weapon which can be used to change the world.

Information and communication technologies (ICT) not only enable deployment of education in a scalable manner but are also poised to provide effective administration and governance of educational institutions. Tearle (2004) developed a framework to identify important factors in relation to the implementation of ICT schools; that particular study deals with a UK secondary school. The approach is characterized by considering the process of implementing use of ICT across a whole school for teaching and learning as a special case of implementing change (Tearle, 2004).

One of the important challenges in the education sector in India is the number of students is increasing at a rapid pace. Coupled with this challenge is the need to manage and administer the educational institutions in an efficient and effective manner. Senior administrators including school Principals, Directors, and Administrators are continuously working to understand and deal with the management of their institutions. ICT reaches these students in terms of educational contents, but also provide effective measures in terms of educational delivery, administration, and the ongoing challenge of optimization in a highly dynamic environment. There are a few options in terms of utilizing the ICT systems in education. In this chapter, we explore the opportunities in school education in India through the use of ICT such as Cloud-based deployments, Teacher–Student Collaboration, Data Analytics-based measurements, predictions, and corrective actions related to managing and administering effective educational institutions (Unhelkar, 2018). Furthermore, we reflect on the impact of these systems on the teaching–learning outcomes and on formulation of policies and procedures for the education sector in India. We present this as a scholarly paper with detailed thoughts and strategies based on the hands-on experience of the lead author.

## 20.2 ICT AND EDUCATIONAL INSTITUTION'S MANAGEMENT

ICT systems provide many significant opportunities in the education domain. ICT has been specifically studied by Said et al. (2010) in the context of how it can enable education to change or improve the lives of people, with particular emphasis on developing regions and underserved communities. Our observations lead us to theorize that ICT-based systems enhance the many business processes in educational institutions including management and administration.

A school may not be fully virtual as it is also meant to develop social skills that would otherwise be lacking. Studies by Askarzai et al. (2014) indicate that virtualization of any organization (in this context a school) is influenced by the biases—such as those between school management and teachers, and between teachers and students.

When it comes to business processes, in particular, the scheduling of teachers, classrooms, labs and various other activities in a typical school are highly complex—matching the degree of complexity of managing the schedules of airline pilots and specialist doctors. If schools have to be student centric, then the corresponding administrative and management processes also need to be designed and implemented keeping the student as the key stakeholder in mind (Unhelkar, 2015). Furthermore, the dynamicity of the situation is such that there can be changes on a daily basis to a carefully laid out schedule. Therefore, hand-held mobile devices are most likely to impact school administrative and business processes as well as delivery of learning objectives (Unhelkar, 2006).

Following are some of the key challenges arising out of the complexity of managing a typical school—particularly in the Indian context:

1. Increasingly larger number of students and reduced number of teachers per class.
2. Myriad government rules and regulations requiring compliance from the educational institutions.
3. Constant interruptions of government agencies that interfere & change the pre-planned calendar of activities and overall operation.
4. Complexity and dynamicity of educational business processes that are made up of numerous factors that are also continuously changing.
5. Continuous and unexpected changes occurring due to the volatile social and cultural environment.
6. Increased demands from parental groups in terms of reporting on progress and its variations.

Need to plan at both tactical and strategic level in the midst of ongoing school operations.

## 20.3 FOUR OPTIONS FOR SCHOOL MANAGEMENT

Based on the experience of the lead author, we identified four high-level groups of options available and being used by educational institutions (typically schools) for day-to-day and strategic management. Following are the four options:

1. *Existing Tool Suite:* Use of available tools such as Google suite (G-sheets, GDocs, GDrive, etc.), Dropbox, and home tools. Excel and Google sheets bring a lot of power because of their inbuilt capabilities. These tools provide customizability—because they enable the users to build processes and data entry, filtering, and analytics. User entry of data is collated in the form of a report which results in actionable insights. The challenge faced by school executives is receiving various reports, in multiple visualizations and finding enough material to make administrative and academic decisions. This data is not easy to visualize through these tools because the data is distributed among multiple systems, entry of data happens at multiple points (redundancy) and the speed of analytics is not always fast enough to handle the window of opportunity. Furthermore, the data is neither historically sufficient nor in the right format to enable planning. Descriptive analytics are used in order to understand historical data and create insights for long-term and strategic planning. This is not easily possible through tool suites. For example, holidays, exam schedules, and classroom capacity planning that is included in the calendar is not easy to create with the current data and systems. A school calendar is neither visible nor dynamic when a principal is using her diary for the planning process. Embedding vacation, holidays (vacations and holidays that are fixed or preplanned and included in the calendar for planning), sick leave, etc., to the calendar provides visibility and metrics (achieving learning objectives over the number of working days) to management.
2. *Medium-level Enterprise Resource Planning (ERP) systems:* Use of medium-level ERP systems (ground up)—may require data entry. The key challenge with these ERP systems is that they try to become an all-encompassing solution for many different problems. Their attempt

to provide all solutions that come with these systems is dispersed. For example, school transport does not integrate with the timetabling system of the school. However, the accounting and finance module is their strongest (e.g., receiving fees and expenses). Management is interested in the financial aspect, rather than the timetabling, attendance, learning outcomes and examinations—as these are not under the direct focus of management and, therefore, substandard. For example, if the aforementioned systems are not available, management tends to use manual systems to get work done. Thus, while ERP is available, it is not used in decision making in many aspects of school operations . Another example, a finger impression in a biometric machine, should result in calculation of salary including the leave taken by the person, sick leaves, overtime performed and so on. Substandard ERPs currently available are not able to seamlessly perform such basic functionalities.

3. *Comprehensive ERP:* Use of comprehensive ERP (PeopleSoft, SAP, Oracle)—require comprehensive data conversion. These systems are typically high cost that require large investments in cost, time, and training.
4. *Collaborative Engine:* Use of an overall collaborative Engine on top of all existing and new systems (e.g. Timetabling, Tally, Attendance, Parental) based on expertise of each system, followed by an artificial intelligence (AI) Engine to collaborate and visualize the data analytics (Gonsalves, 2017; Unhelkar, 2018) . This will require customization—and Cloud is the means to handle these systems. Cloud-based services can be implemented across these systems and producc collaborative results provided the systems are on a single cloud platform. The interrelationship between these systems is made possible through Cloud-based services which require customization at ICT systems level.

## 20.4 COMPARISON OF THE OPTIONS FOR SCHOOL MANAGEMENT

Table 20.1 shows the changing nature of educational management and administration. Owners and principals at the individual school level need to consider and explore the opportunities and risks associated with the use of one of the groups of technologies highlighted in Table 20.1. The concept of overall education delivery itself is rapidly changing. Classrooms today are moving from Chalk-and-Talk approaches that are based on One-to-All methodologies toward implementation of collaborative many-to-many methods

**TABLE 20.1** Comparison of Four Types of ICT Systems to Support Educational Institution Administration and Management

| | **1—Existing Tool Suite:** | **2—Medium-level ERP systems:** | **3—Comprehensive ERP:** | **4— Collaborative Engine:** |
|---|---|---|---|---|
| Data (volume, velocity and variety) | Already available as entered by various stakeholders | Needs to know sources of data—as external sources are involved | Provides detailed reference data from third-party and government sources | Mixed data—in house and external that needs to be put together in a sensible manner |
| Cost (initial and operating) | Minimal—as the suite exists | Manageable by medium-sized schools | Only affordable by large, typically private institutions | Incurs costs of creating and managing a collaborative platform |
| Time (for changeover) | No time needed | Typically 3 months to switch | Typically 1 year to switch | Can range from 6 months to a year—in a phased manner |
| Educational Process Agility | Not very agile due to dispersed data sitting in silos | Moderate agility as data is placed in common database | High agility due to commonality of data and processes | Moderate agility depending on the phase of collaboration |
| Measuring Teaching-Learning Outcomes | Distributed and uncoordinated measures | Easy measurement if outcomes are stable | Improved measurement if outcomes are changing | Improved measurement provided collaborative platforms are stable |
| Policy and Procedure Formulation | Challenging to enter policies and procedures in dispersed systems | Easy to enter policies and procedures but they are not comprehensive | Easy to enter and manage policies and procedures in a comprehensive manner | Flexibility in policies and procedures—entry and management |
| Compliance (Ease of storage, audit and reporting) | Ineffective in demonstrating compliance | Effective in demonstrating compliance | Effective in demonstrating compliance | Requires customization of platform to demonstrate compliance |
| Acceptance (teachers, student, parents, admin) | Accepted without resistance and training as already being used | Requires basic training for all stakeholders to start using the systems | Requires advanced training for stakeholders; | Requires onsite management of collaborative platform in addition to the training |

**TABLE 20.1** *(Continued)*

| | **1—Existing Tool Suite:** | **2—Medium-level ERP systems:** | **3—Comprehensive ERP:** | **4— Collaborative Engine:** |
|---|---|---|---|---|
| Technical (Cloud services) | Basic technology around 'home computing' with possible data storage in the cloud | Usually hosted on the Cloud but can also be on local servers. | Invariably hosted on the Cloud; Service-oriented architecture | Comprises Services on the Cloud together with local, in-house applications |
| Security and Privacy | Not secured due to lack of user awareness and basic support from technology | More secured that stand-alone applications; | Highly secured but susceptible to cyber attacks | Requires customized Security and attention to Privacy of stakeholders—based on in-house technical knowledge |

that are based on effective capitalization of technologies. ICT systems that are being explored here need to support the changing nature of education as follows:

- Collaborative Learning rather than one-teacher to many-student format. This is the type of learning that is facilitated by the teacher but delivered through interactions among students. ICT systems facilitate collaborative learning by the ability to relate students independent of geographic and socio-cultural divides.
- Teachers moving away as the deliverer of information to the facilitator for research at grass-root level and, thereby, developing the skills for self-learning.
- Flipped Classrooms wherein teachers play the role of a service provider and solutions are discovered based on dynamic questions.
- From delivery of information to development kills, or 21st century skills, needed to excel in today's workplace.
- Enquiry-based Learning by making the classes highly modularized and based on specific questions/enquiries.
- Project-Based Learning that enables students to understand the start and the end of a learning challenge resulting in a project with goals, methods and resources.
- Critical Thinking approach facilitated by systems supporting the opportunity to think and analyze problems.

ICT systems and technologies play a crucial and pivotal role to implementing the above aspects of progressive educational pedagogies. ICT systems are to be used to manage and administer education—but can also able to interact with teaching–learning tools like whiteboards, notebooks and writing instruments. ICT is a tool to deliver content, and also a tool than create content by students.

School processes include addressing the needs of all the stakeholders, creating the policies, training and deployment of ICT, etc. Increasingly, AI has started to play a role in helping schools maneuver their processes by anticipating the likely disruptive events (see studies by Gonsalves, 2017). Coupled with upcoming Internet of things devices (Santofimia, 2018), school business processes are poised for high-end automation.

Large technical organizations focus on developing products specific to education, catering to the needs and challenges of the sector. One organization is Google which developed the Google Suite for Education with Classroom tools (on the software side) to Chromebooks (at the hardware front). Use of ICT in administration, management and reporting of educational processes at the Government/State Level is also facilitated through ICT as these systems provide auditability and traceability; in turn leading to effective teaching–learning outcomes on a larger scale.

## 20.5 INSIGHTS OF CURRENT ORGANIZATION IN UTILIZATION OF ICT SYSTEMS

The comparison of the four groups of technologies and the implementation of the collaborative platform is being tried out at a local, private school in the Delhi/Ghaziabad area. With over 2000 students and close to 100 staff and teachers, the school is experimenting with collaborative technologies to bring together the existing plethora of systems under one platform. The advantages of this effort are as follows:

1. Improved exchange of information between systems.
2. Ability to handle unexpected changes such as strikes, elections and sporting events—and rescheduling the school activities dynamically.
3. Unification of data and elimination of redundancies.
4. Improved traceability and auditability of transactions.

The challenges in the use of a collaborative platform are as follows:

1. Need for greater understanding of technologies and systems.
2. Ongoing training and coaching of staff and parents.
3. Dependency on the system to a level where it becomes a single point of failure.

Most educational institutions in India have grown organically. The systems and processes built to tackle operations and challenges are very unique. The cost of building comprehensive ERPs through systems such as SAP/Oracle/PeopleSoft is not feasible for most institutions. Kumar and Sundarraj (2018) argue about the value of disruptive innovations in business, and Sathi (2012) specifically talks about Big Data analytics as a game changing disruptive technology. These are the technologies likely to provide significant advantages in focused analytics for schools as well as development and implementation of government policies and procedures.

On the other hand, medium-level ERPs are unable to account for the unique challenges associated with educational institution. With experience, it is notable that the best systems are the ones that are built using Existing Tool Suite, tackling individual aspects of delivery and management (as mentioned in Option 1). To overcome the challenges of that system, it is most suitable to build a common database on top for these individual systems. Over and above these, an Intelligent AI-Engine makes sense of the Big Data generated by the individual suite. The analysis/dashboard/report generated by this modern system helps relevant stakeholders in decision-making. Specifically, school business processes housed on the Cloud are most likely to provide opportunities to assimilate data for analytical purposes (Murugesan and Bojanova, 2016; and Unhelkar, 2018).Based on our observations and experience, the ideal system is Collaborative Engine (Option 4) built on top of the Existing Tool Suite (Option 1).

## 20.6 CONCLUSIONS AND FUTURE DIRECTIONS

In this chapter, we have positioned the need for ICT-based educational systems to be compared for their various advantages and challenges. We outlined four groups of ICT-based education management and administrative systems. Based on our observations, experience and scholarly studies, we identified option 4, the collaborative option, as the most ideal option. There are numerous advantages and challenges in the use of such collaborative educational platforms as highlighted here. We are conducting further experiments and validating the robustness of our approach. We are also outlining a method to help educational institutions transition from option 1 (the most likely option currently being used in schools, particularly in India) to option 4.

## KEYWORDS

- **cloud-based deployment of educational contents**
- **challenges in school education**
- **education in India**
- **educational policies and procedures**
- **educational process optimization**

## REFERENCES

Askarzai, W., Lan, Y., Unhelkar, B.: Challenges of a virtual organisation: Empirical evidence from Australian SMEs. Global Journal of Finance and Management 6(9), 919–924 (2014).

Gonsalves, T.: Artificial intelligence: A non-technical introduction. Sophia University Press, Japan (2017).

Kumar, V., Sundarraj, R. P.: The value of disruptive innovations: Global innovation and economic value. Springer, Switzerland (2018).

Murugesan, S., Bojanova, I.: Encyclopedia of cloud computing. Wiley-IEEE Press, New Jersey (2016).

Penni Tearle: A theoretical and instrumental framework for implementing change in ICT in education, Cambridge Journal of Education, 34(3), 331–351 (2004).

Said Assar, Redouane El Amrani, Richard T. Watson. ICT and education: a critical role in human and social development. Information Technology for Development, 16 (3), 151–158 (2010).

Santofimia, M. J. Enabling smart behavior through automatic service composition for Internet of things-based smart homes. International Journal of Distributed Sensor Networks, 14(8) (2018).

Sathi, A. Big Data Analytics: Disruptive technologies for changing the game. MC Press, Idaho (2012).

Severi, S. M2M Technologies: Enablers for a Pervasive Internet of Things. Proceedings of the 2014 European Conference on Networks and Communications (EuCNC). IEEE, New York (2014).

Shah, S. A., Horne, A., Capella, J.: Good data won't guarantee good decisions. Harvard Business Review, April (2014).

Unhelkar, B.: Handbook of Research in Mobile Business: Technical, Methodological and Social Perspective. IGI Global, Pennsylvania (2006).

Unhelkar, B.: Customer-centric business as an interdisciplinary affair. In: Proceedings of IIBA Conference. Anahei Publishing, Florida, p. 349 (2015).

Unhelkar, B.: Big data strategies for agile business. CRC Press, Taylor and Francis Group/an Auerbach Book), Florida, (2018).

## CHAPTER 21

# Effectiveness of Developed Learning Management System in Terms of Achievement of B.Ed. Teacher Trainees

DIWYA JOSHI[1,*] and SHANTI TEJWANI[2]

[1]*School of Education, DAVV, Indore, 452001, Madhya Pradesh*

[2]*Shri Vaishnav College of Teachers Training, Indore, 452009, Madhya Pradesh*

[*]*Corresponding author. E-mail: diwyajoshi01@gmail.com*

### ABSTRACT

The present research work is associated with Information and Communication Technology which involves the incorporation of Internet services in the teaching methods to provide all round fortification of education. With the use of technology and Internet in teaching–learning has shown noteworthy changes, as they provide new ways of gaining knowledge. Today the students prefer to learn informally rather than to get formal education. Also, during this fast pacing life most of the teaching methods skip the needs of slow learners and backward child. To overcome these flaws of today's teaching methods, one of the ways of teaching widely to endorse knowledge consists in the use and creation of virtual ambience around the learner which is available online in various formats, which can be achieved by Learning Management Systems (LMS). This chapter is about a study whose objective is to study the effect of LMS in terms of achievement for B.Ed. Teacher Trainees. The type of research design was Single-Group Pretest–Posttest Design. The sample consists of 48 B.Ed. Teacher Trainees of second semester who were selected by random sampling. Single group was taught by LMS and achievement test was applied before and after teaching through LMS. The tool was developed by the researcher that is, an achievement test. Appropriate statistics that is, correlated *t*-test was used for the analysis of data. The results of the present study reveal that LMS is effective in terms of achievement and significantly affect the achievement of B.Ed. Teacher Trainees. These results are valuable for augmenting achievement using LMS–MOODLE.

## 21.1 INTRODUCTION

### *21.1.1 LEARNING MANAGEMENT SYSTEM*

The Learning Management System (LMS) is a computer application that is used for arrangement, distribute, circulate, and consign self-paced online courses. LMS works as fundamental repositories to address all type of instructive necessities. The foremost areas addressed by LMS operation are:

1. *Course preparation*: according to the syllabus of the sample.
2. *Immediate assessment*: using various features of MOODLE app and Google forms.
3. *Student commitment*: through notifications.
4. *Content organization*: as per the units, the theories, and the course.

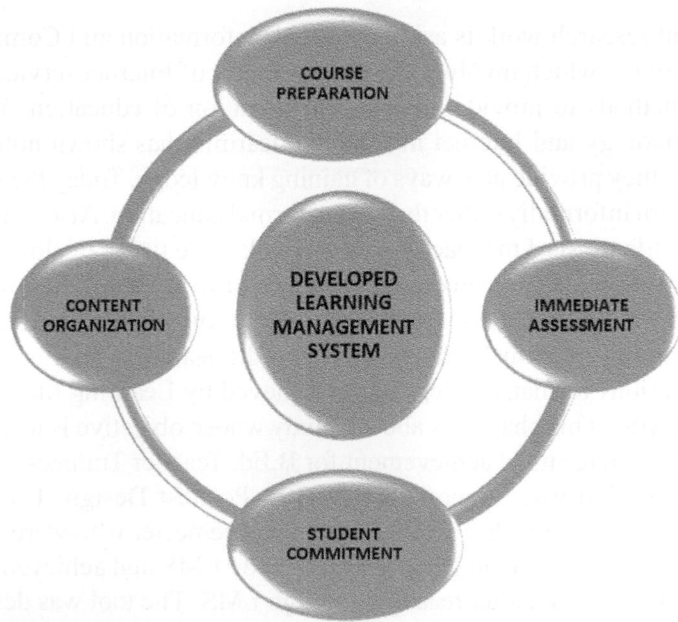


**FIGURE 21.1** Areas of developed learning management system.

### *21.1.2 MODULAR OBJECT ORIENTED DYNAMIC LEARNING ENVIRONMENT (MOODLE)*

MOODLE is an ellipsis for Modular Object Oriented Dynamic Learning Environment. It is used as LMS to continue and support users involved in growing student-centered educational surroundings. An effective LMS can have following functions:

1. Strong management
2. Proper commands and controls, and
3. Fruitful conversation between teacher and learner.

### *21.1.3 LMS AND ACHIEVEMENT*

A widespread way to measure the extent of learning is to assess learner's achievement. Assessing learner's achievement in e-learning surroundings requires exceptional awareness. Test results, as achievement scores are frequently used as the measuring bond for student encroachment to the next rank and as an estimate for judging the excellence of the college and the educators who work in them. The strongest predilection noted in a study done by Buzetto-More (2008) was toward the online compliance of assignments, with students overpoweringly noting that they like having the facility to check their assignment grades online. It has been established that there is a correlation between academic involvement, discussion forums, and grade.

## 21.2 RATIONALE

Reigeluth (1994), Abdallah Arman et al. (2009), Jo et al. (2015), and Mehmet (2016) have studied LMS and independently recognized and analyzed the views of learners to determine whether the LMS had any persuasion on their educational achievement. The fallout revealed that approximately all of the learners thought LMS can increase educational achievement.

In Indian perspective, very few studies had been conducted. This created a gap for the researcher to design the present LMS in a collaborative manner for its effectiveness and to measure achievement by using LMS. Further, the researcher has found a common thing in all these researches as most are for technical students and very few LMS are for B.Ed. Teacher Trainees in India. This draws attention of the researcher toward the present situation and decided to develop an LMS for B.Ed. Teacher Trainees.

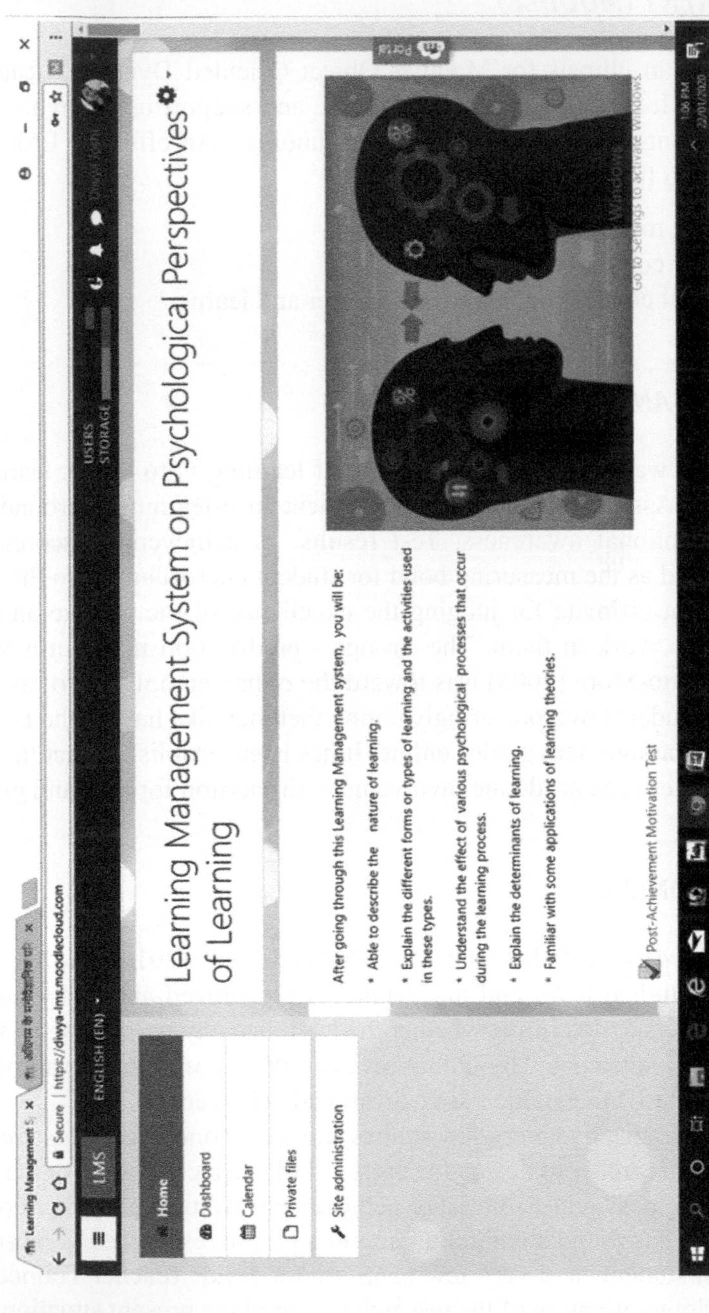


**FIGURE 21.2** Overview of developed learning management system.

## 21.3 NEED AND SIGNIFICANCE

LMS can be used widely for different curriculums. Specifically, the researcher would like to suggest that LMS can work even better if some modifications can be done in its assessment design. Due to which the faculty can apply various techniques to assess achievement and that designs can come under collaboration based assessment designs. LMS tools should be improved by upholding tasks and careful examinations of prearranged instructor and user, and peer interactions on the basis of these tasks. LMS involves communication tools, like chat, discussion boards, collaboration of Google docs, and Google forms, thus, improving the relations among LMS users.

## 21.4 DESIGN

In the present study, *Single-Group Pretest–Posttest Design* was used. The layout is:

O X O

where,

O = Pre-test and Post-test observation

X = Treatment

## 21.5 OBJECTIVE

To study the effectiveness of developed LMS in terms of achievement for B.Ed. Teacher Trainees.

## 21.6 HYPOTHESIS

There will be no significant effect of LMS in terms of achievement for B.Ed. Teacher Trainees.

## 21.7 METHODOLOGY

### *21.7.1 SAMPLE*

The present study was experimental in nature. Single group was taken from randomly selected B.Ed. colleges of Indore (Madhya Pradesh). The sample was consisted of 48 students of B.Ed. second semester.

### 21.7.2 TOOLS

#### 21.7.1.1 ACHIEVEMENT TEST

Achievement test was used to assess the achievement in psychological perspectives of learning of B.Ed. Teacher Trainees. Achievement CRT including 35 items was designed and developed by the researcher including items from theories of learning, through Google forms. Students have filled that form on the app developed by the researcher using MOODLE, asynchronously, or synchronously.

### 21.7.3 PROCEDURE OF DATA COLLECTION

An LMS was developed by the researcher using MOODLE. The permission of the principal of the college, Shri Vaishnav College of Teachers Training, Indore (Madhya Pradesh) was taken for the research work. Before the treatment, dependent variable; achievement was assessed. Then treatment was given to 48 students of the single group of B.Ed. Teacher Trainees. Then the same group was treated through LMS developed using MOODLE.

## 21.8 RESULTS AND INTERPRETATION

### 21.8.1 EFFECT OF DEVELOPED LMS FOR B.ED. TEACHER TRAINEES IN TERMS OF ACHIEVEMENT

The data were analyzed with the help of correlated *t*-test. First of all, the scores of achievement were tested for the assumptions of normality and homogeneity of variances. Then correlated *t*-test was performed using IBM-SPSS software.

### 21.8.2 SUMMARY OF CORRELATED T-TEST OF ACHIEVEMENT SCORES FOR B.Ed. TEACHER TRAINEES

From Table 21.2 it is clear that the observed value of correlation with df (47) is 0.851, whose two-tailed significance value is 0.000, which is less than 0.01; hence, is significant at 0.01 level of significance. Therefore, the null hypothesis "there will be no significant effect of LMS for B.Ed. Teacher

Trainees in terms of achievement" is rejected. Hence, it can be concluded that treatment is effective in terms of achievement. Table 21.1 shows the standard errors of the scores of B.Ed. Teacher Trainees before and after the treatment with LMS.

**TABLE 21.1** Paired Samples Statistics

| | | Mean | N | Std. Deviation | Std. Error Mean |
|---|---|---|---|---|---|
| Pair 1 | PreAch | 11.21 | 48 | 3.649 | 0.527 |
| | PostAch | 18.1458 | 48 | 3.76428 | 0.54333 |

**TABLE 21.2** Paired Samples Correlations

| | | N | Df | Correlation | Sig. (2-tailed) |
|---|---|---|---|---|---|
| Pair 1 | PreAch and PostAch | 48 | 47 | 0.851 | 0.000 |

## 21.9 FINDINGS

The major finding of the present study is as follows:

The LMS was found to be effective in terms of achievement when the single group was matched with respect to pre and post-achievement scores.

## 21.10 CONCLUSIONS

The results of the present study conclude that an LMS can be used to enhance achievement by using various tools. In this chapter researcher has developed an LMS using MOODLE for teaching theories of learning to the B.Ed. Teacher Trainees of second semester. Students taught through LMS–MOODLE have scored more in achievement than before and there is a positive correlation between the pre and the post-achievement scores. One of the reasons for this is MOODLE App offers freedom to learn anytime and anywhere to the students; thus, it is more flexible. The tools used in the LMS–MOODLE have increased the motivation of students, and is the fundamental reason behind the augmented scores of achievement brought after being taught through developed LMS on MOODLE. Going through the findings of this study, we are a bit confident that a LMS system can effectively and satisfactorily increase achievement while teaching theories of learning to the B.Ed. Teacher Trainees of second semester.

**KEYWORDS**

- **Learning Management System**
- **MOODLE**
- **achievement**

## REFERENCES

Al-Otaibi W. H.; *The Effectiveness of Blackboard-Based Blended Teaching in the Development of Academic Achievement, Study Skills and Self-Confidence among Students of Princess Nourahbint Abdulrahman University*. International Education Studies; Vol. 10, No. 11; 2017 ISSN 1913-9020 E-ISSN 1913-9039 Published by Canadian Center of Science and Education. (2017). Retrieved on Aug 11, 2018 from https://doi:10.5539/ies.v10n11p100.

Arman, Abdallah & Taha, El-Arif & Elgazzar, Abdul-latif. The Effect of e-learning Approach on Students' Achievement in Biomedical Instrumentation Course at Palestine Polytechnic University. Communications of the IBIMA. (2009).

Buzzetto. N. *Student Perceptions of Various E-Learning Components*. Interdisciplinary Journal of e-Skills and Lifelong Learning. (2009), 4. 10.28945/370.

Cavus, N., Uzunboylu, H. and Ibrahim, D., *The Effectiveness of Using Learning Management Systems and Collaborative Tools in Web-Based Teaching of Programming Language.* Paper presented at the 3rd ISEECE 23–25 November. 2006, Near East University, Lefkoşa, Cyprus.

Cook, J., *The Role of Dialogue in Computer-Based Learning and Observing Learning: An Evolutionary Approach to Theory*. Journal of Interactive Media in Education, 2001 (Theory for Learning Technologies). (2002), 2, 5. http://www-jime.open.ac.uk/2001/cook/cook-t.html

Dougiamas, M. and Taylor, P.C., *Moodle: Using Learning Communities to Create an Open Source Course Management System*. (2003) Proceedings of the EDMEDIA 2003 Conference, Honolulu, Hawaii. Retrieved June 11, 2018, from: http://dougiamas.com/writing/edmedia.

Firat, M., *Determining the effects of LMS learning behaviors on academic achievement in a learning analytic perspective.* Journal of Information Technology Education: Research. (2016), 15, 75–87. Retrieved from http://www.jite.org/documents/Vol15/JITEv15ResearchP075-087Firat1928.pdf

Fallerio, S., *A Study of the Effectiveness of Learning Management System on Student Engagement, Motivation and Performance in Higher Education.* (2014). Unpublished PhD thesis, SNDT Women's University, Mumbai.

Kulshreshta, T. and Kant, R., *Benefits of Learning Management System (LMS) in Indian Education.* (**2013**), Vol. 4, 1153–1164.

Lopes, A.P., *Teaching With LMS in Higher Education: Institute of Accounting and Administration–ISCAP*, Polytechnic Institute Oporto—IPP, Portugal (2011)

Monarch Media, *Open-source learning management systems: Sakai and Moodle* (2010). Retrieved August 11, 2018 from http://www.monarchmedia.com/wp-content/uploads/2015/01/opensource-lms-sakai-and-moodle.pdf

Mtebe, Jo et al. Learning Management System success: Increasing Learning Management System usage in higher education in sub-Saharan Africa. International Journal of Education and Development using Information and Communication Technology (IJEDICT). (2015), 11, 51–64.

Reigeluth, Charles. The Imperative for Systemic Change. (1994), 67, 9–13.

## CHAPTER 22

# ICT in Education and Sustainable Development: Prospects and Challenges

SUNAKSHI CHADHA

*Department of Management, IITM Janakpuri,*
*Dehi, 1100058, India. E-mail: sunakshichadha@gmail.com*

## ABSTRACT

In the society where environment and education have become two most important paradigms to change "Go Green" has become the major mantra in each and every aspect of society. There is a need of change toward a better economy and this chapter is focused more or less on conducting a review of how Information and Communication Technology (ICT) has led to carbon footprint reduction and what all are the prospects of virtual learning and e-learning environment development. The objective is to identify the relationship between sustainability indicators and the effect of ICT dimensions. In depth study of tripod model is done to effectively measure the relationship between the two paramcters. Sustainability indices like index of ecological and reduction of carbon footprint and index of sustainability are used for the study of relationship and supply of ICT-based infrastructure like hardware products, media, audio, video, and other content and other remote sensing technologies whether permits more effective monitoring or helps in mitigation of environmental risks as well as whether it led to better learning and monitoring leading to value education or not. The study is to see the prospects and possibilities of ICT in social development and the components required to leverage ICT for sustainable economic development. Thus, this chapter presents the design and development of virtual learning environment and its impact on sustainability.

## 22.1 INTRODUCTION

Information and Communication Technology (ICT) has a vital role to play by taking into account the quality of the content that is being provided and it also helps to improve the teachers' ability, content, and quality of delivering lectures making them updated and administrators as well. The role of ICT has been acknowledged and appreciated all across. ICT is playing major role in the effectiveness of teaching, learning, evaluation, and assessment mechanism. Also, there have been certain issues over the effectiveness and applicability of ICT tools in education. ICT is a helping hand in generating greater literacy and is also helping in reducing the carbon footprint and ecological balance. It enhances the scope of education by promoting and facilitating mobile learning and providing value education through advanced mechanism of smart classes. The major issue regarding this is that equal importance is not given to promoting this culture of learning both at school and at home in order to reduce the differences amongst students, teachers, and parents. ICT provides greater flexibility and accessibility in education to ensure that students, researchers as well as academicians can have access to knowledge anytime and from anywhere as Internet has turn out to be the major source of information accessible to anyone and everyone just on a click of a button. ICT also impacts the way knowledge is imparted and delivered and how students learn and recapitulate from the given information. There are various countries who have adopted new and virtual techniques to make their economy knowledge-based economy and India has moved the focus like e-literacy skill development, e-participation, and e-business skills.

## 22.2 REVIEW OF LITERATURE

**Reid (2002):** The author has explained that how ICT and its integration in education has its advantages as well as disadvantages. The use of ICT and its tools will not only lead to changing the ancient ways of teaching, but it also mandates as well as required the teacher or the tutor to be innovative, proactive in assimilating as well as modifying and upgrading their own teaching methodologies as well as materials and strategies with proximity to the changed and upgraded technology.

**Abbott and Faris (2008):** The author through this paper demonstrates that if we talk about all the teaching methodologies as well as strategies, collaborative rather than classroom learning and problem-based and critical thinking.

**Palak and Walls (2009):** This paper corresponds with the suggestion that integration of technology in education will not deliver the desired and resultant effect without having followed student-centered classroom practices and methodologies. So, the idea of integrating the technological upgradation and new communication technologies in education cannot be implemented in seclusion; and therefore, the impact of teacher methodology and content as well as the student response to the adaptation of modern techniques should be taken into account. When it is applied taking into account various diverse and different teaching methods and approaches; learning outcomes, results, and evaluation may be more successful.

**Whelan (2008):** The author has suggested that the findings will be more successful only if the suggestions for the use of ICT are invited from the teachers and scholars as at the stage of implementation; teachers are going to play the major role. In addition to this, the schools should also be well structured in providing some advanced learning support and system while integrating technology in their curriculum as well as assessment and instruction.

**Staples, Pugach, and Himes (2005):** The author has postulated through the paper that schools as well as colleges are suggested to come up with the advance workshops, seminars, and conferences for their teachers to improve their ICT skills and also to train them well for coming across and facing the possible challenges and problems while merging technology in their curriculum.

**Al-Ruz and Khasawneh (2011):** The author through this paper discussed the problems that are generally encountered while adapting modern technologies and the problems that are most commonly faced are access to computers and software as they are not within the reach of everyone, insufficient and lack of time for the planning of course, so stretching the focus onto these will result in the reduction of quality of content imparted and however there is also lack of adequate technical and administrative support for the implementation at the ground level, and also there is lack of drive for change in the mindset of top level authorities making the adaptation even more difficult.

The author through this paper also explained that there are also certain internal factors that impact the performance of students not merely just the adoption of ICT and some of these factors are teachers' attitude, confidence level of the teachers, and the way the content is delivered as well as the authenticity of the information that is being taught. However, through intensive research it is also found that there are certain external factors as well that impacts the use of ICT models. However, there has been very less research into the intensity of relationship between the internal and external factors and how far these relationships change in relation to the variables used. However, there is that examining and monitoring these relationships will just not only help teachers, students, and administrators understand but it will also help them all in reducing the challenges of using and adapting ICT better.

**Chen (2008):** The author here shows that there is no relationship between teachers' beliefs and attitudes and what they actually practice and follow at the time of integrating technology in the classroom.

**Chai, Koh, and Tsai (2010):** There have been very less chance for any author or researcher to study or to investigate the reciprocal relationship between teachers' attitudes, beliefs, and their practice.

## 22.3 OBJECTIVE

1. To study how digital revolution brings risks and benefits.
2. To study the influence of ICT in quality education and literacy drive.
3. To study the impact of ICT tools in reducing carbon footprint.

## 22.4 ROLE OF ICT IN SUSTAINABILITY

There have been limited studies regarding how ICT can be used to enable new strategies for sustainable innovations and demonstrate a significant enhancement in their competitiveness. There are several areas that ICT has addressed. These are economic areas resulting into reducing carbon footprint and thus reducing costs and creating quality initiatives. ICT has also resulted efficient resources consumption by bringing in the practice the innovative technologies. It has also improved the teaching learning as well as evaluation and assessment methodology resulting in quality education. ICT plays major role in fostering innovation and also reduces inequality between countries by facilitating social and economic progress. It offers innovative technologies ensuring smarter cities, smart water management, smart waste disposal, e-building, and efficiency in energy mechanism. However, digital revolution brings in the risks and benefits both. The key to integrate the ICT for improving the environment condition is to spread education and skilling is the key to adaptation because in the knowledge-based economy, it is only the ability to apply and implement the techniques that comes into picture, so various barriers can be reduced as far as the economy is educated thus, digital revolution will be of better importance in that case.

## 22.5 ROLE OF ICT IN EDUCATION

- *Help students in providing access to digital and online information efficiently and effectively*
  Information communication and technologies ensure that students have an access to the e-data and information as well as resources which help them to be more interactive also it will help and assist the students in their respective learning areas through engaging and grabbing their attention in the application of ICT.
- *ICT encourages and creates an innovative and virtual learning environment*
  ICT helps in developing students' mindset and critical thinking through creating interests in technical areas of learning. ICT provides several solutions to various problems that are encountered at the time of manual task doing and learning methodologies by making it more interesting and virtual. For example, in a smart class, there will be e-books and electronic ways of learning which encourages virtual learning.
- *ICT provides several opportunities and ways to develop higher order thinking skills among students*
  ICT helps students focus more on what is important and peculiar rather than the concepts which are of lesser importance. However, it is also proven that there was a significant relationship between the studying and adoption of ICT and improvement in the critical and higher order thinking skills of students.

## 22.6 BARRIERS AND CHALLENGES

Barriers to effective technology integration include:

- Low level of expectations of teacher and lack of clarity in the goals for the using of ICT and integration of ICT in education making it more difficult for the adaptation. ICT technologies are not prevalent and expectations of teacher are not transparent, so lack of clarity makes it vague to implement.
- A lack of support from the administrative staff and also the lack of insight among the coordinating teachers make it more difficult to implement.
- Lack of time to learn and assimilate the new techniques or integrate ICT during a class period: There is lack of time to effectively master the technologies that are coming regularly, so updating self is again a difficult task.

- Insufficient and inadequate knowledge and skills for managing teaching materials: The teaching fraternity lacked the skills of managing teaching material electronically because of lack of workshops and training sessions.
- Competence level in the operational part of software and digitalization is still missing and only the old and traditional ways of assimilating information are practiced.
- Excessive focus on teaching technical or operational skills rather than course content, if extreme focus is laid on the technology implementation then somewhere the content and quality of education is going to deteriorate.
- There is also a social pressure to improve the scores in the examinations which ultimately diverted the focus to the learning by not knowing the practicality; however, Indian education system and mind set always focus more on the quantitative improvement and only on improving the grades so adaptation of ICT is only for the sake of mandate.

  The instructors are more or less focused on the improvement of content and improving the scores and grade card of the students rather than enriching the practicality aspect.
- Also, there is lack of appropriate and adequate administrative support and assistance for the effective usage of ICT.
- Administrative mandates to improve examination results, which shift the focus away from using ICT to engage students in higher order thinking activities.
- A lack of appropriate course content and instructional programs.
- A lack of appropriate hardware, software, and materials: There is lack of effective tools and appropriate mechanism for the implementation and adaptation of ICT.

## 22.7 ICT INITIATIVES IN EDUCATION

### *22.7.1 SARANSH*

With the idea to "improve children's education by enhancing interaction between schools as well as parents and providing data driven decision support system to assist them in taking best decisions for their children's future," Central Board of Secondary Education, has come up with the decision making support and assistance mechanism called "Saransh." The main motive of this tool is to identify and find out the areas where improvement can be done both in students, teachers as well as the curriculum. This mechanism will give the parents and students also an opportunity to look at and also compare their results between various schools and colleges even at the state and national level.

### 22.7.2 THE e-PATHSHALA

It is an initiative of Ministry of Human Resource Development, Government of India and National Council of Educational Research and Training and this have been initiated for providing, inculcating, and spreading across all the innovative mediums like e-book, e-journal, online magazines periodicals, and tablets as well as study material through Internet and a variety of other digital resources to the students to make them more updated.

### 22.7.3 SWAYAM

It is the platform that provides methods for self-learning and e-learning; providing opportunities for a life-long learning. Though this medium learner or the student can choose from hundreds of courses, virtually every course that is being taught at the university/college/school level and this is the massive open learning mechanism and these shall be offered by best of the teachers in India and elsewhere. This will generate employment also for those providing the content.

### 22.7.4 PINDICS

This is the initiative for performance analysis and appraisal and this can be adopted by teachers for assessing their own performance and it will also suggest them the ways of how to make continuous efforts to reach the highest level. This method can also be used by the appraisal committee for providing the feedback of teachers on various parameters that are checked in this mechanism.

### 22.7.5 ICT INITIATIVES IN SUSTAINABILITY

1. Smart City: ICT has come up with the initiatives which have ensured green building and e-resource allocation mechanism improving the transportation mechanism.

2. Smart Transportation: New technology has resulted into efficient fuel utilization resulting in reduction of carbon footprint.

## 22.8 CONCLUSION

School curriculum, generally focuses merely on the contextual knowledge and because of this the learners do not know much about the IT, computer technology, and their applications in education. If we use ICT for educational purposes in schools, colleges, or university as a learning subject, it will enhance learner's level of understanding and achievements in other subjects. By introducing ICT in learning processes, it will also help to encourage creative, integrative teaching, and learning which can ensure that learning should be focused and based on creative ideas. It is the individualized initiative directed toward various learning ways, so as to achieve the goals and aims of various nations. Facilitator's or educator capacity and knowledge have a vital role to play in sustainable development for growth, development, and progress of the societies and communities. They not only circulate knowledge but also create and generate new knowledge. ICT integrated teaching and professional growth of facilitators may open a new door for users for being in further contact, using technology, with their peers, and experts in the field, which may lead to ESD. Their knowledge and understanding of environment help in promoting ESD. Ample provisions are needed to be made in the curriculum and subject specific syllabus for optimum utilization of ICT in schools, along with professional development of facilitators, for achieving the goals in reality.

## KEYWORDS

- **virtual learning**
- **sustainability**
- **carbon footprint**
- **digital revolution**

## REFERENCES

Abbott and Faris (2000). Integrating technology into preserve literacy instruction. Journal of Research on Computing in Education, 33, 149–161.

Al-Ruz and Khasawneh (2011). Jordanian preservice teachers' and technology, Educational Technology and Society, 14, 77–87.

Anderson, J. (2005). IT, e-learning and teacher development. International Education Journal, 5, 1–14.

Anderson, R.E., and Dexter, S. (2005). School technology leadership: An empirical investigation of prevalence and effect. Educational Administration Quarterly, 41(1), 49–82.

Ayodele O.O. (2007). Building sustainability science curriculum in Nigeria: Accommodating local adaptation leveraging technology and enhancing areas of improvement for quality assurance. Paper presented at the proceeding of the Science Teachers Association of Nigeria.

Chai, Koh and Tsai (2010). Facilitating teachers' development of technological, pedagogical and content knowledge. Educational Technology and Society, 13, 63–73.

Reid (2002). The integration of ICT into classroom teaching. Alberta Journal of educational Research, 48, 30–46.

Role of ICT in Education: https://ictcurriculum.gov.in/mod/page/view.php?id=1254

Role of ICT in Sustainable Progress: https://ecsdev.org/ojs/index.php/ejsd/article/view/301

The utilization of ICT in education for sustainable development. Available at www.learntechlib.org/noaccess/115092

What is ICT in education? Available at https://ictcurriculum.gov.in/mod/page/view.php?id=1254

Whelan (2008). Use of ICT in Education in the South Pacific. Distance Education, 29, 53–70.

## CHAPTER 23

# ICT Persuaded Educational Platform: Pragmatic Study on Asian Countries

VIKAS BHARARA

*Department of Management, Institute of Information Technology and Management, New Delhi, 110058, India.*
*E-mail: vikas.bharara@iitmipu.ac.in*

## ABSTRACT

Education is a social context oriented commotion and eminence education has conventionally been allied among educators having soaring degrees of individual contact with apprentices. Information and Communication Technology (ICT) role in education is becoming more and more imperative, as the world is poignant promptly into digital media and information and this significance will carry on to nurture and enlarge in the 21st century. This chapter endeavors to emphasize the escalating role of ICT in higher education for Asian countries, namely, India, China, Japan, and South Korea. This chapter highlights the diverse impacts of ICT on higher education and investigates prospective developments and the role of ICT in transform education. It also seeks out to investigate how future expansion by ICT in converting education will impact on those manner programs which will be accessible and conveyed in the universities as well as in colleges of future. The chapter also recommends that besides for educational development of any nation, ICT in higher education is also a way of socioeconomic development for that nation.

## 23.1 INTRODUCTION

Around the world, for the precedent few decades, numerous people have intuitively looked toward Asia to get indications and impending into what the subsequent wave of consumer technologies might seem like and do and how youth make use of them. Numerous imperative purposes can be serving up in education through nationalized strategies on information technology (IT) or on information and communication technology (ICT) in teaching. Premeditated policies are able to endow with not only an underlying principle or a set of aspirations but also an apparition intended for how education schemes can work among ICT introduction. Not only this, with the help of ICT in education, scholars; educators; parents; and common populace, be benefitted. The benefits of these premeditated strategies are that they are being able to stimulate, amend, and harmonize in congruent efforts to pave the way for a nation's educational goals on the whole.

To have a look at international perspective, three foremost policy lines are requisite for a composed strategy to precede ICT impact on teaching and learning:

1. Fundamental acquaintance and expertise about ICT must become accessible in education. Not only schooling ICT knowledge and skills but following its day by day utilization in higher education should be encouraged. It should be depend on the echelon of development of a country.
2. Educators must become colleagues by means of their apprentice in requisites of approach and proficiencies toward ICT. For this an informal teacher networks should be supported and facilitated in policy creation.
3. Policy ought to provide utilization of ICT for novel creation. Capitalization on Internet admittance should not be merely in schools but also in libraries, sport facilities, and homes.

An inimitable yardstick of the intensity of ICT development in countries globally is the International Telecommunication Union (ITU) ICT Development Index (IDI) (ITU, 2016). IDI coalesce 11 pointers on ICT access, utilize and dexterities to capture vital aspects of ICT development in one assess (Allan & Timothy, 2018). It permits comparisons across countries over the time. In Figure 23.1, provincial averages as well as ranges of IDI 2018 are shown. IDI 2018 covered 175 economies universally in comparison to IDI 2017. It highlights the advancement and importunate partitions in the worldwide information civilization. Out of 175 economies, Africa; Arab States; Asia; and the Pacific; Commonwealth of Independent States (CIS), Europe and America are grouped.

In comparison to 2017, although all countries enhanced their IDI values in 2018, considerable disproportion persevere among more and fewer associated countries. Economic development and ICT development are strongly associated with each other, among the slightest urbanized nations at a fastidious drawback. The mean IDI value augment by 0.25 points to 4.98 points (out of 10), amid slighter enhances at the peak and at the base of the list.

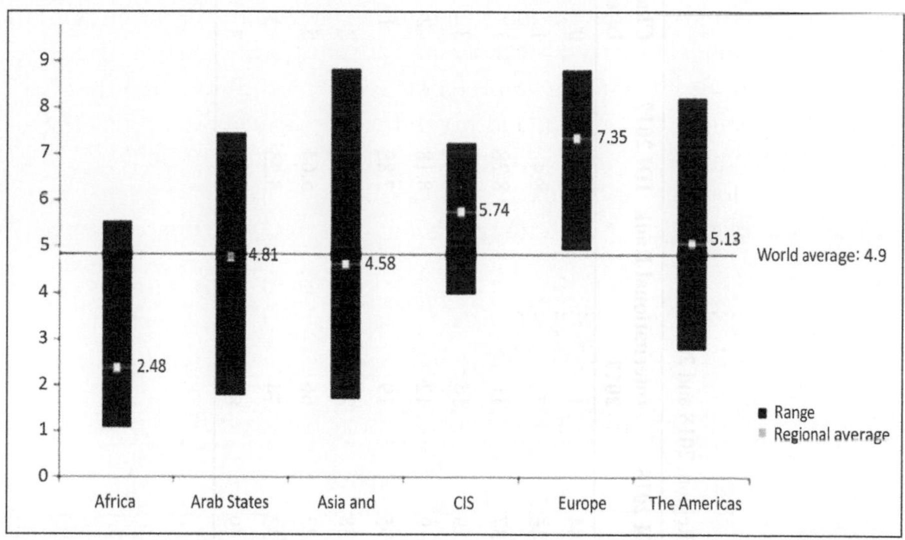


**FIGURE 23.1** IDI 2018 country comparison with global average (adapted from ITU).

Republic of Korea is the topper among other economies in IDI rankings for 2018. Gap among the uppermost and lowermost-performing countries is one of the measures of digital divide. This stayed nearly unaffected at 7.76 points in IDI 2018. The Asia-Pacific region and seven European countries are among the top 10 countries are also included.

IDI positions and values of top 10 economies of Asia-Pacific province are shown in Table 23.1. China displacing Thailand in tenth place in 2018, or else pinnacle 10 positions in provincial rankings for 2018 is just about indistinguishable as for 2017.

Apex 7 economies in the region have IDI values above 7.5 and inhabit uppermost quartile of the IDI rankings. All these economies are elevated revenue economies and ever since the foremost publication of Index they all have upheld high IDI performance. These findings analyzed that among middle ranking countries, Asian countries are having superior upgrading in IDI values than among countries in top and bottom quartiles. It suggests that Asian region is observing a diminution in the digital divide among developed and most of the developing countries.

**TABLE 23.1** Abstract of IDI Rankings and Values, Asia and Pacific Region, 2018 and 2017

| Economy | Provincial Rank 2018 | International Rank 2018 | IDI 2018 | International Rank 2017 | IDI 2017 | Change in International Rank |
|---|---|---|---|---|---|---|
| Republic of Korea | 1 | 1 | 8.84 | 1 | 8.78 | 0 |
| Hong Kong, China | 2 | 6 | 8.46 | 7 | 8.4 | 1 |
| Japan | 3 | 10 | 8.37 | 11 | 8.28 | 1 |
| New Zealand | 4 | 13 | 8.29 | 16 | 8.05 | 3 |
| Australia | 5 | 14 | 8.19 | 12 | 8.18 | –2 |
| Singapore | 6 | 20 | 7.95 | 19 | 7.88 | –1 |
| Macao, China | 7 | 28 | 7.58 | 26 | 7.47 | 2 |
| Malaysia | 8 | 61 | 6.22 | 66 | 5.64 | 5 |
| Brunei Darussalam | 9 | 77 | 5.33 | 74 | 5.25 | –3 |
| China | 10 | 81 | 5.19 | 84 | 4.8 | 3 |

The Asian province, in terms of ICT expansion and by contrasts the most diverse, IDI ranging from 1.73 to 8.84. Particularly for putting together and supporting ICT across numerous domains, together with education, the Asian region furthermore demonstrates considerable economic disparity. Due to these dissimilarities and differences, it is confront to endow with suitable exposure and inclusive discussion of ICT in education policies in Asia.

Table 23.2 reflects a glimpse of ICT platforms provided in Asian countries with respect to higher education. All the above-stated countries are trying their best to provide latest and updated platforms for their students in higher education.

**TABLE 23.2** ICT Platforms in Higher Education in India, China, Japan, and South Korea

| India | China | Japan | South Korea |
|---|---|---|---|
| Campus connectivity | CERNET | ANDES | CLS |
| e-ShodhSindhu | GAOKAO | el-Net system | Colango |
| e-Yantra | ICT4E | LA platform | Edufine |
| MOOCs | MOOCs | LMS | IAMCLASS |
| NDL | Propaganda 2.0 | LRS | Knowre |
| NAD | The hukou system | MOOCs | MOOCs |
| SWAYAM | Udemy | MINCS-UH | NEIS |
| Spoken tutorial | World Class 2.0 Project | NIME | Udemy |
| Udemy | | Udemy | |

## 23.2 OBJECTIVES

1. To highlight the increasing role of ICT in higher education for the Asian countries viz. India, China, Japan, and South Korea.
2. To study the impact of ICT on higher education of India, China, Japan, and South Korea.
3. To know how ICT in higher education is also a mean of socio-economic growth of any nation.

## 23.3 METHODOLOGY

Research is based on an exploratory study and includes secondary sources of data collected from various websites and journals. Its scope is limited to India, China, Japan, and South Korea only.

## 23.4 FINDINGS

### *23.4.1 ICT ROLES IN HIGHER EDUCATION*

Diversification, internationalization, massification, and marketization are higher education issues in Asian countries where role of ICT in higher education is probable. While attempting these issues, role of ICT in higher education to ensure reachable, effectual, and competent higher education few important questions are to be addressed: What is to be learned by students and how will they learn, at what time and place students learn, who will be the student's innovative countenance and innovative faces of lecturers andwhat are the techniques to dapper down the cost of education.

#### *23.4.1.1 WHAT IS TO BE LEARNED BY STUDENTS AND HOW WILL THEY LEARN?*

Conventionally, university courses have accentuated content and textbook centric. Teachers taught all the way through lectures and presentations whereas for rehearsing and consolidating, tutorials and assignments are tools frequently used by teachers. To encourage curriculum focus on proficiency and performance, enveloping occurrence of ICT must united not only with existing educational orientation but with instructional technologies also (CDC & HKEAA, 2015). These curriculums emphasized not only on competencies but also put significance on the usage of information and that is why it necessitates admittance to a horde of information basis and information types. ICT usage in higher education has produced result in a budge from teacher-centered deliverance and transforms learning to student-centered. To facilitate students to be responsible for personal learning, as an information origin and cognitive tools ICT provides its supporting functions. Among academician in higher education environment, appearance of ICT as education technologies generates consciousness on necessitates moving ahead of behaviorist learning theories.

Higher education systems ought to also place significance on their alumnae comprising generic skills, to make certain that scholars achieve apposite acquaintance and expertise in content areas. In precedent, common skills included competences like the knack to explanation, solve troubles, converse, supervise time and resources, act as a team, and work in teams.

### 23.4.1.2 AT WHAT TIME AND PLACE STUDENTS LEARN?

Conventionally, the study is to be completed within a specified time-frame by students and they have diminutive say on time, place, and manner about the delivery of programs. Due to two most important factors, advancement in ICT and transformation in landscape of higher education, students of numerous institutions are now having supple options on what, where and at what time they desire to gain knowledge. For those higher educational institutions who are offering distance learning programs over many years, ICT development encompass extended the reach and scope for them. ICT inclusion in higher education system made spacious inside programmed agendas and timetables. This litheness, exclusive of time restraint, able the apprentices to take part in learning activities, and for this reason, students have further prospects to engage themselves in formal learning programs. Recent and upgraded technologies like mobile and seamless communication technologies facilitate learning environments to shore up actual time and deferred involvement in communicative tasks. Students are able to access upgraded courses and programs from their place of work; this process is termed as work-based learning. Work-based learning is having advantages of convenience and cost effectiveness as there is no requirement of travelling and there is no time away from work. Not only has this, work-based technology also supported learning and training on a needs basis. Moreover, skills and acquaintance achieved are evocative and appropriate in the place of work.

### 23.4.1.3 WHO WILL BE THE STUDENT'S INNOVATIVE COUNTENANCE AND INNOVATIVE FACES OF LECTURERS?

Traditionally, to be a teacher in higher education institutions an individual is required to have suitable postgraduate degree qualifications. On the other hand, with an ICT-loaded education environment, institutions can enlarge their scholastic force afar this faction of populace. Instructors, mentors, and professionals from the workplace are termed as diverse individuals. They all are able to now be part of the teaching and learning procedure, this prop up student in an assortment of supple settings. Teachers from diverse institutions and locations are also having prospects to contribute to their experiences and proficiency in a course. Not only these, teachers nowadays have diverse responsibilities and also necessitate novel talents with elevated levels of ICT. Previously, due to distance; job and additional commitments, students were incapable to attend campuses. But today's distance learners are not constrained to this cluster of scholars. Although higher education has constantly played a decisive role in the economic and societal enlargement of a country, in such circumstances, its role turns out to be even more imperative. Edification augments not only creative proficiency of persons but also their earning power.

#### *23.4.1.4 WHAT ARE THE TECHNIQUES TO DAPPER DOWN THE COST OF EDUCATION?*

There is usual thinking that ICT-enabled education would endow with economies and efficiencies resultant in momentous decline in associated costs of deliverance of educational programs, but in practice it has not take placed. On the contrary, there exist different costs which are associated to expansion and deliverance of elevated superiority technology assisted courses. For example, building ICT enabled courses are not simply repackaging accessible materials. In practice, for deliverance of these courses, an appropriate level of student to staff ratio should be there. Not only this student's prospects of gaining accessibility to teachers into their courses and programs are also considered.

### ***23.4.2 RECENT ICT DEVELOPMENTS IN ASIA***

National Policy on Education 1986 of India is tailored in 1992. Stress of policy is on the requirement of employing educational technologies for improvement in the education excellence. Educational Technology and Computer Literacy and Studies in Schools (CLASS) are two foremost schemes in the policy statement and both are sponsored by the Government of India. Both these schemes led advancement for an additional inclusive and centrally supported scheme namely, Information and Communication Technology @ Schools in 2004. GOI also publicized 2010–2020 as decade of innovation. Scheme recognizes that reasoning and critical thinking skills are crucial for modernism. These skills should start nurtured taught in schools as foundation and further augmented at higher education level (GoI, 2012).

China is implementing innovative technologies which are being extensively advocated as effectual mechanisms for expunging discrepancies among apprentices and education communities, predominantly considering transplanting present education into pastoral communities. China's Ministry of Education, in 2000, conducted a momentous meeting on e-learning for school and higher edification. Meeting delivered two significant conclusions, enhancement of ICT infrastructure in schools and universities by initiating the implementation of the campus network construction project is to be initiated and offering curriculum for students which is to be ICT related. Significant outcomes of meeting funneled the Beijing Municipal Commission of Education to delineate e-learning strategies and policies not only for one but for three five-year plans on educational enhancement and development.

In 2010, Japan initiated its project escorted by Consortium for Renovating Education of the Future namely Knowledge Construction with Technology. Primary aim of the project is to transform conventional educational teaching approaches to additional informative and collaborative beneficial approaches. Through the Knowledge Constructive Jigsaw pedagogy, targeted learning school and university students are considered. Results from these school and university students consist of encouraging collaborative problem solving skills.

Republic of Korea, as reached close to the completion of 4th stage of ICT in Education Master Plan announced the 5th phase of the same. The 5th Master Plan for ICT in education, on whole, endeavors to enlarge student's 21st century proficiencies; improving problem solving skills; and strengthen self-regulated erudition (Kulik, 2003). The Ministry of Education chose numerous strategic assignments in various areas from nursery schools continued to elementary andsecondary schools and nurtured till university schools. Areas of research and development, lifetime education, wellbeing, exceptional education, communal information infrastructure, and configuration of a dynamic cyber ethnicity are also integrated with these assignments.

### *23.4.3 CONFRONTS AND SIGNIFICANCE OF RESEARCH FOR STRATEGIES ON ICT IN ASIAN EDUCATION*

While it moves toward to develop plans or strategies for ICT in edification, few queries need to be considered for filament of empirical findings as well as to the impact of ICT. Does ICT access facilitate students to learn their school subjects? What best can be done in use of ICT to support students learn their school subjects? How can ICT be used to foster student's literacy in ICT? Rationale answers of these questions facilitate policymakers to rationalize hefty monetary investments desired to amalgamate ICT into education systems.

Pragmatic findings on the involvement of ICT to education emerge to be varied. According to the two studies conducted in the Asian countries, there is a positive correlation among availability of computers in colleges and test scores of students (Spiezia, 2010). Contrary to this, Organization for Economic Co-operation and Development, 2015 released a report with results of no substantial enhancements in student accomplishment in reading, mathematics or science in countries that had endowed profoundly in ICT for education, yet after accounting for differences in national income and in the socio-economic condition of students and colleges (Cheung, & Slavin, 2013; Delen & Bulut, 2011; NCES, 2001a). However, to some extent, there is an improvement in those students learning who utilized computers fairly at college, one or two times in a week, than students who rarely used computers.

### *23.4.4 EMERGING PERSPECTIVES FOR DEVELOPMENTS IN ASIA*

The Association of Southeast Nations (ASEAN) ICT Master plan 2020 is focused on propelling the region toward a digitally-enabled integrated economy. To concentrate on key education confronts of excellence, even handedness and effectiveness and to develop human capital, ICTs in education proffer prospects for governments in ASEAN and other emerging nations. This is mainly for developing economies experiencing education transformations and with an outsized young demographic. When a holistic approach toward ICT in education is adopted ICTS can be strategically used to resolve the challenges. ICT enlargement in ASEAN diverges significantly. Singapore is ranked 16th globally with an IDI value of 7.90, while Myanmar is ranked 150th with an IDI value of 1.82 (Kong et al., 2014). Only three countries, Singapore; Malaysia, and Brunei, are reported to be above the global IDI average value of 4.77 (Kong et al., 2013). The nation's consciousness to necessitate improving education quality is growing and advancement is apparent in many areas. Though, disparities in eminence teachers, infrastructure, and admittance still subsist both within and between countries. To carry on succeeding toward the United Nations' 2030 Goals for Sustainable Development for quality education (SDGs), it is very important to unearth ways to make available unbiased and comprehensive education, as well as permanent education prospects for all in the economy.

Discussions were made in the HEAD Foundation's ICT Policy Forum held on November 7–8, 2016 and it is apparent from these discussions that each of these ASEAN nations represented is on its own path for ICT expansion. In general, it is reasonable to say that substantial advancement is being made with ICT execution in many universities within ASEAN. Their focus of ICT has been pertinent to the cultural, geographical, political, and educational contexts of the respective nations. International contrasts for benchmarking and modeling are undoubtedly effectual, but the practice of others cannot hand out as a straight substitute for an exhaustive investigation of one's own requirements and contexts. The accessible resources and ICT infrastructure while preparation for ICT integration during education development programs in the coming decade, it is decisive to reflect as a nation on one's own needs. For example, Singapore is more along the path of thoughts throughout the role that ICT will play for its future socioeconomic plans and preparing its future workforce (Teo & Ting, 2010). The other ASEAN nations like India, South Korea, Indonesia, Thailand, Philippines, Japan, and Vietnam may have slower pace in the broaden of ICT infrastructure, but the hefty populations of these countries symbolize momentous markets for ICT, both fixed and mobile in the future. Based on the experiences of other countries in ASEAN, the expanding awareness in Myanmar from worldwide investors and supported associations endow with an exceptional prospect for the country to experiment with a multiplicity of ICT-based programs.

China, one of the Asian countries, has been a pioneer in embracing information and communication technologies for enlightening purposes (ICT4E) in nationwide educational policies. The country, acknowledged the role played by the technology in education in the late 1990s, now surfaced as a global leader in proliferating the benefits of ICT4E. But there is divergence between political ambitions and educational certainties and this mismatch can fundamentally be recognized to incongruities within the Chinese education system, which endeavors to bring together deviating political, social, and educational objectives.

## 23.5 CONCLUSION

To accelerate the pace of socioeconomic development for any country, education undoubtedly is the driving force. Issues like massification, diversification, internationalization, and marketization of higher education must be addressed innovatively by integrating ICT in higher education. In developing countries, administration must make sure that superior excellence; reachable and reasonable higher education is accessible to students through ICT in education.

For developing course materials, conveying and distributing course substance, delivering lectures and presentations, assisting communiqué between lecturers and students, persuading educational modernization, augmenting collaboration and association, carrying out research, improving proficient enlargement, and endowing with managerial and administration services, ICT is being used by more and more higher education institutions nowadays. In spite of the fact that information on how ICT has been and can be used to augment the design, the deliverance and the supervision of higher education curriculums in the Southeast Asian province is not enthusiastically accessible. Additionally, countries in Southeast Asia are at diverse stages of expansion to make use of ICT in teaching.

Countries in the province can be classified into three phases of ICT development. China is already assimilating the use of ICT in the higher education system. Countries like India and Japan are preliminary to apply and test diverse strategies. Lastly, country like South Korea has presently commenced and is more apprehensive with ICT infrastructure. Hence, in Asian countries, not only for educationalists but for administrators also, achievement stories; understanding; and lessons learnt from the usage of ICT in higher education will be of enormous significance at the vanguard of amalgamating ICT for higher education. ICT based learning materials in university teaching included blended learning and e-learning producing extraordinary results. Pedagogic modernization for the usage of ICT toward enhancing higher education in terms of ease of understanding, efficacy, and competence is a need of the hour. ICT and online approaches to be expertise in higher education and ICT projects in higher education are to be taking on for improving the access and eminence of learning.

## KEYWORDS

- **ICT**
- **innovative**
- **integration**
- **MOOCs**
- **policy formulation**
- **quality education**

## REFERENCES

Allan H. K. Yuen, & Timothy K. F. Hew.; Information and Communication Technology in Educational Policies in the Asian Region, Springer Science and Business Media LLC, Chapter 86-1, 2018.

Cheung, A. C. K.; & Slavin, R.; The effectiveness of educational technology applications for enhancing mathematics achievement in K-12 classroom: A meta-analysis. Educational Research Review 9, 2013, 88–113.

Curriculum Development Council and Hong Kong Examinations and Assessment Authority. Information and communication technology. Curriculum and Assessment Guide (secondary 4–6), 2015.

Delen, E., & Bulut, O.. The relationship between students' exposure to technology and their achievement in science and math. The Turkish Online Journal of Educational Technology, 10 (3), 2011, 311–317.

Government of India (GoI). National Policy on Information and Communication Technology (NPICT) in School Education, Department of School Education and Literacy Ministry of Human Resource. India: Development Government of India, 2012.

ITU. Measuring the Information Society Report 2016. Geneva: International Telecommunication Union, 2016.

Kong, S. C., Chan, T. W., Huang, R., & Cheah, H. M., A review of e-learning policy in school education in Singapore, Hong Kong, Taiwan, and Beijing: Implications to future policy planning. Journal of Computer Education 1(2–3), 2014, 187–212.

Kulik, J. A., Effects of using instructional technology in elementary and secondary schools: What controlled evaluation studies say. SRI International. 2003.

Malaysia Ministry of Education, Malaysia Education Blueprint 2013–2025 (Preschool to post-secondary education), 2013.

National Centre for Educational Statistics (NCES). The nation's report card: Mathematics 2000. Washington, DC: NCES, 2001a.

Spiezia, V., Does computer use increase educational achievements? Student-level evidence from PISA. OECD Journal: Economic Studies, 2010, 2010, 1, 1–22.

Teo, Y. H., & Ting, B. H. Singapore Education ICT Masterplans. In C. S. Chai & Q. Wang (Eds.), ICT for Self-Directed and Collaborative Learning. Singapore: Pearson, 2010, 2–14.

## CHAPTER 24

# Role of ICT and Education Level in Financial Inclusion of Rural Population

HIMANSHU AGARWAL[1], and RASHID[2,*]

[1]*Faculty of Commerce and Business Administration, D N (PG) College, Meerut, India*

[2]*Faculty of Commerce and Business Administration, D N (PG) College, Meerut, India*

[*]*Corresponding author. E-mail: rashid.638@gmail.com*

## ABSTRACT

India is a developing economy and financial inclusion has been considered as the primary indicator for the overall development and well-being of the society worldwide. Sustainable economic growth is must required for financial inclusion. Financial inclusion provides an advantageous potential to redevelop the country's economy and increase productivity. It also ensures that a citizen can use thc natural and economic resources of the country equally according to his understanding. Sustainable growth always stands for the growth equally enjoyed by all citizens. Economic development is always seen with production and consumption and it is related to both because the livelihood and needs of the people are linked to it. A massive area of the society still has very little knowledge about financial instruments and its access to these tools is very less. Even today, this class remains dependent on old financial instruments such as relatives, friends, and moneylenders. According to Global Findex, 2014, 62% of eligible people of world had accounts with banks and in India the number was around 53%. Pradhan Mantri Jan-Dhan Yojana increased the bank accounts of adults in banks to over 80%. Financial inclusion relies on two factors Information and Communication Technology and second one is education level of people. In rural India education level of people is very low. Many people in rural areas are illiterate. They do not know how to deal with banking procedures. Nowadays, banks highly rely on information technology. Basic need for understanding the information technology and its services is education. Rural people are unaware with information technology services due to uneducation.

## 24.1 INTRODUCTION

India is a country of various financial diversities. Lack of accessible, reasonable, and acceptable financial services and low financial gain have an impeded effect on the economic condition of the individuals as well as on the economic health of the country. Therefore, for the accelerated economy conditions and growth, it is necessary that every household must have an appropriate access to different banking services.

Financial inclusion has many areas like banking services, credit, payments, remittance, and insurance services for formal inclusive system. In India, the financial inclusion theme is geared toward banking facilities for everyone with minimum one simple bank account per family, financial acquirement, credit, insurance and pension facility, and various advantages of the Social Security schemes mainly the Direct Benefit Transfer (DBT) scheme of the Government through Pradhan Mantri Jan-Dhan Yojana (PMJDY).

Financial Inclusion is financial services should be available to all individuals within a certain time and the under-aged and weaker sections should have a supply of credit when needed at a low cost (Rangrajan, 2008). The opposite of financial inclusion is financial exclusion. It is both symptom and reason for poverty. Many earlier research studies define nature and causes of financial exclusion (Kempson and Whyley, 1998; Bhanot et al., 2012).

Therefore, Indian economy is essentially a rural economy. India consists of 700 million individuals, living in around 649,481 villages (Verma, n.d.). Their main stay is agriculture. Agriculture sector has a regular demand of credit. And, rural households are still facing a number of obstacles that make it difficult to access financial services.

Low level of the awareness and literacy in rural areas are the main culprits that hurdled the uninterrupted access to banking services and laid the base for financial exclusion (Kumar and Kumar Chattopadhyay, 2011; CRISIL Inclusix, 2015). Financial exclusions are a complex set of barriers to financial inclusion. Those making plans for the prevention of these barriers and financial inclusion, the three main financial institutions have done this and the very best. Due to their efforts financial services have been able to expand to some extent. World Bank also set goal of financial inclusion by 2020 at the world level. It is thus clear that financial inclusion is strongly required for the effective and quick economic growth. In the absence of financial inclusion, the incidence of economic growth benefits cannot reach to the larger population.

Thus, India needs a compact and adequate financial literacy and awareness drive to unbanked population. But, to provide financial literacy and awareness to a vast population is not an easy task. There may be other factors for circumscribed financial inclusion. Moreover, technology may also play a chief role in bringing unbanked population underneath the financial inclusion system. Therefore, keeping all this in mind, the researchers made an attempt to know the exact truth behind this problem and to bring out some valid suggestions through this chapter entitled "Role of ICT and Education level in Financial Inclusion of Rural Population." The chapter made a survey that shows rural India households are completely unaware about various other financial services than opening an account.

## 24.2 OVERVIEW OF LITERATURE

The researcher has studied financial inclusion with a number of factors in the context of India. The main reason for financial exclusion is lack of employment in urban areas, poor means of income in rural areas, and old economic activities such as very low income on investment in agriculture (Lokhande, 2014). The ratio in banks of deposits and withdrawals has remained at a very low level due to low revenue in agriculture and nonagricultural activities in rural areas. It was further concluded that it is very important to make banking services available to low-income individuals and nonbanking people at low cost. For this, financial banks will have to play a very prominent role (Pavithran, 2014). The public mainly the rural public is not aware about the "no frill account." It must be broadcast to the greater audience through technology innovations. Moreover, remote areas may be accessed through technology innovations for better dissemination of banking services. The ATM machines should be changed according to illiterate and non-English people. Basic improvements must be made in these machines according to these individuals (Shah and Dubhashi, 2015). Financial inclusion initiatives are necessary for the overall development of the country. In making financial inclusion a reality, the banking sector has to forego the profitability hypothesis and consider it a social work. All matters of the banks cannot be the business every time. Information about the efforts and schemes made by the government for financial inclusion must reach every citizen of the country. The availability of financial services should be seamless for every citizen (Garg and Agarwal, 2014). Financial inclusion requires the delivery of information about financial education and financial services to the people at a large scale. All financial institutions of the country must take necessary steps in this direction. The responsibility of financial inclusion in the country also applies to financial institutions (Datta, 2012; Lusardi and Michigan, 2005; Hung et al., 2009). As a result of financial inclusion in the country, the standard of living of the people increases, the pace of economic development is fast, and everyone gets equal facilities. After looking at all the schemes to achieve the goal of financial inclusion, it can be said that one day all individuals in India will have bank accounts and will be a part of financial inclusion (Lokhande, 2014). Women should be given the responsibility of operating the right price shop through Anganwadi centers so that they can become a part of financial inclusion. Banks and related NGOs should also train for financial inclusion to the self-help group in both villages and cities (Lokhande, 2009). Banks will have to simplify their loan security conditions so that all individuals can get loans from banks. Banks should introduce new loan schemes for the entire country so that the money can be properly and fully utilized (Tamilarasu, 2014). The financial services availability such as savings, insurance, and remittances are extremely important for poverty alleviation and development (Singh and Tondon, 2015). It is very important to have competent laws and regulations for financial inclusion in India. Financial services should reach every citizen through different routes. India still has a long way to go for financial inclusion (Dangi and Kumar, 2013). There are certain problems like lower financial literacy, lack of awareness, the cost of transaction and customer acquisition is high and it is not at all low cost. RBI has taken many steps to strengthened financial inclusion. Through technology, banks are establishing their reach to unbanked individuals (Mol, 2014).

## 24.3 OBJECTIVES OF THE STUDY

Present research study has the following objective:

a) To discuss the concept of financial inclusion in India.
b) To examine the need of financial inclusion for rural India.
c) To study the education level and financial literacy among the economically underprivileged sections of the society.
d) To investigate the major factors affecting access to financial services.
e) To suggest the measures to cater to the needs of the poor people.

## 24.4 METHODOLOGY

a) Time: November 2019
b) Area: Rural areas of Muzaffarnagar District (Khatauli Data)
c) Demography of area: As of the 2011 census, Khatauli Tehsil has a population of 433,910. The urban population according to Khatauli municipality is 104,108. The male–female ratio here is 898 as against 1000. Around 15% of the population of Tehsil is under 6 years of age. The literacy rate here is 73% with 83% for males and 63% for females. The population of Tehsil is 65.7% Hindu, 33% Muslim, 0.2% Sikh, 0.2% Christian, and 0.8% Jain. The main language here is Hindi. The population consists of 54,756 males and 49,352 females.
d) Data type: Primary Data
e) Tool for survey: Questionnaire cum response statement based on Likert scale. For this scale five responsive were registered viz.—Strongly agree, agree, neutral, disagree, and strongly disagree.
f) Statistical methods used: chi-square test.
g) Used sampling: Total sample population is 100.

## 24.5 RURAL INDIA FOR FINANCIAL INCLUSION

Financial inclusion in rural India is a big problem. People of rural India still believe in old financial instruments and facilities. The people living in these areas are of low income group. Financial inclusion and lack of knowledge about financial products is a big reason for this problem. According to the Finance Ministry, till 2013, 52% people did not have bank accounts rural India. Financial inclusion holds a very important place according to India's background. About 25% of India's population is illiterate and lives in below poverty line category. Reaching financial inclusion to these people is a big challenge.

A large part of financial inclusion in India can be achieved only because of information and access to financial products in the population of rural India. A person's bank account enables him to obtain a formal loan and also helps in obtaining information about financial products. In these individuals, the habit of saving for the future also arises. A bank account provides a lot of support in achieving the goal of financial inclusion. The goal of achieving financial inclusion in the absence of an account in the bank becomes very difficult. It may be possible only through effective financial inclusion. It is a well proved fact that an effective financial inclusion can contribute for a better, improved, and sustainable economic development of India.

The financial inclusion can facilitate the government to bring down the leakages and corruption. In the long run, it can reduce poverty and correct income inequality that lead to add value to country's sustainable and inclusive growth. Thus, financial inclusion proved to be a key component to promote balanced, inclusive, and sustainable growth specially for rural India (Goel and Sharma, 2017).

Therefore, to kick start the inclusive and sustainable growth and development in a balanced manner through financial inclusion Prime Minister Narendra Modi announced National Mission of Financial Inclusion for weaker section and low income groups on 15 August, 2014 (Independence Day) Later on, 28 August 2014, another ambitious flagship program of financial inclusion Prime Minister Jan-Dhan Scheme (PMJDS) was announced to facilitate all unbanked households with conventional banking.

The scheme worked well. But, it cannot be said the success of financial inclusion program. Moreover, this PMJDS worked in a limited arena that is, urban and semi-urban areas. According to a report released by the World Bank, "2 billion people in the world do not have general financial services and more than 50% of the people who are from poor families do not have accounts in banks." The majority of PMJDY accounts are opened mainly in the public sector banks where the private sector banks contribute a minimum role in the financial inclusion (Bilas and Chandrasekhar, 2016).

Many people in society still remain unbanked. Individuals who carry out normal transactions in their accounts and conduct their transactions only through old methods should also be classified as unbanked people. These people also do not use the technical facilities provided by banks.

Financial Inclusion is initiated in India for a long time. But, it cannot become effective financial inclusion. Its dissemination is not equal to all. All social sectors and economic sectors are not covered equally under scheme.

## 24.6 FINANCIAL LITERACY AND LEVEL OF EDUCATION

Financial literacy is the knowledge about the financial system and to manage financial requirements effectively and without the help of others. In India, effective, easy, and adequate financial literacy and awareness program can play a biding role for equitable incidence of financial inclusion and further evidently financial stability. As per the Global Survey by Standard and Poor's Financial Services LLC (S&P), "76% of adults in India which serves as a home for about 17% of world's population, do not understand even the basic financial concepts. This could be very detrimental to India's ambition of becoming an economic superpower in the coming years since it is only attainable when there is inclusive development." Financial literacy can help to understand financial risk to spend and save according to their capacity. Understanding the fact that financial inclusion cannot be fully achieved without financial literary, RBI made a catalytic effort to create awareness about financial products and services, good financial practices, going digital, and consumer protection (Kim et al., 2018; Iqbal and Sami, 2017).

The education level of the expecting parties also plays an important role in imparting financial literacy to all. Without understanding the concept of financial literacy, no one can play with financial products and financial materials. And, without the adequate education of an individual, the understanding of information technology and financial literacy cannot be established. In the absence of education, people find it difficult to understand and use even the basic facilities of banks such as deposits and withdrawals.

If seen in a broad perspective and through future perspective, financial inclusion in India specifically financial inclusion of rural areas is the immediate need of the hour. All roads to economic prosperity go through rural economy. And, most of the rural population is unexpectedly lack awareness and educational standards. It is also a hard fact that such a big number of populations cannot be catered quick educational inputs.

Technological advancements have its own handicaps. So, in providing a proper solution, first move should be of simplifying Information and Communication Technology (ICT) processes, quick and effective fraud and grievances redressal mechanism. Only after the financial literacy and awareness is spread over, can the uneducated and unbanked rural population be included in financial infrastructure.

The growth of the volume of transaction through *Unstructured Supplementary Service Data* (USSD)-based mobile banking is very weak in India. The use of mobile banking increased unexpectedly at the time of demonetization while it lately reduced to an optimized level after demonetization. The reason for this type of practice is seen due to the low level of financial-education in rural areas. Now, USSD mobile banking has to extend this facility to low-income people who cannot buy smart phones (Souza, 2018). Another reason for the reduced mobile banking came to knowledge is high transaction cost involved in e-transfers. During demonetization, the individuals used mobile or Internet banking to avoid the long bank queues or uneasiness in banking services due to mob pressure in the banks. Mobile banking may be a good solution for better banking but weak electricity and Internet facility in the rural India is the main hurdle to mobile banking. Apart from this, rural population and senior citizens lack trust in digital mode of payment or the use of mobile banking. A big gap is registered in Internet access in urban and rural regions. In December 2017, 65% of urban households had an internet connection compared to 20% in rural India (Agarwal, 2018). On the other hand, it is a hard fact to understand that technical knowledge is required to use the mobile banking and digital payment services. Even some urban senior citizens fear to use these services due to the complex system of mobile banking. There may be a loss of funds. And, if urban areas are facing such problems, rural mobile banking scenario can be thus, estimated. Mere availability of mobile phones does not ensure the financial services. There is thus, an urgent need for financial literacy first to better cater financial services than easy access to technology alone (Ventouri, 2018).

## 24.7 SURVEY AND FINDINGS

Effective financial inclusion is really a Hercules' task. But, India needs effective financial inclusion urgently. If the people of the country remain financially backward, the country cannot progress. In the last couple of years, the government has made all necessary efforts to strengthen the financial inclusion infrastructure. Moreover, it was also looked after that the coverage of the financial inclusion will reach to each and every area irrespective of urban, semi-urban, or rural.

Apart from this, even today, there are areas where the coverage of financial inclusion cannot reach. Although many agencies and researchers have done lots of surveys and researches in this regard. Here, the researcher opted Khatauli town of Muzaffarnagar District for this survey, Muzaffarnagar is called the Sugar-Bowl of India. Rural areas of Muzaffarnagar District are purely agriculture-oriented areas. Most of rural population bases on the agriculture for their livelihood.

Around 100 such rural inhabitants were randomly selected respondents, who are basically wage-earners and labors. A five-point Likert scale questionnaire containing 15 questions was administered to register their responses over financial inclusion. It is to note here that all these questions were put before them by the researchers themselves in their local language. Further, all the responses were translated into English to analyze result and write conclusion.

**R1: Jan Dhan account serves my banking needs**

In response to Question *Jan Dhan account serves my banking needs*, out of total sample of 100, 30% says they have no account, 13% strongly agree,

21% agree, 10% neutral on this, 13% disagree with us, and 13% strongly disagree with this question.

**R2: My account was not in the bank before Jan Dhan account.**

In response to Question *My account was not in the bank before Jan Dhan account*, out of total sample of 100, 30% says they have no account, 23% strongly agree, 0% agree, 0% neutral on this, *47% disagree* with us, and 0% strongly disagree with this question.

**R3: The bank's savings account is better than the Jan Dhan account.**

In response to Question *The bank's savings account is better than the Jan Dhan account*, out of total sample of 100, 30% says they have no account, 0% strongly agree, *45% agree*, 12% neutral on this, 13% disagree with us, and 0% strongly disagree with this question.

**R4: I have opened Jan Dhan account to avail government benefits.**

In response to Question *I have opened Jan Dhan account to avail government benefits*, out of total sample of 100, 30% says they have no account, *23% strongly agree, 20% agree*, 1% neutral on this, 26% disagree with us, and 0% strongly disagree with this question.

**R5: There was no government benefit from opening of Jan Dhan account.**

In response to Question *There was no government benefit from opening of Jan Dhan account*, out of total sample of 100, 30% says they have no account, *63% strongly agree, 6% agree*, 1% neutral on this, 0% disagree with us, and 0% strongly disagree with this question.

**R6: I operate my account myself.**

In response to Question *There was no government benefit from opening of Jan Dhan account*, out of total sample of 100, 30% says they have no account, *46% strongly agree*, 1% agree, 10% neutral on this, 13% disagree with us, and 0% strongly disagree with this question.

**R7: I have got the account passbook.**

In response to Question *I have got the account passbook*, out of total sample of 100, 30% says they have no account, *55% strongly agree*, 1% agree, 11% neutral on this, 13% disagree with us, and 0% strongly disagree with this question.

**R8: I have ATM Card.**

In response to Question *I have ATM Card*, out of total sample of 100, 30% says they have no account, *40% strongly agree,* 3% agree, 1% neutral on this, 3% disagree with us, and 23% strongly disagree with this question.

**R9: I do not operate my ATM card myself.**

In response to Question *I do not operate my ATM card myself*, out of total sample of 100, 30% says they have no account, *25% strongly agree,* 0% agree, 0% neutral on this, 1% disagree with us, and 44% strongly disagree with this question.

**R10: I know about opening zero balance accounts by the bank.**

In response to Question *I know about opening zero balance accounts by the bank*, out of total sample of 100, 30% says they have no account, *32% strongly agree,* 24% agree, 1% neutral on this, 13% disagree with us, and 0% strongly disagree with this question.

**R11: I run my ATM card myself.**

In response to Question *I run my ATM card myself*, out of total sample of 100, 30% says they have no account, *45% strongly agree,* 1% agree, 1% neutral on this, 10% disagree with us, and 13% strongly disagree with this question.

**R12: I have invested in a government insurance scheme by the bank.**

In response to Question *I have invested in a government insurance scheme by the bank*, out of total sample of 100, 30% says they have no account, *0% strongly agree,* 0% agree, 1% neutral on this, 35% disagree with us, and 34% strongly disagree with this question.

**R13: I know about the overdraft facility on zero balance Jan Dhan account.**

In response to Question *I know about the overdraft facility on zero balance Jan Dhan account*, out of total sample of 100, 30% says they have no account, *21% strongly agree,* 0% agree, 24% neutral on this, 25% disagree with us, and 0% strongly disagree with this question.

**R14: I know how to operate a bank account through Internet banking.**

In response to Question *I know how to operate a bank account through Internet banking*, out of total sample of 100, 30% says they have no account, *21% strongly agree,* 0% agree, 26% neutral on this, 23% disagree with us, and 0% strongly disagree with this question.

**R15: I have transferred funds with the help of Internet banking facility.**

In response to Question *I have transferred funds with the help of Internet banking facility*, out of total sample of 100, 30% says they have no account, *21% strongly agree, 10% agree*, 0% neutral on this, 26% disagree with us, and 13% strongly disagree with this question.

**R16: I pay for my daily expenses and needs through digital transactions.**

In response to Question *I have trouble running my account due to being uneducated*, out of total sample of 100, 30% says they have no account, 0% strongly agree, 0% agree, 0% neutral on this, *57% disagree with us, and 13% strongly disagree* with this question.

**R17: I am aware of all the financial facilities offered by the bank.**

In response to Question *I am aware of all the financial facilities offered by the bank*, out of total sample of 100, 30% says they have no account, 21% strongly agree, 0% agree, 23% neutral on this, 26% disagree with us, and *0% strongly disagree* with this question.

**R18: Why did your family members open a bank account?**

In response to Question *Why did your family members open a bank account?* Out of total sample of 100, 30% says they have no account, 35% savings, 15% business, and 20% other reason with this question.

**R19: Who helped you to open an account?**

In response to Question *Who helped you to open an account?* out of total sample of 100, 30% says they have no account, 52% self, 08% bank, and 10% other with this question.

**R20: How much do you save per month in your account?**

In response to Question *How much do you save per month in your account?* Out of total sample of 100, 30% says they have no account, 29% less than 1000, 18% more than 1000, and 23% no savings with this question.

**R21: I have trouble running my account due to being uneducated.**

In response to Question *I have trouble running my account due to being uneducated*, out of total sample of 100, 30% says they have no account, 24% strongly agree, 0% agree, 0% neutral on this, 10% disagree with us, and *36% strongly disagree* with this question.

**R22: Only the educated person can avail Internet facilities provided by banks.**

In response to Question *Only the educated person can avail internet facilities provided by banks*, out of total sample of 100, 30% says they have no account, 49% strongly agree, 21% agree, 0% neutral on this, 0% disagree with us, and 0% strongly disagree with this question.

**R23: I transfer money from my bank.**

In response to Question *I transfer money from my bank*, out of total sample of 100, 30% says they have no account, 36% strongly agree, 0% agree, 10% neutral on this, 24% disagree with us, and 0% strongly disagree with this question.

**R24: I have no problem in filling the bank form.**

In response to Question *I have no problem in filling the bank form*, out of total sample of 100, 30% says they have no account, 25% strongly agree, 11% agree, 10% neutral on this, 0% disagree with us, and 24% strongly disagree with this question.

100 respondents are surveyed in the present study. Their socioeconomic status is registered. It is significant here because financial inclusion and use of ICT are directly linked to the socio-economic status.

These socio-economic status data (Table 24.1) show that most of the rural population belongs to low-income group. Most of them are either laborers or house wives. As much as 44% are illiterate (13% more are education in literate category). It means that low-income, illiteracy, and low-occupation profile are the basic hurdles in financial inclusions.

**TABLE 24.1** Socioeconomic Status of the Respondents

| Sr. No. | Particulars | Respondents | Percentage |
|---|---|---|---|
| 1 | *Gender Classification* | | |
| | a. Male | 56 | 56 |
| | b. Female | 44 | 44 |
| | c. Transgender | 0 | 0 |
| | Total | 100 | 100 |
| 2 | *Age Classification* | | |
| | a. Below 30 Years | 34 | 34 |
| | b. 31–40 Years } 31–50 Years | 28 } 51 | 28 } 51 |
| | c. 41–50 Years | 23 | 23 |
| | d. Above 50 Years | 15 | 15 |
| | Total | 100 | 100 |
| 3 | *Marital Classification* | | |
| | a. Married | 67 | 67 |
| | b. Unmarried | 33 | 33 |
| | Total | 100 | 100 |

**TABLE 24.1** *(Continued)*

| Sr. No. | Particulars | Respondents | Percentage |
|---|---|---|---|
| 4 | *Classification* | | |
| | a. Literate | 56 | 56 |
| | • Postgraduate | 14 | 14 |
| | • Graduate | 17 } 56 | 17 } 56 |
| | • Diploma | 12 | 12 |
| | • Below 10th | 13 | 13 |
| | b. Illiterate | 44 | 44 |
| | Total | 100 | 100 |
| 5 | *Family Classification* | | |
| | a. Joint | 34 | 34 |
| | b. Nuclear | 66 | 66 |
| | Total | 100 | 100 |
| 6 | *Occupation Classification* | | |
| | a. Service | 12 | 12 |
| | b. Business | 6 | 6 |
| | c. Labor (male/female) | 48 | 48 |
| | d. House wife (female) | 29 | 29 |
| | e. Agriculture | 5 | 5 |
| | Total | 100 | 100 |
| 7 | *Monthly Income Classification* | | |
| | a. Below Rs. 10000 | 54 | 54 |
| | b. Rs. 10,001–Rs. 20,000 | 19 | 19 |
| | c. Rs. 20,001–Rs. 30,000 | 14 | 14 |
| | d. Rs. 30,001–Rs. 40,000 | 8 | 8 |
| | e. Above Rs. 40000 | 5 | 5 |
| | Total | 100 | 100 |

Table 24.2 shows that out of 100 respondents, 41 respondents know the concept of financial inclusion, 70 respondents are having bank account, 05 respondents are having accounts in co-operative banks, 21 respondents are having two account with the banks, and 21 respondents are having two operative account with the banks (Singh, 2017).

**TABLE 24.2** Opinion of the Customer Toward Financial Services

| Sr. No. | Particulars | Respondents | Percentage |
|---|---|---|---|
| 1 | *Awareness about Financial Inclusion* | | |
| | • Known | 41 | 41 |
| | • Not Known | 59 | 59 |
| | Total | 100 | 100 |
| 2 | *Bank Account* | | |
| | • Have | 70 | 70 |
| | • Not Have | 30 | 30 |
| | Total | 100 | 100 |
| 3 | *Sector-wise Classification* | | |
| | a Public sector bank | 31 | 31 |
| | b Private sector bank | 30 | 30 |
| | c Regional rural bank | 04 | 04 |
| | d Co-operative bank | 05 | 05 |
| | Total | 70 | 70 |
| 4 | *Number of Bank Account in Household* | | |
| | a One | | |
| | b Two | 33 } | 33 } |
| | c Three | 21 } 70 | 21 } 70 |
| | d Four | 10 | 10 |
| | e More than Four | 04 | 04 |
| | | 02 | 02 |

The responses collected through primary data are presented in Table 24.2. This data was further tested through chi-square test. The responses so collected were converted in to scores on the following basis:

| | |
|---|---|
| Agree (A) | 1 |
| Strongly Agree (SA) | 2 |
| Agree (A) | 1 |
| Neutral (N) | 0 |
| Disagree (D) | −1 |
| Strongly Disagree (SD) | −2 |

Response wise values were calculated by multiplying these scores as shown in Table 24.3.

**TABLE 24.3** Responses Scores and Combined Score

| **Responses** | | | | | | **Scores** | | | | | **Combined Score** |
|---|---|---|---|---|---|---|---|---|---|---|---|
| Q | SD | D | N | A | SA | SD × −2 | D × −1 | N × 0 | A × 1 | SA × 2 | Σ |
| Q 1 | 13 | 13 | 10 | 21 | 13 | −26 | −13 | 0 | 21 | 26 | 8 |
| Q 2 | – | 47 | – | – | 23 | – | −47 | 0 | – | 46 | −1 |
| Q 3 | – | 13 | 12 | 45 | – | – | −13 | 0 | 45 | – | 32 |
| Q 4 | – | 26 | 1 | 20 | 23 | – | −26 | 0 | 20 | 46 | 40 |
| Q 5 | – | – | 1 | 6 | 63 | – | – | 0 | 6 | 126 | 132 |
| Q 6 | – | 13 | 10 | 1 | 46 | – | −13 | 0 | 1 | 92 | 80 |
| Q 7 | – | 13 | 1 | 1 | 55 | – | −13 | 0 | 1 | 110 | 98 |
| Q 8 | 23 | 3 | 1 | 3 | 40 | −46 | −3 | 0 | 3 | 80 | 34 |
| Q 9 | 44 | 1 | – | – | 25 | −88 | −1 | 0 | – | 50 | −39 |
| Q 10 | – | 13 | 1 | 24 | 32 | – | −13 | 0 | 24 | 64 | 75 |
| Q 11 | 13 | 10 | 1 | 1 | 45 | −26 | −10 | 0 | 1 | 90 | 55 |
| Q 12 | 34 | 35 | 1 | – | – | −68 | −35 | 0 | – | – | −103 |
| Q 13 | – | 25 | 24 | – | 21 | – | −25 | 0 | – | 42 | 17 |
| Q 14 | – | 23 | 26 | – | 21 | – | −23 | 0 | – | 42 | 19 |
| Q 15 | 13 | 26 | – | 10 | 21 | −26 | −26 | 0 | 10 | 42 | 0 |
| Q 16 | 13 | 57 | – | – | – | −26 | −57 | 0 | – | – | −83 |
| Q 17 | – | 56 | 23 | – | 21 | – | −56 | 0 | – | 42 | −14 |
| Q 18 | – | – | 57 | – | 13 | – | – | 0 | – | 26 | 26 |
| Q 19 | – | – | 26 | 23 | 21 | – | – | 0 | 23 | 42 | 65 |
| Q 20 | – | – | 25 | 25 | 20 | – | – | 0 | 25 | 40 | 65 |
| Q 21 | 36 | 10 | – | – | 24 | −72 | −10 | 0 | – | 48 | −34 |
| Q 22 | – | – | – | 21 | 49 | – | – | 0 | 21 | 98 | 119 |
| Q 23 | – | 24 | 10 | – | 36 | – | −24 | 0 | – | 72 | 48 |
| Q 24 | 24 | – | 10 | 11 | 25 | −48 | – | 0 | 11 | 50 | 13 |

Table 24.2 shows that out of 100 respondents, 41 respondents know the concept of financial inclusion, 70 respondents are having bank account, 05 respondents are having accounts in co-operative banks, 21 respondents are having two accounts with the banks, and 21 respondents are having two operative accounts with the banks.

Combined scores so calculated, seen in Table 24.3 in the most right column are used as sample variables to test the hypothesis by chi-square method:

$$\chi^2 = \frac{\Sigma(x-\bar{x})^2}{\sigma^2} \quad \text{where, } \sigma^2 = \frac{1}{n}\left[\Sigma d^2 - (\Sigma d)^2\right]$$

Calculation of Standard Deviation ($\sigma^2$)

| Question | x | d ($x - \bar{x}$) | $d^2$ |
|---|---|---|---|
| 1 | 8 | −19 | 361 |
| 2 | −1 | 28 | 784 |
| 3 | 32 | 5 | 25 |
| 4 | 40 | 13 | 169 |
| 5 | 132 | 105 | 11,025 |
| 6 | 80 | 53 | 2809 |
| 7 | 98 | 71 | 5041 |
| 8 | 34 | 7 | 49 |
| 9 | −39 | 66 | 4356 |
| 10 | 75 | 47 | 2209 |
| 11 | 55 | 28 | 784 |
| 12 | −103 | 130 | 16,900 |
| 13 | 17 | −10 | 100 |
| 14 | 19 | −8 | 64 |
| 15 | 0 | −27 | 729 |
| 16 | −83 | 110 | 12,100 |
| 17 | −14 | −41 | 1681 |
| 18 | 26 | −1 | 1 |
| 19 | 65 | 38 | 1444 |
| 20 | 65 | 38 | 1444 |
| 21 | −34 | 61 | 3721 |
| 22 | 119 | 92 | 8464 |
| 23 | 48 | 21 | 441 |
| 24 | 13 | −14 | 196 |
| $n = 24$ | $\sum x = 652$ | $\sum d = 3$ | $\sum d^2 = 74,897$ |

**Source:** Primary data.

$$\bar{x} = \frac{652}{24} = 27.17 = 27 \text{ (Rounded Off)}$$

$$\sigma^2 = \frac{1}{n}\left[\sum d^2 - (\sum d)^2\right] = \frac{1}{24}\left[74,897 - (3)^2\right] = \frac{1}{24}\left[74,897 - 9\right]$$

$$= \frac{1}{24}(74,888) = 3120.33$$

The square standard deviation will now be used for calculation of chi-square test.

The Hypothesis of the present study as well as for the chi-square test is given in Section 24.5. It is also given here:

$H_0$ = ICT and education level play a chief role in financial inclusion of rural population.

Calculation of chi-square ($\chi^2$)

| Question | $\bar{x}$ | $\bar{x}$ | $(x-\bar{x})$ | $(x-\bar{x})^2$ |
|---|---|---|---|---|
| 1 | 8 | 27 | −19 | 361 |
| 2 | −1 | 27 | −28 | 784 |
| 3 | 32 | 27 | 5 | 25 |
| 4 | 40 | 27 | 13 | 169 |
| 5 | 132 | 27 | 105 | 11025 |
| 6 | 80 | 27 | 53 | 2809 |
| 7 | 98 | 27 | 71 | 5041 |
| 8 | 34 | 27 | 7 | 49 |
| 9 | −39 | 27 | −66 | 4356 |
| 10 | 75 | 27 | 47 | 2209 |
| 11 | 55 | 27 | 28 | 784 |
| 12 | −103 | 27 | −130 | 16,900 |
| 13 | 17 | 27 | −10 | 100 |
| 14 | 19 | 27 | −8 | 64 |
| 15 | 0 | 27 | −27 | 729 |
| 16 | −83 | 27 | −110 | 12,100 |
| 17 | −14 | 27 | −41 | 1681 |
| 18 | 26 | 27 | −1 | 1 |
| 19 | 65 | 27 | 38 | 1444 |
| 20 | 65 | 27 | 38 | 1444 |
| 21 | −34 | 27 | −61 | 3721 |
| 22 | 119 | 27 | 92 | 8464 |
| 23 | 48 | 27 | 21 | 441 |
| 24 | 13 | 27 | −14 | 196 |
| $n = 24$ | $n = 24 = \frac{\Sigma x}{652}$ | | $\Sigma(x-\bar{x}) = 3$ | $\Sigma(x-\bar{x})^2 = 74897$ |

$$v = (n-1) = (24-1) = 23$$

$$\chi^2 = \frac{\Sigma(x-\bar{x})^2}{\sigma^2} \text{ where, } \sigma^2 = 3120.33$$

$$\chi^2 = \frac{\Sigma(x-\bar{x})^2}{\sigma^2} = \frac{74897}{3120.33} = 24.0 \text{ (at 95\% of significance level)}$$

The table value of $\chi^2 = 35.1725$

If calculated value < table value (24.0 < 35.1725), it means the Hypothesis is accepted.

It hence, proves that ICT and Education level play a chief role in financial inclusion of rural population.

It means that full financial inclusion of rural population is possible only through appropriate ICT and education level.

## 24.8 CONCLUSION

It is evident from the above discussion and survey data that financial inclusion so expected and initiated by the government, cannot be achieved till the other impediments that are in the way are not overcome. Bank branches per population density, complex procedures and regulations, and other governing pitfalls are some burning issues that must be picked up fast and first. However, government and RBI have made necessary improvements in the governing policies and programs to simplify the banking procedures and implemented new schemes to better cater to the financial needs of the public. PMJDY, Digitalization of Banking services, Priority Lending, Kisan Credit Card and some other relevant programs to spread financial literacy are some of the new schemes broadcast by the government. In today's India, financial inclusion and further financial literacy are the key drivers of the economic growth and economic stability. Financial inclusion blended with effective and adequate financial literacy can only help to eradicate poverty and to sustain self-reliant in the country. In the absence of customer centric financial independency, country cannot seek any sustainable inclusive economic development. And, the basic objective of the development of the country will defeat.

Internet, basically the high speed Internet is another area of hurdle for real time and relevant financial issues to operate. In a country like India where coverage of vast area and catering to dense population has always been a challenge. ICT, there can prove to be panacea but weak Internet speed becomes an issue rather than a solution. The Internet provider companies who are providing good Internet services are costly. Internet is really a big issue to discuss because it works two ways—One, Bank's Internet and other, customer's Internet. The combined interface of both the Internet works for the financial delivery. This way, urgent need is of a comprehensive equal Internet speed and access for all.

The cost of financial facilities from mobile banking comes to 50 paise per transaction. The government must offer some incentive packages for mobile banking facilities. The proliferation of mobile banking facilities is accomplished only through seamless technology. Reducing the problems of technology is also a very important subject.

Dissemination of digital education in rural India is very important. It is very important to encourage the youth of the regions to use the Internet. The India Net project in partnership with Google by the Government of India is a step toward achieving this goal. In this project, Wi-Fi facilities in rural areas are being provided by the Government of India. It is very important to make aware of the importance of specialty technology to various persons in rural areas such as landlord school dropouts and under age groups. The villagers of these areas can be encouraged to open an account with banks through the self-help group. Agents of banks should also be trained to achieve the goal of financial inclusion in rural India. The agents in the banks work wherever I am from the same area because they are well aware of the geographical and economic information of that area. Financial literacy is urgently needed for rural population to ensure their financial inclusion through Jan Dhan-Aadhar-Mobile.

To complete the campaign of financial inclusion it is very important that we inculcate a tendency to learn financial education among the people. Financial education can only be learned through education. Therefore, the first goal should be to educate those who are illiterate irrespective of their age. We should take steps like adult education to educate people again. Banks should also move toward simplifying their forms so that people do not feel any difficulty in filling the forms. Banks should make their services accessible to the people through technology and according to very simple technology. Banks should also make some fundamental reforms in the structure of mobile banking. Many people in the survey have reported difficulty in reading the messages sent by banks.

Model for SMS to Illiterate or Low Educated Rural Population

| Sign | Amount |
|---|---|
| + (Deposit) | xxxxx |
| – (Withdrawal) | xxxx |
| = (Balance) | xxxx |
| ? (Narration) | Name/etc. if any |

The banks should deposit the money deposited by the customers and send the rest of the money in their account to the customers in a very easy language so that even the less educated and uneducated people can read those messages easily. Banks should give their messages according to the plus when the money is deposited and minus when the money comes out. Banks should set up a window in each bank separately to provide information and support to financially ill-educated and illiterate persons. Financial education by the Reserve Bank should reach every customer through the bank branch. Financial inclusion will help in achieving this through joint efforts of education and technology.

## KEYWORDS

- **financial inclusion**
- **PMJDY**
- **social revolution**
- **rural economy**
- **ICT**
- **education**
- **financial literacy**

## REFERENCES

Agarwal, S. (2018). Internet and Mobile Association of India: Internet Users in India Expected to Reach 500 million by June: IAMAI—The Economic Times.

Bhanot, D., Bapat, V., & Bera, S. (2012). Studying financial inclusion in North-East India. *International Journal of Bank Marketing*, *30*(6), 465–484. https://doi.org/10.1108/02652321211262221

Bilas, S. K., & Chandrasekhar, N. C. (2016). Financial inclusion in India—a look. *Journal of Indian Journal of Research*, *5*(7), 118–120.

CRISIL Inclusix. (2015). *CRISIL Inclusix An index to measure India's progress on financial inclusion An initiative by CRISIL Developed with Support from Ministry of Finance,* Government of India and Reserve Bank of India.

Dangi, N., & Kumar, P. (2013). Current Situation of Financial Inclusion in India and Its Future Visions. *Xplore International Research Journal Consortium Www.Irjcjournals.Org*, *2*(8). Retrieved from www.irjcjournals.org

Bagli, S., & Datta, P. (2012). A Study of Financial Inclusion in India. *Journal of Radix International Educational and Research Consortium*, *1*(8), 1–18.

Garg, S., & Agarwal, P. (2014). *Financial Inclusion in India-a Review of Initiatives and Achievements 16*, 52–61. Retrieved from www.iosrjournals.org

Goel, S., & Sharma, R. (2017). Developing a Financial Inclusion Index for India. *Procedia Computer Science*, *00*, 0-000. https://doi.org/10.1016/j.procs.2017.11.459

Hung, A. A., Parker, A. M., Yoong, J. K., & Yoong, J. (2009). Defining and Measuring Financial Literacy. *SSRN Electronic Journal*. 1–28. https://doi.org/10.2139/ssrn.1498674

Iqbal, B. A., & Sami, S. (2017). Role of Banks in Financial Inclusion in India. *Contaduria y Administracion*, *62*(2), 644–656. https://doi.org/10.1016/j.cya.2017.01.007

Kempson, E., & Whyley, C. (2000). In or out? Financial Exclusion: A Literature and Research Review. 1–100. Retrieved from http://www.pfrc.bris.ac.uk/Reports/In_or_out.pdf.

Kim, M., Zoo, H., Lee, H., & Kang, J. (2018). Mobile Financial Services, Financial Inclusion, And Development: A Systematic Review of Academic Literature. *The Electronic Journal of Information Systems in Developing Countries*, *84*(5), 1–17. https://doi.org/10.1002/isd2.12044

Kumar, S., & Kumar Chattopadhyay, S. (2011). *Munich Personal RePEc Archive Financial Inclusion in India: A Case-study of West Bengal Financial Inclusion in India: A Case-study of West Bengal*.

Lokhande, A. (2009). *(PDF) Microfinance Initiatives In India*. 16–18. Retrieved from https://www.researchgate.net/publication/267630791_MICROFINANCE_INITIATIVES_IN_INDIA

Lusardi, A., & Michigan, O. S. M. (2005). Financial Literacy and Planning: Implications for Retirement Well-being. In *Financial Literacy: Implications for Retirement Security and the Financial Marketplace*. 1–17. https://doi.org/10.1093/acprof:oso/9780199696819.003.0002

Mol, S. (2014). Financial Inclusion: Concepts and Overview in Indian Context. In *Abhinav International Monthly Refereed Journal of Research in Management & Technology*. *3*, 28–35. Retrieved from www.abhinavjournal.com

Lokhande, M.A. (2014). Financial Inclusion Initiatives in India. *IMPACT: International Journal of Research in Business Management (IMPACT: IJRBM)*, *2*(12), 22–33. Retrieved from http://www.impactjournals.us/journals.php?id=78&jtype=2&page=33

Pavithran, R. M. P. and K. B. (2014). Role of Commercial Banks in Financial Inclusion: A Study in Respect to Indian Economy. *Journal of Business Management & Social Sciences Research (JBM&SSR)*, *3*(5), 75–81.

Rangrajan, C. (2008). *Report of the Committee on Financial Inclusion*.

Shah, P., & Dubhashi, M. (2015). Review Paper on Financial Inclusion—The Means of Inclusive Growth. *Chanakya International Journal of Business Research*. *1*, 37–48. Retrieved from www.iimpcijbr.com

Singh, A. (2017). Role of Technology in Financial Inclusion. *International Journal of Business and General Management (IJBGM)*, *6*(5), 1–6.

Souza, R. D. (2018). Examining Mobile Banking as a Tool for Financial Inclusion in India. *ORF Issue Brief*, (265), 5.

Tamilarasu, D. A. (2014). *Role of Banking Sectors on Financial Inclusion Development in India—An Analysis. 2*(2), 39–45.

Singh, A., & Tondon, P. (2015). Financial Inclusion In India: An Analysis. *International Journal of Marketing, Financial Services & Management Research*, *6*, 41–54.

Ventouri, A. (2018). Bank Competition and Regional Integration: Evidence from ASEAN Nations. *Review of Development Finance*, *8*(2), 127–140. https://doi.org/10.1016/j.rdf.2018.08.002

Verma, R. (2017). India Unclear How Many Villages It Has, And Why That Matters | India Spend-Journalism India | Data Journalism India | Investigative Journalism-IndiaSpend. Retrieved from https://archive.indiaspend.com/cover-story/india-unclear-how-many-villages-it-has-and-why-that-matters-56076.

# CHAPTER 25

# Role of Information and Communication Technology in Developing Northeast Region of India and Some Aspects of e-Governance

HIREN KUMAR DEVA SARMA

*Department of Information Technology, Sikkim Manipal Institute of Technology, Sikkim, 737136, India. E-mail: hirenkdsarma@gmail.com*

## ABSTRACT

Northeast region of India is relatively under developed in comparison to the rest of the country. Information and communication technology (ICT) can play a vital role in the development process of this region. ICT can contribute in economic growth as well as in other aspect of social growth. In this chapter, a road map has been shown about how ICT can contribute in overall growth of the Northeast region of the country. Proposals are made considering the unique geographic constraints and other environmental factors prevailing in this region. Some aspects of e-Governance practices applicable to North Eastern region are also mentioned.

## 25.1 INTRODUCTION

The easternmost region of India is generally referred to as Northeast India. This region includes eight states of India and those are Arunachal Pradesh, Assam, Manipur, Meghalaya, Mizoram, Nagaland, Sikkim, and Tripura. It is apparent that this region of India suffers from under development. The term development has multiple dimensions. Here, the issue development refers to dimensions like overall infrastructure, road and transport facilities and infrastructure, communication facilities, medical facilities, educational infrastructure, economic growth, and natural disaster mitigation provisions. Although the term development covers a very broad spectrum, the ultimate goal of development should be to provide a sophisticated life style to the people of the region with greater happiness. Now the terms like sophisticated life style and greater happiness are quite qualitative and also difficult to quantify. We assume the usual meanings of these terms. The objective of this chapter is to explore how the modern technology like information and communication technology (ICT) can be exploited to bring development to a region. Off-course, each region has its own specific problems and advantages and thus region specific solutions are more adaptable than a general solution in order to address the issues of the region. As already mentioned development has many dimensions, it is important to have developments in balanced manner in all possible dimensions in order to achieve overall growth. ICT is relatively a modern technology which has penetrated significantly in the society in last part of 20th century. Interestingly this particular paradigm has changed the human society in a big way. Information technology (IT) has impact in all aspects of human life and at the same time it is strongly believed that IT can bring development to the people of a particular society or geographic region if IT is used to address the society specific or region specific issues. Thus, IT can play a major role in developing a region. This chapter shows a roadmap how IT can be exploited to address some region specific issues of Northeast India. The theme of this chapter is to give some guidelines which will be necessary in order to achieve development in Northeast India through IT. The rest of this chapter is organized as follows: Section 25.2 highlights the background on Northeast India, followed by Section 25.3 in which the problem undertaken in this chapter is formally stated. Section 25.4 shows how regional growth can occur through various agencies. Section 25.5 summarizes what is IT, followed by Section 25.6 in which the roadmap regarding how IT can be exploited for overall growth in a region like Northeast India. Section 25.7 deals with the role of an individual in developing a region followed by Section 25.8, in which the investment and associated risks of an IT-based business are discussed. Section 25.9 summarizes about what IT cannot do. Section 25.10 outlines some aspects of e-Governance applicable in NE region, and finally the chapter is concluded in Section 25.11. Terms IT and ICT are used interchangeably throughout the chapter.

## 25.2 BACKGROUND

The North Eastern (NE) region of India is famous for its unique cultural heritage, handicrafts, tribes living in this region, and above all the scenic beauty of this region. Some portion of the NE region falls into eastern Himalayas. Similarly, some portion of this region falls into Patkai-Naga Hills and Lushai Hills. This region has a modest climate neither very hot nor very cold. The rainfall in this region of India is severe. Rivers of this region never dry out and remain flowing throughout the year. The mighty Brahmaputra flows across the NE region and meets the Bay of Bengal. The NE region is very resourceful in terms of natural resources reserves like petroleum, natural gas, coal, etc. The petroleum and natural gas reserves of this region constitute a fifth of India's total potential. The soil of NE region is very fertile and potential for agriculture in this region is very high. Jhum cultivation is the way of agriculture in the hilly parts of this region. More than 200 ethnic groups with their respective unique culture live in this region. These groups have very rich traditional knowledge and methods applicable in various fields like medicine, agriculture, disaster mitigation, etc. The art and culture exhibited by the people of this region is also very rich and unique.

The NE region shares its international border with China and Nepal in the north, Myanmar in the east, Bangladesh in the southwest, and Bhutan to the northwest. The NE region has more than 90% of its entire border as international border shared with the above-mentioned countries. Therefore, in this age of globalization, the NE region has better prospect and ease to interact with the rest of Asia. International trade may bring economic growth to this region very fast. Such strategic geographic location of this region in fact makes NE region a candidate for faster growth. The scope for development in this region in the era of globalization is vast but it needs careful planning and policy by the government and economic integration with the rest of Asia. Therefore, mainly due to the geographic location of this region it has potential for becoming:

- International Trade Hub (Global)
- International Educational Hub (Global)
- International Industrial Hub (Global)
- International Tourist Destination (Global)

## 25.3 PROBLEM STATEMENT

The summarized statement for the problem undertaken in this chapter may be "NE region of India needs development in order to keep pace with the rest of the world."

Although development covers a very big range, it may be narrowed down to certain scale and a region may be identified as a developed one if it has economic growth, developed infrastructure, employment generation, modernization and development in agriculture/health/education sector, developed transportation facilities (road/rail/air), and people of the region lead sophisticated life style with happiness. Moreover, the region should be free from insurgencies and human caused disturbances.

The objective of this chapter is to explore the potential of IT that is applicable to a region like Northeast India in order to bring development to the region.

## 25.4 WAYS FOR SOCIETAL/REGIONAL GROWTH

The growth in the society or in a region may come through the efforts of various agencies. The government who is the ruling mechanism of a region may put effort to bring development to the region. Practically, all kinds of power of a democratic governance system are concentrated with the ruling government. The government system can exercise its power to bring development to a specific region although it needs careful and need-based planning and policies. Moreover, execution of the planning is another important factor in bringing development to a region. In fact, the ruling government is the most resourceful entity and also responsible for the management of the resources of a state, and therefore, this entity plays a vital role in the overall growth of the region. The government may contribute in multidimensional development of a region through proper planning, policies, and execution of the planning.

An individual may also contribute in regional growth. Naturally, an individual will have limited resources and also power to contribute toward the growth of a region. As an individual, someone may be able to identify the areas for the overall regional growth and as per his or her capability and capacity; the individual may put effort for achieving the growth objectives. Such kinds of development activity will be area specific and domain will be narrow. For example, an individual may try to establish one or two good schools in remote areas of a region where there is no good academic infrastructure. But this effort may not propagate to a larger region since it is effort of only an individual.

Development in regions is also possible through the joint effort of government and individuals. Under many circumstances this has proved as a better approach. This needs suitable policy from government side and also motivated individual from the other side. Nongovernmental organizations may be considered as an example of this model. Even there are many organizations in India operating under Public–Private Partnership model which are successful in contributing to the regional growth.

It is worth mentioning that the use of computers and Internet has penetrated in different states of NE India although not highly significant. Data presented in Table 25.1 depicts how the NE region is becoming ready for the ICT revolution in the years to come.

**TABLE 25.1** Availability of Computers and Internet in the Households of NE region

| State | Households | Computers | % | With Internet | % | Without Internet | % |
|---|---|---|---|---|---|---|---|
| Assam | 6,367,295 | 592,158 | 9.3 | 101,877 | 1.6 | 490,282 | 7.7 |
| Tripura | 84,2781 | 60,680 | 7.2 | 8428 | 1 | 53,095 | 6.3 |
| Manipur | 507,152 | 45,644 | 9 | 10,650 | 2.1 | 34,993 | 6.9 |
| Meghalaya | 538,299 | 40,911 | 7.6 | 8074 | 1.5 | 32,836 | 6.1 |
| Arunachal Pradesh | 161,614 | 21,452 | 8.2 | 5232 | 2 | 16,220 | 6.2 |
| Mizoram | 221,077 | 33,604 | 15.2 | 5527 | 2.5 | 28,077 | 12.7 |
| Sikkim | 128,131 | 14,735 | 11.5 | 4228 | 3.3 | 10,507 | 8.2 |
| Nagaland | 399,965 | 35,597 | 8.9 | 6799 | 1.7 | 28,797 | 7.2 |
| India | 246,692,667 | 23,189,111 | 9.4 | 7,647,473 | 3.1 | 15,541,638 | 6.3 |

**Source:** India 2011 census data; state wise Internet users.

The ratio in regard to the use of computer and Internet has to increase significantly in order to prepare NE region for Digital India.

## 25.5 WHAT IS INFORMATION TECHNOLOGY (IT)?

IT is a sophisticated mechanism for information acquisition, information processing, information storage and retrieval, information distribution, and information sharing. IT started becoming popular in the middle of 90s of 20th century. IT may be called as one of the significant inventions of 20th century. This field of knowledge is growing with time but with pace. Today IT has penetrated in all stages of our life. IT has influenced everybody's life in a big way. Communication is an aspect of life in which the influence of IT is very much visible. The invention of World Wide Web has brought lot of changes to the society. Probably, today no knowledge domain is free now from the influence of IT (Leon et al., 1999; Halsall and Kulkarni, 2007).

## 25.6 SECTOR WISE DEVELOPMENT THROUGH IT

In this section, we discuss how IT can be utilized for the development of various sectors. Various sectors considered in this study are education, health, natural resource management, disaster management, agriculture, tourism, automation, and employment generation. Figure 25.1 summarizes these sectors. If the above-mentioned sectors in a particular region like NE India can be improved significantly, then this can be considered as a meaningful ingredient in overall growth of the region. In this study, we consider that IT can be exploited to develop IT-based products and to extend IT-based services in order to accomplish certain tasks and goals. IT-based products may be classified as certain software systems which shall be used for accomplishing some specific tasks more efficiently. Similarly, IT-based service means getting certain tasks done with the aid of IT. A user might be in the need of IT-based products as well as IT-based services depending on the type of tasks he has. In the following part of this section, we will discuss how IT-based products and IT-based services can be developed in order to meet the needs of various sectors as mentioned above. The use of IT-based products and IT-based services will definitely improve the functioning of various sectors. As the same time, such initiatives will also open up lot of IT-related business avenues along with employment generation and wealth creation.

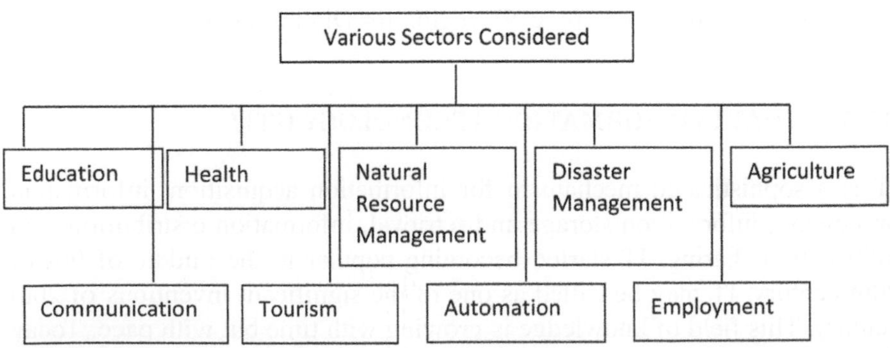


**FIGURE 25.1** Various sectors considered for adaptation of IT.

### 25.6.1 EDUCATION

IT can be used for smooth functioning of educational institutions. Various IT-based products and IT-based services can be used in educational institutions ranging from elementary level to University level. Although, there are many countries utilizing IT in cducation sector, it is observed that NE region of India is yet to adapt IT more seriously in the education sector. Since, every region has its own constraints and also own system as a whole, it is necessary to consider the unique characteristics of the system under consideration at the time of development of the IT-based products and services.

#### 25.6.1.1 PRODUCT

*Software packages for educational institutions:* The governance system of an educational institution may be automated fully or partially. Thus, IT-based products may be developed for smooth governance of the educational institutions. Moreover, web-based systems may be developed and deployed for control and easy dissemination of information.

*Software packages as educational aid:* Software packages may be developed as educational aid for the instructors. There is a scope to develop IT-based products which will help the teachers in delivering their lectures and also managing the class room in a better way. Even students will find it easier to copy the lecture content of the teacher inside the class room. In fact, there are many products available in the market in the name of smart class room or digital class room. Of course, these products cannot replace a teacher but these products can be used as teaching aid by the teachers.

#### 25.6.1.2 MSERVICES

*IT infrastructure development:* In order to exploit the power of IT, it is essential to build up IT infrastructure inside the campus of an educational institution. IT infrastructure, at nutshell, may refer to networking inside the campus in terms of local area network (LAN) (Tanenbaum, 2006) or Wi-Fi (Murthy and Manoj, 2005) apart from high end computing facilities. Moreover, Internet facilities should be available inside the campus. The availability of IT infrastructure inside the campus of an educational institution will not only enrich the institution in terms of modern technology but also will improve the work culture inside the institution.

*Training:* If not all, at least some educational institutions should have IT wing which also can provide training on various aspects of IT. IT is a vast field today. The IT wing as mentioned above should be capable of providing training on some specific areas of IT, like networking, database technologies, programming languages, etc., to the clients or users if IT.

*Digital content development:* There are lots of advantages of having digital copies of books, printed materials, etc. Digital content is easy to distribute, easy to store, easy to search and retrieve, cost-effective, and also durability is very long. The textbooks or other reading materials can be converted into digital form and then these can be utilized in the educational institutions as per the requirement and convenience.

The above-mentioned IT-based products and services are only a few from within the pool of products and services applicable to education sector. Use of these IT-based products and services will not only enhance the efficiency of an educational institution but also it will possibly make it easy to achieve the goals of the educational institutions.

### 25.6.2 HEALTH

Health is a very important sector to be concentrated at present in a country like India. It is one of the prime duties of the government to provide better health and medical services to the citizens of the country. IT can be exploited significantly in improving the health sector. There can be numerous IT-based products and services that can be developed and deployed for overall development of this sector.

#### 25.6.2.1 PRODUCT

*Software packages as an aid to the practices of hospital/doctor/nurse, etc.:* Various software packages may be developed and deployed for smooth administration and functioning of hospitals. Governance in hospitals can significantly be improved by using these software packages. Moreover, there is a scope to develop software which can help doctors and nurses in carrying out their duties like diagnosis, monitoring, etc. For example, there can be some digital image processing-based software system which will help doctors in properly analyzing X-ray plates, MRI-images, etc. (Gonzalez and Woods, 2005).

*Health monitoring system:* It is very important to monitor the condition of health of patients regularly. In the current time, there are various IT-based products which are used in sophisticated hospitals for continuous health monitoring of patients. For example, there are systems based on sensor networks which are deployed for such purposes (Zhao and Guibas, 2007).

*Traditional knowledge-based software system:* In the society, especially in the NE India, there are traditional knowledge-based systems highly popular and used to treat the patients. Although this form of knowledge may be different from modern medical science but it may be good to utilize some knowledge of this kind along with modern medical science. Knowledge-based software systems can be built using traditional as well as modern medical science which shall be of great help for medical practitioners. Expert systems (Bhattacharya, 2008) with respect to the common deceases of the region can also be built to assist the doctors.

#### *25.6.2.2 SERVICES*

*IT infrastructure development:* It is essential to develop IT infrastructure in the hospital premises in order to fully exploit IT. Even the hospitals of a particular district or a state may be interconnected through wide area network or virtual private network (Leon-Garcia and Widjaja, 2003; Stallings, 1999). This type of interconnected system is beneficial from many perspectives. For example, doctors' expertise may be shared among the hospitals very easily. Hospital Information Systems may be developed and deployed over the LAN.

*Data management:* Patients' data is an important asset for a hospital. Based on these data, future policies are fixed. Thus, data management is a very important activity for hospital administration. Through properly designed Hospital Information Systems, it is possible to manage data very efficiently and generate timely and appropriate reports.

The above-mentioned IT-based products and services are only a partial list of what all are possible through IT. There is a vast scope to use IT for development of health sector also. Proper application of IT in health sector will improve the functioning of hospitals significantly.

### ***25.6.3 NATURAL RESOURCE MANAGEMENT***

Natural resources reserve in NE region is very rich. Proper management of these resources can cause heavy raise in the revenue earned by the state as well as the nation. Although there are various government departments responsible for preservation, maintenance, and management of these resources, there can be lot of discrepancies as well as lack of transparency in case manual systems operate in place. In fact, that is the situation, where all records are maintained manually. IT can again be exploited for better management of these resources. As a result, the resources can be easily traced, tracked and also it may significantly contribute in enriching the nation.

#### *25.6.3.1 PRODUCT*

*Suitable software packages:* Software systems can be built in order to keep track of the natural resources in a particular district or state or a region. For example, there are lots of expensive trees available in various zones of the NE region. The records like the total number of such specific trees in a region are generally maintained manually. This manual system can be replaced by a software package. Through the software system, it becomes easy to update, maintain, and also it is possible to make the records easily available to different authorities. Such a system can be made applicable to all kinds of resources by all respective government departments.

*Simulation of river interlinking project:* Water is a natural resource which everybody knows as an ingredient of daily life with extreme importance. At present time, there is a plan by Government of India to interlink some major rivers of the country with an idea that once the rivers are interlinked the water requirements of dry regions will be fulfilled by the water content of some rivers which have plenty of water throughout the year. This idea may not work so straightforward. Moreover, there is a huge cost involved with such projects. Again people of the affected region are also not supporting this idea. The outcome of such river interlinking project is really difficult to predict accurately. But an effort can be made to simulate the situation through computer programs and then predict the effect of such interlinking of rivers by giving realistic data to the simulation program (Banks et al., 2004) as an input. Such result obtained through simulation may be of extreme importance in making policies for future by the government.

#### *25.6.3.2 SERVICES*

*IT infrastructure development:* The respective departments for the management of natural resources should develop IT infrastructure in terms of LAN or Intranets (Leon-Garcia and Widjaja, 2003; Stallings, 1999; Halsall and Kulkarni, 2007). This will enable the departments for better management of the resources. Moreover, there will be a requirement of suitable software system to run over these networks in order to exploit the power of such IT infrastructure. The responsible departments should take initiative to adapt IT for better management.

*Resource monitoring system:* It is extremely important to preserve the natural resources. Therefore, monitoring of such resources is also very important. There are IT-based natural resource monitoring systems already developed and in place in many advanced countries. For example, wireless sensor network-based systems (Zhao and Guibas, 2007) are deployed for tasks like environment monitoring, wild life tracking, etc. These technologies can be adapted in order to monitor highly expensive and rare natural resources in the NE India.

The above-mentioned list of IT-based products and services gives an overview of what IT can provide for better management and preservation of the natural resources. Thus, there can be number of applications of IT in the management of natural resources.

## 25.6.4 DISASTER MANAGEMENT

Natural calamities like earthquake, flood, etc., are unavoidable. But if enough precautions are taken the post-effect of such disasters can be minimized. There are modern technologies coming up which are used for minimizing such effects. There can be some IT-based products and services which may come out to be extremely helpful in such situations. NE region of India is prone to earthquake. Again state like Assam is also badly affected by flood. In the following part of this section we discuss how IT-based products and services can be useful in handling such situations.

### 25.6.4.1 PRODUCT

*Alarming system:* Alarming systems for natural calamities specific to NE region, although it is very challenging, may be developed. Such systems may be installed in suitable places and any alarming situations may be broadcasted in the required zones.

*Post-disaster rescue assistance:* Post-disaster rescue operations are required to be very smart. Because the natural disaster like earthquake is generally difficult to predict but if highly effective post-disaster rescue operations are adapted then probably the loss of lives and properties may be minimized. For example, ad-hoc networks (Murthy and Manoj, 2005) may play a vital role in post-disaster recovery operations.

*Simulation package for earthquake effects:* There are software systems that simulate the condition of a geographic region, for example, a town or a city under the influence of earthquake. The software takes the physical condition of the region under consideration as one of the inputs and then based on the intensity of the earthquake; it predicts the amount and type of damage that may occur in that region. Such study may be useful for making strategies regarding how to face earthquake of different intensities such that the damage can be minimized. This kind of study may be carried out with respect to different specific places within NE region of India and accordingly strategies may be planned.

#### 25.6.4.2 SERVICES

*Infrastructure development:* The departments responsible for disaster management need to develop IT infrastructure in terms of communication network and high-end computing systems. These IT infrastructures again need to be utilized properly for efficient functioning of the department.

*Training/awareness aid:* The citizens should be made aware of the causes of natural calamities like earthquake, etc. Then they are to be trained about dos and don'ts for such events. Such awareness will definitely reduce the amount of damage that can be caused by earthquake like disasters. IT can be exploited for efficient training program for such purposes. IT can play a role of training aid for such training programs.

The above-mentioned products and services are not the complete list of applications of IT in disaster management sector. The responsible department may adapt such IT-based initiatives to handle natural disasters in future.

### 25.6.5 AGRICULTURE

India is basically an agriculture-based country. The agriculture sector is an extremely important one for a country like India. The economy of NE of India is also based on agriculture. There has always been effort by government to increase the productivity of the soil and such responsibilities are entrusted to the agriculture department of a state. By adapting scientific approaches it is possible to improve the agricultural productivity of the soil of a region. The scientific reports say that the soil of NE region is fertile and there is scope to escalate the productivity in this region. Once agricultural products are ready, it is again important to have a better trade with suitable customers so that the farmers get maximum benefit out of these agricultural products. In this section, we will see how IT can facilitate agricultural sector for its development. IT has been applied even in the agricultural sector in the Western countries and benefits have been derived out of it. Those solutions may not be directly applicable here in the NE region as this region has unique climatic and soil conditions. But there is scope to apply IT in an appropriate fashion for the development of the agricultural sector in this region.

#### *25.6.5.1 PRODUCT*

*Need-based water supply and manure supply:* Adequate supply of water and manure at right time is very important for better growth of crops and any agricultural entity. There are systems in place in paddy fields especially in Western countries which can monitor the requirements of water and different manure in the paddy fields regularly. Then depending on the requirements, appropriate amount of water and manure may be supplied. For example, wireless sensor networks are deployed for such purposes (Zhao and Guibas, 2007).

*e-marketing solution:* It is another important activity to sell off the agricultural products in appropriate price in the market. Suitably designed web portals can be useful here.

*GIS-based system for agricultural land discovery and management:* The NE region is mostly covered by forests. There might be huge plot of land in this region which still is unutilized for agricultural purpose due to ignorance. Effort may be put to discover such suitable for agriculture but unexplored land by using technology like Geographic Information System.

#### *25.6.5.2 SERVICES*

*IT infrastructure development:* IT infrastructure needs to be developed at various regions that include administrative offices, paddy fields, etc., to have better monitoring.

*Agri-knowledge dissemination through e-community center:* The involved people in the agricultural sector need modern knowledge regarding agricultural science. This is another continuously evolving area. The people can be made aware of the latest developments, modern knowledge, and related stuff through IT-based community center. The IT-based community centers through web portals and information systems (Mcleod and Schell, 2008) will have information access worldwide. This is perhaps the most suitable mechanism for rapid distribution of information.

The above-mentioned IT-based products and services are only a partial list. There are novel applications of IT coming up every day. It is important to exploit these opportunities and such initiatives will definitely help in growing a sector like agriculture.

### *25.6.6 TOURISM*

The geographic location, climate, scenic beauty, indigenous culture, and different tribes of the NE region can make this place an exotic tourist destination. But there is a need to make this region popular in the world through information distribution in a right way. IT can play a vital role in popularizing this region in the world. The accurate information about the region is to be made available in front of the people. Moreover, there is a need to facilitate tourists by giving web-based facilities to book accommodation, to book tours, etc. In this section, we see how IT can be helpful in developing tourism sector in the NE region.

#### *25.6.6.1 PRODUCT*

*Web-based information system:* Web-based information system is highly essential in this age in order to distribute information among the tourists. Web-based information will not only disseminate information but it will also facilitate tourists in booking hotel facilities or tours, etc., in a particular region. Such facilities will easily attract the tourists to this region.

*Mobile-phone-based system:* Nowadays even mobile phone applications are coming up for distributing information. Mobile phones are also having Internet connectivity at present time. Such systems may be exploited for distributing tourism related information among the users.

#### *25.6.6.2 SERVICES*

*Tourist assistance systems:* Tourists are required to be facilitated in terms of accommodation, transportation, security, etc. Information systems may be deployed in public places so that tourists can have easy access to these systems and acquire necessary local information. This may be in addition to the web portals available in Internet.

The above-mentioned products and services are again only a partial list regarding applications of IT in the tourism sector. IT can play a very big role in the development of tourism sector. The government departments and right authority of a region need to exploit it.

### *25.6.7 AUTOMATION*

Automation of various processes in various systems is necessary in the current time. Automation has several advantages which include rapid product development, flawless operation, better efficiency, higher throughput, etc. Automation is required almost in all sectors to keep pace along with the fast changing world. Automation in the operation of various systems is a need of the hour. As such automation has a very vast domain. If the NE region of India is considered then there is a huge necessity regarding automation of processes in different domains such as offices, industries, institutions, etc. IT plays a vital role in the automation process. In summary, it may be mentioned that IT may be adapted for automation of various systems in this region which in turn will contribute to the overall growth of the region directly and also indirectly. This automation issue needs detail discussion and here in this chapter, we just introduce the idea.

### *25.6.8 EMPLOYMENT*

The unemployment is a major problem in many countries. This is one of the root causes of insurgencies in different regions. India and in particular, NE region is also not free from the problem of unemployment. Employment generation is an extremely important issue in a region like NE India. IT started become popular in the late 20th century. It has already been witnessed all around that IT can generate employment without disturbing current employment opportunities. IT is totally a new technical domain which is creating enough employment opportunities. IT industries are knowledge-based industries. The workers in this kind of industries need to be skilled enough. Along with time IT is influencing everyone's life significantly. Novel applications of IT are coming up every day. And this trend will be on for quite some time in the future. Along with the growing demand of IT-based applications in the society, there is also an increase in the number of employment opportunities. If IT is adapted in various sectors as discussed above in a region like NE India, this in turn obviously shall generate enough employment opportunities. In fact, the majority of such employment opportunities will be for IT educated people. IT can create wealth through knowledge-based industries. IT can play a significant role in creating employment opportunities in a region like NE India. IT can be a great weapon for enabling 3Es (Education, Empowerment, Employment) in a country like India.

### *25.6.9 COMMUNICATION*

In this modern age, the communication systems have become indispensable in everyone's life. Due to the technological advancements, the communication systems have become cheaper and easily available in the society. Internet has narrowed down the world in a sense. On top of everything, social networking sites like Facebook, has made it possible to reach out any one at any time so easily and at almost no cost. The most important technical requirement in this situation is the connectivity which in fact dependent on the communication infrastructure. NE states have unique geographic attributes, for example, hilly terrain spread across the entire region. Such attributes make the communication infrastructure inefficient to provide high quality connectivity at lower cost to the users. Since, the economic return from the sparse users of some hilly terrain in this region is expected to be less, the communication companies also find it difficult to invest high, in communication infrastructure to provide high-end connectivity service throughout. Overall, the communication scenario and connectivity status in this region is not of very high order. There is a scope to do enough research and development activities in order to provide quality communication service to geographically typical NE states at low cost. Novel low cost communication systems can be designed aiming at the unique geographical characteristics of this NE region, using various technologies like ad-hoc networks, mesh networks, sensor networks, etc., so that the overall communication scenario in this region is improved.

## 25.7 ROLE OF AN INDIVIDUAL

An individual can also play an important role in contributing toward the overall growth in the society. In the above-mentioned section, we have given a roadmap how IT can be adapted for overall growth in a region like NE India. An individual can put effort to exploit IT for overall growth in the society. Individuals can become IT entrepreneur. Being an IT-based entrepreneur one can not only generate wealth, employment opportunities but also he or she can contribute reasonably toward the regional development. The necessary products and services in different sectors can be offered by an IT-based entrepreneur. Thus, a motivated entrepreneur may serve the society through IT-based business also. The prospective entrepreneurs need to have smart thinking, intelligence, sense of social responsibility, integrity, and honesty apart from all other important attributes.

## 25.8 INVESTMENT AND RISK

For becoming an entrepreneur or to start any business an initial amount of money is definitely necessary. To start any IT-based venture apart from initial money, the domain knowledge is very important. The prospective entrepreneur should have an intellectual capability and for becoming a successful IT-based entrepreneur, one must be capable of foreseeing the application domain of IT. Innovation is highly essential in any IT-based venture. Compared to other business sectors, a modest IT-based business may not need huge amount of investment in the form of money, but important factors are time and domain knowledge.

Every business involves certain amount of risk. Another important direction to mention is that since the amount of money to be invested initially is not very high, the risk involved in IT-based business in terms of loss of money is also not high. IT-based businesses are totally technology and knowledge-based ventures, and that is why someone's brain or intellectual capability may play a very vital role in the success of such businesses.

## 25.9 WHAT IT CANNOT DO?

IT is an ever growing field. New dimensions of IT are coming up along with time. And therefore, this field of knowledge is yet to be matured in many areas. It is also important to understand that IT cannot do magic. Return against investment in the domain of IT may be very high but it also demands enough hard work. It is already mentioned that IT industries are driven by knowledge. Therefore, it is necessary for someone involved in IT-based business also to keep updated about the latest happenings in the field. Without innovation it may be difficult to sustain in the competition and therefore, innovation has to be a culture in the IT-based businesses. Without above-mentioned attributes, it is impractical to expect very good return from IT-based business.

## 25.10 DIGITAL INDIA, e-GOVERNANCE, AND NORTHEAST REGION

Transforming India into Digital India is one of the focal points of present government of India. There have been some papers reporting various dimensions of e-Governance in the context of India (Yadav and Singh, 2012; Athalye, 2013; Beniwal and Sikka, 2013; Malik et al., 2014; Khan et al., 2015; Kumar, 2016). Chetia analyses present scenario of e-Governance in Northeast India (Chetia, 2016). The present Government of India has taken several initiatives for making India digital. Digital India is a flagship program initiated by Honorable Prime Minister of India, Sri Narendra Modi (2015). However, the NE region of India is far behind in terms of ICT infrastructure also. Internet connectivity is a major challenge in this region. In spite of all challenges there has been effort by the state governments of NE region and central government to bring ICT-based practices and e-Governance in this region. Capacity building in the government departments, aiming at e-Governance in the days to come, is yet another challenge. National Institute for Smart Government is working in this regard for last couple of years, in this region. Short-term and also long-term program on capacity building for e-Governance and making NE region ready for Digital India are offered and also conducted by NISG for various state governments of the region. Some of the major challenges prevailing in NE region for preparing this region for Digital India and also for implementing e-Governance to its maxima are as mentioned below:

- Lack of ICT awareness among the citizens
- Poor ICT infrastructure
- Limited resources for ICT-based education
- Poor Internet connectivity
- Hilly geographic terrain
- Very limited software industry set up in the region.

As a part of the whole solution to the problems mentioned above, author feels that there is a scope and in fact requirement of an institution like e-Governance Academy in NE region, which can cater various services to the states of the NE region regarding e-Governance. Such an institution can also support government to make the dream of Digital India fulfilled.

Adoption of technology by citizens is yet another issue and government may have to take steps to address this issue also (Dwivedi et al., 2017; Rana et al., 2018; Sengupta et al., 2019). Moreover, access to the Internet by citizens in the region like NE India has always been an issue that needs immediate attention. Developing Internet infrastructure as well as user-friendly web portals of government departments, may be in regional languages, is an important task at the moment (Henman et al., 2019). Because, unless technology is adopted by the citizens e-Government practices shall not be successful.

## 25.11 CONCLUSION

IT can be utilized as a weapon for regional development. In this chapter, we have discussed how IT can be exploited to develop various sectors like education, health, agriculture, etc. If the above-mentioned sectors in a specific region like NE India are developed significantly then it is going to be a major part in an overall development of the region. A roadmap is given regarding how IT can be adapted in various sectors which ultimately will significantly contribute to the regional development. Effort in this direction may come from not only government side but an individual also can take part in the initiatives. An individual can become IT-based entrepreneur and significant contribution may come from an individual also in the region development initiatives. It is important to decide what is possible and what is not possible and then to act accordingly. In case of IT-based businesses, it needs maximum thought and minimum money as investment. It is believed that IT can be utilized for regional development also.

## KEYWORDS

- **information and communication technology**
- **region development**
- **social development**
- **e-Governance**
- **digital India**

## REFERENCES

Athalye, S.M.; "e-Governance: issues and challenges," *Episteme: An Online Interdisciplinary, Multidisciplinary & Multicultural Journal,* vol. 2, no. 2, September **2013,** pp.1–10.

Banks, J.; et al.; *Discrete-Event System Simulation,* Pearson Education, ISBN 81-7808-505-4, 2004.

Beniwal, V.S.; Sikka, K.; "e-Governance in India: prospects and challenges," *International Journal of Computer & Communication Technology,* vol. 4, no. 3, **2013**, pp. 1–5.

Bhattacharya, S.; *Artificial Intelligence,* University Science Press, ISBN 978-81-318-0489-6, 2008.

Chetia, S.R.B.; "e-Governance in North-East India," *Journal of Political Sciences & Public Affairs,* vol. 4, no. 2, **2016**, pp. 1–3.

Dwivedi, Y.K.; Rana, N.P.; Janssen, M.; Lal, B.; Williams, M.D.; Clement, M.; "An empirical validation of a unified model of electronic government adoption (UMEGA)," *Government Information Quarterly,* **2017**, pp. 1–20.

Gonzalez, R.C.; Woods, R.E.; *Digital Image Processing,* Pearson Education, ISBN 81-7808–629-8, 2005.

Halsall, F.; Kulkarni, L.G.; *Computer Networking and the Internet,* Pearson Education, ISBN 81-7758-475-8, 2007.

Henman, P.; Graham, T.; "Towards a taxonomy of government web portals," *ICEGOV2019: Proceedings of the 12th International Conference on Theory and Practice of Electronic Governance,* April **2019**, pp. 12–20.

Khan, I.; Khan, N.; "e-Governance reforms in India: issues, challenges and strategies-an overview," *International Journal of Computer Science Issues,* vol. 12, issue: 1, no. 2., January **2015**, pp. 42–53.

Kumar, S.; "e-governance in India," *Imperial Journal of Interdisciplinary Research,* vol. 2, no. 2, **2016**, pp. 480–491.

Leon, A.; Leon, M.; *Fundamentals of Information Technology,* Leon Press & Vikas Publishing House Pvt. Ltd. ISBN 0-81-259-0789-0, 1999.

Leon-Garcia, A.; Widjaja, I.; *Communication Networks,* Tata McGraw-Hill, ISBN 0-07-040235-3, 2003.

Malik, P.; Dhillan, P.; Verma, P.; "Challenges and future prospects for E-governance in India," *International Journal of Science, Engineering and Technology Research,* vol. 3, no. 7, July **2014**, pp. 1964–1972.

Mcleod, R.; Jr. Schell, G.P.; *Management Information Systems,* Pearson Education, ISBN 978-81-317-1949-7, 2008.

Murthy, C.S.R.; Manoj, B.S.; *Adhoc Wireless Networks,* Pearson Education, ISBN 81-297-0945-7, 2005.

Rana, N.; Luthra, S.; Rao, H.R.; "Developing a Framework using Interpretive Structural Modeling for the Challenges of Digital Financial Services in India," *PACIS* **2018**, Yokohama, Japan.

Sengupta, S.; Misra, D.C.; Chaudhary, M.; Prakash, O.; "Role of Technology in Success of Rural Sanitation Revolution in India," *ICEGOV2019: Proceedings of the 12th International Conference on Theory and Practice of Electronic Governance,* April **2019**, pp. 6–11.

Stallings, W.; *Data and Computer Communications,* Prentice-Hall of India, ISBN 81-203-1240-6, 1999.

Tanenbaum, A.S.; *Computer Networks,* Prentice-Hall of India, ISBN 81-203-2175-8, 2006.

Yadav, N.; Singh, V.B.; "E-Governance: past, present and future in India," I*nternational Journal of Computer Applications,* vol. 53, no.7, September **2012,** pp. 35–47.

Zhao, F.; Guibas, L.; Wireless Sensor Networks, Elsevier, ISBN 1-55860-914-8, 2007.

## CHAPTER 26

# Integration of Human Resource and Knowledge Management Initiatives in Higher Education

ALEENA ILYAZ

*PaperPedia Private Limited, Noida, Uttar Pradesh, 201301, India.*
*E-mail: aleenailyas2801@gmail.com*

### ABSTRACT

In a knowledge economy, higher education institutions (HEI) are the central core of generation and sharing of knowledge. The most crucial asset in higher education (HE) is the human capital and their intellect which needs to be organized, disseminated, and retained. With the growth of information and communication technology (ICT) and information technology (IT) infrastructure in the HE environment, the necessity of integrating knowledge management (KM) processes is increasing. Using ICT tools and techniques, knowledge is continuously generated at all levels in the Institutions, both formally and informally. In this regard, the human resource (HR) department of HEI has to manage and develop the intellect capital for building a competitive and sustainable HE system. Since, there is limited study on the linkage between HR, IT-based KM processes and HEI, the chapter aims to explore the positive outcomes of integrating KM initiatives with HR strategies in HEI. For achieving so, the chapter has identified different functional domains where HR must integrate KM processes in the presence of ICT networks. To end this, the chapter critically reviews the literature to draw emphasis on the importance of KM through HR in the HE sector for enhancing knowledge sharing culture in HEI in the future.

## 26.1 INTRODUCTION

Higher education (HE) is the central medium of learning processes and developing societies. Higher education institutions (HEI) like colleges and universities play a central role in exploring scientific and professional knowledge in different streams of life (Bratianu and Vatamanescu, 2016). HE is the source of enormous knowledge generation. This means that knowledge management in HE is needed for sustaining and expanding the present knowledge effectively (Argote, 2013). With the changing landscape and emergence of a knowledge-based economy, it becomes crucial to focus on the intellect of human capital (Stukalina, 2008). Further, with the advent of the Internet and information and communication technology in HE, it is important to find a mechanism for global interaction and the sharing of knowledge and skills that will ensure continuous learning. In this regard, most of the studies in the past focus on the importance of KM in HE with a broader perspective. There is a limited study done on the integration of KM strategies particularly with the human resource department of the HEI (Nel et al., 2004). In this chapter, we focus on the need for KM from the HR perspective in HE. This is because the HR Department of HEI is responsible for managing the knowledge of its human capital (Nel et al., 2004). Thus, KM processes must be collaborated with HR for formulating strategies that will render a sustainable learning environment at all levels of HE.

### *26.1.1 BACKGROUND*

Past studies and researches suggest that the role of KM in HE was solely the responsibility of librarians (Hawkins, 2000). However, such a limited approach for KM needs to be shifted to a broader view. In addition to library sources, the key players include the staff and students who engage in knowledge sharing and exploration. Today, the goal of HE is not only to impart knowledge to students, but there is a dire need for better strategies to help students and researchers evolve (Chalmers, 2012). HE, especially in developing countries, needs competitive and sustainable KM initiatives to strengthen their knowledge depositories. For this purpose, it becomes crucial to manage the knowledge of all the key players in HE (Toro and Joshi, 2013). In addition to this, there is an increasing pressure on HEI to enable themselves for minimizing risks and empowering their competitive edge on a global scale (Larner, 2015). Concerning this, knowledge is the strongest pillar for any HEI to remain globally competitive and continually innovative (Poonkothai, 2016). This implies that the greatest human asset in HE needs to be managed with its knowledge generation capacities. Thus, knowledge created through different human assets in HE needs to be substantially managed.

## 26.2 SIGNIFICANCE OF THE CHAPTER

This chapter has already highlighted the fact that KM is necessary at all levels in HE along with the library. To integrate knowledge at all levels, a cohesive HR environment is needed for implementing KM initiatives. This, in turn, will help HEI to fill the knowledge gaps and disseminate information in a pervasive manner. Although, HE is robustly using ICT in teaching and learning methods; however, sustaining exceptionally skilled human assets is still a challenge. For this purpose, there is a need for developing a KM framework from the HR Department perspective which can be implemented in HEI to sustain continuous learning. A robust HR Department will help to fill knowledge gaps at all levels and implement HR and KM strategies for better KM and sharing. Not only this, but the HR Department will also help to align the vision and mission of institutions with the flow of knowledge. Also, the chapter helps to pay heed to the need of developing strategies that will sustain the stock of expert knowledge of faculty and students so that that the institutions do not suffer a setback when the human capital exits. Thus, the chapter will help to understand the relationship between KM and HR strategies in HE.

## 26.3 OBJECTIVES OF THE CHAPTER

The main objective of the chapter was to focus on the KM processes of the human capital through HR strategies using ICT tools and techniques in HE.

Objectives of the chapter are outlined below:

- To study the use of IT for KM in HE.
- To analyze the major locus of ICT-based KM processes in HE among different generators and users of knowledge like researchers, faculty, administration, and others.

- To examine the key factors highlighting the integration of KM processes and HR initiatives in HE.
- To specify the need for a competitive and sustainable HR in HE for developing employability skills, retaining and managing knowledge, and use of KM across different domains.
- To highlight HR strategies that will help to integrate KM in HEI like the development of a learning-centric organizational culture and formation of a talent management Advisory Board.
- To highlight the indispensability of ICT infrastructure in HE for KM and implementation of HR strategies.
- To determine various technical barriers and challenges at the individual, group, and institutional levels for the implementation of KM initiatives by HR in HE.

## 26.4 IT-BASED KM IN HE

KM is an integrative approach for capturing, disseminating, and implementation of the organizational knowledge while enhancing its value (Petrides, 2004). KM in HE helps to collaborate with the knowledge generated through numerous academic and administrative activities. For this purpose, it is very significant to implement the use of the right set of IT strategies which meet the current demands (Nagad and Amin, 2006). Further, there are two dimensions to KM in HE, including tacit and explicit knowledge which are developed and applied by individuals distinctively (King, 2009). Tacit knowledge comprises of the experiences and conscious learning which occupy the heads and is required for the overall learning growth (Nunes et al., 2009). Such knowledge needs to be deciphered so that it becomes easy to express (Chugh, 2013). Hence, KM helps to transform implicit into explicit knowledge so that it can be used widely by different members pursuing HE. Thus, KM forms an essential part in HE for enabling the sharing of acquisition, transformation, sharing, storing, and utilization of knowledge.

### *26.4.1 LOCUS FOR KM IN HE*

In a knowledge economy, the main asset in HEI is the human capital as all the knowledge is generated through human efforts in the form of research, learning, or teaching (Namdev Dhamdhere, 2015). The same knowledge generated through academic and administrative activities is used by different agents of the Institution like students, researchers, faculty, and office administration (Coukos-Semmel, 2003). In majority of the past researches, the locus for KM in HE comprises of faculty members, administrative employees, librarians, institutional context, students, and researchers (Kumar, 2015). From the viewpoint of faculty members and researchers, KM initiatives are needed for developing effective teaching and research activities including the use of technology that encourages sharing of existing and new knowledge (Santosh and Panda, 2016). Also, KM helps in increasing organizational effectiveness by integrating the knowledge generated through educational activities with the programs and policies of the institution (Shaikh and Aktharsha, 2016). All such KM practices when successfully implemented according to the different needs across HEI results in developing sustainable competitive advantage (Madan and Khanka, 2010). Thus, to become a successful HEI, KM should be made pervasive at all levels.

## 26.5 KEY DRIVERS FOR INTEGRATION OF KM WITH HR IN HEI

### *26.5.1 NEED FOR DEVELOPING EMPLOYABILITY SKILLS*

In a knowledge economy, the academicians are empowered through HE by the enhancement of employability skills (Frunzaru et al., 2018). This is the reason that HE is seen as a gateway to fight unemployment because knowledge and learning provide development opportunities (Hassler, 2013). Through KM, the institutions offer their prospects the required knowledge and skills that will meet the demands of the employer's market. In this regard, the HR Department in HEI is entrusted with managing the career paths and also develops career development plans for researchers, academicians, and staff (Nilsson and Ripmeester, 2016). This needs an in-depth study of the labor market for understanding what type of hard skills and soft skills are needed to be developed. Hard skills are the job-centric skills that require technical knowledge and practical application of HE learning (Bozionelos et al., 2016). Soft skills are the people skills that represent the interpersonal attributes of an individual. After they are identified, the HR Department must enable ICT Tools and knowledge-sharing platforms for developing employability skills. Thus, KM strategies must be integrated with HR identifying and developing employability skills.

### 26.5.2 RETENTION OF KNOWLEDGE EXPERTISE

The environment in HE involves the continuous sharing and dissemination of knowledge from one person to another or from one department to another. There is no doubt that knowledge stored in hard copy form can be easily restored as when and required like from the library. Also, the digital knowledge depositories have successfully implemented KM through the use of ICT which users can access. Further, the past studies highlight that electrical knowledge needs a robust system of ICT tools which forms an integral component of KM (Alavi and Leinder, 2014). However, knowledge is continuously transformed in HE through creative interaction of individuals (Nonaka and Takeuchi, 1995). It was further discovered that knowledge sharing is quicker in personal communication rather than rigid lines of IT-based formal methods (Koch et al., 2002). This implies the need for HR Department who can integrate such initiatives for KM through informal conversations. In addition to this, it becomes important for HR to devise knowledge retention strategies in case the staff with expert knowledge leaves the institution (Alvesson, 2000). In such cases, the HR Department will devise strategies like frequent interviews with the concerned for retaining expertise and managing the knowledge for future needs (Ahmed et al., 2002).

### 26.5.3 ICT AND KM INTERVENTION IN DIFFERENT DOMAINS OF HE

HEI consist of numerous functional domains that collaborate to develop a cohesive learning environment. In this regard, the use of IT tools and software has helped in integrating KM across the domains. Previous research has identified that successful intervention of KM with ICT enhances the performance of HEI across various functional domains. Domains like planning and development, research, placement services, teaching and learning Process, administrative services, performance evaluation of faculty, and student affairs (Bhusry and Ranjan, 2011). Under different domains, numerous factors are identified which require KM intervention for developing a competitive edge. However, there exists a knowledge gap between these domains when KM is implemented without integrating it with HR. HR helps to align the objectives of different domains with the overall processes and goals of HEI (Bhusry and Ranjan, 2011). Such KM through HR across domains ensures better exploration of knowledge, well-structured knowledge, effective knowledge sharing with different stakeholders, and quick location of the source of knowledge

(Kevin and Evaristo, 2004). Thus, HR helps to align KM across different domains with the overall goals of the Institution.

## 26.6 HR DEPARTMENT STRATEGIES FOR INTEGRATING KM IN HEI

### *26.6.1 DEVELOPING ORGANIZATIONAL CULTURE*

To enable KM to enhance the value of HE, the institutions need to look beyond the ICT. This implies that to turn HEI into robust and collaborative knowledge sharing centers, the overall culture of assessing and sharing knowledge are required (Ranjan and Khalil, 2007). In this regard, HR needs to develop such a culture that encourages communication and easy transfer of knowledge. This implies that leadership and management techniques are required for encouraging KM activities in HE. Even with the implementation of robust ICT tools, there might be resistance to adopting the same in HE. In such cases, HR needs to strategize leadership and management tactics for enabling everyone to support KM beyond their personal objectives (Govender et al., 2018). As suggested above, HR must devise open communication channels for the free flow of ideas and experiences among individuals. The culture in HE should carry a common belief of knowledge sharing and management which can be built through trust and understanding among members of the institution (Bechky, 2003). Such a culture-building will enable a change in the attitude of KM in HE. Thus, developing a knowledge-sharing culture can be the first initiative implemented by HR in institutions.

### *26.6.2 TALENT AND EDUCATION MANAGEMENT STRATEGIES*

HE in India is in the developing phase and is faced by the continuous challenge of developing and managing its pool of human intellect. Only limited research is present concerning talent management practices integrated with KM especially in India. Talent and education management is the differentiating factor that elevates the professional and administrative capacity of an individual in HE (Evans and Chun, 2012). In this regard, HR needs to devise an advisory board that will be responsible for devising developmental opportunities for the human capital in HE (Riccio, 2010). This implies that the Talent Management Advisory Board must work in sync with KM tools for evaluating the market state and academic demands at the national and global levels. In addition to this, talent management initiatives will open up learning opportunities in HE through idea generation, the better engagement between staff and students. Also, measures for improving training, better learning experience, and developing opportunities for exploring new information will enable HR to integrate KM in HE. Thus, talent management and developing the human capital asset will foster better KM integration in HE.

## 26.7 USE OF ICT FOR KM IN HR DEPARTMENT IN HEI

The requirement of ICT tools and techniques is indispensable to develop and manage knowledge. Concerning this, a large proportion of digital knowledge is managed through computer databases and highly capable hardware and software infrastructure (Hansen and Haas, 2002). Managing and dissemination knowledge through ICT tools saves time, effort, and also brings down budget (Markus, 2001). Implementation of KM initiatives is almost impossible without ICT because IT tools and applications enable sharing of knowledge across different time zones and enormous distances (Kim and Lee, 2006). However, the process of KM and sharing must be scrutinized and filtered for the most effective results. If the information is shared in raw form without any linkage, then it cannot be rendered as useful knowledge. Thus, the HR Department needs to look into the use of ICT for enhanced KM and sharing across the institution.

ICT infrastructure proves to be very supportive in developing a knowledge-rich learning environment. This means that when ICT helps in faster sharing and communication of knowledge, then it increases the performance and productivity of the HEI (Lee, 2004). The same needs to be tracked by HR for formulating plans and policies. It has been proposed in various researches that the implementation of ICT for KM in HE needs to be explored more (Soto-Acosta and Cegerra-Navarro, 2016). It is because of the presence of the Internet and Intranet enables the members of the HEI to exchange current knowledge and also discover new knowledge (Shih and Chiang, 2005). This implies that the use of ICT for KM helps in continuous innovation and development of learning environment (Meyer, 2002). The same needs to be integrated with the HR Department for tracking the performance of students and staff. Further, it will help HR to plan for rewards and compensation of staff in the presence of effective knowledge sharing and management. Not only this, the stakeholders at different levels in HE can easily report to HR with a faster response time to their problems (Govender et al., 2018). Thus, for the HEI to become the epitome of learning institutions, collaborative ICT and KM initiatives must be integrated with HR Department needs.

## 26.8 CHALLENGES FOR IMPLEMENTATION KM INTEGRATED HR STRATEGIES

### *26.8.1 TECHNOLOGICAL BARRIERS*

There exists a correlation between KM and HR which helps in improving the competitiveness of HE. Every HEI involves the enormous generation of knowledge at different levels which need to be stored, organized, and managed. Past research suggests that to initiate knowledge sharing, the use of the latest ICT tools and application is of utmost importance. A robust IT infrastructure including Internet, Intranet, software, portals, and open learning platforms like MOOCs is needed for developing a strong learning environment (Madan and Khanka, 2010). However, the unavailability of such resources and the absence of a strong infrastructure budget result in the fatal implementation of KM initiatives by HR. In addition to this, the lack of training for the use of IT-enabled mediums used for knowledge sharing and management might be challenging in HE.

### *26.8.2 INDIVIDUAL AND GROUP BARRIERS*

In HE, communication among individuals is the key to KM practices. This implies that an easy and flexible communication strategy among individuals and groups are a must for sharing and managing tacit and explicit knowledge. In such cases, rigid and formal communication lines pose a threat to a learning environment in HE. Further, KM needs continuous involvement of different stakeholders who can readily share tacit and explicit knowledge (Little et al., 2002). However, resistance is faced due to time constraints and lack of encouragement (Madan and Khanka, 2010). Not only this, in one of the studies it was found that individuals have personal motives due to which they resist from sharing knowledge in HE (Storey and Barnett, 2000). Politics and competition induce individuals to restrain new knowledge for appreciation, awards, and promotion (Ranjan, 2008). Thus, it is a challenge for HR in HE to devise awards and recognition strategies to encourage knowledge sharing and management.

### *26.8.3 INSTITUTIONAL BARRIERS*

In the context of HEI, institutional culture poses a great hindrance to knowledge generation and sharing. For this, the absence of knowledge-centric culture results in a low level of commitment and trust among different members of HE for acquiring new knowledge and sharing the existing one (Frappaolo, 2006). Along with culture, the structure in HEI also poses a challenge for implementing KM practices. In this regard, HEI in India are adopting flatter structures which mean more decentralization fostering more integrated teams (Dess and Picken, 1999). However, such structures are backed with formally laid down policies and manuals. Such rigid culture and structures pose a threat to implementing KM initiatives that enhance knowledge generation in HE.

## 26.9 IMPLICATIONS FOR KM AND HR PRACTICES

KM initiatives from the perspective of HR Department has widespread implication on individual, group, as well as organizational behavior. In this regard, the HR Department integrating KM initiatives will be able to understand academic individuals better. This implies understanding the market and devising strategies that enhance the employability factors to develop new soft and hard skills for both faculty and students. Not only this, the HR Department will be able to use knowledge for devising employee-specific programs that boost up motivation and trust level among them. From the context of group behavior, KM and HR initiatives will ensure that the spirit of knowledge sharing and management becomes a primary responsibility for inducing creativity and innovation in knowledge generation. This implies that HR must create linkage among different groups from the information available to implement group activities like conducting peer-to-peer sessions for harnessing critical thinking and a better learning environment. HR when links KM plays a central role in organizational development and sustainability. In this regard, HR will be responsible for integrating KM with organizational vision, mission, culture, and policies. Thus, a knowledge-centric framework needs to be developed by HR to promote knowledge creation and sustainable management at all three levels.

## 26.10 RECOMMENDATIONS AND SCOPE FOR FUTURE WORK

This chapter focuses on the integration of ICT-based KM initiatives with the perspective of HR in HEI. In this regard, a further in-depth research is required to study their relationship in the context of Indian Education Economy. As compared with the past, the Government of India is continuously taking initiatives for building IT infrastructure in Universities. Also, programs like SWAYAM, MOOCs need more acceptance in HE. When the research is done specific to a region, then the impact of government support can also be studied. In addition to this, linkage needs to be drawn between the HE in India and contributions made by foreign academicians in boosting KM processes at all levels in the Institutions. HE in developed countries like the United States and the United Kingdom also needs to be studied. This will help HR in Indian Institutions to consider more advanced IT systems and learn from the academic structure and policies. ICT-based knowledge is always evolving and numerous initiative steps are undertaken to make the human capital more competitive globally.

Currently, the research on the integrated relationship between KM, HR, and ICT in HE is limited. Most of the studies are conducted with a qualitative approach and that too not specific to the HR domain. Keeping this in mind, the research could be done on establishing a statistical relationship between different factors of HR. Such relationships can be examined at individual, group, and organizational levels using quantitative research techniques. Further, a comparative framework that fosters KM processes can be developed according to the current employability skills as identified in the education market. Thus, future research will foster a more effective way to integrate KM processes with HR strategies in HE.

## 26.11 CONCLUSION

This chapter explored the use of ICT infrastructure for KM about HR strategies in HEI. Through the research, it is concluded that HE is the central core of knowledge generation whose most vital asset is human intellect. ICT-based KM is the need of the hour for developing a robust learning environment that is both globally competitive and sustainable. Previous researches focused on the role of KM only with the libraries in HE. However, the chapter shifts the focus to the functional domain of HR in the HEI that devises strategies and develop the human capital more effectively. Further, it was found that knowledge needs to be shared using IT-based tools at both academic and administrative level including students, faculty, and employees of the HEI. Also, it was discovered that KM processes must be integrated with HR as HR helps to devise strategies for enhancing employability in the global education market. Further, HR is required to retain the expert knowledge so that the Institution does not suffer a loss when such faculty leaves. Also, HR initiatives help bridge the knowledge gap among different functional domains of the HEI like placement, research, teaching, administration, and others.

The findings of the chapter also concluded that KM requires a shared organizational culture beyond a well-developed ICT infrastructure. This is possible by enhancing the level of trust and commitment to encourage knowledge sharing among everyone in HE. Leadership and management strategies help to fight resistance shown by employees due to personal or political reasons. Further, talent and education management of intellect capital in HE would open learning opportunities through better integration of KM initiatives in HE. The chapter also resulted in discovering barriers like technological, resistance to share, absence of knowledge sharing culture, and others that HR has to face in implementing KM processes. For future work, aspects like government initiatives and international educational contributions also need to be studied specifically for the HE Market in India.

## KEYWORDS

- **information and communication technology (ICT)**
- **higher education (HE)**
- **knowledge management (KM)**
- **human resource (HR).**

## REFERENCE

Ahmed, P. K., Lim, K. K., & Loh, A. Y. (2002). *Learning through knowledge management.* Oxford: Butterworth-Heinemann Ltd.

Alavi, M., & Leinder, D. E. (2014). Knowledge management and knowledge management systems: Conceptual foundations and research issues. *MIS Quarterly*, *25* (1), 107–136.

Alvesson, M. (2000). Social identity in knowledge-intensive companies. *Journal of Management Studies*, *37* (8), 1101–1123.

Argote, L. (2013). *Organizational learning: Creating, retaining and transferring knowledge.* Springer, USA.

Bechky, B. (2003). Sharing meaning across occupational communities: The transformation of understanding on a production floor. *Organization Science*, *14* (3), 312–330.

Bhusry, M., & Ranjan, J. (2011). Implementing knowledge management in Higher Educational Institutions in India: A conceptual framework. *International Journal of Computer Applications*, *29* (1), 34–36 https://doi.org/10.5120/3527-4805.

Bozionelos, N., Kostopoulos, K., Van der, H., Rousseau, D. M., Bozionelos, G., & Hoyland, T. (2016). Employability and job performance as links in the relationship between mentoring and career success: A study in SMEs. *Group & Organizational Management*, *41* (2), 135–171.

Bratianu, C., & Vatamanescu, E.-M.(2016). Students' perception on developing conceptual generic skills for business. In S. Moffett, & B. Galbraith (Ed.), *17th European conference on knowledge management* (pp. 101–108). UK: Academic Conferences and Publishing International Limited.

Chalmers, D. (2012). *Teaching for learning at university*. London: Routledge.

Chugh, R. (2013). Workplace dimensions: Tacit knowledge sharing in Universities. *Journal of Advanced Management Science*, *1* (1), 24–28. 10.12720/joams.1.1.24-28.

Coukos-Semmel, E. (2003). *Knowledge management in research Universities: The processes and strategies*. Chicago: American Educational Research Association.

Dess, G., & Picken, J. (1999). *Beyond productivity: How leading companies achieve superior performance by leveraging their human capital*. New York: American Management Association.

Evans, A., & Chun, E. (2012). Creating a tipping point-strategic HR and TM in HE. *Association for the Study of Higher Education-Higher Education Report*, *38* (1), 1–143.

Frappaolo, C. (2006). *Knowledge management*. West Sussex: Capstone Publishing Ltd.

Frunzaru, V., Vatamanescu, E.-M., Gazzola, P., & Bolisani, E. (2018). Challenges to higher education in the knowledge economy: anti-intellectualism, materialism and employability. *Knowledge Management Research & Practice* https://doi.org/10.1080/14778238.2018.1493368.

Govender, L. N., Perumal, R., & Perumal, S. (2018). Knowledge management as a strategic tool for human resource management at higher education institutions. *South African Journal of Information Management*, *20* (1), https://doi.org/10.4102/sajim.v20i1.966.

Hansen, M., & Haas, M. (2002). Different knowledge, different benefits: Toward a productivity perspective on knowledge sharing in organizations. *Academy of Management Proceedings*, *1*, 1–6.

Hassler, S. R. (2013). Employability skills and the notion of "self." *International Journal of Training and Development*, *17* (3), 233–243.

Hawkins, B. (2000). *Libraries, knowledge management, and Higher Education in an electronic environment*.

Kevin, C. D., & Evaristo, J. B. (2004). Managing knowledge in distributed projects. *Communications of the ACM*, *47* (4), 87–91.

Kim, S., & Lee, H. (2006). The impact of organizational context and information technology on employee knowledge-sharing capabilities. *Public Administration Review*, *66* (3), 370–385.

King, W. R. (2009). *Knowledge management and organizational learning*. Springer, New York.

Koch, H., Paradice, D., Chae, B., & Guo, Y. (2002). An investigation of knowledge management within a University IT group. *Information Resources Management Journal*, *15* (1), 13–21.

Kumar, D. R. (2015). Knowledge management in higher educational institutions in India: A conceptual framework. *International Journal of Business Management and Scientific Research*, *9*, 7–12.

Larner, W. (2015). Globalising knowledge networks: Universities, diaspora strategies, and academic intermediaries. *Geoforum*, *59*, 197–205.

Lee, N. L. (2004). *Knowledge management: Its application in IT projects*. Johannesburg, South Africa: Zytek Publishing (Pty) Ltd.

Little, S., Quintas, P., & Ray, T. (2002). *Managing knowledge: An essential reader*. The Open University, Sage Publications, UK.

Madan, P., & Khanka, S. (2010). Contribution of knowledge management practices in creating sustainable competitive advantage for business schools in India. *Journal of Information & Knowledge Management*, *9* (4), 387–397.

Markus, M. L. (2001). Towards a theory of knowledge reuse. *Journal of Management Information Systems*, *18* (1), 57–93.

Meyer, M. (2002). *Managing human resource development: An outcomes-based approach* (2 ed.). South Africa: LexusNexis Butterworths.

Nagad, W., & Amin, G. (2006). Higher education in Sudan and knowledge management applications. *2006 2nd International Conference on Information & Communication Technologies*, Damascus, pp. 60–65, doi: 10.1109/ICTTA.2006.1684345.

Namdev Dhamdhere, S. (2015). Importance of knowledge management in the Higher Educational Institutes. *Turkish Online Journal of Distance Education*, *16* (1), 162–183.

Nel, P. S., Van Dyk, P. S., Haasbroek, G. D., Schultz, H. B., Sono, T., & Werner, A. (2004). *Human resources management* (6th ed.). Oxford: Oxford University Press.

Nilsson, P. A., & Ripmeester, N. (2016). International student expectations: Career opportunities and employability. *Journal of International Students*, *6* (2), 614–631.

Nonaka, I., & Takeuchi, H. (1995). *The knowledge-creating company*. Oxford: Oxford University Press.

Nunes, M., McPherson, M., Annansingh, F., Bashir, I., & Patterson, D. (2009). The use of e-learning in the workplace: A systematic literature review. *Journal of Applied Research in Workplace e-Learning*, *1* (1), 97–112.

Petrides, L. A. (2004). *Knowledge Management, Information Systems and Organizations*. EDUCAUSE, Center for Applied Research, Research Bulletin.

Poonkothai, R. (2016). Knowledge management as an important tool in library management. *International Journal of Information Technology and Library Science*, *5* (1), 9–14.

Ranjan, J. (2008). Knowledge management in business schools. *Journal of Information and Knowledge Management*, *7* (1), 55–62.

Ranjan, J., & Khalil, S. (2007). Application of knowledge management in management education: A conceptual framework. *Journal of Theoretical and Applied Information Technology*, 3 (3), 15–25.

Riccio, S. (2010). *Talent management in Higher Education: Developing emerging leaders within the administration at private Colleges and Universities*. Educational Administration.

Santosh, S., & Panda, S. (2016). Sharing of Knowledge among Faculty in a Mega Open University. *Open Praxis*, *8* (3), 247–264.

Shaikh, A. A., & Aktharsha, D. U. (2016). Dynamics of human resources management practices and knowledge management processes in service sector: An empirical study. *The International Journal of Business & Management*, *4* (6), 64–77.

Shih, H., & Chiang, Y. (2005). Strategy alignment between HRM, KM, and corporate development. *International Journal of Manpower*, *26* (6), https://doi.org/10.1108/01437720510625476.

Soto-Acosta, P., & Cegerra-Navarro, J. (2016). New ICTs for knowledge management in organizations. *Journal of Knowledge Management*, *20* (3), 417–422.

Storey, J., & Barnett, E. (2000). Knowledge management initiatives: Learning from failure. *Journal of Knowledge Management*, *4* (2), 145–156.

Stukalina, Y. (2008). How to prepare students for productive and satisfying careers in the knowledge-based economy: Creating a more efficient educational environment. *Technological and Economic Development of Economy*, *4* (2), 197–207.

Toro, U., & Joshi, M. J. (2013). A review of literature on knowledge management using ICT in higher education. *International Journal of Computer Technology and Applications*, *4* (1), 62.

# CHAPTER 27

# College Automation Security Management

KAUSHAL MEHTA[1*], ANMOL SHARMA[2], and LAKSHYA BHALLA[2]

[1]*Department of CSE, Graphic Era University, Dehradun, Uttarakhand*

[2]*Department of MCA, Bhai Parmanand Institute of Business Studies, Shakarpur, New Delhi*

[*]*Corresponding author. E-mail: Kpu_713@yahoo.com*

## ABSTRACT

With increase in the energy consumption and population, there is a high need to save energy in all aspects. We unable to access and control the appliances from a remote location are the major reasons for the loss of energy in our daily life. College is the best place to educate someone the basic system or methods to conserve energy. There are various systems available in the world nowadays (Zig-bee, Bluetooth, GSM, Wi-Fi, etc.), but no system provides security or actual conserve energy, as we are now in an era of digitalization, we need to think various innovative ideas to conserve energy and save energy for the needy ones on the other hand ensuring their privacy also.

College security is essential for people's protection and convenience. At an initial point the system must be secured and this is the main purpose to make this particular system. This chapter aims to develop a low-cost security system. In the College security system we use international mobile equipment identity (IMEI) number (identity number of smartphone) as an initial password for users.

## 27.1 INTRODUCTION

A computer smart system etc. consists of electrical and electronic setup. A phone accessible setup is an atmosphere in which specific gadgets that are connected to our system can be remotely/mobile accessed and controlled using software-systems and web applications. Some specific similar programs are available in the world but with lots of disadvantages. This chapter aims to give innovative ideas to remove these drawbacks of the available systems and give a system idea which can remove most of the drawback from the existing system (Gill et al., 2009).

The proposed system provides a way to safeguard essential and initial point of college like organizations from hackers and crackers. Nowadays all the top organizations take security system modern services in the order to achieve high security and unwanted data access from unwanted access. Most of the organizations rely only on camera system which is actually not enough for the point of security. College automation ways to automate the college appliance such as by controlling the college lighting applications, other electrical services, etc., with the help of the proposed system, we can achieve the automation target which includes microcontroller based on Arduino and cryptography. The main focus is the main entry gate of the college while developing the security system.

The entry provided to only those who have International Mobile Equipment Identity (IMEI) and default password of the smartphone. The confidential password provided by the system to the matched user. For the authentication of mobile phone, the IMEI number is store into the system for the on-demand verification of user mobile phone (Sriskanthan et al., 2002).

By using SMS service instructions, the motive is to automate and control lights of college also to be assurance of authentic mobile number. Based on an embedded system add on with microcontrollers to achieve automation and security in the college environment. Advantage of this system is that it can operate using cellular phones over GSM technology. We implement a microcontroller-based system to receive command and instructions from mobile handheld devices over GSM technology. After that microcontroller carries out commands will transfer to run connected devices and appliances.

Rest of the chapter is organized as follows: Section 27.2 contains a brief literature survey; in Section 27.3 equipment used for the proposed work are explained; in Section 27.4 proposed work is explained; in Section 27.5 the possible future scope of this project is given; and finally in last section conclusion is provided.

## 27.2 LITERATURE SURVEY

A GSM-based automation device must provide Internet access only. Such a system is easy to install. Only then a GSM-based automation device can be commercially available. Easy-to-plug and easy-to-play capability will be a bonus to such system. Automation with personal computer and network they are secured and can use their network securely for accessing of remote devices. High-speed network can be used to reduce execution time. The system also provided with feedback facility to the users.

The Arduino ATMEGA328 microcontroller can be used for various uses such as industrial, educational, security purposes, and laboratory purposes. During the study of IMEI, we found that there is not much study available about the topic in the world. IMEI number is only used for mobile identification or the device identification for which IMEI number is given (Humphries et al., 1997).

## 27.3 EQUIPMENT USED

### *27.3.1 COLLEGE AUTOMATION USING WIRELESS CONTROL SYSTEM*

In this system Wi-Fi is used to integrate the system. Through this system, we can connect remote appliances by our smartphone and can enjoy access from a remote location. By this system, we can keep an eye on that part or location where currently we are not present. Through this system, we can also help in conserving energy and can contribute our concern toward the nation energy crisis.

This system uses Open Service Gateway Interface, the application that we can connect with different networking technologies. The user application layer makes use of Internet. This system has the capability to add some control milestones. This control milestone (Figure 27.1) can automatically sense the extra consumption of energy and automatically switch off the unnecessary devices that are running along (Alkar and Buhur, 2005).

### *27.3.2 ARDUINO*

Arduino is an open-source computer hardware and software-system corporation, venture, and user group that made and produce single-board microcontrollers and microcontroller kitbag for making digital devices and interactive object that can sense and control object in the physical world. The project's products are distributed as open-source software-system and hardware, which are registered under the "GNU General Public License," "GNU Lesser General Public License" permit the manufacture of Arduino boards and software-system distribution by anyone. It saves data on FLASH, EEPROM.

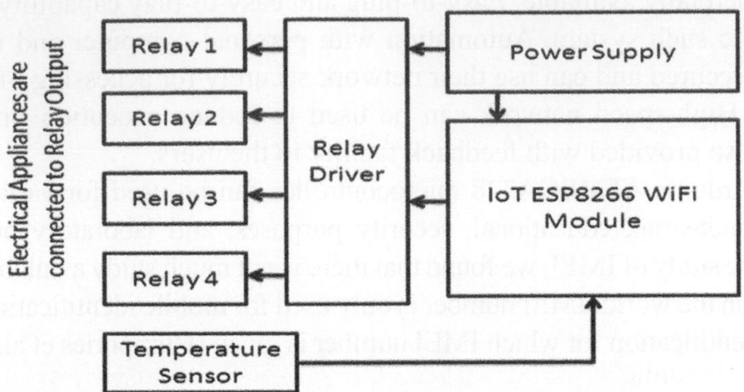


**FIGURE 27.1** Simple Wi-Fi milestone automation device.

By using Arduino controller, we can make our appliance more secure to use as now we can insert some security check in our system by using Arduino. We can insert two security checks firstly password from the user side and secondly the IMEI number of the user smartphone. We can use user smartphone IMEI number as security check

This will make our system more secure and reliable. Now, no intruder can intrude into our college without faculty permission and we can keep a check on every corner in our college (Baraka et al., 2013).

Figure 27.2 shows the Arduino embedded with the college automation Wi-Fi milestone and serves as a security milestone in the device.

**FIGURE 27.2** Arduino controller board.

### *27.3.3 OPEN SOURCE*

Open source refers to something people can update and share because it is made for the public use. The word is originated in software-system development to give a specific way of creating computer programs in today's world. "Open source" has mediated a broader set of values as "the open-source way." Open-source project, product or facilities celebrate on the principle of open sharing, open swap of data, prototyping, team, and transparency oriented development (David et al., 2015).

### *27.3.4 IMEI*

IMEI is a unique identification number given to every mobile equipment and uniquely identifies an individual mobile device. The IMEI format is given by telecommunication standardization authorities and composition by the BABT3 and composition of IMEI. Composition of IMEI and IMEI Software-system version—The IMEI consists 15 decimal digits that is 14 digits plus a check digit or IMEISV (16 digits), it includes information of the origin, model, and serial number of the mobile device. The model and mobile phone brand are represented by the initial eight digits of the IMEI, Called as Type Allocation Code (TAC) and seven remaining digits are defined by manufacturer, six are serial number and one is a check digit. By the end of 2003, the format of the IMEI is DD-CCCCCC-BBBBBB-A (Al-thobaiti et al., 2014).

TAC NUMBER-DD-CCCCCC, SERIAL NUMBER –BBBBBB CHECK DIGIT-A.

## 27.4 PROPOSED WORK

The Future activities planned for the project is that the system will be maddened such that the IMEI number is used as a security check for the college automation device Embed the Arduino microcontroller with the Wi-Fi milestone to upgrade the existing system into highly secured device by using user IMEI smartphone number as a security check method which is highly secured and cheapest way to provide security.

In this, the IMEI number is saved in Arduino and used as a security check (Figure 27.3). It only allows the signals coming from the authentic IMEI number to be executed by the system and stops the intruders to intrude in the premises of the user (Launey et al., 1992).

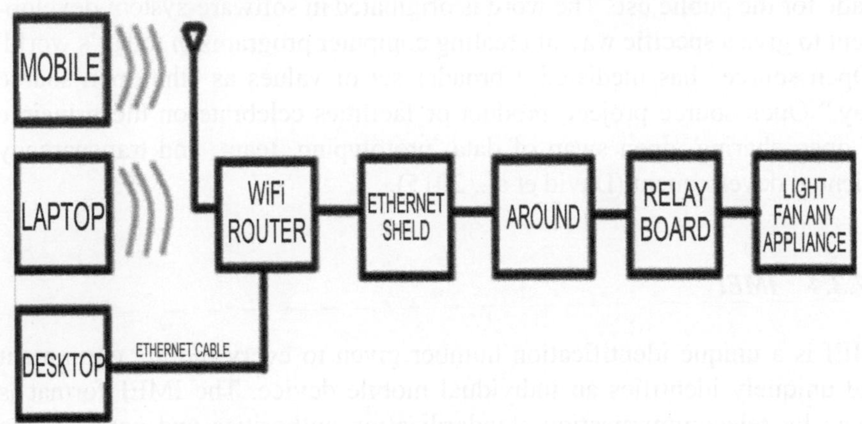


**FIGURE 27.3** Automation device with upgraded Arduino security check system.

## 27.5 FUTURE SCOPE

This system can be used in that area where security is the first priority and automation is the need of the hour so, now automation will be getting place in every corner of the world but by this system we can feel secure.

We can also use cryptography and IMEI security system to give more secured environment to the user and make his premises more secure than ever.

## 27.6 CONCLUSION

We have achieved security in college automation by embedding Arduino microcontroller in the existing wireless automation system and using mobile identification (i.e., IMEI) in smartphones as a password (security check) to give better security and ensure that no intruder can intrude into user premises.

This type of technology is the upgraded version of the existing technology which provides a high level of security and makes user privacy and information secured.

## KEYWORDS


- **Arduino system**
- **wireless college system**
- **IMEI number**
- **security check**
- **password**
- **safe environment**


## REFERENCES


Alheraish, A. "Design and implementation of home automation system." IEEE Transactions on Consumer Electronics 50(4) (2004): 1087–1092.

Alkar, A.K.; Buhur, U. "An Internet based wireless home automation system for multifunctional devices." IEEE Transactions on Consumer Electronics 51(4) (2005): 1169–1174.

Al-thobaiti, B.M.O., et al. "Design and implementation of a reliable wireless real-time home automation system based on Arduino Uno single-board microcontroller." International Journal of Control, Automation and Systems 3(3) (2014): 11–15.

Baraka, K., et al. "Low cost Arduino/android-based energy-efficient home automation system with smart task scheduling." 2013 Fifth International Conference on Computational Intelligence, Communication Systems and Networks. IEEE, 2013.

David, N., et al. "Design of a home automation system using Arduino." International Journal of Scientific & Engineering Research 6(6) (2015): 795–801

Gill, K., et al. "A zigbee-based home automation system." IEEE Transactions on Consumer Electronics 55(2) (2009): 422–430.

Humphries, L.S., et al. "Home automation system." U.S. Patent No. 5,621,662. 15 Apr. 1997.

Javale, D., et al. "Home automation and security system using Android ADK." International Journal of Electronics Communication and Computer Technology (IJECCT) 3(2) (2013): 382–385.

Launey, R.O., et al. "Expandable home automation system." U.S. Patent No. 5,086,385. 4 Feb. 1992.

Morotomi, N., et al. "Home automation system." U.S. Patent No. 4,959,713. 25 Sep. 1990.

Sriskanthan, N., Tan F., and Karande A. "Bluetooth based home automation system." Microprocessors and Microsystems 26(6) (2002): 281–289.

Wilson, B.B., et al. "Home automation system and method." U.S. Patent No. 8,516,087. 20 Aug. 2013.

CHAPTER 28

# Impact of ICT on Leveling the Ethnicity Divide in Order to Promote Student Engagement in the Education Sector

TEJAL NATHADWARAWALA[1*], and BHUVAN UNHELKAR[2]

[1]*M.S. University of Baroda, Vadodara, India*

[2]*University of South Florida, Sarasota-Manatee, FL, 34242, USA*

[*]*Corresponding author. E-mail: chandaranatejal@gmail.com*

**ABSTRACT**

A vital contribution of information and communication technologies (ICT) is to bridge the social divide between various categories of students, teachers, researchers, and administrators. This is because ICT provides the leveling field between individuals with diverse backgrounds. An in-depth study of the impact of ethnicity was carried out by the lead author of this chapter in the context of hospitals in the National Health Service in the United Kingdom. Valuable results were derived based on that study. This particular chapter aims to extend and apply that study in the context of education. Multiple educational processes dealing with teachers and students are identified as challenging as these processes can potentially be impacted by ethnicity, gender, affluence, and regional biases of teachers and students. Defining these potential biases and how they are likely to be overcome with ICT-based education is the core premise of this chapter. We also outline the approach to developing educational systems and processes that alleviate the impact of ethnic bias on education.

## 28.1 INTRODUCTION TO CHALLENGES OF STUDENT ENGAGEMENT AND ETHNIC DIVIDE IN EDUCATION

Education is a social phenomenon that impacts the fabric of a society. Nelson Mandela, the former South African President and Noble Laureate, once observed that education is the most powerful weapon which can be used to change the world. Education, however, needs to facilitate necessary engagement by the students on a consistent basis in order to achieve learning objectives. Education also has to wrestle with the challenges of delivering content to a broad and varied cross-section of recipients. According to the Pearson Voice of Teacher Survey (Businessworld, 2016), only 55% of Indian students are actively engaged in learning. We observe that if the delivery of content is made without due considerations to the ethnicity and biases of the receiving cross-section of students, there is arguably an immediate loss of student engagement (SE). Particularly in the context of India, the student population comprises myriad ethnic groups, disparate financial groups, and groups disadvantaged in the past. Each group has its own values and biases which can lead to engagement or disengagement of students from the education process.

The challenges of ethnic divide in education are as follows:

- Ability to access educational content based on available resources—ethnicity encompasses language, race, religion, among others. Without going into the specific details of each factor, we argue that education is not equally accessible to all students.
- Once educational contents are delivered, there is a need to evaluate whether the learning objectives have been achieved or not. Biases based on ethnicity and background of a student group can potentially play a role to skew the evaluations.
- There is usually a gap between the specifications of the learning objectives and actual achievement. This gap can be a result of biases in delivery, receiving, and application of content to and by student groups. Ethnic biases can potentially play a role in increasing or reducing the aforementioned gaps.
- Ethnic groups are subject to variable speeds in receiving and absorbing content. This variation can be due to education through the vernacular medium. Therefore, there is a need to adjust the speed with which the content is being delivered. This variability requires an understanding of biases carried by ethnic groups as well as biases from the deliverer and administrator of educational institutions against such groups.

- Students could also demand education based on their own ethnic group and the corresponding values. Educational content needs to be highly flexible in order to meet those demands. Language can be a major barrier in understanding the content being taught, thus requiring mother tongue, national language, or local dialect to be included in the teaching process.
- Vast geographical distances make the delivery of unified educational content a challenge. Furthermore, specific to the Indian context, challenges to traversing even smaller distances can be a challenge to students. Various ethnic groups handle this challenge differently.
- Female education, especially in the rural Indian context, is a big challenge—primarily because of lack of facilities for female students, especially at primary school level (K-12). Furthermore, ethnic biases promote or demote education resulting in considerable challenges to the delivery of learning objectives.
- Authentication of results and transcripts, and making results available over a long period of time as the student traverses through primary, secondary, and tertiary education, is an administrative challenge.

This chapter is based on our scholarly study of the education system through the prism of ethnicity and SE. The lead author conducted a detailed study on ethnicity and its impact on employee engagement in hospitals of the National Health Service in the United Kingdom. The findings of the study were quite relevant in developing an understanding of how ethnicity divides and disengages employees. In this chapter, we apply the study to SE. We start this chapter with the literature on ethnic divides and engagement criteria. We follow that with the challenges affecting SE in modern-day society. We discuss the opportunities provided by ICT to bridge the gap between the receivers of education and its providers. The chapter concludes with the key points discussed and opportunities for research directions.

## 28.2 LITERATURE ON ETHNIC DIVIDES AND EDUCATION

Ethnicity is considered an important economic, global, social, and political subject as it characterizes the challenges and opportunities prevalent in contemporary societies (Healy and Oikelome, 2011). There is an increase in the multiethnic workforce due to social, political, and technological advancements (United Nations Statistics Division, 2009; Giddens, 2009; Bisin et al., 2010) which, in turn, supports immigration and demographic shifts (Ferdman,

1992)."One of the most important challenges facing modern societies, and at the same time one of our most significant opportunities is the increase in ethnic and social heterogeneity in virtually all advanced countries" (Putnam, 2007).

The realization that increased interactions facilitate the dynamic nature of the social world has resulted in an increase in analytical attention for ethnicity (Karlsen, 2006). Social action in certain circumstances and societies is guided by ethnic identity and catalyzed due to migration (Fenton, 2010). Many nations, Europe in particular, have hosted a mixture of ethnicities for many decades, largely due to the migration from former colonies after the Second World War followed by significant inflows to fulfill labor needs (Hussein et al., 2014). India too has many different ethnic groups based on language, financial position, and gender, to name a few. Study of ethnicity is considered a relevant subject as it characterizes not only the challenges but also the opportunities (Healy and Oikelome, 2011; Putnam, 2007) prevalent in the increasingly multiethnic workforce (United Nations Statistics Division, 2009; Giddens, 2009; Bisin et al., 2010). Literature (Stokes et al., 2015) suggests that certain ethnicities have a greater emphasis on education, leading to keeping knowledge and skills up to date. Moreover, research has also shown that the diversity of ethnic groups help stimulate creativity and language proficiency (Maestri, 2017). This increasing ethnic diversity of populace requires education content generators and providers to understand the nuances of these groups, create sufficiently flexible content, and respond appropriately to the needs based on agility in educational processes.

## 28.3 SE AND ICT-BASED OPPORTUNITIES

The seminal review is a prudent way to gain a depth of understanding, context, and insight into the evolution of engagement (Shuck and Wollard, 2010). There are various views on the concept of user engagement with an organization, perhaps because of multiple origins and varied conceptualizations of the idea of engagement. Interpreting and defining engagement provides necessary context to understand the issues surrounding SE in educational institutions. This context can be the basis for creating ICT-based educational platforms, populating those platforms with data, and delivering the learning objectives using the Cloud and personalized devices (e.g., IoT—Internet of Things) (Unhelkar and Sharma, 2017).

Kahn (1990) has been largely accredited (May et al., 2004; Kular et al., 2008; Shuck and Wollard, 2010; Schaufeli and Bakker, 2010; Bakker and Leiter, 2010; Welch, 2011; Shuck, 2011; Truss et al., 2014) as the founder of the concept of engagement of individuals working in the industry. We extend the theoretical frameworks discussed by the aforementioned authors and correlate them to the context of how individual students engage or disengage themselves to varying degrees, through their physical, cognitive, and emotional selves. Kahn (1990) conceptually builds from Goffman (1961), who suggested that attachment and detachment of people to their roles varies. These variations could be a result of ethnic upbringing, values, and biases based on multiple stakeholders' interactions. Kahn insisted that an individual's adjustment of self-in-role is personal engagement and disengagement. We explore the opportunities provided by ICT-based educational contents delivery in enhancing SE and reducing ethnic biases.

These concepts integrate Maslow's (1954) and Alderfer's (1972) idea of individuals requiring self-expression and self-employment in their work lives, without the individual consciously contemplating whether they want it or not (Kahn, 1990). Kahn identified three psychological conditions as influencers to an individual's engagement; *"psychological meaningfulness* [which] *is the sense of return on investments of the self-in-role performances, psychological safety* [which] *is the sense of being able to show and employ the self without fear of negative consequences, and psychological availability* [which] *is the sense of possessing physical, emotional, and psychological resources for investing the self in role performances."* (ibid: 705). Building from this, in 1992, Kahn conceptualized personal engagement at work. Here, the psychological conditions are mediated through an individual's psychological presence before it manifests into moments of personal engagement at work (Kahn, 1992). Each element of Kahn's conceptual framework is applicable to students, teachers, and administrators of education. The impact of each of these elements on SE can be potentially ameliorated and the engagement improved with the use of ICT-based educational content creation and delivery.

## 28.4 DISCUSSION ON ETHNICITY AND SE

Maestri (2017) suggests that diversity of ethnic groups not only stimulate creativity among students, but also lessen the feeling of ethnic identification and its resultant effects along with encouraging to adopt the instructional language and culture. ICT-based education platforms can also be used effectively to reduce ethnic identification of students and teachers and, thereby, increase SE. Depending on the location and parental endowments, there is also a correlation between ethnicity and educational attainment (Sander, 1992). Based on the empirical evidence from research (Nathadwarawala,

2019), it can be surmised that individuals of certain ethnicities potentially have a greater emphasis on education. We observe that even partial delivery of education through Cloud-based ICT applications has the potential to increase SE independent of ethnic groups.

In particular, some Asian participants explained that within their ethnicity, it was considered normal for parents to insist on higher education. For example, in the same study by Nathadwarawala (2019), participants pointed out,

> *... Asian parents tend to be quite umm forceful when it comes to academic umm achievements, and I think that's still continued ... I think part of that ambition has probably come down in, through my upbringing ...* [British Asian, P24]
>
> *...but I think by virtue of umm sort of growing up and being brought up as a Chinese person, a lot of emphasis was placed on education and doing well in school. That is the basically the only thing I can—laughs—it's either that or abject failure (ya) when you are growing up... probably being brought up knowing education is important* [British Hong Kong Chinese, P32]

Evidently, the socially inherited values through ancestry could become an integral part of the values and beliefs of participants. In particular, the value of higher education emerged as a characteristic of participants who identified as having an ethnicity associated with Asia. The analysis of the responses of the semistructured interviews only found this particular group of ethnicities as having this characteristic. Along similar lines, Hochschild and Shen (2014) found Anglos and Asians attaining and achieving more years of schooling than Blacks and Latinos.

On the other hand, where there was an increased representation of co-ethnics on the school boards along with administrators and teachers, researchers (Fraga and Elis, 2009) found Latino and African American students achieved more favorable educational outcomes.

We find that delivery of educational content on the Cloud provides significant flexibility enabling SE based on the ability of the student to absorb the content. We propose that Cloud-based content delivery is a leveler of ethnic biases because the opportunity to physically express biases is greatly reduced due to the online nature of content delivery.

The need for a student sitting in a virtual classroom to factor in his or her ethnicity is reduced. Therefore, the SE is likely to increase with this study.

The following factors play a role in delivery of education based on ICT:

- Data—including the volume, velocity, and variety of data that provide opportunities for analytics and enable ongoing improvements in decision making (Unhelkar, 2018).

- Processes—including Cloud-based platforms that provide significant flexibility to deliver educational content.
- Devices—including IoT devices that make it possible for students to access the content. The IoT (IoT Paradigm) is a generic term used to describe any sensor-based gadget that collects and sends data to a repository—usually residing on a Cloud (Bassi, 2013). The IoT forms the basis for a large number of devices and corresponding applications. IoT devices are being extended to machine-to-machine (Severi, 2014), transportation, healthcare, nanorobotics, and education domains.
- Cloud—to provide the platform for delivery as well as control and manage the efficiency of delivery. In general, the Cloud enables centralization of what would otherwise be a highly dispersed set of data drawn from multiple sources and in varying formats. Cloud computing is akin to a grid (like electricity) that charges metered rates for processing time (Murugesan and Bojanova, 2016), which is most helpful in developing educational content that utilized various types and sizes of data and provides a variety of analytics.
- Crowd-sourcing—including creation and distribution of contents by bringing together teachers from across regions and pooling their collective knowledge (e.g., Khan Academy).

Furthermore, based on the aforementioned ICT elements, following are the opportunities to bridge the ethnic divide and improve student education:

- Service-based education creates opportunities for providing educational content as services on the Cloud. The packaging of services enables flexibility and modularity in delivery. Student groups are able to customize the services to suit their needs and their abilities, resulting in improved SE.
- Automation in the evaluation of learning objectives through ICT-based services enables speed as well as the elimination of bias in student scores.
- Analytics to identify gaps in the delivery of educational content enabling rapid corrections to gaps, in particular, based on ethnic differences.
- Ability of ICT to deliver education at variable speeds to suit the SE style.
- ICT's reach across geographical distances enables student cross-section from rural areas to access the content at their convenience. Furthermore, IoT devices enable delivery of educational content in remote areas.
- Potential to hide identity and only use nonidentifiable features during manual evaluations as provided through ICT systems.

- Ability to store transcripts for long periods of time through the use of potential technology like Blockchains to authenticate transcripts.
- Bridge the physical gap between students and teachers by providing collaborating platforms.
- Enable content creation from a variety of sources such as news media, crowdsourcing, and automated machine sensors.
- Ability to offer labs on Cloud-based platforms (PlatiFi.com).

Such ICT-based interventions can contribute in bridging the gaps in education among myriad ethnic groups. Increased engagement can potentially reduce the biases based on ethnic values and vice versa. Additionally, barriers such as speed, language, and teachers' biases can be eliminated with such ICT systems.

## 28.5 CONCLUSIONS AND FUTURE DIRECTIONS

In this chapter, we have highlighted the importance of understanding the ethnic diversity in the education domain. We have further suggested the opportunities provided by ICT in order to bridge the ethnic divide and improve SE. Our observation is that ICT-based delivery of educational content has the potential to reach a vast and growing cross-section of student populations across the world. In particular, we look forward to conducting a further detailed study of ICT-based education in the context of the Indian education system that will help improve our contribution in utilization of ICT for education. In particular, a qualitative study similar to that conducted by Nathadwarawala (2019) in context of education would provide valuable insights to the facets of the impact of ethnicity on SE. Additionally, investigating the impact of ethnic biases of teachers and administrators would enhance the understanding of how ICT systems can contribute in reducing these biases.

## KEYWORDS

- **ethnic divides in education**
- **ICT and education**
- **student engagement**
- **education in India**

## REFERENCES

Alderfer, C., P., Human Needs in Organizational Settings, New York: Free Press of Glencoe, (1972).

Bakker, A., B., and Leiter, M., P., Work Engagement: A Handbook of Essential Theory and Research, Psychology Press, Hove (2010).

Bassi, A. Enabling things to talk: Designing IoT solutions with the IoT architectural reference model. Springer. Switzerland (2013).

Bisin, A., Patacchini, E., Verdier, T., Zenou, Y., Bend it like Beckham: Ethnic identity and integration, European Economic Review, 90, 146–164 (2010).

Businessworld, 2016. http://www.businessworld.in/article/Only-55-Per-Cent-Indian-Students-Are-Actively-Engaged-In-Learning-Survey/02-09-2016-105179/fourth edition of Pearson Voice of Teacher Survey, 2016. Accessed 2nd January, 2020.

Fenton, S., Key Concepts: Ethnicity, Polity Press, London, (2010).

Ferdman, B., M., The dynamics of ethnic diversity in organizations: Toward integrative models, Advances in Psychology, 82, 339–384 (1992).

Fraga, L., R., and Elis, R. Interests and representation: Ethnic Advocacy on California School Boards, Teachers College Record, 111 (3) 659–682 (2009).

Giddens, A., Sociology, 6th edition, Wiley, London, (2009).

Goffman, E., Encounters: Two studies in the sociology of interaction, Bobbs-Merrill Co., Indianapolis, (1961).

Healy, G., and Oikelome, F., Diversity, Ethnicity, Migration and Work: International Perspectives, Palgrave Macmillan, London, (2011).

Hochschild, J. L., and Shen, F., X. Race, ethnicity, and education policy, in Oxford Handbook of Racial and Ethnic Politics in America, Oxford University Press, New York (2014).

Hussein, S., Manthorpe, J., and Ismail, M., Ethnicity at work: the case of British minority workers in the long-term care sector, Equality, Diversity and Inclusion: An International Journal, 33 (2) 177–192 (2014).

Kahn, W., A., To be fully there: psychological presence at work, Human Relations, 45 (4), 321–49 (1992).

Kahn, W.A., Psychological conditions of personal engagement and disengagement at work, Academy of Management Journal, 33 (4), 692–724 (1990).

Karlsen, S., I., A quantitative and qualitative exploration of the processes associated with ethnic identification, Thesis (PhD), 2809076940, University of London, (2006).

Kular, S., Gatenby, M., Rees, C., Soane, E. and Truss, K., Employee engagement: a literature review, Working Paper Series No 19, Kingston University, (2008).

Maestri, V. Can ethnic diversity have a positive effect on school achievement? Education Economics, 25 (3) 290–303 (2017).

Maslow, A., Motivation and personality, Harper and Row, New York, (1954).

May, D., R., Gilson, R., L., and Harter, L., M., The psychological conditions of meaningfulness, safety and availability and the engagement of the human spirit at work, Journal of Occupational & Organizational Psychology, 77 (1) 11–37 (2004).

Murugesan, S., Bojanova, I. Encyclopedia of Cloud Computing. Wiley-IEEE Press, New Jersey, (2016).

Nathadwarawala, T., L. The impact of ethnicity on doctors' responses to employee engagement practices in English NHS Hospital Trusts, Doctoral thesis, University of Hertfordshire (2019).

PlatiFi.com, Accessed 3rd January, 2020.

Putnam, R., D., E pluribus unum: Diversity and community in the twenty-first century the 2006 Johan Skytte Prize Lecture. Scandinavian political studies, 30 (2), 137–174 (2007).

Sander, W. The effects of ethnicity and religion on educational attainment, Economics of Education Review, 11 (2) 119–135 (1992).

Schaufeli, W., B., and Bakker, A., B., Defining and measuring work engagement: bringing clarity to the concept, in Bakker, A.B. and Leiter, M.P. (Eds), Work Engagement: A Handbook of Essential Theory and Research, Psychology Press, Hove, (2010).

Severi, S. M2M Technologies: Enablers for a pervasive Internet of Things. Proceedings of the 2014 European Conference on Networks and Communications (EuCNC). IEEE, New York, (2014).

Shuck, B., and Wollard, K., Employee engagement and HRD: A seminal review of the foundations, Human Resource Development Review, 9 (1), 89–110 (2010).

Shuck, B., Four emerging perspectives of employee engagement, Human Resource Development Review, 10 (3) 304–28 (2011).

Stokes, L., Rolfe, H., Hudson-Sharp, N., and Stevens, S. A compendium of evidence on ethnic minority resilience to the effects of deprivation on attainment, National Institute of Economic and Social Research, Research Report, Department for Education, UK, (2015).

Truss, C., Delbridge, R., Alfes, K., Shantz, A. and Soane, E., (eds.), Employee Engagement in Theory and Practice, Routledge, London, (2014)

Unhelkar, B., Sharma, A. Innovating with IoT, big data, and the cloud. Cutter Business Technology Journal 30 (3), 28–33 (2017).

Unhelkar, B. Big Data Strategies for Agile Business. CRC Press, (Taylor and Francis Group/ an Auerbach Book), Boca Raton, FL, USA, (2018).

United Nations Statistics Division, Ethnocultural characteristics. Available at: http://unstats.un.org/unsd/demographic/sconcerns/popchar/default.htm, (2009) [accessed on: 1st December 2016]

Welch, M., The evolution of employee engagement concept: communication implications, corporate communications: an international journal, 16 (4) 328–346 (2011).

# CHAPTER 29

# Exploring the Role of Cloud-Based Deployment of Classrooms in Handling the Scalability and Reachability Challenge of Education in the Indian Context

EKATA MEHUL,[1*] and BHUVAN UNHELKAR[2]

[1]*Blazing Arrows, Vadodara, India*

[2]*University of South Florida Sarasota–Manatee, Sarasota, FL 34242, USA*

[*]*Corresponding author. E-mail: ekata.mehul@blazingarrows.org*

## ABSTRACT

Scalability of education delivery remains one of the top challenges of providing education at all levels in India. Although the Indian education system works toward creating educational institutions of excellence, particularly in the cities, the challenges of education and literacy within a large cross section of society in cities and villages still remain at the fore. This is mainly because educators need to be connected to students across geographical distances and in large numbers. Upcoming technologies such as cloud-based deployment of online educational materials that are then made available to students using smart, handheld devices, offers opportunities to scale-up education in India. In this chapter, we do a comparative literature study of scalability of education through use of technologies in the Indian context. We study the student-to-teacher ratios across primary, secondary, and tertiary educational institutions; we then compare the ease or difficulty of deploying online education; we also study the need to provide a combination of online and face-to-face education at various levels in the system. Finally, we critically examine the existing policies and procedures in Indian education system and provide scholarly recommendations on their improvement to enable scalability, which also includes one already implemented successful model of cloud-based system in combination with local teachers.

## 29.1 INTRODUCTION TO THE CHALLENGES OF EDUCATION IN INDIA

Education challenges range from creation of contents, identification of experts, processes of delivery, and verification of learning outcomes, to name but a few. Handling these challenges is crucial for the development of individuals, society and, in turn, the nation. India is a developing country with a large population that is rapidly growing. Therefore, the challenges for the education system are further exacerbated by the need for scalability. Design of the curriculum and development of good quality content is not enough. India also requires the dispersal of content to remote areas, along with experts to deliver content, and enhance the literacy of the nation. Thus, the scalability challenge is coupled with a reachability challenge.

In this chapter, we argue that cloud-based deployment of educational content holds the possibility of handling the scalability as well as the reachability issues. The shareable services offered primarily on the cloud have the ability to expand and shrink the capacity, depending on the demand, holds the promise of handling the rapidly growing student population. The ability to deliver those shareable educational services over Internet of Things (IoT) devices (such as handheld phones) enables education to reach students dispersed across large geographical lands (Unhelkar and Sharma, 2017). As the business models enabling sharing of data and analytics improve, so does the business agility of the user organizations; in this case, the educational organizations such as schools and colleges.

The fundamentals of the cloud as shared services are integral to the strategic adoption of Big Data (Unhelkar, 2018). As the ease of and excellence in connectivity increases, educational data and corresponding applications continue to shift to the cloud. This storage on the cloud is highly beneficial in managing large amounts of high velocity data. Cloud-based deployment also enables analytics across varied groups of datasets. Analytics can also be performed across a wide range of resources including the handheld devices with students in remote areas. Cloud-based deployment of educational content can source large suites of external data that need to be included in the analytical processes on an as-needed basis. Thus, approaches to enhancing the information and knowledge on the cloud can enhance the delivery of educational contents to a large cross section of students. It also allows accessing the data from any location and at any time. Heterogeneous data generated from any IoT devices can also be easily segregated and then can be analyzed upon, as it is stored in cloud.

This chapter explores the role of cloud-based deployment of classrooms in handling the scalability challenge of education in the Indian context. Key factors affecting the deployment of education contents on the cloud include the creation of content through multiple sources, validation of content in line with learning objectives, compliance and regulatory requirements mandated by the government (including security and privacy of data), and evaluation of student performance. This chapter further considers the opportunities provided by Big Data, its analytics and corresponding usage by educational institutions. Starting with an understanding of the cloud characteristics and Big Data in the context of education, this chapter explores the sources, hosting, and deployment of educational contents on the cloud. An important part of the literature study is the advent of IoT. These IoT sensor devices generate high-velocity data that is not all generated by the user. For example, these devices automatically generate the availability of student and his/her engagement with the educational content. A case study in the education domain is presented as a practical application of the concepts outlined in the chapter. Deployment challenges are then outlined and the chapter concludes with the key points discussed and the opportunities for future research directions.

## 29.2 EXPLORING CLOUD AND BIG DATA CHARACTERISTICS IN THE CONTEXT OF EDUCATION

As mentioned in Section 29.1, cloud-based deployment is pivotal in enabling shared educational content over a large cross section of student population. As the cloud deployment models based on sharing of data and analytics improve, so does the business agility of the educational institutions.

Figure 29.1 shows the various sources of Big Data that are provided and stored on the cloud for analytical purpose. Each source of data shown in Figure 29.1 has some common and other unique characteristics that influence the potential to deliver educational contents. These data types and their potential to impact education are mentioned in the following.

1. *Structured data*: the existing transactional data that is usually stored in relational formats. Typically, this is the administrative data such

as student and parent details, names and addresses, and transactions such as fees. Analytics on this data for historical and transactional information provide insights for management and administration of schools.

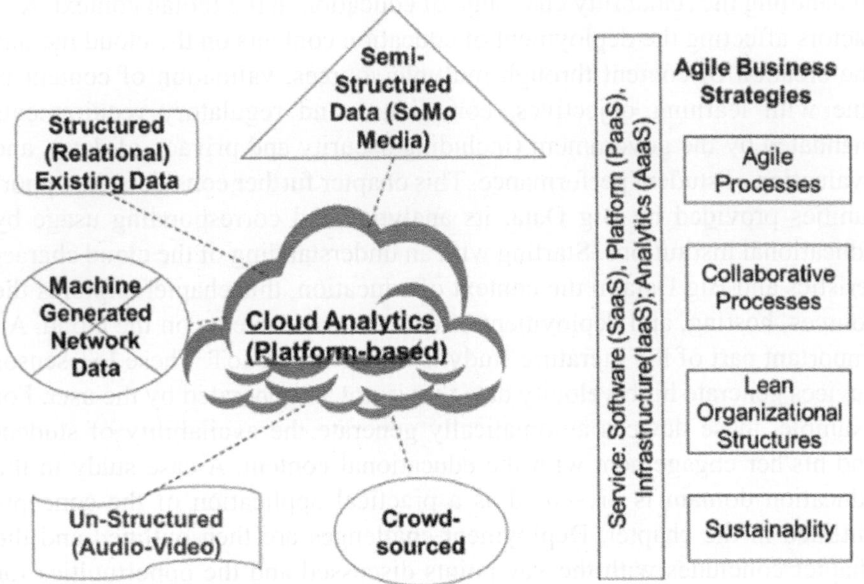


**FIGURE 29.1** Sources and types of data on the cloud, and their impact on business agility (Unhelkar, 2018).

2. *Semistructured data*: made up of data extracted from social media (SoMo) and mobile interfaces. This data may not be owned by the school. While it is more challenging to analyze this data, it offers a view of interesting patterns that help school administrators identify trends and ascertain the views of parents and policy makers outside the school boundaries.
3. *Unstructured data*: again from SoMo and mobile as well as various audio (IVR) and video data; this data is easy to store on the cloud in high volumes and provide opportunities to create contents for education. Typical video lectures that can be close captioned and that encourage student engagement are a part of this type of data. This data is of course most difficult to analyze, as it is not well structured.

4. *Machine-generated data*: typically from IoT devices connected with the enterprise. This is high velocity streaming data that requires utmost attention in the overall cloud-based deployment of education. The personalized IoT can provide excellent, customized analytics but, at the same time, also require high-speed processing. Creating and populating Chatbots with large numbers of student questions is a part of capitalizing on this type of data. The importance of IoT to Big Data and ensuing analytics is reviewed in the literature in this chapter.
5. *Crowd-sourced data*: that is made available by the mobile devices used by the crowd (e.g., these could be unregistered users uploading audio, video, and pictures using SoMo). This type of data in the education sector is a combination of contents generated by the teachers and the contents available from third parties and government bodies.

The right side of Figure 29.1 also lists how Big Data on the cloud affects agility of an organization. This agility translates into rapid responses of the educational systems to dynamically changing external situations.

1. *Agile processes*: Cloud-based Big Data platforms facilitate agility in educational processes and their deployment. This is because through cloud-based analytics, educators can anticipate and prepare for changes; as well as respond to changes that occur unexpectedly.
2. *Collaborative processes*: through utilizing collaborating organizations and/or publicly available free data (e.g., government data). This is the data shared between collaborative vendors. Combining this data with the existing school data leads to collaborative educational processes.
3. *Lean (and flattened) organizational and team structures*: the ability to scale-up and scale-down the team structures contributes toward a lean business model for schools.
4. *Mass personalization (and customization)*: due to enhanced abilities to customize a solution to the needs of a user through analytics.
5. *Sustainable work environment and ethics*: resulting from a lean-agile process with minimum waste (Unhelkar, 2018). Cloud is the basis for virtualization of resources, including configurability, shareability, and scalability—eventually contributing toward sustainability due to reduction in wastage of resources.

By its very nature, Big Data analytics is both storage and computing intensive. In the context of cloud computing, Big Data analytics requires careful consideration of storage, integration, security, and pricing. Storing and securing large volumes of high-velocity data is not easy for medium-sized schools. Therefore, outsourcing the challenge of storage and security to the cloud vendors is an important part of educational organization strategies. Schools are better off focusing their resources on core business functions rather than managing data. Schools neither have interest nor expertise in managing and administrating Big Data. With strategic use of the cloud, management and administrative activities related to data can be offloaded to the cloud and, thus, free up resources to focus on the core processes of content creation and delivery.

In general, the cloud enables centralization of what would otherwise be a highly dispersed set of data drawn from multiple sources and in varying formats. Cloud computing is similar to an electricity grid, where charges are based on electricity used; the cloud charges metered rates for processing time (Murugesan and Bojanova, 2016), which is helpful in developing Big Data strategies because of the aforementioned vagaries in data size, type, and analytics. The cloud also enables distributed and parallel computing as it provides the necessary infrastructure for Hadoop Distributed File System with relative ease. Thus, the cloud has a major role to play in the deployment of educational solutions and, in turn, improve the reach of the contents to a large number of students.

## 29.3 SCALING EDUCATION DEPLOYMENT WITH THE CLOUD

Cloud-based deployment of education content creates significant opportunities to scale-up education. This is because of the following reasons:

1. Cloud enables relatively easy uploading of content from multiple sources.
2. Cloud-based deployment of content is accessible wherever a student has Internet connectivity.
3. Deployment of courses is not time bound as compared with classroom delivery.
4. Contents on the cloud are amenable to analytics as the data related to the student engagement is easily available.
5. Cloud-based deployment is easy to trace, audit, and report on for compliance purposes.
6. Along with the data, cloud also provides the opportunity for experts that "best fit" a problem faced by a student to reach them within the given time by crossing all geographical boundaries.

The cloud-based deployment of educational content can be further improved by incorporating business intelligence. Traditional business applications are time consuming, modular, and linear in nature (Moss, 2003). For example, well-organized data (placed in rows and columns) requires substantial technologies and statistics to produce analytical solutions. This same approach of analyzing rows and columns runs into even greater challenges in the world of Big Data. According to Sathi (2012), there is not only a quantitative increase in volume and processing complexity but, with Big Data, there is a qualitative jump in the challenge of handling the high volume, high velocity and of wide-variety (the three "V"s of Big Data). The 4th V—Veracity (or quality) is added to create the contemporary definition of Big Data (IBM, Big Data, 2011). As mentioned earlier, all these types of data are imposed on educational content and, therefore, subject to the scrutiny of Big Data. For example, automation of data-to-data connectivity has the potential to have correlations between student groups, teachers, and administrators that are not easy to envisage by the human mind. A cloud-based approach together with ML is thus important to enable automation in ascertaining information and undertaking decisions in a school environment.

## 29.4 END-USER (END-STUDENT) COMPUTING AND INTERNET OF THINGS

The characterization of Big Data as high Volume–Velocity–Variety also points to the most typical source of such data—the IoT. This is primarily the machine generated data shown earlier in Figure 29.1 together, with the crowd-sourced data. The IoT (IoT Paradigm) is a generic term used to describe any sensor-based gadget that collects and sends data to a repository—usually residing on a cloud (Bassi, 2013). The IoT forms the basis for a large number of devices and corresponding applications.

While the Mobile–Handheld device (one of the IoT devices) is part of most people, it is easy for any student to not only get the correct lessons from anywhere or any expert at the right time; a student can also share the data in terms of assignments, expert details, or links to other education resources.

IoT is a disruptive technology because it dismantles and reorganizes business processes across the Internet and, in turn, impacts existing business models. Automation in the deployment architecture utilizing IoT is vital because the speed with which a group of IoT devices collect and send data (effectively "stream" data) results in ever-increasing volumes and velocity of data. These data also have variety—including audio, video, graphics, and sensor data—that present challenges of analyzing data together. Furthermore, such data is time sensitive. Once the currency of such data is over, the corresponding analytics lose meaning for business decision making.

Usage of this data can be tracked and parameters for tracking the outcomes can be measured. Outcome measures can include high usage content, "likes" for a particular expert as well as data around feedback, learning quotients, learning pace, and time of day of learning or geographical diversity for specific subjects.

Apart from that, these mobile devices can be used for meetups as well as creating discussing forums with experts and among all the various students across all geographical boundaries.

The challenge is to utilize IoT for business decision making by navigating through the myriad of data types, information exchange systems, applications, hardware, and communication systems. Organizations are keen to quantify consumer behavior, individual tastes, preferences, and behavioral patterns among other things through IoT, and students are no exception.

Analytics of Big Data generated by IoT devices is not limited to technical or statistical challenges. Hence, the use of artificial intelligence as well as machine learning algorithms are needed in order to get the information after accessing this disruptive and huge data.

The data points for IoT devices can be broken down into different categories to provide ease in analysis. One such taxonomy for IoT devices is discussed by Noura and Martin (2018). However, it is important to have the interconnectivity embedded within the device (data point) to enable a search for corresponding data points in other devices or sources of data. This connectivity between data points enriches the flow of information as the analytical process gathers more data from each new stream of data emanating from a variety of IoT devices. Each flow gathers the related information it seeks—depending on the business context or the context of the problem needing analysis—to create a new informational flow. There are now Universities where complete system is been designed for doing this analysis using Data Mining Techniques and once done we can use these generated details for the betterment for the Machine Learning Algorithms

One of the structural shifts taking place in education is the move from a knowledge transfer model to a collaborative, information-sharing system. IoT will have a profound impact on the way we teach, because connected systems free-up teachers from recording and monitoring students, enabling them to facilitate learning rather than merely to regurgitate information. In task-based instruction, students learn by doing and teachers assist when needed. IoT systems provide feedback, assistance, and classroom-level monitoring automatically by signaling teachers for help and increasing difficulty when necessary; as a result, no student falls too far behind nor gets too far ahead, solving a persistent problem in the classroom.

Finally there are many applications for IoT and that is being used apart from the conventional education mechanism, for example, some of the special usages and applications of IoT can lead to the correct development of special education, classroom monitoring using video-as-a-sensor technology, student physical and mental health, learning from home, personalized learning, and many more disruptive ways to learn.

## 29.5 CASE STUDY IN EDUCATION FOR CLOUD DEPLOYMENT

Currently, we are already working on a product named "Bringle Academy" where the focus is to develop a blended learning model combining the benefits of physical learning along with cloud-based knowledge sharing, allowing us the scalability of having 100,000 users and reaching up to 140 countries through cloud channels via. YouTube. The online cloud platform provides the support to develop communities and connect groups of mentors leading Online Meetups. While we have Skill Development Centers in each of the cities in India where the research setup is established, to get the complete, practical hands-on experience as well as interaction with mentors, to support the practical experience.

## 29.6 CONCLUSIONS AND FUTURE DIRECTIONS

In this chapter, we have explored the opportunities to scale-up education based on the technologies of cloud-based deployment. While numerous attempts are made at reaching out to student masses, we observe that ICT-based education content delivered on the cloud can complement the face-to-face delivery of education, particularly in the Indian context. We have also highlighted the risks associated with this type of education delivery that include compliance and regulations, privacy and security, and quality of content delivery. These risks can be mitigated by combining the existing infrastructure with that of the cloud. The best model will be the blended version. Furthermore, we observe that ICT-based education opens up opportunities for collaboration independent of geographical regions and time differences. Therefore, cloud-based platforms for education delivery provide the best option to scale-up education.

## KEYWORDS

- **cloud-based deployment**
- **challenges of scalability in education**
- **education in India**

## REFERENCES

Askarzai, W.; Lan, Y.; Unhelkar, B. Challenges of a virtual organisation: Empirical evidence from Australian SMEs. *Glob. J. Financ. Manag.* 2014, *6*(9), 919–924.

Bassi, A. *Enabling Things to Talk: Designing IoT Solutions With the IoT Architectural Reference Model.* Springer: Switzerland, 2013.

Dey, I. *Qualitative Data Analysis: A User Friendly Guide for Social Scientists.* Routledge: New York, 2003.

Gonsalves, T. *Artificial Intelligence: A Non-Technical Introduction*. Sophia University Press: Japan, 2017.

IBM, Big Data. 2011. http://www.ibmbigdatahub.com/infographic/four-vs-big-data. (accessed March 25, 2019).

Kumar, V.; Sundarraj, R. P. *The Value of Disruptive Innovations: Global Innovation and Economic Value*. Springer: Switzerland, 2018.

Moss, L. T. *Business Intelligence Roadmap: The Complete Project Lifecycle for Decision-Support Applications.* Addison Wesley Professional: Boston, 2003.

Murugesan, S.; Bojanova, I. *Encyclopedia of Cloud Computing.* Wiley-IEEE Press: New Jersey, 2016.

Njeru1a, A. M.; Omar, M. S.; Yi, S.; Paracha, S.; Wannous, M. Using IoT Technology to Improve Online Education Through Data Mining; IEEE-ICASI 2017—Meen, Prior & Lam (Eds) ISBN 978-1-5090-4897-7-515.

Noura, M. A.; Martin, M.G. Interoperability in internet of things: Taxonomies and open challenges. *Mob. Netw. Appl.* 2018, 1–14.

Pinka, K.; Kampars, J.; Minkevičs, V. In *Case Study: IoT Data Integration for Higher Education Institution*, Proceedings of the 2017 IEEE International Conference on Applied System Innovation, December 2016, vol. 19, pp. 71–77, ISSN 2255-9094 (online).

SAS. http://www.sas.com/en_us/offers/sem/statistics-machine-learning-at-scale-variant-107284/download.html#. (accessed March 25, 2019).

Sathi, A. *Big Data Analytics: Disruptive Technologies for Changing the Game.* MC Press: Idaho, 2012.

Severi, S. In *M2M Technologies: Enablers for a Pervasive Internet of Things*, Proceedings of the 2014 European Conference on Networks and Communications (EuCNC). IEEE: New York, 2014.

Shah, S.A.; Horne, A.; Capella, J. *Good Data Won't Guarantee Good Decisions.* Harvard Business Review, April, 2014.

Unhelkar, B. *Customer-Centric Business as an Interdisciplinary Affair.* In Proceedings of IIBA Conference. Anahei Publishing: Florida, p. 349, 2015.

Unhelkar, B. *Big Data Strategies for Agile Business.* CRC Press, (Taylor and Francis Group/ an Auerbach Book): Florida, 2018.

Unhelkar, B.; Sharma, A. Innovating with IoT, big data, and the cloud. *Cutter Business Technology Journal* 2017, *30*(3), 28–33.

CHAPTER 30

# Higher Education in Capacity and Capability Building for the Information Economy

KEITH SHERRINGHAM[1*], and BHUVAN UNHELKAR[2]

[1]*A.C.N. 629 733 633 Pty. Ltd., Sydney, NSW, 2000, Australia*

[2]*College of Business, University of South Florida Sarasota-Manatee Campus, Sarasota, FL, 3424, USA*

[*]*Corresponding author. E-mail: keith.sherringham@gmail.com*

## ABSTRACT

Educational institutions are rising to the challenge of enabling organizations and society to transform, and to adopt and adapt to the uncertainties and opportunities arising out of rapid changes in technology. Moving beyond the technical and subject matter expertise, offerings for skilling and training need to include an emphasis on the essential professional skills (like people management, problem-solving, relationship management, and financial management). Technology based learning offerings are expanding to include support for the operations and management of technology and its services as well as addressing the business integration and adoption of technology. Business centric and other nontechnical learning offerings are including the role of technology and the business application and transformation from technology. The automation of knowledge workers (from artificial intelligence or real-time decision making or machine learning) and the provision of a knowledge worker services from the cloud (like Tax as a Service or Audit as a Service or Project Management as a Service) are also emerging for which learning offerings will be required. Skilling and training for the necessary capacity and capability building (including adaptiveness, responsiveness, and resiliency) to support transformation is increasingly expected of educational institutions. This chapter brings the industry experience of the authors in business transformation around technology, with their investigations in the role of higher education, to help shape emerging offerings for capacity and capability building for transformation.

## 30.1 INTRODUCTION

For a student undertaking three years of study, the technology used at the start of the study is likely to have changed significantly by the end of the study. While the "how we do it" changes quickly, the "what we do" changes slower. A student still needs to learn how to manage people and work with others, but whether they learn how to do this with a given application or make use of artificial intelligence to help in predicting how people respond is what is changing faster. Managing technology obsolescence, business use of legacy systems, and the established proven pragmatic business principles will still need to be part of their study.

The Internet, Mobile Computing, Cloud Computing, Social Media, Big Data, and Cloud-based services are all converging to form the core platform off which businesses and societies operate. The Internet of Things (IoT), real-time decision making, machine learning, and artificial intelligence are all becoming part of this emerging core platform. This core platform needs to be managed and integrated into business, with issues like regulatory, privacy, security, and profitability all to be managed. Jobs around the core platform for which a student is being trained may no-longer exist at the end of a study period, but new and diverse roles are likely to be created. Irrespective, capacity, and capability building to be adaptive, responsive, and resilient is required. The current technology-focused cloud services like Platform as a Service (PaaS), Infrastructure as a Service (IaaS), Database as a Service (DBaaS), and Software as a Service (SaaS) are expected to be automated further and become more extensive in use within business and educational institutions. Starting with the routine and moving to the more complex, knowledge worker services are also likely to undergo automation and be provided from the cloud (on-demand as pay-per-use) with changes in the provision and management of education services, amongst others. Services like Tax as a Service (TXaaS), Audit as a Service (ADaaS), Project Management as a Service (PMaaS), legal services, and many others are set to be cloud-based, with the provision of devices, servers, databases, applications, data management, processes, frameworks, governance, best practice, reporting, routine administration, the training (how to do), and skilling (ability to do), as well as resourcing and other specialist services and expertise.

The transformation of knowledge workers (Sherringham and Unhelkar, 2020a) sees organizations (business, government, educational, Not for Profit) managing the risks associated with transformation against the need to maintain operations and sustain business through change as part of their risk-based approach to business. Educational institutions are faced with making their own transformations around technology with revised operations and service models, whilst providing ongoing upgrades to studies and courses. The way students are engaged and providing the skills and expertise which students will bring to new roles, is the opportunity and market differentiator for educational institutions around technologies.

Businesses are often behind the "cutting edge" in technology adoption because of the need to overcome the cost of incumbency, sustain business, managing risk, and to learn the lessons from the early adopters. Conversely, educational institutions are often required to be the early adopters and thought leaders, and to manage out their own incumbency whilst occurring costs through being at the "cutting edge" and with the need to include lessons learned and innovation within offerings. Staff providing the courses are faced with maintaining relevancy, whilst students who are seeking innovation and leadership are expected to manage through the legacy and be accepting of technology change by the end of their study.

The transformation of operations and services around the technology is driven by markets, regulations, customers, and costs. Vested interests and the need to overcome incumbency also impact. Businesses need to manage the risk of transformation against the need for continuity of service. Delivering business transformation is often a series of projects managed across the business addressing infrastructure, data, processes, operations, stakeholders, and roles and responsibilities, with the required skilling (ability to do) and training (how to do). To prepare and implement business transformation often requires capacity and capability building in areas from project management, to change management, and through to training. The ongoing operations and improvement of the business also often requires capacity and capability building, especially with skills in adaptiveness, responsiveness, and resiliency (Figure 30.1).

This chapter takes a technology-agnostic approach to the adoption, integration, and transformation around technology within educational institutions. The industry experience of the authors is brought in this chapter to help with the capacity and capability building around emerging technologies and the adoption and adaption within educational institutions. The focus of this chapter is on the capacity and capability building to manage the uncertainty that results from rapid changes in technology through the application of the combination of strategy and leadership, to influence the environment, to instill the behaviors, and strengthen with skilling to shape the pride, ownership, and empowerment within all of us. The role of skilling and training and the use of artificial intelligence are considered alongside the people transformations and the management of the adoption and adaption to technology. Some future trends are also identified with the intention of shaping the emergent behavior and environment for transformation through professionalism, the pride in who we are and what we do, and to bring forth the future that lies within our hands.

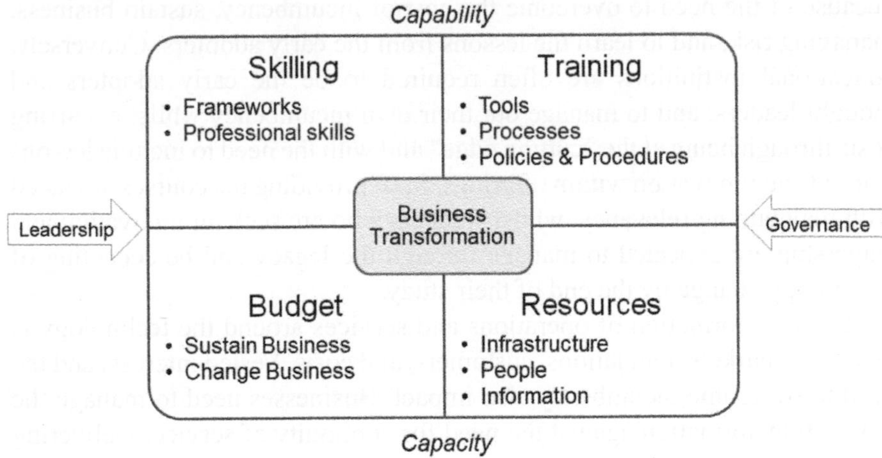


**FIGURE 30.1** Capacity and capability building for business transformation (from Sherringham and Unhelkar, 2020a).

## 30.2 SKILLING AND TRAINING

Even though skilling and training is often a cost to business (subject to cuts for profitability), the transformation from technology sees skilling and training as a core issue for businesses in managing organizational change. The rapid changes in technology are impacting how skilling (ability to do) and training (how to do) is provided to both current and emerging work forces, as well as increasing the demand for skilled workers and for ongoing skilling and training. Educational institutions are evolving their offerings and service models to meet the emerging opportunities.

### *30.2.1 THE DEMAND*

As reported by the Australian Computer Society (2019), "Australia will need an additional 100,000 technology workers to meet employer demand by 2024" which will require reskilling of existing workers as well as new workers. In addition, a report by Australia's leading scientific research organization, the Commonwealth and Scientific Industrial Research Organization (Hajkowicz et. al., 2016) outlines the role of automation in changing roles of knowledge workers and the role of skilling and training in the transition (with similar trends are seen in other countries). Although the impacts of automation are expected to vary (from the near complete automation of roles impacted by automated vehicles through to minimal short-term impacts in service industries like nursing), there is consistency in the types of skills needed for knowledge worker professionals who will need to transition to new roles as well as for the skills needed by those entering the workforce. This is the demand being asked of educational institutions by employers and society and is what students are expecting.

The Australian Computer Society (2017) also identified that professional skills (such as people management, financial management, vendor management, relationship management, strategy and planning, risk management, project management, problem-solving, management of change in the business, management of ambiguity, governance, compliance management, cross-disciplinary collaboration, ethics, and communication and presentation) are a must-have in current and emerging opportunities. Educational institutions are increasingly expected to provide both the technical training (how to do) and the skilling (ability to do) through professional skills development and strengthening. Both employers and students are expecting this from educational institutions.

The business consumption of technology is driving demand for technical expertise in Information and Communication Technology (ICT), alongside the service management (Sherringham and Unhelkar, 2016a), and with the business application and integration of technology. On the business side, the demand is for the business application of technology, the adoption of technology into the business, and the use of the technology within current and emerging business operations. Business is also increasing demand for the "Specialist" with deep knowledge within a given area (e.g., network engineers or data scientists or cyber security) of technology and which can be kept current, but who can also interact and engage with a wider audience. With increasing automation and the use of artificial intelligence, the specialization is increased, but the interdependencies also become more complex.

Therefore, business is also increasing the need for "Generalists" who can interact with the specialist areas, but also work across the areas, and operate end-to-end to see that the interdependencies are managed. "Generalists" require the ability to engage and understand the specializations whilst being able to see across and work through the interdependencies.

To meet emerging opportunities and changes in demand, educational institutions are faced with the challenge of:

- Skilling and training of those entering the workforce as well as those within the workforce.
- Provisions for the increasing numbers entering and needed within the workforce.
- Supporting the demand for both "Generalists" and "Specialists" across a range of technologies and business areas.
- Adoption of business courses to include technology and the business application of technology within the offerings.
- Adaption of ICT operations and services within technology courses as well as the business integration and adoption of technology knowhow into offerings.
- Supplying customized skilling and training that can be accommodated in a variety of ways in a diversity of offerings.

To meet the demand, offerings need to be both integrated and standalone as well as assisting and supporting:

- Refresher—Ongoing and periodic to strengthen capacities and capabilities as well as keeping current with contemporary practices.
- Onboarding—As part of the new start and onboarding process or when a role changes.
- Compliance—Part of compliance-based training (e.g., financial crime).
- General—As part of career development and the ongoing development.
- Business specific—Specific training when joining a business area or a project or program.

Educational institutions are also rising to meet the demand for changes in skills and expertise as operations are automated.

### *30.2.2 FROM "RUN THE BUSINESS" TO "CHANGE THE BUSINESS"*

As operational roles become more automated, especially those in the "routine" processing roles that keep a business running ("Run the Business"), less of these roles are expected. Those in "Run the Business" roles are expected to transition to other roles, and "Run the Business" roles will require a higher value skill set to problem solve when things go wrong and to manage stakeholders (i.e., a premium on professional skills). Those involved in roles that improve the business and work on the business ("Change the Business") are set to increase in the numbers, with greater diversity of roles, and increased complexity of roles. "Change the Business" roles place a premium on skills for: strategic analytical problem-solving, change management knowhow, project management proficiency, cross-silo expertise, and operational and process improvement. "Change the Business" requires increased professional skills and use of the "Generalists" alongside the "Specialists."

Customers of educational institutions will expect to see the championing of transformation and adoption within their own activities, but to also see capacity and capability building provided for "Change the Business" roles and for professional skills (alongside the technical) for those moving into the workforce as well as for those transitioning within the workforce. ICT course offerings will need to move beyond the technology to address ICT operations and services as well as business integration. Development of professional skills (like problem-solving, project management, and vendor management) is an expected default offering. For business courses (like business administration, or engineering, or agriculture, or arts and social-based), the need for inclusion of the role of technology is required, together with how to use the technology within operations. Business courses will also provide professional skills development to compliment the subject expertise.

The expectations of educational institution customers and of business in general, are that offerings are more customer-centric and meet the emerging opportunities and service:

- For those entering the workforce, the technology and business of adoption of ICT around "Run the Business" and the "Change the Business" is expected within offerings.
- For those transitioning within the workforce as roles are automated, offerings provided by educational institutions can support this transition.
- The development of professional skills is seen as an integral outcome from courses as well as specialist offerings to capacity and capability building of professional skills across business and technology.
- The provision within offerings for the business focus of technology as well as the varying needs of specialists and generalists.

### 30.2.3 TECHNOLOGY IN SERVICE PROVISION

The rapid changes in technology including knowledge worker services from the cloud as well as automation and artificial intelligence impact the services provided by educational institutions (Table 30.1).

One of the major uses of technology (subject to respective permissions and safeguards) is in the personal profile management and preferences of those studying. The personal profiles developed can include staff feedback, student feedback, reviews, management feedback, collaboration results, and profiles on social networking sites, as well as socio-economic details. In the profiles developed, the attributes, values, aspirations, and learning types can be established. This information is then used in the customization of the offerings, suggestions, adaptions to learning style (e.g., different ways to attain an assessment). Consider a highly introvert network engineer who is comfortable increase their technical skills but feels their career is not progressing or feels a lack of recognition. Through profile management, incremental professional skills development can be undertaken without "fear of failure" in an adaptive and supportive environment to help their career advancement.

Alongside the use of profiles are peer pressure and the role of people of influence. People of influence with aligned values and interests are often of more impact in the skilling and training process than other sources of information (either positive or negative). Artificial intelligence, real-time decision making, and Analytics as a Service, can all be used through people of influence, to guide peer pressure, and facilitate the skilling and training. Other technologies can also be used including:

- Bots—The use of bots to automate replies with different personality traits to assist with tests or answering questions in role-play over messaging.
- Real-Time Feedback—Assessment of answers in real-time with suggestions of alternatives.
- Difficulty—Changing the difficulty of the questions in tests based on the comparative success to responses and against other team members.
- Rewards—Use of artificial intelligence to provide rewards and incentives in the learning process aligned with the preferences of the participants.

The emerging cloud-based knowledge worker services like Business Analysis as a Service, Testing as a Service, Operations as a Service, PMaaS, TXaaS, ADaaS impact educational institutions as follows:

**TABLE 30.1** Technology Impacts on Service Provision

| Operational Area | Technology Use | Business Benefits |
|---|---|---|
| Skilling and training needs and analysis | Use of automation in analysis of needs, previous study, results, and other personal profile material so that the customized skilling and training can be provided | • Assist with sales<br>• Course offerings more appropriate to customer<br>• Customize courses enable higher completion rates with beneficial impact to customer and institution |
| Reporting | Automation of routine reporting to stakeholders for performance management and other business areas as well as ease of specialist reporting | • Higher quality feedback to customers for their development, improvement, and reinforcement.<br>• Simplified business operations and lower cost<br>• A diverse range of value added information for individuals, business areas, and the overall business in training, skilling, as well as the overall capacity and capability development |
| Monitoring | Application of artificial intelligence to monitoring for students and other business areas for provision of value added information services | • Monitoring of satisfaction and performance for ongoing development and improvement.<br>• Information source for new product and services development<br>• Tailoring of offerings and specializations for better returns |
| Baselines | Automation and analysis for establishing and validation of baselines and for performance assessment against base lines | • Use of baselines for self-assessment and improvement tool offerings.<br>• Easier metrics quantification and performance management providing a competitive advantage offering |
| Assessment | Real-time decision making and artificial intelligence in making assessments of skilling and training and identify offerings | • Enable higher value propositions to customers<br>• Diversified revenue streams to the institutions<br>• Research opportunities |
| Career matching | Use of analytics for improved career suggestion, career mapping, and alignment to employer needs | • Appeal to students as an offering.<br>• Institution has greater student appeal<br>• Stronger partnerships with industry and business |

- Adoption of the services within the institute for the management of their services and operations.
- Skilling and training on the establishment and management of cloud-based knowledge worker services.
- Addressing the business integration and adoption of cloud-based knowledge worker services.
- Inclusion of cloud-based knowledge worker services as tools within the study process (e.g., students managing their own projects use PMaaS with an assessment on the use of PMaaS as well as the study outcome).

Just as technology can be used in a supportive and engaging role, technology can be used to subvert as well as detect (e.g., plagiarism). Addressing the processes, policies, procedures, governance, security, privacy, audit, and regulatory is required in the implementation and management. All of these also form areas for skilling and training and for additional offerings for educational institutions.

## 30.3 MANAGING THE TRANSFORMATION

From the analysis of the failure of ICT projects by the IEEE (2015) through to high profile implementation failures noted by Connolly (2014), the shortcomings in the adoption of technology relate mainly to the business implementation, support, and people issues; rather than the technology per se. For a specific issue like security in the IoT, it is also the adaptiveness and responsiveness to service management and operations (Sherringham and Unhelkar, 2020b) that are integral. It is the capacity and capability building for successful adoption and adaption that is the transformational challenge around technology which educational institutions are addressing.

### *30.3.1 EMERGENT BEHAVIOR*

For an educational institute there is the need to:

- Transform their own operations.
- Provide leadership to the community on the adoption and adaption of technology.
- Develop new offerings around emerging technologies.
- Play a wider guidance role in managing organizational change
- Make offerings to customers in these areas as a source of revenue.

All of these needs require the application of the combination of strategy and leadership, to influence the environment, to instill the behaviors, and strengthen with skilling to shape the pride, ownership, and empowerment within all of us (Figure 30.2). While funding and resources are required, much of the capacity and capability building comes from the actions of individuals to form an emergent behavior and environment for transformation through professionalism, the pride in who we are and what we do. It is building the emergent behavior within the organization around the environment to instill behaviors and promoting through the offerings and courses through which capacity and capability for transformation is developed.

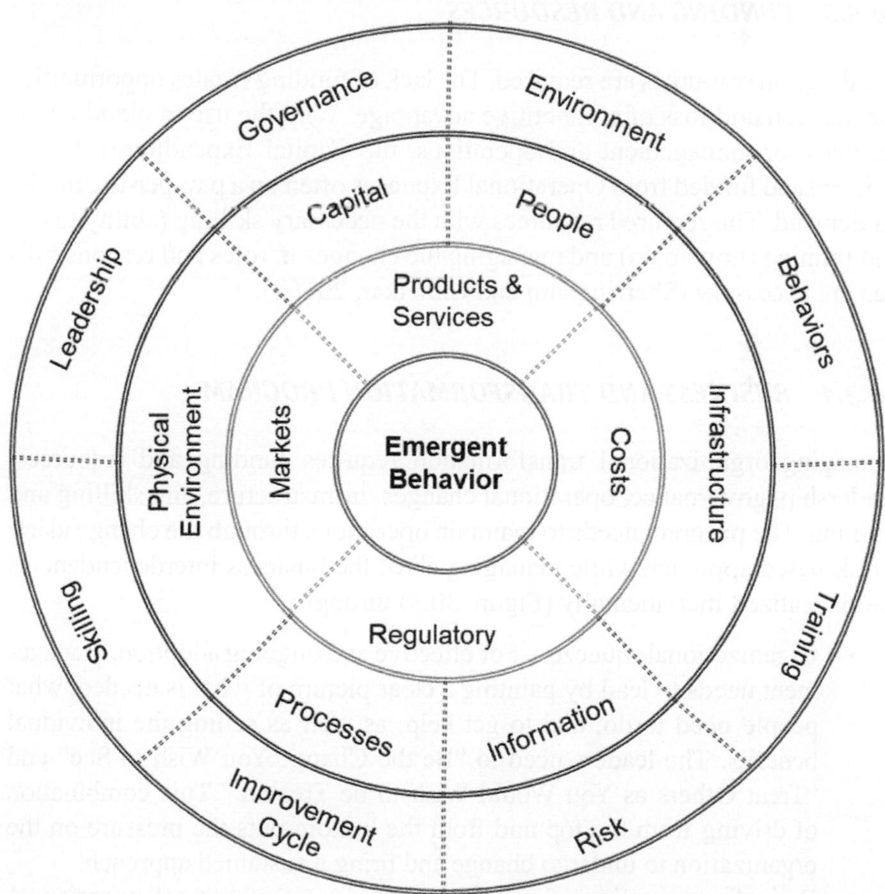


**FIGURE 30.2** Shaping the emergent behavior for business transformation.

### 30.3.2 BOARDS AND EXECUTIVE

Board and Executive Management are needed to lead the capacity and capability building and to prioritize the skilling and training. They are tasked with changing the environment and instilling the behaviors to enable the educational institute. Both technology and organizational change expertise and representation are required at the Board level (McConnell, 2018) for the management of strategic issues and priorities. Similar principles occur in organizations of all sizes, types, (business, government, educational, and not for profit), markets, and jurisdictions.

### 30.3.3 FUNDING AND RESOURCES

Funding and resources are required. The lack of funding creates opportunities for inaction and loss of competitive advantage. With the use of cloud-based services for management and operations, the Capital Expenditures can be reduced and funded from Operational Expenses often on a pay-per-use model on demand. The required resources with the necessary skilling (ability to do) and training (how to do) and managing the changes in roles and responsibilities are necessary (Sherringham and Unhelkar, 2016b).

### 30.3.4 BUSINESS AND TRANSFORMATION PROGRAM

Managing organizational transformation requires funding and resources, leadership, governance, operational changes, infrastructure, and skilling and training. The program needs to maintain operations through the change using a risk-based approach while managing all of the business interdependencies and is realized incrementally (Figure 30.3) through:

- Organizational squeeze—For effective and ongoing adoption, management needs to lead by painting a clear picture of what is needed, what people need to do, and to get help, as well as selling the individual benefits. The leaders need to "Be the Change You Wish to See" and "Treat Others as You Would Wish to be Treated." This combination of driving from the top and from the bottom puts the pressure on the organization to undergo change and bring a sustained approach.
- Rails for operation—Implementation is not a one-off exercise. A sustained approach (rails for operation) for implementing change

and its ongoing management is required. Changes come through the building of momentum, accepting difference in the adoption and transition, taking an iterative approach and building the environment and behaviors through ownership and empowerment. The implementation has to be good enough to get buy-in support whilst allowing people to take ownership and improve.

- Building momentum—Adoption and adaption may go through stages and maybe a series of starts and stops, but it is about an ongoing capacity and capability to change through sustained momentum.

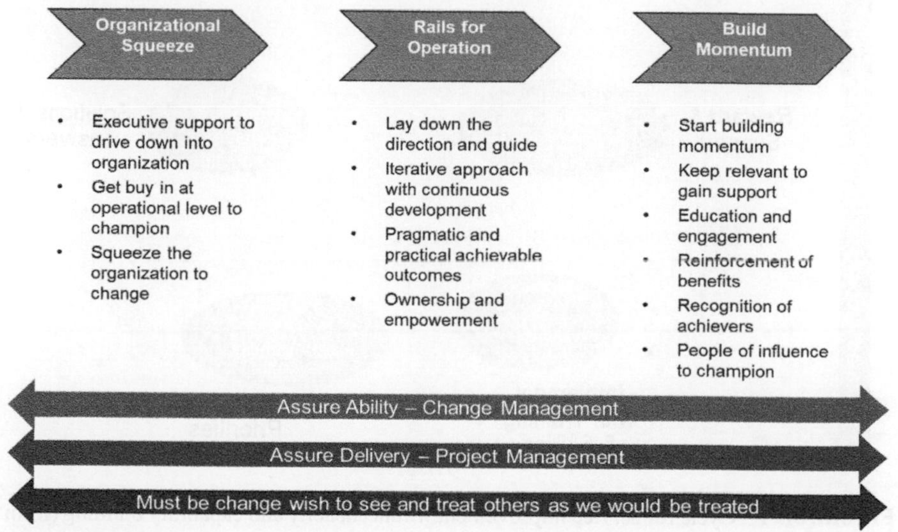


**FIGURE 30.3** Pragmatic implementation of organizational change (from Sherringham and Unhelkar 2020a)

### *30.3.5 PROCESS FOR IMPROVEMENT*

Once established, a process for ongoing improvement is required (Figure 30.4) to assure the business and technology response to threat changes, evolving business needs, and rapid variations in technology. The improvement cycle requires adoption across the impacted areas of business and ICT operations and services (part of the implementation project as well as ongoing) with the required improvements adopted.

The need for process improvement is ongoing as part of business operations. Offerings from educational institutions that omit embedded improvement across the offerings, including research, are doing a disservice to businesses, societies, and diminishing their value to customers.

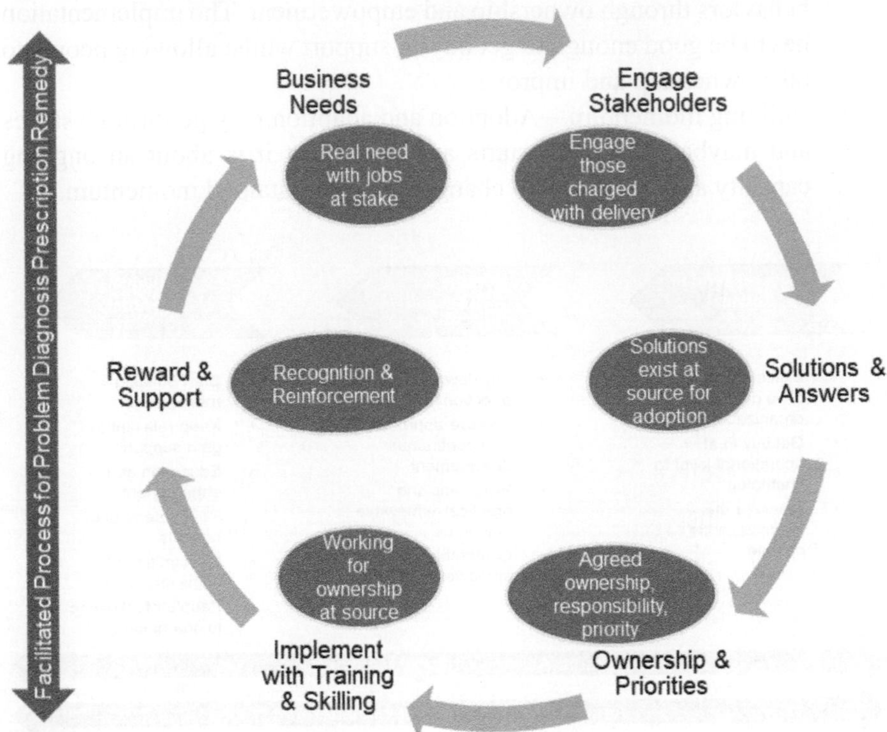


**FIGURE 30.4** Cycle for service improvement within capacity and capability building (from Sherringham and Unhelkar, 2020a).

## 30.4 FUTURE TRENDS

Selected emerging trends for which capacity and capability building within and by educational institutions is required for responding to changes in technology and from which new offerings will emerge include:

### *30.4.1 ADOPTING TO TRANSFORMATION*

The provision of knowledge worker services from the cloud (like PMaaS, ADaaS, TXaaS) and their business integration and adoption, alongside with their automation (including artificial intelligence and real-time decision making) is transforming educational institutions and their offerings. Educational institutions are undertaking their capacity and capability building and skilling and training their own resources to undergo their own transformation and provide new offerings. In addition, the leadership role of educational institutions is likely to see direction and offerings in the following areas amongst others (Table 30.2):

The trends from Table 30.2, as well as other emerging business areas, form some of the many operational aspects of a business that are being automated as well as providing opportunities for revenue and market differentiators for educational institutions. A key priority is not just the development of the technology and ICT-centric offerings, but the wider business and societal including:

- Addressing the business integration and business adoption (including the processes, policies, procedures, governance, security, privacy, audit, and regulatory).
- Assisting with the frameworks and regulatory regimes that need to be developed and applied.
- Researching the adoption, integration, and societal impacts.
- Providing a diverse range of offerings in support of the emerging trends.
- Information assurance including access, quality, privacy, and security.

These priorities and their interdependencies show the need for an integrated approach across the teaching, advising, and research (educational activities) of educational institutions (Figure 30.5). The drivers of the educational institutions are impacted by the emerging areas (often stemming from the work of the educational institutions) as well as influencing the delivery of the educational activities. The emerging offerings (from the emerging areas) within the activity areas are more than the ICT and include the business and societal aspects, which provide additional value (through the educational activities) to customers. Technology changes and the resulting business impacts are often seen to reinforce the current risk profile, revenue streams, and reputations, but also provide opportunities for market changes (e.g., the rise of the Chinese Universities).

### *30.4.2 FUNDING*

With technology transforming markets and customer expectations, educational institutions are faced with corresponding funding changes, especially in the near future, in the sourcing of sustainable funds for longer-term activities,

**TABLE 30.2** Emerging Trends around Technology for Educational Institutions

| Trend | Trend Description | Educational Institution Role |
|---|---|---|
| Decision making | Empowering decision making at source in real-time using multiple information sources, experience, analysis, and authenticated assumptions. | • Research on decision making technology.<br>• Research and bench marks for testing.<br>• Business trends and adoption research.<br>• Technology and Business courses, including integration and service management.<br>• Developing the frameworks to provide the required trust and support. |
| Personality assistant | Adoption of personal profile information and related information to help assess expected responses in real-time. | • Psychological modeling and profiling research.<br>• Behaviors prediction research.<br>• Technology and Business courses, including integration, business benefits, and service management. |
| Leadership development | From confidence building measures to responsiveness and decision making using real-time information analysis to help leaders in operational decisions. | • Research on leadership technology.<br>• Business trends and adoption research.<br>• Technology and Business courses, including integration and service management.<br>• Analysis of leadership and response changes. |
| Performance management | The routine monitoring, assistance with assessment, and engagement for performance management. | • Research on the human response to the use of the technology.<br>• Monitoring of business use and adoption.<br>• Development of the management frameworks and advising government on legislation. |
| Management of the risk-based approach | Managing risk for business within a risk-based approach with real-time risk assessment tools. | • Maturing risk-based approach models for business.<br>• Adoption of the models within technology.<br>• Courses on the use and adoption within a risk-based approach to business. |

**TABLE 30.2** *(Continued)*

| Trend | Trend Description | Educational Institution Role |
|---|---|---|
| Benchmark testing | Benchmark setting and testing of automation to ensure performance and integrity with independent auditability of self-learning and artificial intelligence. | • Research on artificial intelligence for self-testing and diagnosis.<br>• Research on artificial intelligence for bench mark monitoring, assurance of performance, and exceptions management.<br>• Development of analysis tools and governance.<br>• Offerings around artificial intelligence testing. |

within more volatile markets whilst maintaining independency and academic rigor. Specialization in response to funding is also expected with specialization in cross-disciplinary approaches and strategic issues also emerging. Funding challenges include:

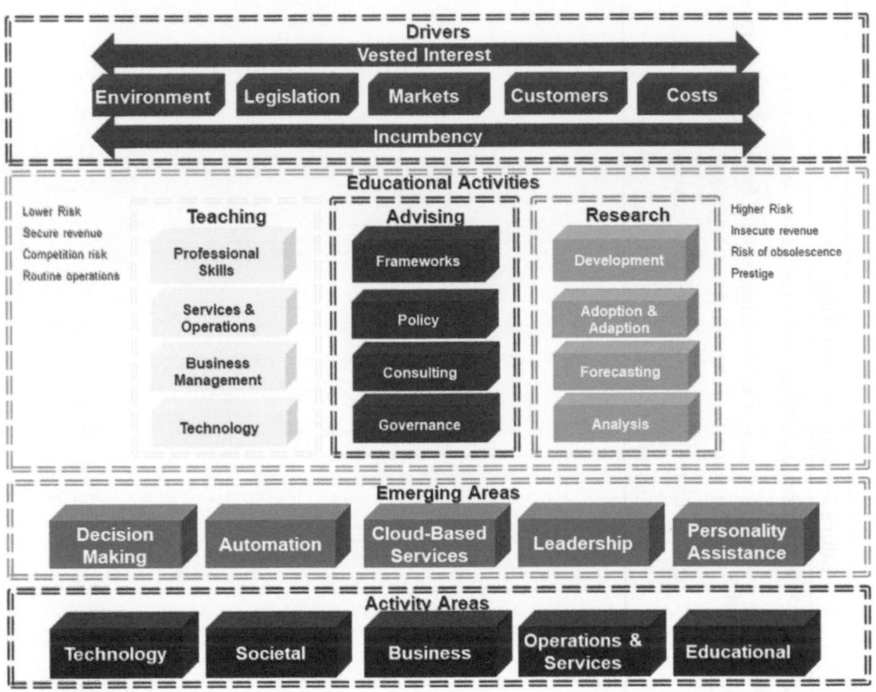


**FIGURE 30.5** Influencing the offerings of educational institutions.

- Global competition—Competition for research and teaching is global with offerings to global markets. The public institutions are competing with private providers and this trend is set to continue. Technology increases the competition, empowers the consumers, and increases expectations. The ability to respond quickly to changes is the increasing norm. The increasing demands of government from tax revenues are likely to strengthen the global markets and funding impacts.
- Government funding of teaching—The main stay of government funding is expected to continue, but revised priorities and relative fluctuations in funding levels are expected. Greater variability in funding levels and priorities is expected, with the anticipation of more rapid responses. Major changes in funding will occur in response to

government priorities occur (e.g., defense, environmental, geopolitical factors) with corresponding impacts on offerings.

- Private funding of teaching—Pay-per-use by domestic and overseas students is market driven and is set to remain a key element of funding. Governments are set to use private funding as a substitute for tax-based funding. Private funding from business for services is also expected to be an increasing revenue source, but more volatile.
- Advising—The role of educational institutions in advising government (and businesses) is expected to continue with additional revenue from pay-per-use services provided globally. Educational institutions are expected to service these needs and manage the commercial impacts of revenue dependency and vested interest.
- Government funded research—Government-funded research is an at-risk activity and the changes in technology are increasing the expectation and response times. The significance placed on research for economic or prestige or national priorities is a key influencer of funding which is intensified by the rapid adoption of technology. Sustained funding for long-term activities and strategic initiatives is at risk.
- Government funded development—Increased pressure to commercialize and apply research, on a faster time scale, is expected for both funding and meeting government expectations. The pressure for the formation of commercial operations aligned to national interests is increasing.
- Private funded research—Is an at-risk activity on a global market driven by global competition that is reinforced through technology changes.
- Private funded development—Is an at-risk activity on a global market driven by global competition that is reinforced through technology changes. The expectation is more commercialization of core research through technology changes.
- Cross-sector collaboration—Addressing the needs of business and of society is increasingly complex and multi-stakeholder. Cross-sector, cross-country, and multiple participant collaboration is expected. Success in these areas brings its own funding sources.

The changes in technology often serve to drive the volatility in funding, which in turn is facilitating innovation and revised offerings. Conversely, the assurance of quality and strategic needs is impacted. Educational institutions are expected to accommodate these trends within their businesses, their offerings, as well as research and to provide leadership for. Educational institutions are faced with capacity and capability building for their own needs as well as to serve emerging needs.

### 30.4.3 GEOPOLITICAL

Educational institutions, both public and private, are increasingly subject to geopolitical trends, which are intensified by technology changes for which capacity and capability building is required to respond:

- Weaponization—From their role in national security, to cyber attacks by external parties, to vested political interests; educational institutions are being weaponized in a variety of ways. The rapid changes in technology reinforce the opportunity for this. The response from educational institutions is to prepare for this and to be able to manage out as weaponization occurs.
- National priorities—The funding dependencies arising through technology changes and the increased funding volatility which results, makes educational institutions more vulnerable to changes in national priorities. The need to meet short-term demands, the expectation of more rapid responses, and meeting vested interests is the risk to be managed.
- Political—Changes in political views is an inherent risk for educational institutions. From the "echo chamber" of social media to the changes in expectations about acceptable outcomes because of technology, the overall risk profile of politics on an educational institution is increased. Educational institutions are faced with political risk and its operational management, including the weaponization occurring.
- Staff—Technology changes enable staff to move more easily between educational institutions. Recruiting high profile researchers that can deliver key outcomes for governments whilst increasing the prestige of an educational institution is easier to achieve and to reorganize markets. Targeting staff and the people risk is also part of the weaponization occurring which educational institutions are required to manage.
- Information—From cyber-security attacks to gain the competitive advantage to controlling the release of information which is not looked on favorable by vested interests, technology is changing the access and use of information. Information is a key part of weaponization, reputational risk, people risk, and political risk for educational institutions. The role of technology is to increase the risks.
- Intellectual property—Changes in technology make it easier to copy information and technology with corresponding changes in the management and value from intellectual property. From the inclusion of educational institutions in free trade agreements to restrictions on

academics, managing intellectual property is increasing in complexity, changing the risk profile of educational institutions, and is part of the weaponization.

Major policy changes, global events, environmental impacts, demographic changes, and wealth distribution activities; all play a role in what influences educational institutions. Whilst technology changes often serve to intensify these impacts, ICT also plays a major role in the preparation and response. Educational institutions are expected to accommodate these trends within their businesses, their offerings, as well as research and provide leadership for.

## 30.5 CONCLUSION

Beyond providing the technical offerings around automation and cloud-based knowledge worker services, educational institutions need to look within and transform their operations, services, and offerings. Addressing the business integration and business adoption of the technology (including the processes, policies, procedures, governance, security, privacy, audit, and regulatory) is part of the transformation as well as forming the basis for additional offerings which need to support:

- Skilling and training of those entering the workforce as well as those within the workforce.
- Provisions for the increasing numbers entering and needed within the workforce.
- Supporting the demand for both generalists and specialists across a range of technologies and business areas.
- Adoption of business courses to include technology and the business application of technology within the offerings.
- Adaption of ICT operations and services within technology courses as well as the business integration and adoption of technology knowhow into offerings.
- Supplying customized skilling and training that can be accommodated in a variety of ways in a diversity of offerings.
- Enabling those entering the workforce and those transitioning within the workforce to have skills and expertise in the technology and business of adoption of ICT around “Run the Business” and the “Change the Business” is expected within offerings.

- The development of professional skills is seen as an integral outcome from courses as well as specialist offerings to capacity and capability building of professional skills across business and technology.
- The provision within offerings for the business focus of technology as well as the varying needs of specialists and generalists.
- Addressing the business integration and business adoption (including the processes, policies, procedures, governance, security, privacy, audit, and regulatory).
- Assisting with the frameworks and regulatory regimes that need to be developed and applied.
- Researching the adoption, integration, and societal impacts.
- Information assurance including access, quality, privacy, and security.

Educational institutions are also capacity and capability building for:

- Managing the volatility of revenue, while supporting diversification of funding sources, and supporting Teaching, Advising, Research, and meeting the demand for increased commercialization.
- Responding to the weaponization of educational institutes.
- Adjusting to evolving national priorities and managing the risk to meet short-term demands, the expectation of more rapid responses, and meeting vested interests is the risk to be managed.
- Managing the political risk which is increased through the use of technology.
- Maintaining staff in a global economy.
- Responding to the information risks, including loss of information whilst supporting information sharing, which is also part of the weaponization.
- Preservation of intellectual property, including its weaponization, while realizing the commercial opportunities.

Adaptiveness, responsiveness, and resiliency are needed, along with the strengthening of professional skills (like people management, problem-solving, relationship management, and financial management). The automation of knowledge workers and the provision of these services from the cloud (like TXaaS or ADaaS or PMaaS) require the consistent and persistent application of proven business practices and principals applied pragmatically.

Educational institutions are the enabler (catalyst, leader, and facilitator) for organizations and societies to transform, to adopt and adapt to the uncertainties and opportunities coming from rapid changes in technology requires capacity and capability building. Like campaigns to change societal behavior (e.g., health or road safety), the capacity and capability building supplied by educational institutions needs to be integrated and sustained to shape the emergent behaviors. Although resources and funding are of influence, the main determinant is the desire and actions of individuals through the pragmatic changes they can bring on a daily basis.

While we may not know what specific technologies are to be used, we can bring the combination of strategy and leadership, to influence the environment, to instill the behaviors, and strengthen with skilling through which we shape the pride, ownership, and empowerment within all of us; forming the emergent behavior and environment for transformation. Shaping the future lies within our hands, within our professionalism, and within our pride in who we are and what we do.

## KEYWORDS

- **business transformation**
- **knowledge workers**
- **technology services**
- **higher education**
- **information economy**

## REFERENCES

Australian Computer Society (2017). *The one must-have skill for tomorrow's ICT jobs.* Information Age (https://ia.acs.org.au/article/2017/the-one-must-have-skill-for-tomorrows-ict-jobs.html last viewed Aug-2019).

Australian Computer Society (2019). *ACS Australia's Digital Pulse 2019* (https://www.acs.org.au/content/dam/acs/acs-publications/Digital-Pulse-2019-FINAL-Web.pdf last viewed Sep-2019).

Connolly, B. (2014). "*Top 10 Enterprise IT Disasters*", CIO Magazine (https://www.cio.com.au/article/542245/top_10_enterprise_it_disasters/ last viewed Aug-2019)

Hajkowicz, S., Reeson, A., Rudd, L., Bratanova, A., Hodgers, L., Mason, C., and Boughen, N., (2016). *Tomorrow's Digitally Enabled Workforce.* Report of the Commonwealth and Scientific Industrial Research Organization Australia112 pp (https://research.csiro.au/lifelong/lifelong-participation-digital-technology/ last viewed Aug-2019).

IEEE (2015). "*Lessons from a Decade of IT Failures*", Institute of Electrical and Electronics Engineers, Piscataway, NJ (https://spectrum.ieee.org/static/lessons-from-a-decade-of-it-failures last viewed Aug-2019)

McConnell, P. (2018). *Is there a Governance Deficit in Australia's largest Banks?* (https://financialservices.royalcommission.gov.au/Submissions/Documents/interim-report-submissions/POL.9100.0001.0641.pdf last viewed Aug-2019).

Sherringham, K. and Unhelkar, B. (2016a). *"Service Management in Big Data"*, Proceedings of the System Design and Process Science (SDPS2016) Conference, 4–6 Dec, 2016, Orlando, FL, USA.

Sherringham, K. and Unhelkar, B., (2016b). *"Human Capital Capacity and Capability for Big Data"*, Proceedings of the System Design and Process Science (SDPS2016) Conference, 4–6 December, 2016, Orlando, FL, USA.

Sherringham, K. and Unhelkar, B., (2020a) *Crafting and Shaping Knowledge Worker Services in the Information Economy*. Palgrave Macmillan Singapore, p. 500.

Sherringham K. and Unhelkar, B., (2020b) *Business Adoption and Service Management for the Internet of Things*. In Sharma, K.S., Bhushan, B., and Debnath, N.C. (Ed). Security and Trust Issues in Internet of Things: Blockchain to the Rescue. CRC Press–Taylor Francis, NY, in press.

## LIST OF TERMS

The following terms are used:

- AaaS—Analytics as a Service. The emerging cloud service from the use of Big Data, analytics, real-time decision making with artificial intelligence and machine learning.
- ADaaS—Audit as a Service. The sourcing of audit services from the cloud including software, processes, procedures, governance, templates, and other project management capacities and capabilities. Typically, a pay-per-use model.
- BAaaS—Business Analysis as a Service. The use of business analysis services including tools, frameworks, processes, information, and resources from the cloud for business analysis.
- Change the Business—Activities that relate to changing and improving the business. Mainly refers to resources allocated to activities that change a business.
- Core Platform—The core platform off which businesses operate resulting from the convergence of the Internet, Mobile Computing, Cloud Computing, Social Media, Big Data and cloud-based services, with real-time decision making, machine learning, artificial intelligence, and the Internet of Things.
- DBaaS—DataBase as a Service. Database applications and maintenance are provided out of the cloud as a service. Application owners do not have to install and maintain the database themselves. Instead,

the database service provider takes responsibility for installing and maintaining the database, and application owners are charged according to their usage of the service.

- IaaS—Infrastructure as a Service. Hardware is provided and managed on a pay-per-use model. This may be physical hardware or virtual hardware.
- ICT—Information and Communications Technology.
- ICT Operations and Services— The provision and management of ICT as a consumable service from infrastructure to consulting services to the business with all of the required processes, policies, procedures, frameworks, governance, reporting, management, and operations.
- IoT—Internet of Things. A network of Internet-connected physical devices and everyday objects able to collect and exchange data.
- Knowledge Workers—Workers who take information from various sources and process it or use it to provide products and services.
- OaaS—Operations as a Service. The use of cloud-based services for ICT operations and management and other related services. Typically, a pay-per-use model.
- PaaS—Platform as a Service. A category of cloud computing services that provides a platform allowing customers to develop, run, and manage applications without the complexity of building and maintaining the platform. Typically, a pay-per-use model.
- PMaaS—Project Management as a Service. The sourcing of project management services from the cloud including software, processes, procedures, governance, templates, and other project management capacities and capabilities. Typically, a pay-per-use model.
- Run the Business—Activities relating to the ongoing management and operations of a business. Mainly refers to resources allocated to maintaining operations.
- SaaS—Software as a Service. A software licensing and delivery model in which software is licensed on a subscription basis and is centrally hosted. A common example of SaaS is email services supplied by the likes of Google or CRM software accessed as a service like Salesforce.
- TaaS—Testing as a Service. Testing services including tools, frameworks, processes, information, and resources from the cloud.
- TXaaS—Tax as a Service. The management of taxation as a service from the cloud.

CHAPTER 31

# ICT in Higher Education: Overcoming the Challenges

VAISHALI DUBEY and VINOD KUMAR KANVARIA*

*Department of Education, University of Delhi, Delhi, 110007, India*

**Corresponding author. E-mail: vinodpr111@gmail.com*

*Track #5: Education Reforms and Prospects*

*Subtrack: Strategies for overcoming challenges of ICT in Higher Education*

## ABSTRACT

Information and Communication Technology (ICT) has become an integral part of today's education system. Be it school education, higher education, or teacher education, the use of ICT in classroom teaching cannot be undermined. Learning through smart boards, laptops, computers, and mobile phones has become a latest trend in the educational world today. In this changing world, the teachers need to be well equipped with the changes taking place in the world around. Although teachers usually appreciate the benefits of ICT in the teaching–learning process, they are the ones facing the most challenges in dealing with it. No doubt the use of ICT in education has become an important area; there are still so many hurdles and challenges that are being faced. This chapter highlights the common challenges faced by the educators while attempting to integrate ICT in the classroom teaching, and also offers certain possible solutions to these problems. Examination of these problems will be helpful to the current and future educators, teacher educators, and the educational ICT researchers.

## 31.1 INTRODUCTION

The onset of the era of information and communication technology (ICT) has resulted in the "renovation" of every field. It is, undoubtedly, having a profound impact on our lives. It is also true that one cannot escape it, even if he/she wants to. No doubt, ICT has become an inevitable part of almost every sphere today. It is very likely that the influence of ICT will increase further in the years to come. The workplace and public spheres are completely dependent on ICT now (Sjøberg, 2001). The education sector is also not lagging behind. The earlier or traditional system of education followed a traditional and teacher-centric approach. It completely relied upon that approach where the teacher was considered to be the epitome of knowledge and the sole purpose of the teacher was to transfer knowledge to the learners. The paradigms shift with time. This shift can be seen in educational field also where the teacher-centric approach has been replaced by the child-centric approach and the role of the teacher has changed from being the only source of knowledge to being a facilitator. With time, the use of ICT as an aid for teaching–learning also increased. Slowly, ICT became one of the strongest factors shaping the world of education. The recent trends in the educational field not only give a clear view of the technological advancements in educational field, but also give a glimpse of the future ahead. Nowadays computers and educational software have been introduced at almost all levels of education. It is quite clear that the introduction of ICT is a big change and we, as human beings, need to adapt ourselves to changes. Therefore, the complete adoption of ICT is based upon the level of adaptation by us. If we talk specifically about the field of education, it is the teachers and the learners who need to adapt to the new changes taking place.

## 31.2 REVIEW OF RELATED LITERATURE

One can witness a lot of recent trends in the educational field. Some of them are—cooperative learning, collaborative learning, individualized learning, learning through mobile apps, smart class, flipped classroom, blended learning, etc. All these changes and trends somewhere put a "necessary pressure" on the teachers to adapt to them and adopt them. In recent years teachers have had to adapt to comprehensive schools, to large schools, to new methods of teaching, to new mathematics, to team teaching and to educational ICT. ICT is becoming an integral part of the education system today. The policymakers are paying huge attention toward including them in the policies (UNESCO, 2011). The countries worldwide are paving their ways to incorporate AI or artificial intelligence in their education systems (UNESCO, 2019). The teachers are required to be on their toes always and be ready to learn new things. This becomes important as change is the need of time and being ready to adapt is the only way out for the survival. The chapter discusses only about the changes taking place in the field of educational ICT and the challenges that come up in front of the teachers. Gupta (2019) quotes that till the end of the last century, the education system in India worked on the traditional approach which did not give the learners an opportunity to interact with the peers and take part in the interactive sessions. With the evolving time, the digital education has made things easier for both the learners and the teachers. This poses the question—"Are the things actually easier for the teachers or we have just assumed it?"

The proper implementation of ICT in the field of education requires a number of supportive factors. A lot of work has to be done in the Indian context. This chapter highlights the current scenario in the use of ICT in the classrooms. It also focuses upon the challenges that are faced and the tentative or possible solutions that can be provided for the issues.

## 31.3 THE REALITY

No doubt, the world is experiencing a wave of ICT and new technological inventions. The digital technologies provide the opportunities of collaborative learning, individualized or self-directed learning, improving communication, and thereby enhancing learning. ICT skills can also help in developing capable and future-ready citizens. Keeping these advantages in mind, the teachers have been expected to integrate digital technologies in the classroom teaching–learning.

This era often is termed as the "21st century" and the learners are called the "21st century learners". The learners, of thc 21st century, are born and grown up in the era of ICT and are aware about its usage. These learners have been in the realm of ICT since their births. They are far more advanced in their knowledge about it as compared to the adults. Therefore, they are sometimes termed as, "digital natives" who are comfortable with and immersed in ICT. These learners still depend on the teachers to learn through digital means. There can be many possible reasons for this. One of them can be the lack of resources.

Sharma (2019) lists a number of advantages of using ICT in the classroom. On the other hand, he talks about the disadvantages or the challenges that occur during this use. According to him, with the increase in the use of ICT, the learners do not need teachers when they have Internet and Google. They give less importance to the teachers and this results in the dilution of the role of the teacher. He also clearly mentions that teachers and professors might require to be retrained to make them stay abreast with ICT. The teachers who have been teaching all their lives using the traditional methods may not be comfortable and susceptible to the changes that are being applied. The teachers also believe that the constant use of ICT reduces the attention span of the learners and also reduces their social interaction. This again refrain the teachers from using the ICT in the classrooms.

UNESCO (2011) emphasizes on the fact that ICT is an important factor that can contribute in making a change in education and all other spheres. The policymakers are paying immense attention toward the incorporation of technology in all the spheres. If seen closely, the major concern for the policymakers and policy-making is the policy implementation. UNESCO had taken up several case-studies in the countries—Singapore, Namibia, Jordan, Uruguay, and Rwanda. The case study analyses aimed at reflecting upon the importance of having clear policy goals, and their translation into appropriate strategies and plans. The case studies conducted in different countries suggest that the effective ICT in education policies depends upon:

- Access to ICT infrastructures and equipment
- Teacher capacities, and
- Monitoring

It reiterates the importance of equipment, networks, and quality resources as a prerequisite for the deployment and utilization of ICT. Thus, it is important to note that the integration of technologies in the education system requires a supportive environment. This, in turn, lays stress upon the need and importance of policy consistency and the need to take up a broader movement for ICT infrastructure development and its implementation. Therefore, in many countries, it can be seen as a future implication of forging innovative alliances between the public and private sectors. The private sector or private companies often control most of the ICT sector. Therefore, ICT in education policies may potentially give rise to multiple public–private partnerships. Only after the technological infrastructure is ready, the next major challenge remains the preparation of teachers and building their capacities to use the ICT opportunities to their fullest for teaching. This whole process involves developing their capabilities and professional capacities. Furthermore, even after developing the infrastructure and giving adequate professional training to the teachers, the proper usage of ICT for teaching depends upon the motivation of the teachers. The major challenge remains motivating the teachers enough to be able to effectively use technology in the classroom. This again can be traced back to the improvements in the teacher training received by the teachers. This involves a cultural change for the teachers which is a slow process and cannot happen rapidly.

Bingimlas (2009) addresses the fact that teachers are eager to integrate ICT and technology in the classroom, but they face a number of barriers. According to him, the teachers face barriers like lack of confidence, lack of competence, and access barriers. He reiterates the fact that the teachers should be provided with proper hardware, software, and technical support to the effective integration of technology in the classroom.

According to the ICT@School evaluation, conducted by the CIET, NCERT (CIET, 2015) in Karnataka, 35% of the high schools had nonfunctional computers/hardware. It also states that while 65% of the schools had functioning Internet, during the study only 19 schools were found to have a functional Internet facility. The report also clearly indicated that the schools reported a wide use of ICT apart from its use for training learners in ICT. It included record keeping, examination, library management, accounting, admission, and correspondence. It was also evident that the range of software and educational content on the systems was very low. Teachers also did not get significant time to use the facility for teaching–learning due to the only infrastructure being the thin client. It was also seen that 10–19 teachers declared themselves low on their competencies. It was also observed that very few teachers used ICT in the teaching–learning process.

On the other hand, if we talk about the teachers, it has become a necessary requirement that they must be well-equipped with the recent technologies and their usage in the classroom. The curriculum also requires teachers to develop learners' general ICT capabilities across all fields of study, alongside the 'technologies' curriculum.

## 31.4 THE CHALLENGES

The National Policy on Information and Communication Technology in School Education (Department of School Education and Literacy, 2012) highlights the major challenges that are there in front of the Indian Education system in the integration of ICT in the schools. The first and foremost challenge is the access and reach of education and the other challenges are the infrastructure and capacity building of the in-service teachers, pre-service teachers, school heads, and the education department.

ICT and its integration are new concepts in the Indian classrooms. Every new change has challenges in its implementation. When it comes to ICT, there are a number of challenges faced by the teachers (Kanvaria and Kumar, 2019). These challenges faced by the teachers in the integration of ICT in the classroom are of two types (Johnson et al., 2016):

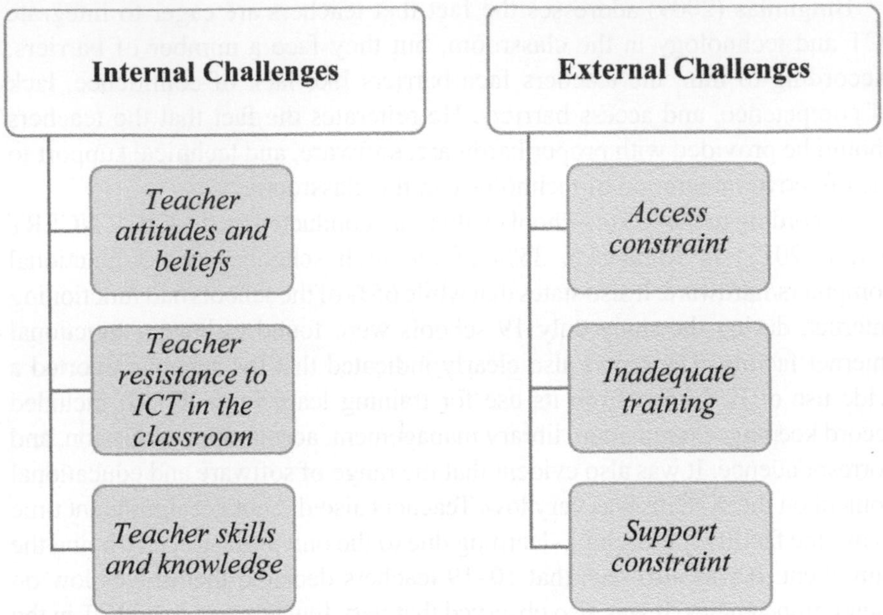


**FIGURE 31.1** Challenges in the integration of ICT.

## *31.4.1 INTERNAL CHALLENGES*

Internal challenges occur at the personal level of the teachers. No doubt there is an advancement of ICT in the classrooms but ultimately the individual teacher is responsible for the implementation (Johnson et al., 2016). Personal beliefs and knowledge of the teachers vary from teacher to teacher. Therefore, it is difficult to address these issues broadly. However, an overview can be provided.

Some of the internal challenges faced by the teachers are as follows:

### *31.4.1.1 TEACHER ATTITUDES AND BELIEFS*

Attitudes and beliefs about both educational ICT and pedagogy in general will ultimately influence how teachers implement ICT. Many teachers do not feel confident about their skills and knowledge about using skills and knowledge in the classroom. The teachers also have different beliefs regarding the use of ICT in the classroom. Some of the teachers do not approve of using ICT in the classroom as they find them as a hindrance in their teaching rather than thinking of them as an aid.

#### *31.4.1.2 TEACHER RESISTANCE TO ICT IN THE CLASSROOM*

Most of the teachers are satisfied with their current lesson plans; therefore, they find it useless to use ICT in the classrooms. They are satisfied with their lesson plans. If they find effective learning in the classroom due to their lesson plans, they are less motivated to use ICT in the class.

#### *31.4.1.3 TEACHER SKILLS AND KNOWLEDGE*

Many teachers lack the skills and knowledge about the use of latest technologies. They have never been trained for the same. Due to this lack of knowledge and skills they cannot figure out which ICT is to be used in the classroom to teach a specific concept.

### *31.4.2 EXTERNAL CHALLENGES*

External Challenges are the challenges faced by the teachers at the institutional and implementation level, for example at the school level. These are the challenges related to the resources and their usage. Some of the challenges are:

#### *31.4.2.1 ACCESS CONSTRAINT*

Access constraint means insufficient equipment and connectivity. There are schools that have ten learners per computer in the computer lab. The basic availability of the ICT is not fulfilled. In this case, even the teachers are helpless as they are unable to use the ICT. Several countries (for example, St Lucia) are taking steps to provide laptops and tablets to the students whereas, the developing countries still have limited broadband access. This is a major blockage to the ICT integration in education in the developing countries (The Commonwealth Education Hub, 2015).

#### *31.4.2.2 INADEQUATE TRAINING*

Inadequate training means the teachers lack in their professional skills when it comes to using ICT in the classrooms. The teachers have no effective professional development on new technologies therefore, they feel pressurized and overburdened when they are asked to use ICT in the classrooms. Therefore, there is a need of adequate training and re-training for the teachers, which is not taking place.

#### *31.4.2.3 SUPPORT CONSTRAINT*

The use of ICT in the classroom requires an adequate technical support and administrative peer support. If the support is absent, it becomes difficult for the teachers to access the ICT.

## 31.5 METHODOLOGY

The chapter included a primary research work wherein telephonic interviews of 10 educators/teachers were taken. They were asked about the challenges they face in the incorporation of technology in their teaching in the classroom and the possible solutions to these challenges. The interview questions were made based upon the following themes:

- Institutional support in the use of technology
- Training in the use of technology
- Comfort/confidence in teaching through technology
- Views and beliefs about the use of technology
- Level of motivation in the use of technology.

The interviews of the teachers were transcribed and analyzed based upon the themes chosen and the literature reviewed.

### *31.5.1 ANALYSIS OF DATA*

The data collected through the telephonic interviews of the teachers/educators is thematically analyzed in this part.

#### *31.5.1.1 INSTITUTIONAL SUPPORT*

It could be interpreted from the interviews that the teachers/educators had limited institutional support when it comes to technology. The support was limited to computer labs and smart boards. In certain institutions, as reported by the teachers, the support was not sufficient or inadequate when the class size was referred to. On the other hand, the private institutions had an additional benefit of having a support assistant but the government institutions rarely had it.

### 31.5.1.2 TRAINING IN THE USE OF TECHNOLOGY

It could be inferred from the interviews that the teachers/educators received no special training for the use of technology. The teachers operated with the help of the computer teacher in the school. They were dependent on their own skills and knowledge. UNESCO (2018) reiterates the fact that the use of new technologies requires the adoption of new skills and roles by the teacher which in turn embraces new pedagogies and approaches to teacher education. The complete and successful integration of ICT in the classroom will depend upon the teachers' abilities to plan out, adopt, and structure new ways and ideas to merge technology appropriately with their pedagogy. For many teachers, this will look like an entirely new concept and will definitely require developing a new set of skills and abilities. Therefore, the role of teacher education becomes multifold here. Teacher professional learning will play the most important part here.

### 31.5.1.3 COMFORT/CONFIDENCE IN TEACHING THROUGH TECHNOLOGY

When asked about their preference for their own lesson plans or technology for teaching, most of the teachers preferred their own lesson plans and techniques for teaching. They found technology less reliable. However, a few were ready to experiment with technology. It was seen that the age factor played a significant role here. The younger educators were more enthusiastic about using new trends and techniques in their classrooms as compared to the older educators, who remained stuck to their own pedagogical techniques.

### 31.5.1.4 VIEWS AND BELIEFS ABOUT TECHNOLOGY

Almost all the teachers agreed to the point that technology is effective in teaching–learning. They agreed that the students respond well and are eager to learn when taught using technology.

#### *31.5.1.5 LEVEL OF MOTIVATION IN THE USE OF TECHNOLOGY*

The level of motivation is not so much as the teachers rely upon the lesson plans and their teaching skills. Not all of the teachers seemed to be motivated enough to use technology in their classrooms.

### *31.5.2 POSSIBLE SOLUTIONS*

It can be clearly seen that although the road to ICT is good and required, it is not an easy one. The road toward ICT is clearly a road toward the future, but far ahead. There are still a lot of challenges that are being faced and need to be tackled. Some of the possible solutions for these challenges are:

- The teachers are the major stakeholders in the learning of the learners. Therefore, the say of teachers should be given importance in what technologies are to be used. They should be consulted and their say should be valued.
- The technologies available for teaching–learning are not organized and therefore become inaccessible to the teachers for using. Therefore, the ICT and the materials should be better organized and made easily available to the teachers.
- Many times, the schools or colleges are poorly funded due to which the basic infrastructural needs are not fulfilled. Therefore, the funding for infrastructure and maintenance should be properly funded.
- It should be ensured that adequate technical, administrative, and peer support is available while implementation so that the teachers can effectively use the ICT.
- Teachers should be properly trained in the use of ICT in the classrooms. Regular teacher training programs and workshops should be organized so that the teachers are well-equipped with the necessary skills required for teaching through ICT. They should be made comfortable in its use.
- Most of the time, the teachers adhere to their own traditional way of teaching. They do not include child-centric approach or individualized teaching styles. They feel more comfortable in using their own methodology and approaches. Therefore, it becomes important that the teacher training should focus on the constructivist area and learner-centered approach.
- The use of TPACK or Technological Pedagogical Content Knowledge (Koehler and Mishra, 2009) should be promoted.

- Strict guidelines should be laid on the policy implementations regarding the ICT in the schools.

## 31.6 CONCLUSION

The use of ICT in the classrooms has become one of the latest and necessary trends. It has become the need of time. The concept of e-learning and ICT in education is getting very popular these days. ICT and its use in the classroom for teaching–learning is no longer an alien concept still there are many barriers—internal and external. The use of ICT can enhance not only the classroom environment, but also promote engagement. For ICT to be used properly and effectively by the learners, the teachers should be well prepared and updated. More and more focus should be laid upon making the use of ICT in the classroom easier. It becomes important that the teachers should be internally motivated and should be supported through the external infrastructure. Therefore, the challenges that are being faced should be tackled and ICT should be made accessible. This would not only aid the teaching–learning process in the classroom but also motivate the teachers to be well updated and motivated to deal with the digital-natives.

## KEYWORDS


- **ICT**
- **education**
- **higher education**
- **challenges**


## REFERENCES

Bingimlas KA. Barriers to the successful integration of ICT in teaching and learning environments: A review of literature. *Eurasia Journal of Mathematics, Science and Technology Education*. 2009; *5*(3); 235–245. Available from http://www.ejmste.com/Barriers-to-the-Successful-Integration-of-ICT-in-Teaching-and-Learning-Environments-A-Review-of-the-Literature,75275,0,2.html.doi https://doi.org/10.12973/ejmste/75275 [Accessed 6 January 2020]

CIET. *ICT@Schools Evaluation*. 2015. Available from slideshare.net/GurumurthyKasinathan/ictschools-evaluation-by-ciet-ncert-karnataka

Department of School Education and Literacy, Ministry of Human Resource Development, Government of India. *The National Policy on Information and Communication Technology in School Education*. 2012. Available from https://mhrd.gov.in/sites/upload_files/mhrd/files/upload_document/revised_policy%20document%20ofICT.pdf. [Accessed on 29 December 2019]

Gupta S. e-Learning—The future of education. *Future of education—An innovative approach in the technotronic era*. Ghaziabad: Swaranjali Publication. 2019

Johnson AM, Jacovina ME, Russell DG, Soto CM. Challenges and solutions when using technologies in the classroom. In *Adaptive educational technologies for literacy instruction*. Routledge. 2016; 13–30. Available from https://files.eric.ed.gov/fulltext/ED577147.pdf https://files.eric.ed.gov/fulltext/ED577147.pdf. [Accessed 25 September 2019]

Kanvaria VK, Kumar S. Teacher education: Key issues and challenges in India. In S. Panda (Ed.) *Global Dimensions of Teacher Education*. New Delhi: Ankit Publications; 2019; pp. 13–27.

Koehler MJ, Mishra P. What is Technological Pedagogical Content Knowledge (TPACK)? *Contemporary Issues in Technology and Teacher Education*. 2009; 9, 60–70. Available from https://www.researchgate.net/publication/241616400_What_Is_Technological_Pedagogical_Content_Knowledge/link/53e2d8840cf275a5fdda688f/download. [Accessed 30 September 2019]

Sharma S. Innovative technology—boon or bane. *Future of Education—An Innovative Approach in the Technotronic Era*. Ghaziabad: Swaranjali Publication. 2019

Sjøberg S. Science and Technology Education Current Challenges and Possible Solutions. Connect. Invited contribution to Meeting of European ministers of education and research. Uppasala. 1–3 March. 2001; Available from http://www.iuma.ulpgc.es/users/nunez/sjobergreportsciencetech.pdf [Accessed 19 October 2019]

The Commonwealth Education Hub. *ICT Integration in Education*. Discussion summary in Education roundtable at 19 CCEM. Bahamas. 2015. Available from https://www.thecommonwealth-educationhub.net/wp-content/uploads/2015/06/ICT-Integration-in-Education-Final-Summary.pdf [Accessed 29 December 2019]

UNESCO. *Transforming Education: The Power of ICT Policies*. 2011. Paris: UNESCO. Available from http://www.unesco.org/new/fileadmin/MULTIMEDIA/FIELD/Dakar/pdf/Transforming%20Education%20the%20Power%20of%20ICT%20Policies.pdf [Accessed 29 December 2019]

UNESCO. *ICT Competency Framework for Teachers*. 2018. Paris. Available from https://www.open.edu/openlearncreate/pluginfile.php/306820/mod_resource/content/2/UNESCO%20ICT%20Competency%20Framework%20V3.pdf [Accessed on 29 December 2019]

UNESCO. *Artificial Intelligence in Education: Challenges and Opportunities for Sustainable Development*. 2019 Paris: UNESCO. Available from https://unesdoc.unesco.org/ark:/48223/pf0000366994 [Accessed 29 December 2019]

CHAPTER 32

# Fostering ICT-Based Education for Sustainable Development of an Inclusive Classroom Setting

FR. BAIJU THOMAS*, and S. LOGESH KUMAR

*Ramakrishna Mission Vivekananda Educational and Research Institute, Faculty of Disability Management and Special Education, Vidyalaya Campus, SRKV Post, Coimbatore, 641020, India*

**Corresponding author. E-mail: rtobaiju@gmail.com*

## ABSTRACT

In the modern world, information and communication technology (ICT) has emerged as an essential component in the lives of every human being in society. In present days, we need to open our minds toward technological transformations in the world. The contemporary technology has proved that our education system has to overcome its immense difficulties faced by the students in the classroom. ICT plays an enhancing role in overcoming the difficulties in the inclusive classroom setting. ICT can provide a lot of technological support to the learner to be energetic in classroom practices. Sustainable development of an inclusive classroom can be potential through using ICT in their dynamic and collaborative learning approaches into inclusive classroom learning. This study aims at the means and technologies involved in developing an ICT-based education technology for the sustainable development of an inclusive classroom set up for diverse learners. ICT supports a teacher to implement his/her lessons efficiently and able to achieve for the diverse learner at any level of learning curriculum in an inclusive classroom. The innovative role of ICT-based education technology provides learners a quality education, and lifelong learning circumstances in the classroom. ICT provides both teachers and students a lot of opportunities to improve their ways of learning and forcing schools to adapt technical innovations into the inclusive classroom environment. This study describes how ICT-based education technology can create an effective teaching–learning process for the sustainable development of diverse learners in an inclusive classroom setting.

## 32.1 INTRODUCTION

The modern world is overflowing with various technologies, which control the whole world. Education also uses "education technology" with much interest. It suggests that proper use of knowledge and technology in the field of education can attain the necessary outcome of learning and testing. Communication is one of a very significant factor in the lives of individuals for interaction with each other and relationships, facilitates the needs, and benefits everybody in society. The concept of information and communication technology (ICT) indicates a universal term of technologies that are proper to supply, produce, share, and exchange information to one another in an inclusive classroom setting. The word ICT carries out an important role in education and at the same time supports the students to develop their learning and guides the teachers to have better programs in the classrooms. The proper development ICT plays a vital role in the school education system of a developing country like India, to advance the standards of education. ICT can be a dynamic source of an instrument to encounter in the existing problem. ICT can make quality in teaching and learning to help in assessment and evaluation procedures in favor of inclusive education (Tikam, 2013). The method of ICT-based education programs depend on how the teachers are empowering themselves to perform in the inclusive classroom settings.

The term ICT defines into two compounds, that is, information technology and communication technology. "Information technology is in addition to a scientific, technological, and professional discipline and management practice using the current knowledge, its application, and relationship with social, economic, and cultural matters." Communication Technology is the electric system that approves communication between people and the groups, who are not bodily, present in the same room. For this purpose, the following drives are in use such as telephone, telex, fax, radio, T.V., mobile, audio-visual, and modern computer-based technologies which include electronic data exchange and e-mail are involved (UNSECO, 2002). ICT is a mandatory part of most of the institution these days (Zhang and Aikman, 2007). In a short time, ICT has enhanced into one of the learning technology that is mostly elaborate in providing effective and beneficial in the learning process (Oye et al., 2011). "ICTs are networks that offer new preambles for teaching, learning, and training through the transfer of digital content (Prytherch, 2000). ICTs develop and establish several types of technological devises and assets that are used for transfer, distribute, store, and manage information and communication. Thus, ICT advances a new understanding of education that recommends new techniques of enhances learning and professional training to teachers and learners in inclusive classroom settings.

## 32.2 ICT-BASED EDUCATION TECHNOLOGY

Technology has enacted an important role in every sphere of our daily schedules in lives and it is now an unavoidable think about human linking and communication network of digital India. ICT-based education technology can make several modifications in class that needs an appropriate strategy and policymaking. The expansion of ICT is not a single-step, but it consists of continuous supports to teaching, learning, and information technology (Young, 2003). In Addition, ICT provides the help and balancing supports for both teachers and students where it consists of effective learning with the assistance of the computers to figure with the aim of learning process (Jorge et al., 2003). Within this concept, ICT is not a topic of teaching. ICT may be a cultural, Mediastinal tool within the undertaking structure during which students and teachers construct and co-construct new knowledge, in other words, students, and teachers do the work of knowing. Teachers' major role is accepting more significant especially in the usage of ICT in technology that would develop the achievement of the scholars, their creativity, and presentation skills. ICT-based education technology is popular as a big module for social renovation, and an important tool for education. ICT has the prospective to succeed in across the domain to those linked to global nets, and mainly, the web, which is decided as an "inter-network of computer networks" (Collis, 1996).

ICT is placed as a strong tool for educating of technological information for both formal and nonformal organizations of the society mostly covered the spaces of population. The ICTs have assisted the policy designers to form available educational policies, plans, and methods accessible to the teachers, students, administrators, and researchers. UNESCO acknowledges, "The ICT-based tools have balanced and possible for data operation, effective learning, and thus leads to more economical education services" (UNESCO, 2002). ICT-based education technology of learning is often moved to develop the standard of education, create awareness about teaching skills, and tools to improve the teachers for effective teaching. ICTs have developed an advanced technological supports for assuming an arranged role in providing best use of those resources, in moving information where it has preferred, to be vibrant, and in creating information, which leads to effective actions (Walter Fust, 2003). The massive usage of ICT helps and supports the quality of education to update the teaching–learning an active structure that is connected with the current world situation. The implementation of ICT in education will not only enhance the training procedure but also will transform the main content of education, institutional infrastructure, and therefore the strategy of education system. ICT is recognized as an effective tool that offers the training process and gives hope to new outcomes for the challenges that education is facing in the present day (Oduma et al., 2014).

## 32.3 ICT FOR SUSTAINABLE DEVELOPMENT

The sustainable development is focused on the development and diverse needs of future generations. Sustainable development always attempts to balance the economic, ecological, and social extents of development in an on-going and worldwide perception (WCED, 1987). ICT can only promote substantially to the improvement of schooling if it is properly rooted in commanding and cooperating learning environments [established within] the wider framework of [supportive] pedagogy, curriculum, and school administration (Deetya, 1996). Sustainable development is secure by the activities of people from every division of society, and on our capability to learn from one another's efforts and involvements (PCSD, 1997). It should be always built on its former success stories to instruct people on sustainable development. Sustainable development can think about as the complete growth of the economy to bring together the wants of the people of a country on time, moving into concern about the economic, social, and environmental limitations of the country (Ayodele, 2007). It has been observed that development in ICT has become a crucial factor to cater to the demand of changing the education system (Chao, 2015). Sustainable development can only be skillful if development efforts were unfolded about these main features of sustainability. Implication should be given to develop newly advanced ICT strategies to support sustainable development.

Education is seen as an important role in the way of achieving sustainable development. However, it is formal education to contribute to sustainability, traditional pedagogies, and strategies that need to be updated (Huckle et al., 1996; Tilbury et al., 2002). ICT for Sustainable Development directs each person to work with information technology and to find out the problems facing for sustainable development of education in an inclusive society. Moreover, ICT for sustainable development on the other hand represents a systematic process for social change that seeks to foster through education practices and public awareness to values and performances are essential for a sustainable future. Sustainable development is about individuals, communities, groups, corporate, and government to measure and act accordingly, and giving them an understanding of the environmental factor, ethical deeds, and monetary issues involved (Ayodele, 2007). ICT plays a vital role in order to realize quality education and lifelong learning possibilities as enclosed within the sustainable development proceedings.

## 32.4 ROLE OF TEACHER IN ICT FRAMEWORK

A teacher needs to understand the necessity of presenting completely diverse learning experiences in different ways in which by approving updated teaching–learning procedures, that is, ICT. In order to acquire this skill, the teachers and students must determine themselves with proper digital capabilities in life. The important purpose of this study is to know the role of teachers toward the use of an ICT framework in their classroom intervention. "Teachers learn the best way to use technologies for instructional functions if their own learning takes place through such technologies" (Erben, 1999). The teaching profession is an on-going practice of ICT-based development in inclusive classroom settings. Students are more active and energetic in nowadays on the use of computers and electronic devices in the learning process (Castro et al., 2011). ICT enhances students' knowledge about technologies into a new space of information (Chai et al., 2010). ICT plays a vital role in the development of student talents, creativity, and progress (Grabe et al., 2011). Teachers play an energetic role in the whole process of ICT-based education and several ICT-based tools are fostering to action into the teaching–learning procedure more outstandingly. Teachers are more often assessed to express their views across the levels and structures and relaxing to progress and advance. Teachers also should take more interest in developing a quality of prominent role to play in creating the ICT framework in their own institutions.

ICT establishes a more resourceful result in various types of learning queries. Using ICT allows students to communicate, share, and work collaboratively anywhere, any time (Koc, 2005). ICT-based education framework helps teachers and students to concentrate on the advanced level of designs and meaningful tasks in life (Levin and Wadmany, 2006). This provides a motivating parallel to the present work that does not find valuable effects for learners and to the related work on firms where there is an indication that ICT speculation enriches stable output (Machin et al., 2007). Despite enormous efforts to spot ICT as an important view of academic teaching and learning, the fact remains that many school students and faculty make only limited proper academic use of computer technology (Selwyn, 2006). The main goal for teacher professional progress in ICT is to improve classroom practice and then improve learners' accomplishments. Teachers need in-depth, on-going exposure to ICTs to be able to judge and choose the foremost acceptable resources.

## 32.5 ICT ENABLING INCLUSIVE EDUCATION

In the present-day ICT-based framework is increasingly moving the world into digital information and the role of ICTs in inclusive education emerging into more important in the life of every person. The ICT-based technology is the most suitable tool in the life of every student in an inclusive classroom setting. Inclusive education is enabling the participates to be more concerned about learning, and equal opportunities for all especially with or without disabilities and with a special reference to the vulnerable to marginalization and exclusion from society life (Salamanca, 1994). The inclusive education has made a remarkable change in the scope of schools and entire educational settings. ICT entitle a prominent tool for supporting and promoting the teaching and learning in inclusive practices. It constantly helps and supports the system of communication and learning. It helps to breakdown all barriers coming across the learners in inclusive education settings (McFarlane et al., 2007). Teachers in the classroom must have the efficiency to assess student's skills and requirements; fix correct expectations about each student and develop appropriate assignments and practice to meet the necessities of all learners, and offer every tine successes for all students (Mackey, 2012). The modern technologies ensure a great potential to develop the opportunities exposed to a person with diverse needs and overcome the barriers they would otherwise experience in life.

## 32.6 ICT AND INCLUSIVE CLASSROOM TECHNOLOGY

It is an important role and right of each child to play and learn in an inclusive classroom setting that protects the needs of each and every child with diverse needs. It is very important to secure every child's culture, language, ethnicity, and family backgrounds are to be acknowledged and valued in the program (Copple, 2006). It is admitted that technology by itself is neither good nor bad. On the other hand, the triumph and set down of technology always carried out by the way it achieved, and the situation in which it is enacted. Moreover, it is very essential to decide the strength and weakness of technology and differentiates the "suitable setting of technology practices when it is mandatory to make use of technology for teaching and learning" (Bates, 1994). ICT, in its various forms, are held to bridge the gap and approve inclusion for students with diverse needs (Rifai et al., 2006; Brodin, 2010). ICT can be adapted as a good tool for teaching students with diverse needs to improve their classroom activities. The proper practice of ICT-based education in inclusive classroom setting covers of several changes for better development of technological skills. Teachers must require special training with necessary methods and application in the appropriate use of ICT, in supporting teaching and learning. The modern technologies ensured the new potential of reaching out to the unwanted and ignored group of children with diverse needs in society.

It is evident from the training of ICT-based revolution in the classroom, because it promotes the achievement of diverse students in an inclusive classroom setting. The ICTs can progress the quality of education in several approaches that incorporated and often increase the motivation and commitment of students to enabling themselves into the achievement of basic skills and by empowering the preparation of teachers in course of time (Haddad et al., 2002). Most teachers lack the basic knowledge of how to integrate technology properly in the classroom (Doering et al., 2003). Innovative and advanced ICT-based education in teaching and learning is primarily about shifting techniques to teaching and learning (Drent et al., 2008). The important purpose of using technology in an inclusive classroom setting is to give enriched meaning to the training of diverse learners (Miller, 2005). It vital to denote that the use of ICT-based education system could motivate powerful learning and encourages teachers to answer well to the diverse needs of all learners in an inclusive classroom setting. It is acknowledged, to providing ICT-based learning opportunities to all classroom teachers, as the quality of ICT leadership improves, so does the provision of good ICT learning opportunities are upgraded and quality of education approaches are enhanced in schools (Lai et al., 2004). Thus, under ICT initiatives involved in the improvement of learning strategies in inclusive classroom are enhancing access, equity, and quality of education in the schools of India.

## 32.7 CONCLUSION

The ICT is symbolizing as an important component in all the phases of development in modern world. ICT creates several situations to all learners to learn in enhanced and more rapidly in an appropriate environment. It is acknowledges that the ICT-based education technology will extend the understanding ICT into better teaching–learning in the coming generations. The rise of the knowledge of technologies has increased the efforts of teachers in improving teaching–learning of diverse learners in inclusive classrooms setting. The key factor in this study was the sustainable development of the ICT-based education technology for the diverse learners in an inclusive classroom setting. It is evident that the ICT has influenced the teachers to improve and develop their knowledge in connection with their classroom assessment and effective effort to practice the ICT-based learning process for students in an inclusive classroom setting.

## KEYWORDS

- **ICT-based education technology**
- **sustainable development**
- **inclusive classroom**

## REFERENCES


Aguilera Castro A, RiascosErazo SC. ICT tools as support for the management of human talent. Cuadernos de Administración (Universidad del Valle). 2011, *27*(46), 141–154.

Ayodele OE, Egbewale BE, Alebiosu CO. Kidney function and clinical correlates in newly diagnosed hypertensives attending a university teaching hospital in southwest Nigeria. *African Journal of Medicine and Medical Sciences*. 2007, *36*(2), 95–101.

Bates RJ. *Wireless networked communications: concepts, technology, and implementation*, 1994, McGraw-Hill.

Brodin J. Can ICT give children with disabilities equal opportunities in school? *Improving Schools*. 2010, *13*(1), 99–112.

Chai CS. The relationships among Singaporean preservice teachers' ICT competencies, pedagogical beliefs and their beliefs on the espoused use of ICT. *The Asia-Pacific Education Researcher*. 2010, *19*(3), 387–400.

Collis B. WWW-based environments for collaborative group work. *Education and Information Technologies*, 1998, *3*(3–4), 231–245.

Copple, C., and Bredekamp, S. *Basics of developmentally appropriate practice: An introduction for teachers of children 3 to 6*. Washington, DC: National Association for the Education of Young Children, 2006.

Deetya, 1996. The Australian Research Council and the Higher Education Council. Discussion paper, Canberra: DEETYA, 1996.

Doering A, Hughes J, and Huffman D. Preservice teachers: Are we thinking with technology? *Journal of Research on Technology in Education*, 2003, *35*(3), 342–361.

Drent M and Meelissen M. Which factors obstruct or stimulate teacher educators to use ICT innovatively? *Computers & Education*, 2008, *51*(1), 187–199.

Erben T. 15. Emerging research and practices in immersion teacher education. *Annual Review of Applied Linguistics*. 2004 *1*(24), 320.

Grabe W, Schmitt N, and Jiang X. The percentage of words known in a text and reading comprehension. *The Modern Language Journal*. 2011, *95*(1), 26–43.

Haddad L. An Integrated Approach to Early Childhood Education and Care. Early Childhood and Family Policy Series.

Koc H. The level of inclusion of environmental literacy components in the published course books with regard to 2005 geography teaching programmes in Turkey. *International Journal of Academic Research*. 2013, *5*(1).

Lai KW and Pratt K. Information and communication technology (ICT) in secondary schools: The role of the computer coordinator. *British Journal of Educational Technology*. 2004, *35*(4), 461–475.

Levin T and Wadmany R. Teachers' beliefs and practices in technology-based classrooms: A developmental view. *Journal of Research on Technology in Education*, 2006, *39*(2), 157–181.

Machin S, McNally S, and Silva O. New technology in schools: Is there a payoff? *The Economic Journal*, 2007, *117*(522), 1145–1167.

Mackey M. Middle school inclusion: Case studies of three general education teachers.

McFarlane A, Roche N, and Triggs P. Mobile learning: research findings: report to Becta. Becta; 2007.

Miller HJ. What about people in geographic information science. *Re-Presenting Geographic Information Systems,* John Wiley, 2005, 215–242.

Oduma CA and Ile CM. ICT enabled education and ICT driven e-learning strategies: Benefits and setbacks in Nigeria education system. *AFRREV STECH: An International Journal of Science and Technology*, 2014, *3*(2), 108–126.

Oye ND, Noorminshah A, and Rahim NA. Examining the effect of technology acceptance model on ICT usage in Nigerian tertiary institutions. *Journal of Emerging Trends in Computing and Information Science,* 2011, *2*(10), 533–545.

PCSD M. Eco-Industrial Park Workshop Proceedings, October 17-18, 1996, Cape Charles, Virginia (Washington, DC, 1997). The Cornell Work and Environment Initiative coordinates an Eco-Industrial Development Roundtable and tracks the status of several eco-industrial park developments around the country.

Prytherch D, Beard JD, Ridler BF, Earnshaw JJ. Vascular Surgical Society operative outcome study: preoperative physiology predicts outcome. *British Journal of Surgery*. 2000, *87*(4), 507–508.

Rifai N, Gillette MA, and Carr SA. Protein biomarker discovery and validation: the long and uncertain path to clinical utility. *Nature Biotechnology*, 2006, *24*(8), 971.

Salamanca, 1994. Inclusive education in Australia ten years after Salamanca. *European Journal of Psychology of Education*.1994, *21*(3), 265.

Selwyn N, Gorard S, and Furlong J. *Adult learning in the digital age: Information technology and the learning society*. Routledge, 2006.

Tikam MV. Impact of ICT on Education. *International Journal of Information Communication Technologies and Human Development (IJICTHD)*, 2013, *5*(4), 1–9.

Tilbury D, Lian FL, Moyne J. Network design consideration for distributed control systems. *IEEE Transactions on Control Systems Technology*. 2002, *10*(2), 297–307.

UNESCO, 2002, Akbulut Y, Kesim M, Odabasi F. Construct validation of ICT indicators measurement scale (ICTIMS). *International Journal of Education and Development using ICT*. 2007, *3*(3), 60–77.

Young SS. Integrating ICT into second language education in a vocational high school. *Journal of Computer Assisted Learning*. 2003, *19*(4), 447–461.

Zhang P and Aikman S. Attitudes in ICT acceptance and use. In *International Conference on Human–Computer Interaction* (pp. 1021–1030). Springer, Berlin, Heidelberg, 2007.

# Index

## C



## D



## E

## H



## I

Printed and bound by CPI Group (UK) Ltd, Croydon, CR0 4YY
23/10/2024
01777705-0010